Sakal Publi(

A Modern Interp~~~~~~~
Lokmanya Tilak's Gita Rahasya

Prof. Arun Tiwari
Author-Scientist

Arun Tiwari was born at Meerut, Uttar Pradesh in 1955. He did his Masters in Mechanical Engineering from G.B. Pant University and joined the Defence Research & Development Laboratory (DRDL) at Hyderabad as missile scientist in 1982, reporting to Dr. A. P. J. Abdul Kalam.

Under Dr. Kalam's tutelage, he developed India's first Titanium air bottle used in 'Trishul' and 'Akash' missiles and designed Airframes for both the missiles, developed India's first Coronary Stent known as the 'Kalam-Raju Stent' with cardiologist Dr. B. Soma Raju, set up the first link of Pan-Africa e-Network that now connects universities and hospitals across the African continent with their Indian counterparts, and finally became Dr. Kalam's co-author and spiritual pupil.

'Wings of Fire', the autobiography of Dr. A. P. J. Abdul Kalam, published in 1999 and 'Transcendence: My Spiritual Experiences with Pramukh Swamiji', both co-authored with Dr. Kalam, are considered modern classics. They have been translated in to multiple Indian languages and have been read by millions of readers.

Arun Tiwari is Platinum Jubilee Mentor of CSIR-Indian Institute of Chemical Technology, Hyderabad; Director Care Foundation, Hyderabad; and teaches at the School of Management Studies in Hyderabad University as Adjunct Professor.

"Those who look upon our political slavery as the external violence of a band of robbers preying on innocent people have a very narrow conception of history. The historic destinies of people cannot be dismissed so lightly. The British are not brigands who have fallen on India in the highway of her history and bound her hand and foot. British rule is a much deeper phenomenon, reflecting the serious organic defects of Indian society. It is the outward symptom of an inward crisis, of loss of faith, of hideous weakening of our moral life, our indiscipline and disunion, our violence and vulgarity. To use Robert Bridges' phrase, it is our 'crowed uncleanness of soul' that is responsible for our backward condition. This requires to be overcome. We cannot build a new India unless we first rebuild ourselves. The immediate task confronting us is moral purgation, spiritual regeneration..."[1]

Sarvepalli Radhakrishnan (1888-1975)
President of India (1962-1967)

---

1 *Foundation of Civilisation: Ideas and Ideals*, p. 82

A Modern Interpretation of
Lokmanya Tilak's Gita Rahasya

Arun Tiwari

Sakāl
PUBLICATIONS

Sakal PUBLICATIONS

A Modern Interpretation of Lokmanya Tilak's Gita Rahasya

Arun Tiwari (2017)

© All rights reserved.
No part of this publication may be reproduced or transmitted in any form or by any means, electronically or mechanically, including photocopying, recording, broadcasting, podcasting of any information storage or retrieval system without prior permission in writing from the writer or publisher or in accordance with the provisions of the Copyright Act (1956) (as amended). Any person who does any unauthorised act in relation to this publication may be liable to criminal prosecution and civil claims for damages.

Sakal Media Pvt. Ltd.
595, Budhwar Peth,
Pune– 411002, India
www.sakalmediagroup.com
sakalpublications.com
sakalprakashan@esakal.com

First Edition: December, 2017

The views expressed in this book are those of the Authors and do not necessarily reflect the views of the Publishers.

Although the Editor and Author have made every effort to ensure that the information in this book is correct at the time of printing, the Authorsand the Publishers do not assume and hereby disclaim any liability to any party for any loss, damage, or disruption caused by errors or omissions, whether such errors or omissions result from negligence, accident, or any other cause.

ISBN 9781654865436

Cover Design: Madhumita Shinde

Printed in India by Sakal Media Pvt. Ltd.

"Om Namo Bhagavate Vasudevaya"

Shri Krishna, immediately after his birth had revealed Himself as the four-armed, standing Vishnu in front of His parents. Unnikkannan (child Krishna) is the presiding deity at the Shri Krishna Temple in Guruvayur, Kerala.

Contents...

Foreword	11
Preface	17
Introduction	35
Acknowledgements	44
1. The Sealed Nectar	49
2. An Epigram for Every Dilemma	70
3. The Science of Right Action	94
4. Pursuit of Happiness	119
5. An Inside Job	140
6. The Seed and the Soil	164
7. The Riddle of the Universe	190
8. The Mint of the Matter	217
9. Thing-in-itself	245
10. Be Your Own Benefactor	270
11. Good by Choice	300
12. Guiding Souls	327
13. The Path of Devotion	358
14. The Train of Thought	389
15. The Code of Creation	422
Epilogue	453
Image Bibliography	454

Foreword

Sir Arnold Toynbee, one of the greatest historians of world civilisations, observes that during the last ten thousand years, several civilisations arose in the world, reached their peaks and then waned off; but it is only the Indian civilisation that dates back to Vedic times, which presents itself as a living and vibrant civilisation even today. The main reason for this is the fact that Indian civilisation is founded on the understanding of the nature of reality and the purpose of human existence. In this sense, the Indian civilisation is the world's first truly knowledge-based civilisation which attempts to answer fundamental questions relating to human existence in the cosmic eternity and its very purpose. Who am I? What is the nature of reality that I perceive? What is the very purpose of living? Who created this world; how did it begin and how will it end? Why do I experience pleasure and pain? How do I liberate myself from this ever changing experience to realise eternal happiness? Vedas, particularly the Vedanta, literally, the essence of the Vedas, tries to answer these questions. Vedic religion or culture is based on three sacred books, the Prasthan-Trayi, the triad of *Upanishads*, Brahma Sutra and *Bhagavad-Gita*, of which *Bhagavad-Gita*, meaning the Divine Song, is the most popular. The *Gita Rahasya*, literally the Secret of the *Gita*, is one of the most acclaimed commentaries on the *Gita* which was penned by Lokmanya Bal Gangadhar Tilak at the beginning of the last century.

Astronomical evidence cited in the *Mahabharata* places the incidents upon which the *Bhagavad-Gita* is based, around the time 3100-3150 BCE. The Western historians placed the actual writing of the *Gita* in or around the 4th century BCE, when the older *Upanishads* were written. The drama surrounding Arjuna's conversation with Krishna reinforces the inherent theme of the script and reserves a special place in Indian culture, thereby allowing it to become a timeless work, speaking to generations of Indians thereafter.

The *Bhagavad-Gita* revolves around the following questions: How can someone live a life that is spiritually meaningful, without withdrawing from society? What can someone, who does not want to give up on family and social obligations, do in order to live the right way? The *Gita* challenges the general consensus that only ascetics and monks can live a perfectly spiritual life through renunciation. It emphasises the value of an active spiritual life. This message can be considered either distressing or inspiring, but it still addresses some of the concerns we have today, and as a result, its message has now spread all over Asia and across the globe too.

Lokmanya Bal Gangadhar Tilak wrote the *Gita Rahasya* as an extensive commentary on the *Bhagavad-Gita* in order to stoke a feeling of nationalism amongst Indians, who were ruled by the British during those days. A brilliant scholar, Lokmanya Tilak placed the prime reason of India's decline and the surrender of its sovereignty, first to the Muslim rule and later on to the European invaders, to a culture of fatalism and escapism that had taken its root in the Indian society. This was triggered by the popular renunciation-based Buddhist and Jain religions. At one point, Adi Shankaracharya, in his Bhashya of the *Gita*, provided the final seal on renunciation being the most coveted goal of an ideal life. However, Lokmanya Tilak saw it as the sapping of the Energism from the Indian civilisation.

In a highly rational and forceful manner the *Gita Rahasya* proved that the *Bhagavad-Gita* placed primary significance on duty. Each person had his duty to carry out and that had to have supremacy over everything else. In the performance of one's duty it is said that one should not be attached to the results. The reward is inherent in the effort and not in the results of the effort. The ultimate duty of any person is to uphold righteousness and to ensure the destruction of evil. The truth is the heart and soul of righteousness and the truth is God. In other words, the ultimate goal has to be communion with God, beyond pleasure and pain, gain and loss, as well as victory and defeat.

The *Gita Rahasya* is indeed a revelation on how the *Bhagavad-Gita* espoused *Sthitaprajna,* which is a unique state of mental equilibrium and which can be accomplished by withdrawing one's focus from the world of senses to the depth of one's inner self. The sensory world brings attachment, desire, as well as frustration. On the other hand, an inner focus will only move a person closer towards enlightenment. Most of the time, people are engrossed with worldly pleasures and as a consequence, are oblivious to the true reality that lies beyond the material world. The *Gita* argues that one has to swim against the current in order to leave the mundane world and experience the truth within.

When I was studying at the Maharaja Sayajirao University of Baroda, I had an opportunity to read the original *Gita Rahasya*, which was written in the Marathi language. As a youth, who was brought up in a liberal Marathi family, but who was attracted to Western science and technology, I felt two opposite forces acting on my mind. Usually, people embark on a spiritual quest when they are distressed and when they are in pursuit of knowledge or wisdom, or peace and happiness. There are many ways of accomplishing release from the mundane world and achieving union with the absolute. The path that one chooses will depend upon one's calling in life, circumstances, as well as temperament. Men of contemplation usually find God through knowledge and wisdom, while men of action resort to worldly activity. I found my truth through the knowledge-inspired love of God. The *Gita* reaffirms the supremacy of *dharma*. The Divine incarnates as avatars from time to time in order to protect the good and to destroy evil and to re-establish *dharma* in the world.

At a later point in my career at IIT and during the development of the supercomputer PARAM, I internalised how India gave the world an ingenious method of expressing all numbers by ten symbols, each receiving a value of position as well as an absolute value, which is a profound and important idea and which appears so simple to us now that we ignore its true value. Computers would never have been possible without the 'zero' emerging out of the Indian mind. The highly formalised methods of Vedic learning helped inspire the establishment of large teaching institutions such as Taxashila, Nalanda, and Vikramashila, which were the world's early universities and were established in ancient India.

The *Gita* presents yoga as a skill– *Yogah Karmasu Kaushalam*– and proclaims excellence at work– *svadharma*– as the purpose of a human life. It captures, in an amazing way, all three possible approaches to realise this purpose– *Jnana yoga, Karma Yoga* and *Bhakti Yoga*. My personal understanding of the *Gita* is the synthesis of all three approaches so that our *svadharma* (outward life), and *svabhava* (inner being) become complementary to each other. Only through desireless effort (*karma yoga*), our actions can become free, easy and spontaneous leading us to live in God's world as God intends us to live (*jnana yoga*), by placing ourselves in the hands of the Divine (*bhakti yoga*). I feel devotion to knowledge-based selfless action is the essential message of the *Gita*.

I am currently working as the Chancellor of the Nalanda University. We have now embarked on the process of reviving Nalanda to its original glory. Looking back, Nalanda flourished under the patronage of the Gupta Empire in the 5th and the 6th centuries and later under the rule of Harsha. The Nalanda University was very likely ransacked and destroyed by an army of the Mamluk Dynasty of the Delhi Sultanate under Bakhtiyar Khilji, in the year 1200. It was eventually abandoned and forgotten till until the 19th century, when the site was surveyed and the Archaeological Survey of India conducted its preliminary excavations.

This book is indeed timed with the revival of the Nalanda University and in the ushering of the Indian Nation into its original role of a *Vishwa Guru*. In the concluding chapter of the *Gita*, Shri Krishna tells Arjuna, *"yatha icchasi tatha kuru"* (do as you choose). By uniting reason and faith in a higher-dimensional paradigm, the Vedic-wisdom can heal the wound that has torn the human brain and the human heart far apart and thereby usher in a new era of an integrated, holistic development of the world.

I congratulate Prof Arun Tiwari, the worthy pupil of the legendary Dr. A. P. J. Abdul Kalam, and urge him to present the *Gita Rahasya* to the present day readers, particularly the young ones.

This book meticulously retains the structure of the original book while presenting the thoughts of Lokmanya Tilak, in a language and a style that belongs to this time and day. The liberal use of pictures taken from the Internet will succeed in activating 'the right brain' of the reader, which testifies, in a subtle way, the all-pervasive field of consciousness that the *Bhagavad-Gita* presents.

The American professor J.B. Pratt writes in his 1946 book, '*The Religious Consciousness*', that Hinduism is a self-perpetuating religion which shows the way of constant spiritual reinterpretation, leading to a life which is self-perpetuating, self-renewing and which, for the individual, and for the world, may be eternal. Arun Tiwari, through this book, has proved this quite brilliantly. The book ends with the assertion that the driving force for the Indian people is their 'knowledge'. Reflection and self-correction is woven into our DNA. Our freedoms reside within us. The luckiest people on the Earth are the people who are born in India. I am sure this book will act as a beacon for the seekers in New India as well as elsewhere in the world, for generations to come.

Vijay Bhatkar
Pune

Preface

Shrimad Bhagavad-Gita

The *Bhagavad-Gita*! An exceptional episode from history! A guideline which transcends time! A journey leading from the mundane, earthbound realities of life to the lofty peaks of ultimate ideals! A creation that uplifts a materialistic individual to the brahmic state– one of continuous bliss! A revelation that intertwines philosophy and life! A thought process that remains relevant from individual peace to world peace! A force that transforms despondency into happiness! A divine celebration that expels inaction and venerates rightful action! A divine doctrine that elevates menial action to the glorious heights of *Karma Yoga*– Union with God through Action!

'What can the *Gita* teach a country like China?' I was posed this question by a professor during the viva examination for my Ph.D. While introducing the *Gita* to the examiners, I had emphasised that the *Gita* transcends borders of countries and is relevant across all cultures. The question became more poignant as it was asked to a Hindu renunciate. The Professor clarified his stand by saying, "I do not give any importance to sectarian research." A couple of professors among the 20 odd examiners nodded with approval and praised the questioner by passing comments like, "Very good question!" I attempted to grasp the significance of the question as my guide looked at me with anticipation. I knew little about the Chinese civilisation, culture and mindset, however, they were awaiting my reply. I sent a silent prayer to my Guru, Pramukh Swamiji, and began to answer.

"Does anyone in China ever cry?" I asked the examining Professor.

"Yes", replied the Professor.

"Does anyone in China ever become confused about the true nature of his duties?"

"Yes."

"Is China a country without emotion?"

"No."

"Do the Chinese despise inner peace?"

"No."

"Does a frustrated, discouraged person in China prefer to listen to encouraging words which rejuvenate his strength and morale?"

"Yes."

Other professors were smiling at our exchange of words.

"Does China seek the truth?" was my last question.

"Yes," replied the professor who had asked the original question to me.

"Then the *Gita* can give a lot to a country like China. Arjuna had cried, was emotional, yearning for inner peace, confused about the true nature of his duties, seeking the truth, and desired to rejuvenate his courage. In the *Gita*, we observe the manner in which Shri Krishna uplifted Arjuna, through his friendly counsel, and so it seems that the *Gita* can certainly be of some help to every human being in this world", I replied.

As the professor was familiar with the *Gita*, he was satisfied with my answer.

The *Gita* is a psychology, overflowing with the entire panorama of human emotions. Fear is awakened and bravery is conjured. You can observe a painful heart and a blissful mind. Gloom and joy playfully co exist here. There is a competition between shirking of duties and sincere dutifulness. At times doubt emerges, to be replaced by faith immediately. Confusions arise and are resolved forever. The sweet tune of love is in harmony with the rhythm of knowledge. We find friendly coaxing along with candid freedom. We can simultaneously see poverty and affluence, vivacity and steadfastness, sorrow and laughter, doubt and faith, logic and miracle. Truly, the *Gita* is an ocean of human emotions. Nothing is hidden here, there is no deception. Everything is open, without guile and deceit. Everything is candidly revealed. I consider the *Gita* to be an example of a very clear, very honest, completely historical, absolutely sacred, ever-exemplary and ever-perfect manifestation of psychology, and Shri Krishna as a supreme psychologist.

From Passion to Discouragement to Complete Passion

Yes, it is true that the *Gita* begins with great passion, but later it is replaced by discouragement. But ultimately discouragement is kicked out and complete passion recaptures its original place of honour.

In the beginning of the first chapter, Arjuna is full of vigour and energy. The two opposing armies are entrenched on the battle ground as per the strategic configurations planned by their respective commanders. The start of the warfare is signalled by blowing of conches and Arjuna very fittingly gets into combat mode *(Bhagavad-Gita Chapter 1, Verses 20, 21)*. He lifts his bow, named Gandeeva, and asks Shri Krishna, his charioteer, "O Achyuta, take my chariot in the middle of the two armies ready for war. Let me have a proper look at my opponents" *(Bhagavad-Gita Chapter 1, Verses 21, 22, 23)*. These words were full of confidence. Arjuna was fully aware of his capabilities and power. Shri Krishna abides by Arjuna's wish and brings his chariot between both armies eager for battle. Then Krishna said, "O Partha! See these Kauravas who have gathered here." *(Bhagavad-Gita Chapter 1, Verse 25)*. Arjuna started looking at them. This is the moment where the situation takes a dramatic turn. An unforeseen page of history starts unfolding. Suddenly, Arjuna is gripped by an unknown emotion. He becomes sentimental about fighting his own kith and kin. His attachment gets the better of him and he even forgets his natural heroism and starts regretting the situation. He is gripped by delusion and that delusion leads him to despondency. Forgetting his bravery, Arjuna begins to speak in despair. This is described in the *Gita* in the following words.

कृपया परया आविष्टः विषीदन् इदम् अब्रवीत् ।

His body started manifesting his psychological condition.
(Bhagavad-Gita Chapter 1, Verse 28).

At this point of time Arjuna says,

सीदन्ति मम गात्राणि मुखं च परिशुष्यति ।
वेपथुः च शरीरे मे रोमहर्षः च जायते ॥

गाण्डीवं स्रंसते हस्तात् त्वक् च एव परिदह्यते ।
न च शक्नोमि अवस्थातुं भ्रमति इव च मे मनः ॥

He says, "O Krishna... my limbs have grown languid, (my) mouth is parched, my body is trembling and my hair stands on end. The Gandeeva (bow) is slipping from my hand, my skin is burning, my mind is spinning and I am unable to stand."
(Bhagavad-Gita Chapter 1, Verses 28 - 47)

Look at how this sensitive scenario is unfolding! The brave warrior who has Hanuman on his flag, who possesses the bow Gandeeva (gifted by Indra, the King of the gods), who has Krishna himself as his charioteer– is now in tears! His natural personality is subdued and overpowered by emotions!

Today humankind fervently progresses towards personality development. We are living in the age of presentation, performance and perfection. The *Gita* offers a complete panorama of personality development. If people do not learn to conquer their emotions, then in spite of possessing world-class skills of presentation, performance and perfection, they will still deviate from their rightful duty at any moment. Arjuna is the personification of how this can happen.

If a laggard has to recover, and stand on his own feet, he must read the *Gita* very carefully. Indeed Arjuna had gone astray but he found his way back and took to the right path with complete dedication.

Arjuna was blessed to have a Guru in the form of Krishna! Though he was in the guise of a charioteer, he was the ultimate succour for Arjuna. Arjuna knew that He is Divinity in human form. This Divine Guru– Krishna– instilled energy, power and complete passion into Arjuna.

He was invigorated with perfect morale through the clear and precise discourses that Shri Krishna conveyed. *Samkhya*, the art of equipoise, the necessity and inevitability of action (*karma*), the skill of combining action and *yoga*, the importance of establishing and preserving *dharma*, the glory of one's duty and *dharma*, the live experience of being liberated, the solution to controlling one's mind, *abhyasa* (practice) and *vairagya* (non-attachment), the greatness of knowledge, the ultimate goal, the power of equanimity, the principles of *bhakti* (worship) and *seva* (selfless-service), the beauty of wishing for the well-being of all, the importance of friendship and lack of malice– these are but a few of the many messages that Shri Krishna expresses to Arjuna at his lowest point. Hence, Shri Krishna is the focal point of the entire *Gita*. It would be futile to attempt to understand the *Gita* while disregarding Shri Krishna.

The Two Facets of Arjuna

The second Chapter begins with a description of Arjuna as seen by Krishna. He says,

तं तथा कृपयाविष्टम् अश्रुपूर्णाकुलेक्षणम् ।
विषीदन्तम् इदं वाक्यम् उवाच मधुसूदनः ॥

To him (Arjuna) who was overwhelmed by pity, grieving and whose eyes were filled with tears, Krishna spoke. (Bhagavad-Gita Chapter 2, Verse 1)

Consider this to be a photograph of Partha clicked by his charioteer. This reflects the depth of Krishna's perception. Many people in the battlefield might have seen Arjuna's tears and the thoughtful amongst them would have observed his lamentation; but it was only Krishna who was able to perceive Partha's condition of delusion– moha. From a philosophical point of view, this perception of Shri Krishna's is unique. Here Arjuna is engulfed in sorrow, dejection and delusion– a reflection of Arjuna's three bodies. Our Indian philosophy perceives the soul as being bound by three bodies. These bodies are namely (1) the gross body (2) the subtle body and (3) the causal body. The gross body is an individual's physical figure– what one can perceive through the senses. The subtle body is comprised of an individual's mind and intellect, which cannot be physically perceived but is more active than the gross body and also controls it. That which causes the mind and intelligence is known as causal body. The causal body consists of an individual's desires, his or her anger, greed, ego etc. These tendencies bind us to the cycle of birth and death. This body causes us to be born again and again and that is the reason it is called the causal body. Arjuna's tearful eyes represent his gross body. His dejected mind represents his subtle body and his delusion is the causal body.

Arjuna's delusion is the root cause of his disease. This delusion is manifested in the mind as dejection and in the body as tears. Here, Krishna has not only seen the symptoms of Arjuna's disease but also diagnosed its root cause. This is the present situation Arjuna is facing.

A competent doctor possesses a special quality. He can vividly see the present sorrowful status and also the future joyful status of the patient. In the 18th chapter of the *Gita*, Arjuna's future state as foreseen by Shri Krishna is described:

ब्रह्मभूतः प्रसन्नात्मा न शोचति न काङ्क्षति ।

One who has attained brahmbhav is eternally happy. He neither grieves nor desires (materialistic objects).
(Bhagavad-Gita Chapter 18, Verse 54)

The entire discourse of the *Gita* is focused towards uplifting Arjuna to this brahmic state– union with *Brahman*. Once Arjuna is firmly established in this state, constant peace will be experienced and sorrow will naturally be dispelled.

Equanimity (स्थितप्रज्ञता)

"I am unable to concentrate; I am always in two minds. I cannot tolerate even common discomforts; I have become oversensitive. I am scared. In spite of trying honestly, I am unable to give up my bad habits. I cannot prevent my senses from doing something harmful. I am unable to build good relationships with other people. I always have a feeling of emptiness and lack of peace." All those who have one or more of the above complaints about life, must read the portion from the *Gita* which deals with the state of Equanimity.

Equanimity! Equanimity is the ultimate definition of humanity. Within the *Gita*, equanimity is established as a characteristic of *Yoga*.

Preface

The *Gita* considers equanimity as the ideal state and describes it in great detail at the end of the second chapter. Equanimity is nothing but balance of mind. Whether it is worldly activities or spirituality, balance of the mind is crucial. Instability of thoughts, decisions and actions creates chaos. Arjuna had become a victim of instability. Shri Krishna was fully aware of this pitiable condition of his dear friend. That is why he told Arjuna,

श्रुतिविप्रतिपन्ना ते यदा स्थास्यति निश्चला ।
समाधावचला बुद्धिः तदा योगम् अवाप्स्यसि ॥

Your intellect has become unstable by listening to various words of advice. You will attain yoga only when your intellect will become stable in samadhi.
(Bhagavad-Gita Chapter 2, Verse 53)

Shri Krishna has used the term *samadhi*. The state of *samadhi* is described as *Yoga* and from the context of the *Gita*, *Yoga* is firm conviction within the manifest form of God. So *samadhi* according to the *Gita* is the absolute union with the present form of God. Here *Yoga* is described as being in the state of *samadhi* even while performing one's daily activities. Thus we can elevate every activity in life to the state of *Yoga*. The *Gita* teaches us how to transform mundane activities like speaking, sitting and walking into *Yoga*. Arjuna wants to become such a *Yogi* and hence he asks,

स्थितप्रज्ञस्य का भाषा समाधिस्थस्य केशव ।
स्थितधीः किं प्रभाषेत किमासीत व्रजेत किम् ॥

O Keshava! What are the characteristics of a devotee whose mind is entirely focused in samadhi and of one with unwavering conviction? How does one with such unwavering conviction speak? How does he sit? How does he move about?
(Bhagavad-Gita Chapter 2, Verse 54)

These questions did not emerge from Arjuna's casual curiosity; rather it represented his sincere yearning for liberation. His question was an inner heartfelt prayer. The next 18 verses answer Arjuna's prayer by describing the qualities of such a *sthitaprajna* person: one who has renounced worldly desires, being content with the God that resides in one's self, retaining stability in incidents of joy and sorrow through the firm belief that God is the all-doer and being without attachment, fear and anger *(Bhagavad-Gita Chapter 2, Verses 55-57)*. The example of a tortoise describing control over one's senses *(Bhagavad-Gita Chapter 2, Verse 58)* the illustration of strong winds and a boat portraying the power of the senses *(Bhagavad-Gita Chapter 2, Verse 67)* and the paramount stability of the ocean despite the constant influx of countless rivers *(Bhagavad-Gita Chapter 2, Verse 70)* are profound insights that deeply touch the reader. The perils of the five objects of sense pleasure, sound, touch, form, taste and smell, and the necessity of renouncing ego and attached are also openly revealed. *(Bhagavad-Gita Chapter 2, Verse 62, 63, 71)*. Over and above all these qualities, the most principal attribute necessary for being a man of equanimity is devotion to God *(Bhagavad-Gita Chapter 2, Verse 61)*. By this principal attribute, one can easily cultivate the qualities mentioned above and attain the state of equanimity.

Equanimity is The Brahmic State

In this manner, Shri Krishna describes the various aspects of a equanimity and concludes his discourse on this subject by saying,

एषा ब्राह्मी स्थितिः पार्थ नैनां प्राप्य विमुह्यति ।

O Partha! This is called Brahmi Sthitih– the state of being one with Brahman. After attaining this state one never gets deluded again (Bhagavad-Gita Chapter 2, Verse 72)

Equanimity is a quality of *Brahman*; hence, it is appropriate to call a person who has attained equanimity *Brahmaroopa* (*Brahman*-like).

Brahman– The Entity

Brahman is constantly referred to throughout the text as a separate entity. In the third chapter it is said,

तस्मात् सर्वगतं ब्रह्म

Brahman is omnipresent (Bhagavad-Gita Chapter 3, Verse 15)

In the fourth chapter it is said,

ब्रह्मार्पणं ब्रह्म हविः ब्रह्माग्नौ ब्रह्मणा हुतम् । ब्रह्मैव तेन गन्तव्यं ब्रह्मकर्मसमाधिना ।

the offering is Brahman, that which is being offered is also Brahman, the sacred fire is also Brahman, the one performing the rites is also Brahman and in this manner the Yogi who has attained samadhi in Brahman related activities becomes one with Brahman (Bhagavad-Gita Chapter 4, Verse 24)

In the fifth chapter it is said,

स ब्रह्मयोगयुक्तात्मा सुखमक्षयमश्नुते ।

the person who attains Brahma-Yoga, receives everlasting happiness (Bhagavad-Gita Chapter 5, Verse 21)

स्थिरबुद्धिरसंमूढो ब्रह्मविद् ब्रह्मणि स्थितः ।

One, who is established in Brahman, knows Brahman, is with unwavering intellect and is without delusion. (Bhagavad-Gita Chapter 5, Verse 20)

In the sixth chapter it is said,

युञ्जन्नेवं सदाऽऽत्मानं योगी विगतकल्मषः ।
सुखेन ब्रह्मसंस्पर्शम् अत्यन्तं सुखमश्नुते ॥

In this way, a Yogi, who is without wrongdoing, while always uniting with Paramatman, easily enjoys the extreme happiness experienced by Brahman. (Bhagavad-Gita Chapter 6, Verse 28)

In the seventh chapter it is said,

जरामरणमोक्षाय मामाश्रित्य यतन्ति ये । ते ब्रह्म तद् विदुः

Those, who having sought refuge in me, strive to free themselves from old age and death; they realise that Brahman. (Bhagavad-Gita Chapter 7, Verse 29)

Brahman is Akshara

In this way, Shri Krishna uses the word *Brahman* several times while preaching to Arjuna. After repeatedly hearing Shri Krishna say '*Brahman*', Arjuna asks in the beginning of the eighth chapter,

किं तद् ब्रह्म

O Krishna! What is that Brahman about which you are preaching me? (Bhagavad-Gita Chapter 8, Verse 1)

Shri Krishna answers,

अक्षरं ब्रह्म

that which is Akshara is Brahman. (Bhagavad-Gita Chapter 8, Verse 3)

The crux of the matter is that in the *Gita* the word '*Brahman*' is synonymous with *Akshara*.

Purushottam– Beyond Akshara

Now we can observe a very unique philosophical aspect in the *Gita*. In the second chapter, the qualities of a *sthitaprajna* person– a person of equanimity are described as

एषा ब्राह्मी स्थितिः

This state is that of Brahman.
(Bhagavad-Gita Chapter 2, Verse 72)

This same *Brahman* is defined in the eighth chapter as *Akshara*, hence, the eighth chapter is aptly titled 'Aksharabrahman Yoga'. *Aksharbrahman* is an ontologically separate entity from *Parabrahman*. *Parabrahman* is higher than *Aksharbrahman*. This principle is clarified in the fifteenth chapter, where Shri Krishna refers to *Parabrahman* as *Purush*:

द्वाविमौ पुरुषौ लोके क्षरश्चाऽक्षर एव च ।
क्षरः सर्वाणि भूतानि कूटस्थोऽक्षर उच्यते ॥
उत्तमः पुरुषस्त्वन्यः परमात्मेत्युदाहृतः ।

There are two types of purush in the world: kshara and akshara. All beings are kshara and the unchanging is called Akshara. There are two types of entities in this world: perishable (Kshara) and imperishable (Akshara). The greatest purush (Purushottam) is different and is therefore called Paramatman.
(Bhagavad-Gita Chapter 15, Verses 16-17)

The word *Brahman* is used interchangeably with *Akshara* in the *Gita*. This *Aksharabrahman* is distinct from *Parabrahman*. *Purushottam Parabrahman* is the supreme entity and is worthy of worshipful devotion by all. The brahmic state described in the second chapter is the state of *Akshar*. Hence, the essential message of the entire *Gita* is to become *Brahmaroop* or *Aksharroop* (attaining the state of *Brahman* or *Akshar*) and offer devotion to *Purushottam*. This philosophy can be called the '*Akshar-Purushottam Darshana*'.

In this way, upon clearly expounding the entities of *Aksharabrahman* and *Parabrahman* (*Paramatman*), the *Gita* makes the Vedic and *Upanishadic* topic of *Brahmanvidya* its subject. This, in turn, allows the *Gita* to be considered as an *Upanishad* and *Brahmanvidya* (every chapter of the *Gita* concludes with the statement, 'इति श्रीमद् भगवद्गीतासु उपनिषत्सु ब्रह्मविद्यायां योगशास्त्रे

श्रीकृष्णाऽर्जुनसंवादे...'. As a result, a person who is not well versed in the *Vedas* or *Upanishads* would not be able to comprehend the philosophical tenets of the *Gita*– tenets that are capable of permanently resolving every problem in life.

Likewise, the *Gita* is a great philosophy. Along with *Brahmanvidya*, philosophical topics such as the nature of the *Atman*, the distinctness existing between the body and *Atman*, the transitory nature of the world, previous births, reincarnation and liberation are candidly discussed. The beauty of the *Gita* is that while transcending superficial arguments and seemingly intellectual debates, it integrates meaningful philosophy within one's daily life. It is a rewarding journey from information to realisation.

The inseparability of philosophy and life are reflected in verses throughout the *Gita*. Philosophy is the science of understanding life. Superficially, they may seem distinct, but in reality, philosophy and practical life are one. That is why Pramukh Swami Maharaj spread the knowledge of *Brahman* narrated in the *Gita* to even small children. The former President of India, Abdul Kalam himself experienced this when Pramukh Swamiji spoke to 20,000 children about philosophy of the *Gita* in Gandhinagar. He immediately said that Pramukh Swamiji sees a philosopher in every child!

I was first introduced to the *Gita* by my revered Guru, His Holiness Pramukh Swami Maharaj. Very often his discourses contained the deep wisdom of the *Gita*. Pramukh Swamiji strongly emphasised two words of the *Gita*: *Akshara* and *Purushottam*. The eighth chapter contains preachings regarding the word *Akshara* and is named *Aksharabrahman Yoga*. The fifteenth chapter contains preachings regarding the word *Purushottam* and is named *Purushottam Yoga*. When I was in the process of writing my research paper on 'Yoga in the Gita', Pramukh Swamiji personally explained to me that these two words, *Akshara* and *Purushottam*, constitute the essence of the entire *Gita*. I was surprised as I had not come across this principle in either of the traditional commentaries written by the *acharyas* of ancient sects or the interpretations of modern thinkers. However, when I thoroughly researched the *Gita* through this perspective I became convinced that without the understanding of these two–

Akshar and *Purushottam*– it would be impossible to define *dharma*, *sthitaprajnata*, *yoga*, and spiritual practices such as *Karma Yoga*, *Jnana Yoga* and *Bhakti Yoga* of the *Gita*. I must say, it is as though the *Gita* is guiding us into a new direction of philosophy which can be called the 'Akshar-Purushottam-Darshanam'.

I am your Disciple (The Turning Point)

शिष्यस्तेऽहम्

I am your disciple ! (Bhagavad-Gita Chapter 2, Verse 7)

What a profound and meaningful statement! This heartfelt sentiment is the turning point for Arjuna. Here, the principle of discipleship is clearly established. Discipleship is a fundamental principle for seekers of wisdom. Discipleship is the gateway of progress! Discipleship is the source of power, courage and enthusiasm. Discipleship is not a reflection of ignorance or helplessness but rather of enlightenment and energy. A proud person fears accepting discipleship. As a result, doubt, ignorance, helplessness and unhappiness take place. A true seeker of wisdom has a natural tendency for discipleship. Arjuna is a true seeker of wisdom. He dedicated himself to Shri Krishna and accepted him as his *Guru*. It is at this point in the *Gita* that the unique, genuine, affectionate, profound and matured Guru-disciple relationship flourishes. The Guru-disciple relationship is a distinctive marker of Vedic culture. The glory and grandeur of the Guru-disciple relationship is profoundly realised in our *Vedas, Upanishads, Puranas, Ramayana* and *Mahabharata*. The world has received priceless philosophical principles which have been born from dialogues between a *Guru* and a disciple.

From the Vedic age, subjects like the origin and the end of our universe, theories about life and its purpose, the definitions of happiness and sorrow and their connection with life, liberated and disembodied souls have been discussed. Due to the nature of the Guru-disciple tradition, these in-depth discussions were conducted logically, openly, in a healthy manner and balanced with pure reasoning and faith. The *Gita* is one such example of the Guru-disciple tradition.

The Present Day Context

A curious thought naturally enters one's mind while pondering over the *Gita*– is there a Shri Krishna today who is a companion and guiding light to modern day Arjunas like us? Who can uplift us from the deep dungeons of inaction ("न योत्स्ये", "I will not fight" *(Bhagavad-Gita Chapter 2, Verse 9)*) and place us on the pinnacle of rightful duty ("करि वचनं तव", "I will follow your command" *(Bhagavad-Gita Chapter 18, Verse 73)*)? Who can relieve us from the pain of grief ("विषीदन्", "grieving" *(Bhagavad-Gita Chapter 1, Verse 28)*) and offer us the eternal experience of eternal contentment ("प्रसन्नात्मा", "eternal happiness" *(Bhagavad-Gita Chapter 18, Verse 54)*)? Who can understand and resolve our dilemmas and confusions? Who can patiently listen to and settle our inner doubts? Who can hold our hand and guide us on the right path of progress when we fall back? Who can comfort us while rescuing us from discouragement ("मा शुचः", "do not grieve" *(Bhagavad-Gita Chapter 18, Verse 66)*)? Who can instil and establish spirituality within our every action ("अध्यात्म चेतसा", "with a mind that has attained *Brahmabhava*" *(Bhagavad-Gita Chapter 3, Verse 30)*)? Who can convey the importance and loftiness of rightful duty ("स्वकर्मणा तमभ्यर्च्य", "worships *Paramatman* by offering one's actions" *(Bhagavad-Gita Chapter 18, Verse 46)*)?

The answer is very clear– Yes. Yes, indeed!

Yes, Krishna never departs nor does Arjuna. Hence, the *Gita* too is ever present. As long as there is an emotional Arjuna, there will be a Krishna to empower him. As long as there is a grief-stricken, deluded Arjuna, there will be a Krishna to bring joy and provide clarity. As long as there is an Arjuna fallen from his rightful path, there will be a Krishna to inspire rightful action. Arjuna lives today. We all are Arjuna. The *Gita* clearly points to the present day Krishna,

तद् विद्धि प्रणिपातेन परिप्रश्नेन सेवया । उपदेक्ष्यन्ति ते ज्ञानं ज्ञानिनस्तत्त्वदर्शिनः॥

O Arjuna! Know that truth from a wise Guru through prostration, service, and submissive inquiries. The wise who

perceive the truth will impart this wisdom to you.
(Bhagavad-Gita Chapter 4, Verse 34)

The word 'उपदेक्ष्यन्ति' signifies future tense. This future tense links the *Gita* with the present age.

संभवामि युगे युगे ।

I will be ever-present. (Bhagavad-Gita Chapter 4, Verse 8)

These words of Shri Krishna are a divine blessing for every Arjuna reassuring that God will eternally incarnate Himself. A wise and God-realised *Guru* is the present day Krishna. Dedicating oneself as a disciple to such a Guru is the means to attain happiness and fulfilment.

I consider myself extremely fortunate as not only have I read and studied the *Gita* but I have physically seen the living personification of the *Gita*. I have closely observed the dutiful, disciplined and pious life of His Holiness Pramukh Swamiji. Pramukh Swamiji was the present-age Krishna as he uplifted society by inspiring countless Arjunas with his selfless dedication to rightful action. His every action reflected the characteristics of a true *Karma Yogi* as described in the *Gita*. His life embodied the perfect sense of equality ("अद्वेष्टा सर्वभूतानां मैत्रः करुण एव ।" *(Bhagavad-Gita Chapter 12, Verse 13)*, "यस्मान्नोद्विजते लोको लोकान्नोद्विजते च यः " *(Bhagavad-Gita Chapter 12, Verse 15)*, "समः सर्वेषु भूतेषु" *(Bhagavad-Gita Chapter 18, Verse 54)*). Throughout his entire life Pramukh Swamiji had continuously wished and persevered for the well-being of all *("सर्वभूतहिते रताः:" (Bhagavad-Gita Chapter 12, Verse 4))*. Constantly in a state of supreme equanimity, Pramukh Swamiji was the personification of compassion and within him was a complete absence of malice, ego and attachment *("निर्ममो निरहंकारः समदुःखसुखः क्षमी ॥" (Bhagavad-Gita Chapter 12, Verse 13))*. Pramukh Swamiji exemplified a living commentary of the Bhagwad *Gita*. Even today, one can feel the presence of Shri Krishna in Pramukh Swamiji's successor Guruhari Mahant Swamiji. Hence, the *Gita* is ever-present. It was a living and inspiring philosophy in the past, continues today and will forever remain so in future.

Lokmanya Tilak and the Gita Rahasya

It would be rare to find an Indian who may be unfamiliar with Lokmanya Tilak. There are very few people who are still remembered today for their principles and Lokmanya is one of them. He was an inspiring leader in the fight for independence. Lokmanya was very forthright and his expression was without guile. His soul was saturated with love for the nation. He worshipped the idea of an independent India. He made patriotism a lasting virtue through his analysis of the scriptures. The *Gita Rahasya* is its best example.

Lokmanya employed the knowledge of scriptures in the best possible manner to strengthen patriotism. He had a natural flair and competence for the study of ancient texts, research papers, discourses and editorials, critical appreciation and independent thinking.

Lokmanya thought it appropriate to take help from the *Gita* in order to present his thoughts across his fellow countrymen. He focussed on *Karma Yoga* in because that was the need of the hour. He introduced the all encompassing breadth of knowledge in the *Gita* to the readers by writing the book the *Gita Rahasya* . Lokmanya's devotion to the *Gita* is emphasised by the fact that he wrote the book while he was in jail; depending purely on his remarkable memory. He wanted to spread the mantra of 'उत्तिष्ठ भारत'– 'Arise and Awake India' from the *Gita*, all over the country. He wanted to ignite the soul of every Indian with his call– 'Independence is my birthright'. He knew very well that the *Gita* had the power to enlighten the people and remove the darkness of foreign rule from India. Hence, incarceration was a blessing for him. He used his powerful pen to present a fitting interpretation of the *Gita*.

The *Gita Rahasya* gives us an insight into the external glory of the *Gita* as expounded by modern thinkers and at the same time respectfully presents the intrinsic strengths of the *Gita* as revealed by the ancient commentator-sages. As stated in this book, 'The ancient pundits who have written commentaries on the *Gita* have not paid much attention to the external aspects of the text. The reason is that the critiques of extraordinary works like the *Bhagavad-Gita* thought that dwelling on the external aspects of the scripture are similar to counting of the petals of a flower instead of enjoying its fragrance. It is like counting the holes in a beehive instead of tasting the honey when one finds a honeycomb.' (The *Gita Rahasya*, Introduction, Letter No. 7). A critical method which helps one understand the morals of the *Gita* is also given in this book. Seven steps from the *Mimansa Darshan* which guide the student to reach the substance of any text are also quoted here. (*"उपक्रमोपसंहारावभ्यासोऽपूर्वता फलम् । अर्थवोदोपपत्ती च लिङ्गं तात्पर्यनिर्णये॥"*– *Gita Rahasya*, Hindi Edition, Introduction, Letter No. 21).

The *Gita* itself is a complex vessel containing a vast ocean of knowledge, yet, Tilak was able to successfully capture and present the *Gita* through his work. A reader of the *Gita Rahasya* is able to become knowledgeable in all the scriptures.

I believe that it should be compulsory for every child, youth and elderly person of India to be aware of the fire of patriotism, the pains of foreign dependence, the glory of traditional scriptures, the threats of learning distorted history, the necessity of the knowledge of true history, the unlimited strength and power enveloped in national unity and the efforts needed to restore the glory of our nation. The *Gita Rahasya* contains the power to deliver this awareness.

This Book

One can see shades of Arjuna in Mr. Arun Tiwariji. I first saw him devoutly bowing down at the feet of Pramukh Swamiji. As if the words *"शिष्यस्तेऽहम्"* *(Bhagavad-Gita Chapter 2, Verse 7)* from the *Gita* were echoing in his life. Receiving blessings from Pramukh Swamiji is as good as receiving blessings from the *Gita* itself.

Arun Tiwariji was fortunate to have a dear friend and guide in the great scientist Dr. Abdul Kalam. Arun Tiwariji had completely expressed the emotions and aspirations of Dr. Kalam while penning his memoirs. The entire world is witness to this. He has immortalised the life of Dr. Kalam through his words. He has also been showered with the divine blessings of Pramukh Swamiji. Arun Tiwariji assisted Dr. Kalam in describing his deepest and highest feelings for His Holiness Pramukh Swamiji into words. Those words took shape in the book, *Transcendence*, jointly written by Dr. A.P.J. Kalam and Arun Tiwariji.

Arun Tiwariji has a combination of modern education and traditional spiritual upbringing which he lends aptly to his writing. Tiwariji is compassionate and so his words convey kindness. Readers from all walks of life and from all over the world have experienced the joy of reading the books so ably written by him.

It is nearly impossible to simplify a philosophical work without elaborating– simplicity and summary are contradictory. A summary often tends to be abstruse. To express Lokmanya's subtle and deep thoughts in today's parlance with clarity and brevity is a herculean effort.

He has written this book with a lot of love and affection. This is not merely a task of authorship but a devoted worship of the *Gita*. Truly, Arun Tiwariji has completed a difficult project with this new book.

Arun Tiwariji introduced me to this book and urged me to write about the *Gita*, Tilak and this book. I informed our senior saint, Honourable Ishwarcharan Swamiji about this. Honourable Swamiji immediately said, 'Arun Tiwariji is a great soul. It is a great service to write for him. So please him by writing for him.'

I thank Arun Tiwariji from the bottom of my heart for giving me an opportunity to write about a book based on an inspirational scripture like the *Gita*.

I hope this new manifestation of Lokmanya's *Gita Rahasya* will benefit the young generation by giving them determination, good moral values and a sense of duty and responsibility. I once again thank Arun Tiwariji for his pure hearted service towards society.

Affectionately,
Mahamahopadhyaya Sadhu Bhadreshdas
Sarangpur

Introduction

The *Shrimad Bhagavad Gita Rahasya* (hereafter referred to as the *Gita Rahasya*), which is the monumental work of Lokmanya Bal Gangadhar Tilak was first published in the year 1915 in the Marathi language followed by translations in Hindi (1917), Gujarati (1917), Kannada (1919), Telugu (1919), Tamil (1924) and finally, in English in the year 1935. The book received great recognition from internationally reputed orientalists as well as the common man of this country who were groping in the dark, and were looking towards this book for light. There is perhaps no other book that is more beautiful in terms of its work and in which, the more enlightened find greater spiritual comfort.

While there is a plethora of books, films and television serials that show that the hero has to fight against villains, in the *Mahabharata*, which stands in its ample glory containing 700 verses of the *Gita*, there are villains who do the right things for the wrong reasons, or the wrong things for the right reasons. There is no human predicament that is not there in the *Mahabharata*. Generations of Indians were raised to understand and know the difference between right and wrong through the *Bhagavad-Gita*.

The *Gita Rahasya* requires no introduction. Lokmanya Tilak's name and his commentary on the *Bhagavad-Gita* will be remembered and read diligently as long as India takes pride in its past and has a hope for its future. The motivation to present this book, after more than 100 years of the publication of the *Gita Rahasya*, came from the never-ending cognitive surplus thrown upon young minds by the media and the confusion that this has created about what is right and what is wrong. The pendulum of the mind is not allowed to alternate between sense and nonsense or between correctness and the erroneous. Rather, it is fixed on what is right for the production houses of goods and services that control the discourse on the media. The conflict is no longer between right and wrong; it is now between two different kinds of wrongs. Young people are made to celebrate freedom by choosing between two well-known brands discarding the fact that both are injurious to health and are really quite useless.

In the Preface of the *Gita Rahasya*, Lokmanya Tilak writes, "The religion propounded by the *Gita* is true and invincible." A lot has happened since then. Societies, the government and even the value system upheld by the society have gone through not only a profound change, but in certain aspects, a metamorphosis. To some, the central question of the *Gita,* 'whether to act or renounce' does not appear to be an existential issue. The minds of people have been trapped in such a web of spurious alternatives and redundant choices that both, action and renunciation are not very much different from each other. The line between what is good and what is bad is also blurred. Not surprisingly, many people look upon it now as unnecessary.

The conflicting forces of right and wrong have created a collage out of the grand portrayal of the ideal human condition. Affluence now co-exists with poverty; profundity with profanity, and curiosity to know what is right has crumbled under the weight of conformity with the memes, fashions, and trends. But then, the fact is that right is right, and wrong is wrong. But when people start getting it confused with something else, then it means that they need to connect with something that is real and that they can hold on to. This book attempts to provide that real thing to those people who are stuck in their intellectual arguments. The purpose of the *Gita Rahasya* was for people to know and understand the difference between right and wrong instinctively. This book is anchored around that very thought and intent.

Lokmanya described engagement with the world as the central message of the *Gita* by saying, "The original *Gita* did not preach the Philosophy of Renunciation (*Nivrithi*), but of Action (*Karma Yoga*)." He declared, "According to the philosophy of the *Gita*, it is the primary duty of every human being in this world, to acquire the Knowledge of the pure form of God (*Parameshvara*), and thereby to cleanse out and purify his own intellect (*Buddhi*) as far as possible. But, that is not the principal subject matter of the *Gita*. At the commencement of the war, Arjuna was greatly confused about what his duty was, namely, whether he should or should not take part in the war. His heart was burdened with the fear of committing a sin, a blunder by fighting against his own clan and destroying them. In order to clear this doubt, the *Gita* has propounded the device of performing action (*Karma*) in such a way that one ultimately attains release (*Moksha*) without committing sin." Lokmanya declared the purport of the *Bhagavad-Gita* as, 'the *Karma Yoga* founded on knowledge, in which devotion is the principal factor.'

To expound further on the secret (*Rahasya*) that action founded on knowledge comes out of devotion, Lokmanya divided various subjects or doctrines, which one comes across in the *Gita*, into fifteen chapters and included in his book the most important logical arguments relating to them. Lokmanya writes, "I have separated the exposition of the *Gita Rahasya* (esoteric import of the *Gita*) from the translation itself." *Gita Rahasya* therefore, becomes a text with three clear aims:

(1) To show where and in what manner the doctrines of the *Gita* have appeared in the evolution of Indian thought;

(2) To explain the difference between renunciation (*Samnyasa*) and action (*Karma Yoga*); and

(3) To expound the importance of the *Gita* from the point of view of practical action, by comparing the *Gita* with other religious opinions or philosophies.

In a brilliant scholarship, Lokmanya established the *Gita* as the original systemic treaty on the discrimination between the right and the wrong action available to mankind. Debunking the claim that Greek philosopher Aristotle (384-322 BCE), followed by a series of Western philosophers established, what separates right from wrong, Dr. S. Radhakrishnan declared in his translation of the *Bhagavad-Gita*, "The *Gita* has exercised an influence that extended in early times to China and Japan and latterly to the lands of the West. The two chief works of Mahayana Buddhism, *Mahayanashraddhotpatti* (The Awakening of the Faith in the

Mahayana) and *Saddharmapundarika* (The Lotus of the True Law) are deeply indebted to the teaching of the *Gita*." Dr. Radhakrishnan called the *Gita*, 'a popular poem which helps even those who wander in the region of the many and variable.'

The *Gita* bases its message of action on a philosophy of life. It requires us to know the meaning of life before we engage in action. Ethical action is not decreed; it is derived from metaphysical realisation. The message of the *Gita*, that a man cannot commit any sin after the intellect has become equable, as a result of the knowledge of the existence (*Brahman*) echoed in the assertion of Socrates (470-399 BCE) that man commits a sin as a result of ignorance.

Lokmanya brilliantly tracked in the *Gita Rahasya* that the stream of consciousness emanated from the *Gita* and followed through the Epicurean and Stoic traditions of the Greeks, Immanuel Kant (1724-1804) in Germany, John Stuart Mill (1806-1873) and Herbert Spencer (1820-1903) in England. The stream continued even after Lokmanya, in the time of Mahatma Gandhi (1869-1948) who declared, "When disappointment stares me in the face and all alone I see not one ray of light, I go back to the *Bhagavad-Gita*. I find a verse here and a verse there and I immediately begin to smile in the midst of overwhelming tragedies." Aldous Huxley (1894–1963) best summarised the *Gita* as, 'the most systematic spiritual statement of the Perennial Philosophy', which views each of the world's religious traditions as sharing a single, metaphysical truth or origin.

Gita Rahasya is organised into fifteen chapters. The first chapter establishes the position of the *Gita* in to the matrix of Indian philosophy. The next two chapters (2 and 3) dwell upon the desire to know the right action and the science of right action as a desire must precede the provision. In chapters 4 and 5, a theory of happiness is provided and how happiness and unhappiness are discerned. Chapter 6 introduces the idea of the soul and how it is different than the body. In chapter 7, the body-soul idea is expanded, to mutable and immutable and the existential elements in the *Samkhya* philosophy. In chapter 8, existence is explained as cyclic and the cosmos is constructed and destructed, followed by the philosophy of God as absolute and unchanging in chapter 9.

Chapter 10 discusses the effect of *Karma* and the 'freedom of will', and expands it to the choice of renunciation or action in chapter 11, thereby constructing a perfect state of society in chapter 12. In chapter 13, the path of devotion is explained and the superiority of the *Gita* over other scriptures is established. In the last two chapters (14 and 15) the message of the *Gita* is synthesised by reviewing each of the 18 chapters in the *Gita* and finally, chapter 15 summarises the message of the subordination of any pursuit (*Yoga*) to the *yoga* of action (*Karma Yoga*), rather than the *yoga* of sole knowledge (*Jnana Yoga*) or of devotion (*Bhakti Yoga*).

This book presents the gist of each of the 15 chapters in their original format and places them in the contemporary context- a migrant living in an Internet connected, globalised world. In the *Gita Rahasya*, Lokmanya had established the importance of *Sthitaprajna* (Steady-in-Mind) as the foundation of a virtuous life and harmonious community living leading to peace and order in the world. Today, the exact opposite is indeed happening. Almost all the generations living in the year 2017 are hooked to electronic media and grouped in to virtual communities.

In stark contrast to the dilemma of Arjuna– whether to fight against his teachers and elders, the modern generation looks upon its elders with indifference. The emphasis is not on what should be done; it is indeed on what all can be done. A new format of social institutions and communities, as shown on television seems to have captured the collective consciousness.

The narcissist culture unleashed by social media encourages, celebrates and rewards people for their conceit. Instead of discovering the purpose of their lives, people have withdrawn into their cocoons. The pangs of isolation, instead of prompting them to transform in to a new reality like a butterfly, is handled by going after and receiving approvals from other similarly stuck up souls. The 'likes' on Facebook and 'thumbs up' on a YouTube upload have become the new social currency. The incessant exchange of status updates and emoji show the dried and parched emotional hearts of the people who use them, and they are increasing in number by the day. Not only have 'restrictive texting' and Twitter posts destroyed communication skills, especially how to write and express, they have also extinguished the flame of curiosity in the minds of the young. No one wants to search and find; everyone is out to ask and get answers. No wonder, the intellectual space is almost filled with useless ideas and debased inquiries.

Instead of anchoring in to the *buddhi*, an increasing number of people are drowning in to the sea of opinions. The Internet has given every one a false sense of importance by way of providing a platform wherein one can express one's beliefs, feelings and observations without any check on their veracity. There is hardly any contrast left between what is right and what is not. There is hubris everywhere. Deluded people are living in their bogus realities where relations are meant to be 'linked ins'.

Furthest to the concept of *yoga*– the wholesomeness of a being- a majority of people have fragmented personalities. People are living multiple personalities– one at work, another at home, yet another in the community and may be a totally strange one on the Internet. The real-life self is lost in to these various fragments. It is indeed scary to see that if in a few years' time, the Internet could de-individuate multiple generations. What kind of a zombie the next generation is going to be! Submersion of the self into an amorphous culture is the opposite pole of submersion of self into *Brahman*. While the original idea was to be liberated, the modern man is snared in to technology.

It is indeed an irony that the secular format of education in modern India has taken scriptures out of the curriculum, including the *Gita*. There are three streams of general perceptions about the *Gita*, particularly amongst the youth. One view is that the *Gita* is all about doing one's duty. Another view is that the *Gita* is all about not having desires and being detached from the world. Yet another view is that the *Gita* is a metaphysical text dealing with the afterlife. Together, these three views have put off the general youth, who see the *Gita* as impractical in the modern day context, where life is hinged on satisfying desires for success and achievement. What is not talked about the *Gita* is that it presents a road map to perfection and excellence in this world by acquiring skills and living an active life. It presents a way out of human predicament and dilemmas.

Just as the switch must be moved to the 'on' position to enable the electric current to reach the device and energise it, this book calls for a switch 'on'. Many of our present day problems can be solved or can at least be mitigated by opening our hearts to the timeless message of the *Gita*. Today, humanity is facing many challenges such as terrorism, global warming, financial crisis, the disintegration of the family system etc. Becoming a mature and responsible person is very much a part of the solution to the many problems and challenges that we are facing in the world today.

The world has changed significantly in the last 100 years but the mission of explaining what is right remains unchanged. Lokmanya, so passionately concluded the Preface of the *Gita Rahasya*, "I am placing this philosopher's stone (*Raja-guhya*) of the Vedic tradition into the hands of the readers. The observance of this tradition, even to a small extent, delivers a person from great difficulties." What more can anybody want? The universal rule is that nothing happens unless something is done. Nothing that exists is uncaused. The *Gita* was not preached as a pastime. It was revealed by the Blessed Lord in order to render advice as to the true duty of virtuous human beings in worldly life.

Lokmanya has included some incredible stories from the *Mahabharata*. It is important that we tell 'our stories' to our children and make them realise the passage of time since these stories were originally written. Early people, archaic hunter-gathers, considered the local valley and the surrounding mountain chains as their world. Ancient people talked with animals, trees and stones. It was commonplace for the spirits and celestial beings to take human form and get involved in the affairs of the mortal world. Lokmanya has weaved in an amazing tapestry of stories in the *Gita Rahasya* where animals and human beings converse and values and norms emerge out of these conversations. It is important to connect to this incredible lost world. While all this has changed, the mission of living a purposeful life remains unchanged. This life can't be a one-man show– whether in family, at work, in communities or at the national and international levels. We need to understand others and communicate with them.

The Divine Hand poked me first about this mission when I visited Mandalay in Myanmar in 2005 and came to know that Lokmanya was imprisoned at the Mandalay jail from 1908 to 1914. It was here that Lokmanya wrote more than 400 pages of the *Gita Rahasya* book in pencil on the stationery provided by the Jailor who was awed by his radiating brilliance and indomitable spirit. Later, when I assisted Dr. A. P. J. Abdul Kalam on his book, *'Transcendence: My Spiritual Experiences with Pramukh Swamiji',* which was published in the year 2015, a month before his death, I knew that I was destined to write this book. I actually started writing this book after returning from the cremation of Pramukh Swamiji on the 17th of August, 2016. Lokmanya opened the *Gita Rahasya* with the words of Saint Tukaram who was a 17th century poet-saint of the *Bhakti* movement in the state of Maharashtra, "I only repeated the words already uttered by saints. How else can an insignificant man like me know this?" This applies to me even more.

With this book, my tutelage under Dr. Kalam, which is spread over 33 wonderful years and which has brought so much satisfaction to my mind, and through the blessings of Pramukh Swamiji that have filled my heart with peace that had always eluded me, have truly fructified. This book is indeed the divine grace that has reached me through the liberated souls of Dr. A. P. J. Abdul Kalam and Pramukh Swamiji. I am placing this book in the hands of promising readers, with the hope that they will arise, awake and understand the blessings that our ancestors have left behind for us. This book is offered with affection to all those who take pride in being born in India and who have a hope for this civilisation.

Arun Tiwari
Hyderabad

Lokmanya was charged with sedition for his writings celebrating freedom fighters and martyrs in 1908. He was sentenced to a six-year prison and exiled to faraway Mandalay in Burma. Lokmanya famously dared the judge who convicted him saying, "There are higher powers that rule the destinies of men and nations; and I think, it may be the will of Providence that the cause I represent may be benefited more by my suffering than by my pen and tongue." It was during this period that Lokmanya wrote the Gita Rahasya.

Acknowledgements

I consider completing this book as the rationale of my birth and gratefully place it at the feet of my mother, Smt. Upasana Tiwari, and dedicate it to the memory of my father, Shri Krishna Chandra Tiwari, who departed this mortal world in 1979, after giving me education, but without seeing any of my accomplishments that were possible only because of the upbringing he provided me.

I have had the good fortune of being spotted by Dr. A. P. J. Abdul Kalam, early in my youth, when I joined DRDL in 1982. I spent 33 years under his watchful guidance that transformed me from a mechanical engineer to a missile scientist to a translational researcher, to an author and finally, a teacher of our civilisation's heritage and values. His soul in the eternal realm will be very pleased to see this book.

Most revered saints, starting with Sadhu Vivekanandaji of Gurukul Prabhat Ashram, Satpurush Pramukh Swamiji Maharaj and Satpurush Mahant Swamiji Maharaj have blessed me. Sadhu Swayamprakashdas (Doctor Swamiji), Sadhu Ishwarcharandas Swamiji, Sadhu Atmaswarupdas Swamiji, Mahamahopadhyaya Sadhu Bhadreshdas Swamiji, Sadhu Munivatsaldas Swamiji, Sadhu Brahmaviharidas Swamiji and Sadhu Divyamurtidas Swamiji– have put my feet firmly on the spiritual path. This book is indeed dedicated to these saints.

Dr. B. Soma Raju, Shri Govind Lalji Dholakia, Dr. Vijay Bhatkar, and Shri Mahesh Rajojibhai Patel, all true *Karma Yogis*, have helped me comprehend the timeless message of Lokmanya Bal Gangadhar Tilak in using this life for desireless work and for the good of the society.

No one exists in this world alone and even the most subtle transactions are linked to larger happenings in some other space-time. I place on record through this book, the brief presence of some of the finest people in my life, who have all departed, but without whom I would not have been able to write this book. May peace be upon my grandmother, Smt. Javitri Devi, my uncle, Late Shri Jagat Prakash Sharma, my teachers, Prof Arun Prakash, Prof Ajai Kumar Dron, and Prof Sharat Chandra Malviya.

I am grateful to my wife Dr. Anjana Tiwari; my siblings, Smt. Seema Sharma, and Salil Tiwari; and pray that my sons Aseem and Amol and grandson Agastya remain ever grounded in the tradition they are born in. My younger brother, Varun Tiwari, departed on 23 November, 2017, as if breaking the exit queue, but then, there is nothing 'untimely' in the eternal realm and this book will reach him nevertheless.

I sincerely thank Ashutosh Ramgir of Sakal Publications, my publishers, who gave me the opportunity to write this book and my immaculate editor Yogita Vaidya, who put in immense efforts to bring it to its present form.

Finally, my prayers are for the well-being of the readers of this book. The fact that you have this book in your hands and are reading it, is a testimony of our eternal connectedness. We were together earlier and will meet again in some other space-time coordinates.

I have liberally used material posted on the Internet by generous souls to spread the message of the *Gita*. My publishers have taken scrupulous caution in acknowledging the source, but there are sources which could not be traced. With folded hands seeking forgiveness and head bowed in reverence before these contributors, we acknowledge their priceless support.

ॐ सर्वे भवन्तु सुखिनः ।
ॐ सर्व सन्तु निरामयाः ।
सर्वे भद्राणि पश्यन्तु
मा कश्चित् दुःखभाग्भवेत् ॥
ॐ शान्तिः शान्तिः शान्तिः ॥

I pray to the indescribable, impersonal *Brahman*,

May all be happy,
May all be free from disease,
May all see things good, and
May none suffer misfortune.
Let there be peace upon every one, everywhere, every moment.

ॐ

We are grateful to

Translation of the Preface from Hindi into English
Shri. Subhash Phadke

Verification of the Shlokas in Sanskrit
Vaidik Samshodhan Mandal
(Adarsh Sanskrut Shodh Sanstha, Pune)
Dr. Bhagyalata Pataskar (Director)
Shri. Pranav Gokhale (Assistant Director)
Amruta Kulkarni (Research Assistant)

ॐ

1
The Sealed Nectar

सर्वोपनिषदो गावो दोग्धा गोपालनन्दनः ।
पार्थो वत्सः सुधीर्भोक्ता दुग्धं गीतामृतं महत् ॥

All the Upanishads are like the herds of cows; the son of the cowherd Blessed Lord Shri Krishna is a milkman. The intelligent Arjuna is the calf drinking the milk that is the Gita. It is nectar for the human race. [1]

Gita Rahasya's first chapter is simply titled 'Introduction'. It opens with the *Mahabharata's* opening verse:

नारायणं नमस्कृत्य नरं चैव नरोत्तमम् ।
देवीं सरस्वतीं चैव ततो जयम् उदीरयेत् ॥

One should first offer obeisance to Narayana, the God, to Nara, the most excellent among men,
To Devi Sarasvati, the goddess of knowledge, and then begin to recite the 'Jaya', that is the Mahabharata.

There is practice of worshipping *Bhagwan* and the *Bhakta* together in India since time immemorial. They are seen as two poles of a battery. Whenever God appeared in a worldly form (*avatar*), He made a dyad (a social group of two people) with a human being to accomplish the mission of restoring order in the world by setting wrongdoings right. The dyad is called Nara-Narayana, wherein the earthy soul Nara is seen as the eternal companion of the heavenly Narayana. Along with the Badri-Vishala deity at the Badrinath Temple, there are stone images of Nara and Narayana. In Shri Bochavasi Swaminarayan temples, two idols are

---
[1] Swami Chidbhavananda, *Bhagavad Gita*, P. 69

worshipped depicting the God with his right hand in a protecting gesture (*Abhaya Mudra*) and the Man with his right hand in the recipient gesture. In some temples, a third idol of the teacher is added with his right hand in the decretory gesture.

By making the principle of Nara-Narayana the stepping stone of the book *Gita Rahasya*, Lokmanya provided the gist of the entire book right in the beginning in an unmistakeable, short and clear manner. The human being is conceptualised in this book as a crystal that grows out of an invisible seed. This seed does not belong to this world and therefore, is unaffected by the depravity and deception that are inherent aspects of the affairs of the world. While we grew around this, it remains separate from the growth. We cannot access it, change it, or even seek it out. It is indeed beyond human imagination and yet it is– the invisible seed of a crystal! But the human mind, conditioned with making nouns and pronouns for whatever comes its way, must give it a name. This point is called, for want of giving a deification, as 'heart'; not the physiological pump that circulates the blood in our body, but the seat of our emotions. God indeed lives in a pure and humble 'heart', and all sufferings and adversities serve the purpose of revealing the holiness of the soul.

The *Gita Rahasya* presents God as residing in every human heart and says that working and becoming are indeed one. If a carpenter does not work, wood does not become the furniture. If the axe is not doing anything, the tree does not become wood. Without the soil, water, atmosphere and the Sun, the seed does not become a tree. As the becoming and working are essentially coupled, working God and the doer man are also paired.

Man is seen as an instrument, a medium, an agent of the activity that is neither his, nor does he have any control over it. Just like whatever burns becomes ash, giving away all its energy and identity to the fire, man becomes part of the action that is taking place, the change that is becoming, and the phenomenon that is happening, with the inevitable remainder of the ash. Like no ordinary material form can withstand the blazing fire, no human being can affect the unfolding of the world. Kings and beggars, artists and buffoons, geniuses and fools, from the dust they all come and in to the dust they all go! No one has to go away outside oneself to come into real conversations with the soul or with the mysteries of the spiritual world. The eternal is at home, within one's self. Dr. Kalam, once shared a verse of Rumi (1207- 1273) with me:

> *In the presence of His Glory,*
> *closely watch your heart*
> *so your thoughts won't shame you.*
> *For He sees guilt, opinion, and desire*
> *as plainly as a hair in pure milk.*[2]

This chapter now provides the reader with the genesis of the *Bhagavad-Gita*. The *Gita* was not written in a distinct form. It is embedded in to the epic poem *Mahabharata* comprising of 18 books (*parvas*). In the eighteen chapters of the sixth book, titled *Bhishma Parva*, the *Gita* appears as the 700- verses spread over the 25th to the 42nd chapters. These verses, seen as outstanding in content, have been taken out at some point of time and became a cornerstone of scholarship since then. Every learned man of his time wrote a commentary on the *Gita* and it is not surprising that there are widely differing views about what the *Gita* actually conveys. Lokmanya writes, "One can understand which and how many copies, and good and bad imitations, summaries of the *Gita* are to be found in our sacred writings on Hindu mythology and folklore (*Puranas*). These *Pauranika* style *Gitas* which came into existence later on, fall into the shade before the profound and comprehensive brilliance of the *Bhagavad-Gita.*"

Hinduism is also known as *Sanatana Dharma* which means, 'the eternal law' or the 'endless way'. It is useful for modern people to understand how Indian thought has evolved over millennia. There is no Church-like structure or Pope-type of a command that governs the affairs of Hinduism. There are no religious heads such as *mullas, moulvies, mufties* and *moulanas* that administer Hindus. There is a rich repository of what is heard (*Shruti*) and what is remembered (*Smriti*) by the ancient scholars, but no one holy book or prophets for the Hindus.

---

1   Rumi, Mathnawi I, 3144-3145, quoted in: Helminski, Kabir (2000). *The Rumi Collection*, P.66

They can choose to worship any form of God; they can see God in every particle; or, believe in the existence of only one God that created the world, the one who is all-powerful and interferes in the world. There are Hindus who are doubters about the whole idea of God. They feel it is impossible to know about the existence or nature of God. Hindus even consist of atheists, who disbelieve or lack belief in the existence of God.

The origin of Indian thought is the *Vedas*. The Sanskrit term '*Veda*' as a common noun means 'knowledge.' These are considered as revelations as seen by ancient sages after intense meditation. The authorship of the *Vedas* has not been given to any mortal man and these are therefore called *Apauruseya* (not created by man). There are four *Vedas*, namely, the *Rig-veda*, the *Yajur-veda*, the *Sama-veda* and the *Atharva-veda*.

When the flood destroys the world, the sacred texts Vedas are hidden by a demon. God as Matsya (the fish) slays the demon, rescues Manu, the progenitor of humanity, along with seven sages and gives them the scriptures.

The *Brahmanas* and the *Aranyakas* texts followed the *Vedas*. These are primarily the condensation of the *Vedas*, which also incorporate myths, legends, and the explanation of rituals mentioned in the *Vedas*, and in some cases, philosophical concepts are also added. It was only natural that later, scholars expanded the content of the *Vedas* according to their grasp and appreciation. So much akin to the high beat versions of old melodious songs and their modern coarse dance forms, the mysticism of the Vedic *mantras* was lost to expressive rituals and uncouth ceremonies. The content was lost to the style. Over a period of time, the Hindu religion turned ceremonial, replacing contemplation with rituals, and *Brahmanas* and *Aranyakas* became the scriptures supplanting the *Vedas*.

In the 4th century BCE, Rishi Jaimini founded the *Mimamsa* School, promoting ritualism (*Karma-kanda*), which was a counter-movement to the Self-knowledge (*Atman*) suppositions of the *Vedanta* philosophy. Rishi Jaimini performed a *Nag Yajna* for Janmejaya, who is also known as the first ruler of the *Kalyuga* era to seek revenge for his father's death due to the bite of a snake called Takshak. Rishi Jaimini even wrote a version of the *Mahabharata*, which is called the *Jaimini Bharatam*.

Brahmanas and *Aranyakas*, full of opinions and myths did not find favour with the intellectual rigour and that further bound believers to a narrow view of life and human potential. In the course of time, various *Upanishads* were written in the form of a dialogue between a teacher and a student. The word *Upanishad* is derived from the verb 'to sit down beside somebody.' It implies 'confidential communication.' The *Upanishads* contain secret instructions about the real teaching of the *Vedas* imparted to the pupil by his teacher, to prepare, inspire, and lead the student to know and realise the Ultimate Truth of the oneness of beings and God. Each *Upanishad* explains this in its own unique way. The central theme of the *Upanishads* is Monotheism or the depiction of a Supreme Being as the fundamental principle of the universe. The *Upanishads* very forcefully ask the seeker to cast away his intellectual slavery to blind faith, superstitions, sectarian beliefs, and dogmas. There is a saying that the relation of the *Upanishads* to the *Vedas* is that they are 'the life sap of life sap' and '*Amrit* of *Amrit*'.

To avoid further attenuation and even perversion of the Vedic philosophy after about 200 *Upanishads*, an end was put to such writing projects. The term *Vedanta* had come in to being to signify the final culmination of the Vedic ideas. The first dozen or so

Upanishads were given the status of the principal ones. The first four *Upanishads* starting with the *Brihadaranyaka* and the *Chandogya* and followed by the *Taittiriya,* the *Aitareya*, and the *Kaushitaki* were written during 700-600 BCE. Then the writing changed to the poetic form. The *Kena* is the oldest *Upanishad* written in the verse form, followed by the *Katha,* the *Isa,* the *Shvetashvatara,* and the *Mundaka Upanishads.* Two later *Upanishads*– the *Prashna* and the *Mandukya*– were returned to the prose style of writing.

Rishi Badarayana systematised and summarised the philosophical and spiritual ideas in the *Upanishads* in to 555 aphoristic verses (*Sutras*) in the *Brahma Sutra*. Rishi Badarayana strings together the leading concepts of *Vedanta* in an ordered manner. The *Brahma Sutra* is an exquisite garland made out of *Upanishad* blossoms. The contents of the text also acknowledge and analyse the various Vedic schools, and mention the existence of multiple, divergent versions of the same underlying text. The *Brahma Sutra* investigates the *Upanishad* teachings about God, the world, and the soul, in its conditions of wandering and of deliverance, thereby removing apparent contradictions of the doctrines and binding them systematically together. It is also known as the *Vedanta Sutra* as it is especially concerned with defending the *Vedas* and *Upanishads* against the attack of the opponents.

The *Bhagavad-Gita* is the final text that forms the basis of the *Vedanta*. While the *Upanishads* and the *Brahma Sutra* remained quite out of reach for the unaided understanding of a layperson, the *Gita* is relatively easier to approach as it bridges the gap between esoteric philosophy and practical life. We have earlier described the *Vedas* as the testimony of what was revealed by a 'not-man' source and heard and recorded by the man (*Shruti Prasthana)*. The *Upanishads* were composed by sages based on their understanding of the *Vedas* and were termed knowledge that is remembered (*Smriti Prasthana*). The *Brahma Sutra*, the indexed form of all major *Upanishad* teachings was called the logical text (*Nyaya Prasthana*). The *Bhagavad-Gita* was given the appellate of an *Upanishad*. Together, the three canons of Hindu religion are called *Prasthanatrayi* and deciphered as the *Vedanta.*

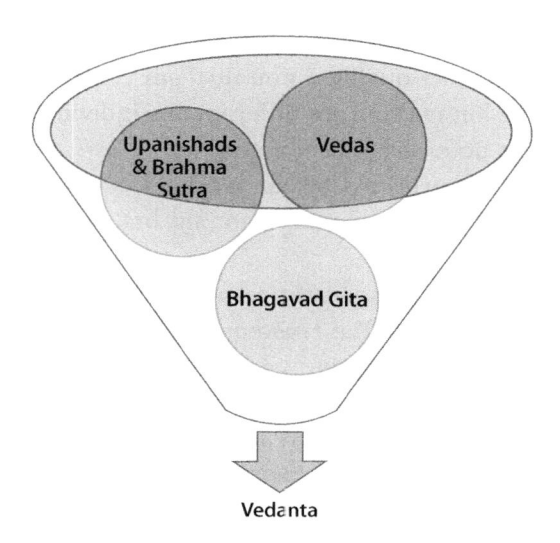

The Vedas and Upanishads along with the Brahma Sutra and the Bhagavad-Gita form the 'Scriptural Trinity' of the Sanatana Dharma culminated in to Vedanta, which answers the fundamental questions of life.

With the authority of the *Prasthanatrayi* firmly established, no maverick school would be accepted and find support of either people or the kings. It resulted in a new trend of interpretation of the *Prasthanatrayi* by different *Acharyas* based on their own analysis and conclusions. The passage of time and change in the socio-political landscape gave rise to multiple variations. The 300-year period that started from the decline of the Buddhist religion triggered by the collapse of the Gupta Empire in the seventh century and continued till the arrival of foreign invaders in the 10th century saw the embellishment of multiple philosophical schools.

The grand Indian one-upmanship show saw the concept of God in its relation to the creation of the universe and the existence of life on the Earth examined from different angles. It was done more in a spirit of discrediting the other viewpoints rather than as the pursuit of the truth. The Monistic (*Advaita*) school called for the unity of origin of all things and that all existing things return to a source that is separate from them. The Dualistic (*Dvaita*) school saw God and the individual souls as distinct and even independent realities. Another school posits qualified non dualism claiming that though the God and the human soul are different, the individual souls carry within them the potential to be identical.

The *Gita* was interpreted by the teachers of these schools, not only in support of their own understanding, but also in refutation of those of others.

This book now presents a historical perspective of the progression of Indian thought beyond the *Prasthanatrayi*. There are four major schools which evolved, starting with Adi Shankara (788-820 CE), followed by Ramanujacharya (1017–1137 CE), Madhavacharya (1197-1276 CE) and Vallabhacharya (1479–1531 CE).

Lokmanya writes, "Shri Shankaracharya was a great sage and had by his brilliant intellectual power refuted the Jain and the Buddhist doctrines which had gained ground on all sides. Shri Shankaracharya established his own Non-dualistic (*Advaita*) doctrine (that Reality or *Brahman* is one without a second) and founded four monasteries (*Mathas*) in the four directions of India for the protection of the Vedic religion contained in the *Shrutis*." According to this concept, the entire world, with its innumerable forms and activities is not real in itself. It seems to be real only for those who live in ignorance (*Avidya*). We are all implicated in this bondage. Our worldly activities and efforts further strangle us in the chain of cause and effect. With the wisdom that we as the individual selves are nothing but a small part of a bigger phenomenon, the ego is dissolved, the wandering ceases and we taste blessedness".

Lokmanya writes, "According to the philosophical aspects of the doctrine, Shri Shankaracharya says that,
(1) The multiplicity of the various objects in the world, such as 'I', 'You', or all other things which are visible to the eye, is not a true multiplicity, but that there is in all of them a single, pure and eternal Highest Self (*Parabrahman*). Various human organs experience a sense of multiplicity as a result of the illusion (*Maya*) of that *Parabrahman*.
(2) The soul (*Atman*) of a man is also fundamentally of the same nature as the *Parabrahman*, and

(3) It is not possible for anyone to obtain 'Release' (from the cycle of birth and death, *Moksha*) except after the complete 'Realisation' (*Jnana*) or personal experience of this identity of the *Atman* and the *Parabrahman*."

Dr. S. Radhakrishnan in his commentary on the *Gita* writes, "Shankara holds that while action is essential as a means for the purification of the mind, when wisdom is attained action falls away. Wisdom and action are mutually posed as light and darkness. He believes that Vedic rites are meant for those who are lost in ignorance and desire. The aspirants for salvation should renounce the performance of ritual works."[3] The knowledge of the *Brahman* does not become perfect unless a man has entirely conquered all root tendencies (*vasana*) and gives up all action emanating from them.

In his *Bhashya* (commentary) on the *Gita*, Adi Shankaracharya drew up a definite conclusion that the teaching of the *Bhagavad-Gita* is the same as his doctrine by quoting such verses from the *Gita* as:

यथैधांसि समिद्धोऽग्निर्भस्मसात्कुरुतेऽर्जुन ।
ज्ञानाग्निः सर्वकर्माणि भस्मसात्कुरुते तथा ॥३७॥

Akin to the process of fire burning all material into ash, the knowledge destroys the mental attachments of a person with this world. (Bhagavad-Gita Chapter 4, Verse 37)

श्रेयान्द्रव्यमयाद्यज्ञाज्ज्ञानयज्ञः परन्तप ।
सर्वं कर्माखिलं पार्थ ज्ञाने परिसमाप्यते ॥३३॥

Actions based on knowledge are superior to the actions carried of impulse. The discrimination of not acting upon the impulses and avoiding such deeds is the true sacrifice.
(Bhagavad-Gita Chapter 4, Verse 33)

Lokmanya further writes, "Shri Shankaracharya has written to show that the *Gita* is not in favour of the combination of knowledge with action, which was prescribed by the previous commentators.

---

3 S. Radhakrishnan, *The Bhagavad Gita*, HarperCollins Publishers, Noida, India, 2014, p. 9.

He has further to show that the Blessed Lord has, in the *Gita*, preached to Arjuna the doctrine of the Shankara cult, that action is only a means of acquiring Knowledge and is inferior and the Release is ultimately obtained only by Knowledge combined with Renunciation of Action. Therefore, we may say that the first attempt to deprive the *Gita* of its *Energetic* form and to give it a *Renunciation* doctrinal form was made by Shri Shankaracharya."

After a gap of more than two hundred years, Shri Ramanujacharya founded the Qualified-Monism (*Vishisht Dvaita*) tradition and similar to Shri Shankaracharya, he wrote independent commentaries (*Bhashya*) on the *Prasthanatrayi*, which of course include the *Gita*. Shri Ramanujacharya refused to see the world as unreal. The world is no deception or illusion, but is genuine and real. The world and God are one as body and soul are one. The absolute dependence of the world on God is underlined through this analogy. God is the supporting, controlling principle of the soul, even as the soul is the supporting principle of the body. God and soul are one, not because the two are identical, but because God indwells and penetrates the soul. God has purposefully created this world and will bestow salvation on the creatures. Shri Ramanujacharya thus refuted the doctrine of Shri Shankaracharya and his path of renunciation of action. Shri Ramanujacharya admitted that the paths of knowledge, devotion and actions are all mentioned in the *Gita*, but emphasised devotion.

Shri Ramanujacharya had indeed affected a change in the cult of Shri Shankaracharya by substituting renunciation with devotion. Lokmanya writes, "If devotion is looked upon as the duty of man from the point of view of mode of life, then the lifelong performance of the worldly duties pertaining to one's particular status, becomes an inferior mode of life. Once the mind has become purified as a result of an Energistic mode of life, and man has attained realisation (*Jnana*), whether he, therefore, remains steeped in the contemplation of the abstract God (*Brahman*) or he is steeped in the unbounded loving worship of the personalised God (Vasudeva), is just the same from the point of view of action (*Karma*). Both are renunciation."

Lokmanya observes, "Although Shri Ramanujacharya may have

been right in saying that Shri Shankaracharya's theory of the Non-reality of Illusion is wrong and that one ultimately attains release only by devotion to Vasudeva, yet, looking upon the God (*Parabrahman*) and the conscious ego (*Jiva*) as 'one' in one way, and 'different' in the other ways is a contradiction in terms and an inconsistency." Therefore, it was imminent that a third school would come in to existence. However, it took another 200 years for that to happen.

Shri Madhavacharya declared that the soul and God are eternally different from each other and any unity between them, partial or entire, is untenable. Considering that the existence of the human soul is grounded in the divine, they are depicted as reflections, images or even shadows of the divine, but never in any way can they be identical with the divine. Discarding the position that all souls will eventually obtain *Moksha*, even if after millions of rebirths, Shri Madhavacharya divided souls into three classes. One class of souls, which qualify for liberation (*Mukti-yogyas*), the next, subject to eternal rebirth or eternal transmigration (*Nitya-samsarins*), and a third class that is eventually condemned to eternal hell (*Tamo-yogyas*).

Mahamahopadhyaya Dr. BNK Sharma observed, "Shri Madhavacharya has rejected much that was defective and outmoded in the conceptions, categories, definitions and methodology (*Prakriya*) of the older schools of *Nyaya*, *Mimamsa* and *Vedanta*. He has propounded a fresh doctrine of the validity of knowledge with special reference to the principle of *Sakshi* as a corrective to all the earlier theories on the subject."[3]

Lokmanya writes, "Shri Madhavacharya has shown in his commentaries on the *Prasthanatrayi* that all these sacred books are in favour of the theory of Duality. Shri Madhavacharya rejected *Jnana Yoga* (path of knowledge) as the means of *Moksha* (release from cycle of birth and death), and considered *Bhakti Marga* (path of devotion) as the only path to salvation. In his commentary on the *Gita*, he says that although desireless action has been praised in the *Gita*, yet desireless action is only a means and devotion is the true and ultimate cult. And once one has become perfect by following the path of devotion, whether one thereafter performs or does not perform action is just the same."

A couple of centuries later, Shri Vallabhacharya declared that the soul is not separate from God, but the various souls are particles of God, just like sparks of fire. The individual soul (*Jiva*) when pure and unblended by illusions, and the Supreme *Brahman* are one. He called his doctrine *Shuddha Advaita* (Pure Non-dualism). In 1493, Vallabhacharya is said to have identified an image of Shri Krishna at the Govardhan Hill at Braj, to the west of the Mathura city in Uttar Pradesh. This image is now called Shrinathji and is located at Nathdwara, Rajasthan.

Advaita (Non-dualism): Symbolised by sugarcane juice, which is the the very essence of sweetness.

Vishishta Advaita (Qualified Non-dualism): Symbolised by sugar that is sweetness processed into a special form.

Dvaita (Dualism): Symbolised by the ant that is separate from the sugar and wishes to enjoy the sweetness.

ॐ refers to the unity of the Atman (soul) and Brahman (ultimate reality). The syllable is often found at the beginning and the end of chapters in the Vedas, the Upanishads, and other Hindu texts. The Bible begins with the words, "In the beginning was the Word, and the Word was with God, and the Word was God."

There is another Vaishnava cult entailing the worship of Radhakrishna, which was promulgated by Shri Nimbarka, who lived after Shri Ramanujacharya and before Shri Madhavacharya. Shri Nimbarka equally emphasised both, the difference and the non-difference between the creator God (Ishvara) and His creation– the souls, the animate (*Chit*) and the inanimate universe (*Achit*). Shri Nimbarka held that the individual soul (*Jiva*), the world (*Jagat*) and the Supreme *Brahman* are different from each other; yet their existence and activity depend on the will of the God. There is a unity in this duality. Shri Nimbarka's disciple Keshava Kashmiri wrote a commentary on the *Gita* called *'Tattvaprakashika'*.

Lokmanya writes, "It is quite clear that these different devotional sub-cults of Duality and Qualified-monism which discarded the Shankaracharya doctrine of *Maya* have come into existence because of the belief that devotion, that is the worship of a tangible thing, loses foundation unless one looks upon the visible objects of the world as real."

The saints in Maharashtra have substantiated the doctrine of 'Devotion' without discarding the doctrines of 'Illusion' and 'Non-duality'. Lokmanya writes, "Saint Tukaram declared 'Devotion' as the easiest of the means by which 'Release' in the shape of realizing the identity of the *Brahman* and the *Atman*, can be obtained." The path of 'Devotion' based on 'Non-duality' is the principal moral of the *Gita* in as much as the Blessed Lord Himself has first told Arjuna:

क्लेशोऽधिकतरस्तेषामव्यक्तासक्तचेतसाम् ॥
अव्यक्ता हि गतिर्दुःखं देहवद्भिरवाप्यते ॥५॥

It is extremely difficult to engage the mind with something that is not manifested in any form. Worshipping a form accessible to the senses is indeed easier. (Bhagavad-Gita Chapter 12, Verse 5)

But the most valuable work relating to the Devotion School is the *'Jnaneshwari'*, a commentary in the Marathi language on the *Bhagavad-Gita* by Sant Jnaneshwar (1275–1296) of the Nath tradition. Shri Jnaneshwar himself called the *Jnaneshwari* the *Bhavarth Dipika*, which means 'light on the inner meaning of the *Shrimad Bhagavad-Gita*'. Indeed the *Jnaneshwari* is a stand-alone book expounding the Indian Philosophy with *Bhagavad-Gita* as the base. Over 8500 *Ovees* (verses) are written to explain the 700 *Shlokas* of the *Bhagavad-Gita*. Every *Shloka* is greatly amplified and its meaning enriched with literary embellishments like *Upama* and *Utpreksha* (similes and metaphors) and *Drishtant* (illustrations). In doing so, the *Jnaneshwari* reaches great literary and philosophical heights.

In a very short life span of 22 years, Sant Jnaneshwar left an everlasting imprint on the sands of time. His commentary on the Bhagavad-Gita, written in Marathi, stands out for its clarity and some remarkable similes, notably those of a tortoise for a Sthitaprajna Yogi, and a serpent that coils round the root of a sandal tree for the pride that goes with knowledge.

After presenting a detailed account of the interpretation of the *Bhagavad-Gita* by various seers, Lokmanya writes, "No one says that the *Bhagavad-Gita* looks upon the *Karma Yoga* as the most excellent path of life." He cites the Marathi poet Vaman Pandit (1608–1695) over the predicament of multiple interpretations by great spiritual giants over a thousand years: "O Blessed Lord, in this *Kalyuga* each one interprets the *Gita* according to his own opinion. Everyone, on some pretext or the other gives a different meaning to the *Gita*. But I do not like their doing this, though they are great; what shall I do, O Blessed Lord?"

Lokmanya now writes, "The *Gita* had been written long before these various schools of thought came into existence, and it was preached by Shri Krishna to Arjuna not to increase his confusion, but to remove it. It contains a preaching of one definite creed to Arjuna and the effect of this advice on Arjuna has also been what it ought to have been."

संन्यासं कर्मणां कृष्ण पुनर्योगं च शंससि ।
यच्छ्रेय एतयोरेकं तन्मे ब्रूहि सुनिश्चितम् ॥१॥

You simultaneously recommend abandonment of the actions and advice to act with devotion. There is a need for explicit direction. (Bhagavad-Gita Chapter 5, Verse 1)

The answer given by Shri Krishna is not ambiguous.

संन्यासः कर्मयोगश्च निःश्रेयसकरावुभौ ।
तयोस्तु कर्मसंन्यासात्कर्मयोगो विशिष्यते ॥२॥

Not performing actions altogether and actions performed with devotion, both lead to the avoidance of wrong and unwholesome actions being done. But the policy of performing actions with devotion is superior way of life.
(Bhagavad-Gita Chapter 5, Verse 2)

Lokmanya wonders why when such a terse reply is given to an equally terse question, there could be so much confusion about the teaching of the *Gita*? He goes on to answer rather lyrically, "Looking at a sweet and nice food preparation, one says it is made of wheat, and another one says it is made of ghee, and a third one says it is made of sugar, according to his own taste. What that food preparation is, remains unsolved. Because as it is possible to mix wheat, ghee, and sugar and to prepare from them various kinds of eatables– *laddus, jalebi, ghivar*, etc.,– the particular eatable cannot be sufficiently defined. Just as when the ocean was churned, one person got nectar, another one got poison, and the other got Lakshmi, etc. Yet, the real nature of the ocean was not thereby fixed. So also, is the case of the commentators who have churned the ocean of the *Gita* on a doctrinal basis and so on. So also the *Bhagavad-Gita* is one and the same; people following different cults see it in a different light."

Lokmanya now quotes a rule from *Mimamsa* School to establish the right message of the *Gita*.

उपक्रमोपसंहारौ अभ्यासोऽपूर्वता फलम्।
अर्थवादोपपत्ती च लिंगं तात्पर्यनिर्णये ॥

If one has to find out the purport of any particular writing, chapter, or book, then the seven things mentioned in the above verse are necessary and have got to be considered. The first two are Upakram and Upasamhar, which mean the beginning and the end of the book. Therefore, it is a given that every writer who writes a book does so with some motive or the other in his mind.

Geometry has defined a straight line as a line, which goes straight from the point of commencement to the last point without severing. The same rule applies to the purport of a book. If there are other roads for going from the beginning to the end, all those roads must be considered as by-paths. One should see which points are covered repeatedly in the book, that is to say, what constitutes an *Abhyasa*. The writer would show numerous reasons in support of it on numerous occasions and will refer to it as a definite proposition over and over again. Now this is the third thing. The fourth and the fifth things are the novelty (*Apurvata*) and the effect (*Phala*) of it. A good book offers something new and there must be a purpose achieved by the writing of that book. The sixth and seventh means are *Arthavada* and *Upapathi*. All possible meanings and perspectives are included in *Arthavada* and in *Upapathi* and all things contrary to the prior stated *Upasamhara* are refuted.

Lokmanya asserts, "As these rules of determining the purport of a book laid down by the ancient *Mimamsa* writers are equally accepted by learned persons in all countries, if we have to extract the true purport of the teaching of the *Gita*, such purport must be consistent with the *Upakarma* (beginning) and *Upasamhara* (conclusion)."

Lokmanya emphatically states, "The Blessed Lord preached the *Gita* to Arjuna at the critical moment before the *Mahabharata* war was actually started. Shri Krishna did not intend Arjuna to go to the woods as a mendicant by making a *Samnyasi* out of him."

The Blessed Lord used the conjunction 'tasmat', i.e., 'for this reason', and asked Arjuna to fight for a cause– *tasmad yudhyasva Bharata*, and throughout the book, a profound reasoning reinforces this initial candid retort.

अन्तवन्त इमे देहा नित्यस्योक्ताः शरीरिणः ।
अनाशिनोऽप्रमेयस्य तस्माद्युध्यस्व भारत ॥१८॥

The true existence of a person is the indestructible, immeasurable, and eternal soul and not the body made out of earthly materials. For this reason, do not get distracted by the physical identities and worldly relationships of your enemies and fight. (Bhagavad-Gita Chapter 2, Verse 18)

हतो वा प्राप्स्यसि स्वर्गं जित्वा वा भोक्ष्यसे महीम् ।
तस्मादुत्तिष्ठ कौन्तेय युद्धाय कृतनिश्चयः ॥३७॥

*In the fight, either your physical body will be destroyed for a good cause thereby your soul gets emancipated, or you will emerge victorious by slaying the wicked and restoring righteous rule. Either way you must fight; your path is clear.
(Bhagavad-Gita Chapter 2, Verse 37)*

तस्मादसक्तः सततं कार्यं कर्म समाचर ।
असक्तो ह्याचरन्कर्म परमाप्नोति पूरुषः ॥१९॥

For this reason, rise above the confusion with worldly identities and relations and act without attachments to them. Actions done in this way only lead one to the realisation of the true purpose of human existence. (Bhagavad-Gita Chapter 3, Verse 19)

एवं ज्ञात्वा कृतं कर्म पूर्वैरपि मुमुक्षुभिः ।
कुरु कर्मैव तस्मात्त्वं पूर्वैः पूर्वतरं कृतम् ॥१५॥

Realising their true identity as the soul, the erudite and wise, in the past have acted upon their duty of maintenance of the world. For this reason, following the established path of the righteous, you too should perform your duty as a warrior to fight the unjust. (Bhagavad-Gita Chapter 4, Verse 15)

तस्मात्सर्वेषु कालेषु मामनुस्मर युध्य च ।
मय्यर्पितमनोबुद्धिर्मामेवैष्यस्यसंशयम् ॥७॥

For that reason, establish your mind in God, and in God alone, at all times (sarveshu kaleshu) and carry out your duty to fight (mam anusmara yudhya) the unjust, the powers of darkness. In this way you will become an instrument of God without a shred of doubt. (Bhagavad-Gita Chapter 8, Verse 7)

तस्मात्त्वमुत्तिष्ठ यशो लभस्व जित्वा शत्रून्भुङ्क्ष्व राज्यं समृद्धम् ।
मयैवैते निहताः पूर्वमेव निमित्तमात्रं भव सव्यसाचिन्॥३३॥

God is the actual doer and you, an expert archer, are chosen as an instrument by God in this war to destroy the unjust and restore order. The end of the wicked you are to going to fight is already sealed. Do not deceive yourself as if you are going to kill them. (Bhagavad-Gita Chapter 11, Verse 33)

तस्माच्छास्त्रं प्रमाणं ते कार्याकार्यव्यवस्थितौ ।
ज्ञात्वा शास्त्रविधानोक्तं कर्म कर्तुमिहार्हसि ॥२४॥

Scriptures (shastra) stand as a guidepost on the path of duty. Your actions must emanate not from the drive of desires, or even the prescribed social codes, but from a deep insight into the spirit of all life, captured in the timeless scriptures. (Bhagavad-Gita Chapter 16, Verse 24)

एतान्यपि तु कर्माणि सङ्गं त्यक्त्वा फलानि च ।
कर्तव्यानीति मे पार्थ निश्चितं मतमुत्तमम् ॥६॥

Actions are not to be set aside but indeed carried out without selfish attachment or expectations of gains. The choice of renouncing all works is not there. The point is not whether or not to do a certain action, the point is to act without involvement of the personal motives and ego. This is my decided and final view (nishchitam matamuttamam).
(Bhagavad-Gita Chapter 18, Verse 6)

Shri Krishna then takes an acknowledgement from Arjuna.

कच्चिदेतच्छ्रुतं पार्थ त्वयैकाग्रेण चेतसा ।
कच्चिदज्ञानसम्मोहः प्रनष्टस्ते धनञ्जय ॥७२॥

A pointed question is asked: Have you heard what I said with an attentive mind? Has your distraction of thought caused by your ignorance been dispelled? (Bhagavad-Gita Chapter 18, Verse 72)

नष्टो मोहः स्मृतिर्लब्धा त्वत्प्रसादान्मयाच्युत ।
स्थितोऽस्मि गतसन्देहः करिष्ये वचनं तव ॥७३॥

The answer is equally clear: My illusions are destroyed, my doubts are dispelled, and I can now recognise by your grace what is the right action for me. I will carry out my appointed action, not with an egoistic mind, but with self-knowledge. (Bhagavad-Gita Chapter 18, Verse 73)

In the words of S. Radhakrishnan, "This evolution means a great shedding of all pretences and evasions, a stripping of all sheaths, a *vastrapaharana*, the self-naughting of the soul."[4] Thereupon, Arjuna fought and during the course of the war, he killed Bhishma, Karna, Jayadratha, and others as and when the occasion arose. Lokmanya now writes vehemently, "When the prospect of a terrible clan-destruction was staring him in the face, whether to fight or not, and if fighting was the proper course, then how was it to be possible without incurring sin, was the principal question before him. The definite answer to this principal question was given in the following words, namely, '*fight with a disinterested frame of mind*, or *perform action*.'" Lokmanya clarifies, "I do not say that the *Gita* has not preached *Vedanta*, or Devotion or the *Patanjali Yoga* at all. But the combination of these three subjects which has been made by the *Gita* must be such that thereby Arjuna, who was on the horns of a terrible dilemma of conflicting principles of morality, and who had, on that account become so confused about his proper duty as to say: 'Shall I do this or shall I do that?', could find a sinless path of duty

---

4   S. Radhakrishnan, *The Bhagavad Gita*, HarperCollins Publishers, Noida, India, 2014, p. 9.

and feel inclined to perform the duties enjoined on him by his status as a warrior."

The purport of the Gita is to support action. You are born with a purpose as an agent operating on the past to create the future. You are duty bound to act as per the circumstances and your station in life. Find a sinless path of duty.

Summing up the argument succinctly Lokmanya writes, "It is perfectly clear that the proper teaching in this place would be of action (*Pravrtti*), and that, as all other things only support action, the purport of the *Gita* must also be to support action. But no commentator has properly explained what this Energistic purport is and how that implied moral could be authoritatively based on *Vedanta* philosophy. Whichever commentator is taken, he totally neglects the *Upakram* of the *Gita* that is the first chapter and the concluding *Upasamhara*, and the *Phala*. He becomes engrossed in discussing from a Renunciatory point of view how the preaching in the *Gita* about the Realisation of the *Brahman* or about Devotion supports their respective cults. As though it would be great sin to link together a permanent union between Knowledge and Devotion on the one hand and action (*Karma*) on the other."

The greatness of India lies in the freedom that it offers to its people. In the concluding chapter of the *Gita*, the Blessed Lord tells Arjuna– '*yatha icchasi tatha kuru*': do as you choose (Chapter 18, Verse 63). Dr. Radhakrishnan elaborates, "God is seemingly indifferent for He leaves the decision to Arjuna's choice. Man is to be wooed and not coerced into cooperation. He is to be drawn, not driven; persuaded not compelled. The Supreme does not impose His command. We are free at any moment to reject or accept the Divine call. The integral surrender should be made with the fullest consent of the seeker."[5]

Lokmanya wrote the *Gita Rahasya*, during his long prison term in Mandalay, Burma. Away from his people in a far away land, Lokmanya would have examined the existential truths to their barest. Life never unfolds with a plan that is foretold, it remains an enigma even to the most learned. The *Mahabharata* war culminated out of a long drawn process of human errors and mistakes of judgement on the parts of those who held positions of power. Arjuna is one of the thousands of warriors who assembled in the battlefield of Kurukshetra for their own reasons. Arjuna was at best a key part of the cohort. The war would not end if he does not fight. But his decision not to fight the war will mark his end as a warrior. Lokmanya ends this first chapter offering the reader a perfect blend of Indian ethereal and Western epistemological approaches.

Lokmanya concludes the first chapter of *Gita Rahasya* in a brief and clearly expressed manner, "The principle object of the present book is to critically examine the *Gita* to show the complete consistency which is to be found in it. But before I do so, it is necessary to deal in greater detail with the nature of the difficulty experienced by Arjuna as a result of his having been of mutually contradictory ethical principles. Therefore, in order to understand the nature of these difficulties and to decide between action and inaction by being caught in the dilemma of 'Shall I do this, or shall I do that?' we shall now first consider the numerous illustrations of such occasions, which we come across in our sacred books and especially do so in the *Mahabharata*."

ॐ

---

[5] S. Radhakrishnan, *The Bhagavad Gita*, HarperCollins Publishers, Noida, India, 2014, p. 445.

2
An Epigram for Every Dilemma

> To be, or not to be: that is the question:
> Whether 'tis nobler in the mind to suffer
> The slings and arrows of outrageous fortune,
> Or to take arms against a sea of troubles,
> And by opposing end them? To die: to sleep–
> No more; and by a sleep to say we end
> The heart-ache and the thousand natural shocks
> That flesh is heir to.
>
> *Shakespeare*[1]

The most distinguished feature of a human being is the power to reflect upon the surroundings, think about the various experiences and decide about his/her actions. From the most mundane– like what dress to wear, what is to be cooked for dinner, to the serious ones about livelihood and above all relationships, human beings are incessantly making choices. Some of the choices that one makes could have far-reaching consequences and may even decide the further course of one's life, allowing no return. The consequences of certain decisions may even effect the lives of future generations, for example, children of a couple who have migrated to the United States of America would be born as American citizens, or a child born out of wedlock will forever carry the stigma of an illegitimate birth. Of all the decisions, ethical decisions must be made most carefully. Physicist and Nobel laureate Albert Einstein (1879-1955) declared, "The most important human endeavour is the striving for morality in our actions. Our inner balance and even our very existence depend on it. Only morality in our actions can give beauty and dignity to life." French philosopher Albert Camus

---

1 *The Tragedy of Hamlet, Prince of Denmark*; Act III, Scene 1

(1913-1960) said, "A man without ethics is a wild beast loosed upon this world."[2]

The critical position in which Arjuna had found himself before the commencement of the *Mahabharata* war was the result of being caught between two mutually contradictory paths of duty. Therefore, Arjuna becoming doubtful about his proper duty is not something unique. Lokmanya called the second chapter of *Gita Rahasya*, 'The desire to know right action' and opened it with this verse of the *Bhagavad-Gita*:

किं कर्म किमकर्मेति कवयोऽप्यत्र मोहिताः ।
तत्ते कर्म प्रवक्ष्यामि यज्ज्ञात्वा मोक्ष्यसेऽशुभात् ॥१६॥

Even the wise are found bewildered while discerning between what is to be done and what should not be done. Shri Krishna tells Arjuna that He would disclose to him this secret so that he would not suffer this indecision and would stay away from committing any sin. (Bhagavad-Gita Chapter 4, Verse 16)

If life is taken as a tryst with destiny, an opportunity for the evolution of the soul, then facing odds emerges as a natural process and fighting or adapting to these odds is a continuous process of choice-making. There are people who are born in most unfavourable circumstances– poverty, persecution, diseases, homelessness and sometimes without even caring parents– yet, they fight every odd and rise to great heights in their lives. On the other hand, there are also people who are born with silver spoons in their mouths and waste away their lives in addictions, infatuations and lust games and die as paupers, leaving behind their destitute children. In between these two extremes, there are millions of people happily settled in mediocre lives, passively going through the ageing process contributing hardly anything worthwhile to the people around them. Why is it so? There are no easy answers. We are all caught in a maze of conflicting values, and which path leads to the next and where do we face a blocking wall is not immediately known. Even

---

2 Albert Camus (1913-1960), French author, philosopher, and journalist

retrieving steps is not always possible. And finally, there are choices between two alternatives, both undesirable. There are 'take it or leave it' choices; 'out of the frying pan and into the fire' choices; and 'between the devil and the deep blue sea' choices; which are indeed no choices at all. In contrast, when Arjuna got confused he did not suffer indecision; he was filled with a desire to know his proper duty right before the commencement of the war. It was a 'what to do in this situation' inquiry. Arjuna was facing a difficult choice.

It is a fact that great writers have written charming poems and excellent plays based on such puzzling situations of duty and non-duty, which they either found in the annals of history or which were merely figments of their imaginations. The stories of Hamlet and Coriolanus, which were both written by the legendary English poet Shakespeare (1564-1616) are cited to establish the universality of the innate quality of a human being– to know what is right in situations that are difficult, problematic and even perplexing at times.

Shakespeare, in his play 'Hamlet' portrayed the heart-wrenching quandary of a son whose uncle had killed his father and married his mother. Faced with this horrid situation, described by the Shakespeare as 'the slings and arrows of outrageous fortune', the son has to decide whether 'to take arms against a sea of troubles,' and end them by taking revenge from his uncle and mother, or else go in to the 'sleep of death'. Here again, the son is worried about 'what dreams may come' in that sleep. What if the experience of death turns out to be worse than the involvement of life?

Coriolanus is another historical character chosen by Shakespeare to discuss the existential dilemma. Coriolanus was a brave Roman potentate who had been driven out of Rome by the citizens and on that account he joins hands with a neighbouring Italian tribe, the Volscians, who are the enemies of Rome. Coriolanus is caught in web of conflicting loyalties. He wants to serve the idea of Rome, but he is against the Roman people, whom he sees as not good, and to further complicate the matter, his mother's ambition of seeing her son as a king, drives him to join hands with the enemy tribe, who would help him to deliver 'his ideal Rome' from the 'not-so-ideal Roman people.' He is eventually destroyed by his confusion.

Lokmanya writes, "There are numerous other similar examples of persons with the dilemma as to duty and non-duty in the ancient or modern history of the world. But it is not necessary for us to go so far. We may say that our epic the *Mahabharata* is a mine of such critical occasions. What is found here, is to be found everywhere and what cannot be found here can be found nowhere else."

Lokmanya now picks up some 'lofty ideals' of Indian culture and examines the dilemmas that they attract. These are notions that are lofty and therefore, can't be correctly applied in real situations and yet are held as ideals making people inadequate and failures in attempting them. He starts with the percept of Harmlessness (*Ahimsa*). Harmlessness is a principle, which has been accepted as preeminent not only in our Vedic religion but also in other religions. But what does one do when an intruder enters one's house, robs one's wealth or assaults one's family? Should one not attack him? Lokmanya quotes Manu:

गुरुं वा बालवृद्धौ वा ब्राह्मणं वा बहुश्रुतम्।
आततायिनमायान्तं हन्यादेवाविचारयन् ॥

Such an atatayin (offender) should be killed without the slightest compunction and without considering whether he is a preceptor (guru) or an old man or a child or learned Brahmin.
(Manusmriti, 8.350)

A very important point is established here. When the defender kills an offender, the defender does not incur the sin of killing, which has now become the *fait accompli* of the offender. His death has already happened or has been decided by his offence, leaving him with no option but to be executed by the defender. Non-violence is not the absence of violence. The violence involved in the defence of *dharma* is fully justified and accepted as is evident by the pictures and idols of gods carrying weapons and slaying demonic creatures. Goddess Kali, seen as a violent destroyer by the ignorant, is indeed the Divine Mother, created to lap up the blood of the perpetual wicked so that no more demons are formed.

The Hindu mind places the highest value on *Rta* (ऋत), the order of the Creation. The order of this world, *Dharma*, evolves from the order of the Creation, *Rta*. Any attempt to disrupt this order is seen as ignorance and such acts are seen as violence. The message of *Ahimsa* springs out from this understanding. Any violence against those who are out to disrupt *Rta*, or are working against *Dharma* is seen as right action and incurs no sin. When a policeman uses force to arrest a criminal, he is not doing *Himsa*, or a judge who is pronouncing the death sentence to a murderer or rapist is not violating the principle of *Ahimsa*. The Indian civilisation celebrated and revered those who fought and laid down their lives in the line of their duty by upholding *dharma*.

अहिंसा परमो धर्मः
धर्महिंसा तथैव च ।

*Non-violence is the ultimate dharma
So too, is violence in service of dharma.*[3]

In *Sanatana Dharma*, the first line of the phrase is only applicable to the ones who preferred renunciation to action, and secondly, to the ascetic. Even if and when provoked, a *Samnyasi* should not defend himself i.e., even when his life is in danger, he should not resort to violence because he identifies himself with the *Atman* rather than associating with his body. However, it is the second line that is purposefully dropped by the preachers of *dharma* and *ahimsa*.

The word non-violence in English is absolute in its meaning but *ahimsa* means non-violence in a qualified term. In *Sanatana Dharma*, it is the moral duty of a person to resort to violence if it is used to stop a greater violence or evil. For example, in order to keep peace and order in his country, a king has to be strict in his punishment. To practice *ahimsa*, he may even have to kill a man who is, for example, killing and taking away the lives of others.

The ideal of *Ahimsa* is anchored in the universal phenomenon of *Rta* and *Dharma* and therefore, is seen as a matter of restraint

---

3 http://www.hindupedia.com/en/Ahimsa_Paramo_Dharma

over violent drives and animalist impulses entwined with one's own physical body and the mind. Unwholesome mental acts like holding others in contempt, pride, prejudices, frowning, or hating others and plotting to ruin another person's life in any way whatsoever is violation of *Ahimsa*. Also, not succumbing to intimidation by the wicked, to the temptations of lust and greed is the subtle form of *Ahimsa*. Understood this way, *Ahimsa* is the highest form of bravery and not the avoidance of conflict and the path of appeasement of the oppressor.

Lokmanya makes an important point that non-violence is not an absolute principle. Non-violence is neither possible, nor prescribed in our scriptures. In the *Vana Parva* of the *Mahabharata*, Draupadi in exile is discussing the merit of forgiveness with her husbands. There is even a caveat on the highly acclaimed virtue of forgiveness. In the *Vana Parva* of the *Mahabharata*, the king of the Sindhu Kingdom, Jayadratha, with his men kidnapped Draupadi when the Pandavas were away hunting in the forest. Upon their return, the Pandavas set out to rescue her and routed the abductors. Yudhishthira did not kill Jayadratha and let him go. This story later becomes a case study in forgiveness. In another age, when Prahlada's grandson Vali asks him if Yudhishthira was right in setting Jayadratha free, Prahlada said 'no'.

न श्रेयः सततं तेजो न नित्यं श्रेयसी क्षमा ।
इति तात विजानीहि द्वयमेतदसंशयम् ॥६॥
यो नित्यं क्षमते तात बहून्दोषान्स विन्दति ।
भृत्याः परिभवन्त्येनमुदासीनास्तथैव च ॥७॥
सर्वभूतानि चाप्यस्य न नमन्ते कदाचन ।
तस्मान्नित्यं क्षमा तात पण्डितैरपवादिता ॥८॥

Neither the use of might, nor forgiveness are absolute virtues. Forgiving wicked people leads to unfavourable consequences. The weak, the ignorant, and the enemies always belittle the pardon and return with vengeance. Forgiveness as a dharma has not been laid down by the learned. (Mahabharata, Vana Parva, Adhyaya (Kairat Parva) 29. Shloka 6-8)

The phrase *'ahimsa parmo dharma'* is not found in the *Bhagavad-Gita* as is often depicted. On the other hand, Shri Krishna tells Arjuna to get up and fight:

अथ चेत् त्वमिमं धर्म्यं संग्रामं न करिष्यसि ।
ततः स्वधर्मं कीर्तिं च हित्वा पापमवाप्स्यसि ॥३३॥

Running away from the duty of fighting a war against the wicked, be it for sentimentality, weakness or faint-heartedness, is certainly sinful for a warrior. Such action is indeed inglorious. (Bhagavad-Gita Chapter 2, Verse 33)

It is therefore the duty of a man to fight against injustice and evil rather than practice the greater *dharma* of non-violence. If a warrior chooses to become non-violent on the battlefield, it will be a dereliction of duty, and hence, will be classified as a sinful act. Therefore, Shri Krishna states that if Arjuna abandons his duty, considering it to be repugnant and troublesome, he will be committing a sin.

Shri Krishna further says:

परित्राणाय साधूनां विनाशाय च दुष्कृताम् ।
धर्मसंस्थापनार्थाय सम्भवामि युगे युगे ॥८॥

For the protection of the good and the destruction of the wicked, and for the establishment of order in the world, I assume human form in every age and set things right for the good. (Bhagavad-Gita Chapter 4, Verse 8)

At this point, Lokmanya takes up the second proclamation about speaking the truth. He starts by citing the Creation Verse from the *Rig Veda* (Book 10, Hymn 190).

ऋतं च सत्यं चाभीद्धात्तपसोऽध्यजायत ।
ततो रात्र्यजायत ततः समुद्रो अर्णवः ॥१॥
समुद्रादर्णवादधि संवत्सरो अजायत ।

अहोरात्राणि विदधद्विश्वस्य मिषतो वशी ॥२॥
सूर्याचन्द्रमसौ धाता यथापूर्वमकल्पयत् ।
दिवं च पृथिवीं चान्तरिक्षमथो स्वः ॥३॥

Arduous penance (of Brahma) led to truth of thought and truthfulness of speech, which generated the night, the firmament and the watery ocean (arnava samudra).
From the firmament and the watery ocean emerged the order of days and night, which rule every moment.
Dhata, the creator then formed in the due order the sun and the moon, the Heaven and the Earth, and the regions of the air and the light.

The *Vedas* thus established the concept of truth as the existential reality. The noun of '*Satya*' indeed encompasses all that exists, all that which never ceases to exist and that which transcends the past, the present and the future. There is great emphasis laid on penance. It is through penance that Brahma invokes the Creator. Through penance, gods acquired their superiority. Even the luminaries in the firmament, the stars and the sky have got their share of felicity as the result of their atonement.

Lokmanya also cites *The Manusmriti*:

वाच्यर्था नियताः सर्वे वाङ्मूला वाग्विनिःसृताः।
तां तु यः स्तेनयेद्वाचं स सर्वस्तेयकृन्नरः॥

All the activities of mankind are carried on by speech; there is no other means as speech for the communication of thoughts.
That man who sullies this speech, which is the basic foundation of all these activities, is despoiling everything at one strike.
(Manusmiriti, 4.256)

Falsehood, deceit, and misrepresentation are seen as manifestation of the sin, the doing of an imperfect mind. We can cleanse our sins by speaking the truth. Akin to the body cleaned by water, the inner being of the man (*Antahkarna*) is cleaned by the truth. Obedience of the truth indeed purifies the soul. While speaking the truth is an eternal value and does not change with time and space, a caveat is made about the possibility of truth being harmful to the knower– *'satyam bruyat priyam bruyat na bruyat satyam apriyam'*– the truth must be presented in a palatable manner; unpleasant truth is better left unspoken. There is a term 'need to know' in the government, particularly concerning the military activities. There are well-laid procedures restricting the data, which is considered sensitive. If you tell people something on a need-to-know basis, you only tell them the facts they need to know at the time they need to know them and nothing more. Knowing too much can put one in grave danger. However, the teaching is completed by the assertion– *'priyam cha nanrutam bruyat'*– speaking untruth however pleasant it may be is forbidden. Handling truth in this manner is declared the path of eternal morality (*esha dharmah sanatanah*).

The present age is called *Kalyuga*– the age of darkness. It is the final of the four ages– *Manvantara* cycle of human existence (the duration of the progenitor of humanity called Manu) after *Satya Yuga, Treta Yuga, and Dvapara Yuga* have passed. Shri Krishna's departure after the end of the *Mahabharata* war marked the end of *Dvapara Yuga* and the beginning of the *Kalyuga*. The human civilisation would degenerate spiritually during the *Kalyuga* preparing itself for its annihilation and paving the way for the next *Manvantara*. The world is run in this age not by the truth but based upon falsehood. We are indeed drowned in the sea of myths, fibs, and falsifications such that it is extremely difficult to discern the truth. People do not make much sense in practicing truthfulness in this world of make-believes and pretensions. As one can hardly see much in a dark ally and both snakes and ropes appear the same, we are frightened of imaginary threats and unmindful of real dangers.

It appears that our civilisation has reached its point of contra-flexure.

Every civil engineer know that the beam in a building carries load in such a way that there exists a point where the forces causing tension in the beam turns in to the compressive forces. The beam is therefore designed as an intelligent arrangement of

An Epigram for every dilemma

steel rods, that bears the tension, and cement-concrete, that bears the compression. Similarly in life, there are situations when a truth turns in to a falsehood. The industry of manufacturing falsehoods is indeed flourishing. The media excels in presenting partial facts as reality and perceptions as facts. Praying on the human tendency of believing the wise and following the powerful, the modern world has created academies, institutions and information dispensing mechanisms to manipulate public opinions for vested interests.

What one can do in such a world? The task of the soul progressing on its evolutionary path remains unchanged. Each one of us must not confuse the drumbeats of this world with the heartbeats of our body. Our truth is not hidden from us. We can feel our truth in our physiology– panting, racing of the heart, goosebumps and hair-raising. In fact, knowing the truth in *Kalyuga*, though difficult and strenuous, is highly beneficial and carries immense value.

Lokmanya wonders, "If there is so much difference of opinion with reference to Harmlessness (*Ahimsa*) and Veracity (*Satya*) then why should one be surprised if the same line of reasoning is applied to the common law, namely Non-stealing (*Asteya*)?"

Lokmanya narrates the story of how the starving Rishi Vishwamitra stole dog meat from a butcher's house and when the butcher protested, he rebuked him by saying that as cows do not stop drinking water even when frogs remonstrate, similarly, the butcher had no right to preach morality to Vishwamitra. The Rishi declared that keeping alive is better than dying. "But then, keeping alive is not the only thing worth doing in this world. Even crows keep alive for many years eating the *pinda* offering," writes Lokmanya and at this point, cites the story of Vidula.

Vidula was a well-educated and a brave princess. She rebuked her son Sanjaya who lay prostrate and depressed after being defeated by the king of Sindhus, by saying that he could not be her son if he gave way to such despair. He was more of a eunuch than a man if he was unable to carry the burden of his affairs on his own shoulders. She exhorted him to abandon his fears and stop delighting his foes by grieving over his defeat, which left him bereft of all sense of honour. Vidula instead told her son that he ought to think big and not be gratified by small gains. He should range like a hawk ranges the sky and make himself known by his deeds. He must fight in the battlefield and thus free himself from the debt he owed to the duties of the *Kshatriya* order. If he could not display prowess, then what was the meaning of his life. "Even when one's roots are cut off," says Vidula, "one should not give way to despair but act mustering up all his strength and courage."

If one is bound to die either today or tomorrow or at any rate after a hundred years then why be afraid of it or cry or dread or lament? From the metaphysical point of view, the soul (*Atman*) is eternal and never dies. It keeps changing bodies as necessitated by its evolutionary paths. Identifying oneself with the body is like mistaking the attire for a person. The death of the body is like curtains coming down after an act in the drama– another acts commences as one concludes. The story is eternal, the process of the individual soul (*Atman*) immersing back in to the Supreme Soul (*Paramatman*) spanned over countless lifetimes, with bodies keep changing depending upon the regression or the progress in a particular lifetime.

जातस्य हि ध्रुवो मृत्युर्ध्रुवं जन्म मृतस्य च ।
तस्मादपरिहार्येऽर्थे न त्वं शोचितुमर्हसि ॥२७॥

Human life circulates in a perpetual cycle of birth and death. Every one who is born will have to die and take birth in a new body. One must not waste one's verve pondering upon the inevitable. (Bhagavad-Gita Chapter 2, Verse 27)

The lineage of Indian kings has two streams– the Solar dynasty and the Lunar dynasty. The Solar dynasty kings ruled with a stern hand, valued integrity, honour and self-discipline and were ascetic and traditional in their conduct. Shri Rama represents the higher solar side. Rishi Vashistha was the most revered teacher of the Solar dynasty kings. The Lunar dynasty kings were free-spirited, expansionists and lived luxurious lives. Shri Krishna represents the higher lunar side. Rishi Vishwamitra mentored the Lunar dynasty kings.

Emphasising the perishable nature of the body and highlighting how noble souls have willingly sacrificed their lives in the fire of duty, Lokmanya tells the story of King Dilipa of the Solar dynasty. Cursed to be childless by the divine cow Kamadhenu, Dilipa sought help from Rishi Vashistha, who ordained him to nurse the divine cow Nandini, the daughter of Kamadhenu. During this period, a lion pounced on Nandini when she was grazing. Dilipa wrestled with the lion to save the cow, but could not defeat the beast. Defeated but unfazed, Dilipa then pleaded to the lion to eat him but spare the cow. Pleased with the integrity of the king, Nandini removed the curse and blessed Dilipa to have a child soon. Thus, Raghu was born and the linage extended to Shri Rama and beyond.

This body is perishable in any case. Noble souls have willingly sacrificed their lives in the fire of duty. When the cow Nandini was grazing in the field, a lion appeared suddenly and pounced on it. King Dilipa begged the lion to spare the cow and eat him instead.

Continuing further, the stories of Shibi, Dadhichi and Karna follow. Shibi was a famous king of the Lunar dynasty. Shibi got involved in saving a dove that approached him for protection from a predator hawk. The hawk, actually Indra, out to test Shibi, demanded the equal mass of flesh from Shibi in exchange of sparing the dove. Shibi offered his own flesh without hesitation.

When Indra was fighting a losing war with the serpent king Vritra, invulnerable to any known weapon, he came to know that the thunder-containing bones of Rishi Dadhichi only could kill Vritra. The Rishi released his life force, Kamadhenu licked the flesh from the bones and Indra killed Vritra with the spine, which came to be known as the Thunderbolt (*Vajrayudha*).

Karna was born in queer circumstances when the young, unwed princess Kunti (who later became the wife of the Lunar dynasty king Pandu) invoked the Sun god who impregnated her. The son was born with a golden armour as his divine protection. In order to safeguard her honour, Kunti let the child float away on the river to be found by a saviour. The infant was found by a lowly placed charioteer who raised Karna as his own son. Later, Duryodhana bestowed upon Karna a kingdom and made him his friend. In the final stage of the *Mahabharata*, when the battle between Arjuna and Karna became inevitable; Indra begged Karna for his armour in the disguise of a mendicant, to ensure his defeat. Knowing fully the consequences, Karna did not flinch and gave away his armour. "I do not care if I lose my life, but protecting my reputation is my avowed purpose."

Lokmanya now writes, "Consider the questions– 'what is the use of renown after you are dead, though by doing good to others you obtain renown?' or, 'why should a righteous man prefer death to disgrace or, prefer doing good to others to saving his own life?' These questions will not be satisfactorily answered unless one enters into the consideration of the Self and the Non-self (*Atma-Anatma*); and even if these questions are answered otherwise, yet, in order to understand on what occasions it is proper to sacrifice one's life and when it is not proper to do so, one has also to consider the question of the philosophy of action and non-action (*karma-akarma*). Otherwise, far from acquiring the glory of having sacrificed one's life, one will have incurred the sin of having foolishly committed suicide."

Familial conflicts are taken up next. Punishment to erring relatives and family members by a king is examined with a verse from *Manusmriti*:

An Epigram for every dilemma

पिताचार्यः सुहृन्माता भार्या पुत्रः पुरोहितः ।
नादण्ड्यो नाम राज्ञोऽस्ति यः स्वधर्मे न तिष्ठति ॥

May be a father or a preceptor or a friend or a son or a priest, or a mother, or a wife, if he or she have not behaved according to their own duties, they are not free from punishment by the King. The King must give them proper punishment.
(Manusmriti, 8.335)

In this context, the story of King Sagara is now told. Sagara of the Solar dynasty had two wives– Sumati and Kesuni. However, he was childless and so being without progeny, the king solicited the aid of the Rishi Aurva. Foreseeing the patterns of the future, the Rishi offered the wives of the king a strange choice. One wife could have a son; the upholder of his race, and the other wife would have sixty thousand sons. Kesini opted for one son and Sumati had sixty thousand sons.

The only son of Kesini, called Asamanjas, grew up as a vagabond. His father disowned him. However, the sixty thousand sons of Sumati turned out to be no better. When Sagara performed the *Ashwamedha Yajna* to assert the expanse of his territory, on one night, the horse disappeared. The sixty thousand sons located the horse near Rishi Kapila who was sitting in meditation. Arrogant and stupid, they ran towards the Rishi with uplifted weapons. Disturbed out of his meditation, Rishi Kapila burned them all with his divine sight.

Sagara now dispatched Anshumat, the son of Asamanjas, to recover the horse. The astute youth reached Rishi Kapila's ashram and bowed before him for forgiveness. The Rishi returned the horse without ado and pleased with the good manners of Anshumat offered him a boon. Anshumat asked for the resurrection of his uncles. Rishi said they would be resurrected but not immediately. "Let the family conduct itself well and then your grandson will have the opportunity to bring down the river of gods to the earth and immersed in its water, your uncles would come alive," he said. The son of Anshumat was Dilipa, whose son Bhagirath eventually brought the Ganga to the earth.

Bhagiratha performed a thousand-year penance to bring the river of gods– Ganga to the earth. He placated Lord Shiva to absorb Ganga's mighty flow in his matted hair and then release it to flow gently. To commemorate his efforts, the head stream of the river is called Bhagirathi, till it meets Alaknanda River at Devprayag.

Ancient Indians had a knack of conveying the most esoteric and abstract concepts through simple and easy stories that even a layperson could grasp. There is this concept of *Saptarishi* (seven sages) in India. As briefly mentioned in the first chapter, these seven *Rishis* are mind-born sons of Lord Brahma and are created to guide mankind throughout a *Manvantara*, a period of 306,720,000 earth years, spanning over four *yugas*. The *saptarishis* live through the entire period of the *Manvantara* and merge with God when life on earth gets destroyed and a new Manu is created with newly appointed *saptarishis*. The seven stars of the Big Dipper constellation used by navigators to know the true north are named after the *saptarishis*– Vashistha, Marichi, Pulastya, Pulaha, Atri, Angirasa and Kratu.

Lokmanya now shares a story related to *Brahma-Rishi* Angirasa. In reply to the question of a layperson Saunaka who wanted to know 'what is that one knowledge by which one can understand the creation of the universe', *Brahma-Rishi* Angirasa differentiates between two kinds of knowledge, namely the lower and the higher knowledge. The lower knowledge is all about hymns, rituals, *yajnas*, and all sort of arts, crafts and sciences. The upper knowledge is not of this world, once accessed it can lead man to what is eternal and indestructible (*Akshar*).

Brahma-Rishi Angirasa now gives Saunaka an analogy of two birds sitting on a tree on two different branches– one is lower than the other. The bird sitting at the lower branch is very busy, chirping, hopping and tasting various fruits, some sweet, others sour. The bird sitting on the upper branch is sitting with poise, watching the activities of the bird on the lower branch. The bird on the lower branch, tired and bored with its activities, looks above and impressed by the bird sitting there, flies to the upper branch. After meeting the bird at the upper branch, this bird finds the other bird exactly similar to itself. The message is that the existences at the lower branch and on the upper branch are like two states of consciousness of the same soul.

The real purpose of life is indeed the raising of consciousness from a lower level of the physical, gross, coarse, and carnal to a higher plane of the sublime, magnificent, benevolent and virtuous. As succinctly said by Socrates (470-399 BCE), "The unexamined life is not worth living"[4]; mere aging of the body does not make one wise or mature.

---

4 A famous dictum apparently uttered by Socrates at his trial for impiety and corrupting youth, for which he was subsequently sentenced to death, as described in Plato's Apology (38a5-6)

न तेन वृद्धो भवति येनास्य पलितं शिरः ।
यो वै युवाप्यधीयानस्तं देवाः स्थविरं विदुः ॥

Man does not as old become old by virtue of his white hair. If a man may be young, but learned, the gods look upon him as old. (Manusmiriti 2. 156)

Conversely speaking, the man who has become old without acquiring knowledge has lived in vain. In order that a person should become mature, he must have acquired the virtues of veracity, harmlessness, etc. Lokmanya writes, "Lord Buddha has himself permitted that even if a *bhikshu* (mendicant) who may be preaching is young, yet he would sit on a high pedestal and preach the religion to other *bhikshus*, who have been previously been invested in the creed and may be older than him."

Earlier, Prahlada was talking to his grandson Vali about the spurious virtue of forgiveness. This time, the story of Prahlada's father and his uncle is told. Hiranyakashipu was an Asura-kind, indulgent and arrogant, in a way living to his name which meant enveloped in the gold foil. Prahlada was born to Kayadu, the wife of Hiranyakashipu. As it happened, Hiranyakashipu's younger brother was slayed by Lord Vishnu in His Varaha *Avatar*. Naturally, Hiranyakashipu hates Lord Vishnu.

To avoid his brother's fate, Hiranyakashipu even obtained a boon from Lord Brahma that he would not meet his death from any of the living entities created by Him. That he would not die within any residence or outside any residence, during the daytime or at night, neither on the ground, nor in the sky.

Providence made Prahlada a devotee of Lord Vishnu. Having failed to convince his son to refrain from worshipping his enemy, Hiranyakashipu challenged Prahlada to prove the omnipresence of Lord Vishnu and if Lord Vishnu can indeed save him, should Prahlada be assaulted. When Prahlada pointed out that Lord Vishnu is present, right in the pillar there, an enraged Hiranyakashipu smashed the pillar with the powerful blow of his mace only to see a half-man-half-lion Narasimha emerging out of the pillar. Circumventing every condition of Brahma's boon to Hiranyakashipu, Lord Vishnu as Narasimha (neither man nor beast), killed him by holding him in His lap (neither on earth, nor in the sky) and tearing him apart, sitting at the doorstep (neither inside nor outside the home), at twilight (neither day nor night). Lokmanya writes, "Prahlada had disobeyed his father Hiranyakashipu, and won over the Blessed Lord."

Lord Narasimha is a protector of his devotees in times of danger. When a Kapalika, by name Kirakashan, tried to kill Adi Shankaracharya, Narasimha entered the body of the disciple of Shankaracharya– Padmapada and slayed Kirakashan. Shankaracharya composed the powerful Lakshmi-Narasimha Karavalamba Stotram at the very spot in front of the God.

From these stories and examples it will be seen that in view of other important considerations, the relationship between the older and the younger in age, between father and son are unimportant. But if an arrogant son begins to abuse his father, will he not be looked down upon as a brute? Moving on to the obligation of a student towards his teacher, Lokmanya quotes Bhishma's advice to Yudhishthira– "the preceptor is superior even to the mother or the father," and then cites the example of King Marutta.

In this story, Indra, the lord of the *Devas*, and Brihaspati, the priest of Indra, are pitted against a virtuous king, Marutta. When Marutta organises a *Yajna* and invites Brihaspati to preside over as the priest, a jealous Indra plays traunt and persuades Brihaspati to decline the invite. Marutta is heartbroken but approaches Brihaspati's younger brother Samvarta to perform the *Yajna*. With the power of his *mantras*, Samvarta forces Indra to come to the Yajna and receive the sacrifices. Marutta offers the sacrifice to Indra with due respect and sans any ill feelings. The moral of the story is that even a preceptor, who arrogantly takes up the wrong path, deserves reprimand. Valmiki Ramayana mentions:

गुरोरप्यवलिप्तस्य कार्याकार्यमजानतः ।
उत्पथप्रतिपन्तस्य न्याय्यं भवति शासनम् ॥

Arrogance is unacceptable even from a person of high station in life (for example, Indra), venerable for his knowledge (for example, Brihaspati). Similarly, indiscretion and transgression from the right path by such persons are unforgivable.
(Book 2 (Ayodhya Kanda), Chapter (Sarga) 21, Shloka 13)

The fights between Bhishma and Parshurama and between Arjuna and Drona were justified on the same principle and when the preceptors of Prahlada appointed by Hiranyakashipu began to advise him against worshipping the Blessed Lord, he had disregarded their advice on the same principle. Bhishma himself says to Shri Krishna that although a preceptor may be a venerable person, yet he must also be bound by the rules of Ethics.

It is quite clear that the net advice of the *Upanishads* is that even if elders are god-like, they do not escape the binding force of laws. In the *Taittiriya Upanishad*, after asking the student to treat the mother, father, preceptor, and guests as deities, it is said that imitate only such of their actions as are good, and ignore the others.

> देवपितृकार्याभ्यां न प्रमदितव्यम् । मातृदेवो भव ।
> पितृदेवो भव । आचार्यदेवो भव । अतिथिदेवो भव ।
> यान्यनवद्यानि कर्माणि तानि सेवितव्यानि ।
> नो इतराणि । यान्यस्माकं सुचरितानि
> तानि त्वयोपास्यानि । नो इतराणि ॥२॥

Man must observe his duties towards others. The mother, the father, the teacher, and the guests, deserve to be treated as gods. They should be dealt with in a flawless manner.
(Taittirīya Upanishad, 1.11.2)

Hindu tradition places great emphasis on the control of the senses, the action organs, and the mind with the overall objective of living with equanimity. Anger (*krodha*), the foremost destroyer of equanimity is indeed a very complex emotion. It builds over a period of time and shows up in most unpredictable situations. Conversely, equanimity is the antidote of anger. Understanding this process indeed leads to self-discovery. It is very common to see youngsters on a picnic and joy ride driving rashly and unmindful of the other people, objects and vehicles around. But people going to work, travelling on a purpose, are cautious. They leave on time, drive slowly and arrive in time. Understanding the purpose of life well tempers down anger. It also acts as a barrier to passion and greed-propelled actions. The *Gita* declares anger, avarice and lust as the three gates to hell.

> त्रिविधं नरकस्येदं द्वारं नाशनमात्मनः ।
> कामः क्रोधस्तथा लोभस्तस्मादेतत् त्रयं त्यजेत्॥

The soul undertakes the journey of a life as a process of evolution. This is derailed and even reversed by acquisitiveness (kama), antagonism (krodh) and insatiability (lobh), which are described as the triple gates of hell (trividham narakasyedam).
(Bhagavad-Gita Chapter 16, Verse 21)

Lokmanya points out that if all living beings decide to shun *kama*, and observe celibacy, the entire living creation will come to an end within fifty or at the most hundred years, and the silence of death will reign everywhere. Wealth (*artha*) and desire (*kama*) are indeed the engines of progress. They ought to be consistent with justice (*dharma*). Anger (*krodha*) is also essential. If a man does not get angry or annoyed when he has been insulted, it is just the same whether he is your friend or whether he hates you. "He who gets angry on account of injustice and who does not submit to insult is truly a man." The highest civilisation consists in putting restraint on these powerful mental impulses, and not in totally destroying them. In order that the world should go on, there must not be either anger or valour, or forgiveness at all times. Whatever the virtue may be, it is not equally appropriate in all circumstances. The Blessed Lord has made this very clear.

बलं बलवतां चाहं कामरागविवर्जितम्।
धर्माविरुद्धो भूतेषु कामोऽस्मि भरतर्षभ ॥११॥

Shri Krishna discerns the desire and passion (kamaraga) from the desires derived from the true spiritual personality. The desires and activities derived from the true spiritual personality are indeed the manifestation of the Divine will.
(Bhagavad-Gita Chapter 7, Verse 11)

Dharma is described in the *Mahabharata* as consisting of the highest moral qualities such as learnedness, austerity, self-sacrifice, faith, sacrificial ceremony, forbearance, purity of emotions, piety and above all, control over the self. Like honey can't be made without bees collecting nectar from the flowers, digesting it and depositing it in the bee-hive, without performing virtuous deeds in daily life, living by the principles of compassion, forbearance and thrift and giving away the fruits of action for the overall good of the people around (*lokasmgraha*), the evolution of the soul is impossible.

On the advice of Shri Krishna, who saw in Bhishma the perfect integration of thought and action, Yudhishthira approached Bhishma ridden on the bed of arrows to learn *Raja-dharma*.

Bhishma instructed Yudhishthira for six days. These instructions are considered as a repository of principles of good governance and are also peppered with interesting anecdotes and inspiring stories. In one such story, Bhishma talks about Cloud King Kundadhara and a Brahmin. The Brahmin was in the habit of seeking rewards from the gods for his work. Floating between the mortal world of the Brahmin and the gods, Kundadhara gave the Brahmin a spiritual eye so that he could see the fleeting and unreal nature of the wealth that no one can carry beyond one's life. Kundadhara made the Brahmin see scores of mighty kings and prosperous people sunk in hell after their deaths. Bhishma concludes:

देवता ब्राह्मणाः सन्तो यक्षा मानुषचारणाः ।
धार्मिकान्पूजयन्तीह न धनाढ्यान्न कामिनः ॥५४॥
सुप्रसन्ना हि ते देवा यत्ते धर्मे रता मतिः ।
धने सुखकला काचिद्धर्मे तु परमं सुखम् ॥५५॥

The Devas, Brahmins and Yakshas and good men always adore those that are virtuous but never those that are rich or given in to indulgence of their desires. It is indeed futile to plead to the gods for wealth. The gods are truly propitious to you since your mind is devoted to virtue. In wealth, there may be a very little happiness, but in virtue, the measure of happiness is very great.
(Mahabharata, Shanti Parva, Adhyaya 263, Shloka 54, 55).

Having established the superiority of mind devoted to virtue over a mind chasing wealth and pleasures, Lokmanya expands the discussion on what is right and what is wrong adding the dimension of time. With time, changes take place in the laws relating to worldly life; and therefore, if one has to consider the propriety or otherwise of anything pertaining to ancient times, one has to also necessarily consider the ideas of righteousness or unrighteousness prevailing at that time.

अन्ये कृतयुगे धर्मास्त्रेतायां द्वापरेऽपरे ।
अन्ये कलियुगे नृणां युगह्रासानुरूपतः ॥

The laws relating to Krta, Treta, Dvapara and the Kali eras are all different as the yugas (eras) change (Manusmiriti 1.85).

Lokmanya further writes, "Needless to say, there must be different standards for considering the laws pertaining to different times. In the same way, if the laws, which are in force in the present age are changed in the future, then the consideration of the righteousness or unrighteousness of actions in the future will also be on a different basis." While the definitions of right and wrong do change with the passage of time, even at a given time customs prevalent in a country, in a community or even a family, vary from one another. An element of a culture or system of behaviour keeps being passed from one individual to another incessantly.

Lokmanya now writes, "If I go on dealing in this way all the problems about what should and what should not be done and what is righteous and what is unrighteous, I shall have to write a second *Mahabharata* myself." He then concludes this chapter by writing, "*Gita* has become the mystic *Upanishad* and the crown jewel of the *Mahabharata*, and the *Mahabharata* has become an illustrated and detailed lecture on the fundamental action (*Karma Yoga*) enunciated in the *Gita*."

यः शास्त्रविधिमुत्सृज्य वर्तते कामकारतः ।
न स सिद्धिमवाप्नोति न सुखं न परां गतिम् ॥२३॥

Actions impelled by the carnal desires and violating the spiritual commandments and tenets are indeed unwholesome. Such actions forever remain devoid of accomplishment, contentment and even excellence. (Bhagavad-Gita Chapter 16, Verse 23)

तस्माच्छास्त्रं प्रमाणं ते कार्याकार्यव्यवस्थितौ ।
ज्ञात्वा शास्त्रविधानोक्तं कर्म कर्तुमिहार्हसि ॥२४॥

Scriptures (shastras) stand as guideposts on the path of duty. Your actions must emanate not from the drive of desires, or even the prescribed social codes, but from a deep insight into the spirit of all life, captured in the timeless scriptures. (Bhagavad-Gita Chapter 16, Verse 24)

Lokmanya declares, "Although there are numerous treaties like the *Upanishads* etc., which deal with the pure science of Release (*moksha*) that is, with *Vedanta*, or like the *Smritis*, which merely enunciate rules of righteous conduct such as harmlessness, etc., yet there is not to be found, at least in these days, another ancient work in the Sanskrit literature like the *Gita*, which discriminates between the doable and not-doable on the authority of the extremely recondite philosophy of the *Vedanta*." Lokmanya cites *Yoga Vashistha*, wherein *Rishi* Vashistha preached to Shri Rama the path of Energism (*Karma Yoga*) based on Self-Realisation (*jnana*), as has been done in the *Gita*.

ॐ

3
The Science of Right Action

> Every science consists in the coordination of facts; if the different observations were entirely isolated, there would be no science.
>
> *Auguste Comte*[1]

The early scientists were philosophers and many of them were very religious people. English philosopher-scientist Francis Bacon (1561-1626), revered as the father of empiricism; Italian astronomer and mathematician Galileo Galilei (1564-1642), French mathematician Blaise Pascal (1623-1662), German mathematician Gottfried Leibniz (1646-1716), and Austrian botanist Gregor Mendel (1822-1884), called the father of modern genetics were all very religious people. However, a wall separating science from religion started emerging over a period of time. The issues of morality were taken out of the domain of scientific inquiry. Lokmanya pointed out this ominous trend and questioned– if not reality and sound scientific method, what else could be the ground for an act to be called moral or otherwise?

Is morality a part of human nature? Like genes, are moral concepts passed through successive generations? If so, can there be a scientific method to examine moral dilemmas? As established by the English naturalist Charles Darwin (1809-1882) human beings have evolved a deep sense of right and wrong from their primate ancestor species. Modern human beings are naturally cooperative and reciprocate goodness almost spontaneously. Excessive self-regard and greed are universally seen as not good and even depraved. In a first-principle argument backed by plentiful scriptural evidence

---

[1] Auguste Comte, *The Philosophy of Mathematics: "A True Definition of Mathematics"*. Auguste Comte (1798–1857) was the French philosopher who founded the discipline of sociology. He is regarded as the first philosopher of science.

woven through a tightly reasoned narrative, Lokmanya wields a sledgehammer to the 'is-ought fallacy' in this chapter. In spite of the great advances made in the modern age, people are more deluded than any of their earlier ancestors. The cognitive surplus of electronic media makes people think that if things are a certain way, they ought to be that way. The delusion gets compounded with the assumption that because something is not occurring now, means it ought not to occur. Lokmanya defines *Karma*, *Yoga* and *Dharma* in this chapter with factuality and genuineness to help people emerge out of their delusion.

Lokmanya opens Chapter 3 of *Gita Rahasya* with these words: "If a man is not actuated by the desire of acquiring the knowledge of a particular science, he is unfit to study that science, and explaining such a science to such an unfit person is a mere waste of time." The appearance of the aphorism *'Athato brahmajijnasa'* (now one should inquire about *Brahman*) at the beginning of both, the *Mimamsa Sutras* of 4th century BCE scholar Jaimani and the *Brahma Sutra*, composed by Jaimani's guru Badarayana, is cited. Just as the teaching of the *Brahman* is best imparted to a *mumukshu* (one who is desirous of 'Release'), or as the teaching of the law of justice is best imparted to one who seeks that knowledge, so also is the teaching of the 'Right Action' most properly given to the person who has been inspired with the *jijnasa* (desire of knowing) on how to rightly perform action while leading a worldly life. The earlier two chapters of the *Gita Rahasya* are therefore structured in this format– dealing with *athato* (now) in the first chapter and *karmajijnasa* (inquiry about *karma*) in the second chapter. Unless a man has by experience, found where his difficulty lies, he does not realise the importance of the science of getting over that difficulty.

The starting advice of Shri Krishna to Arjuna is:

बुद्धियुक्तो जहातीह उभे सुकृतदुष्कृते ।
तस्माद्योगाय युज्यस्व योगः कर्मसु कौशलम् ॥५०॥

Once the intelligence is yoked to the Divine, good and bad reactions of the action performed become irrelevant. With the

> *mind reposed in God, the art of skillfully carrying out action is called the yoga (yoga karmasu kaushalam).*
> *(Bhagavad-Gita Chapter 2, Verse 50)*

In the normal sense, the term 'life' means performing some activity that people consider proper. Of course, there can be activities that are functioning well and activities that are functioning poorly. The poorly functioning category captures the occurrence of sick, sterile, maladaptive and death as the most extreme description. '*Yoga*' is presented as a skill whereby functions are performed well and not poorly. As the living things devoid of action eventually turn dead, and the inanimate things incapable of action are simply not alive, a life of no action is not a life at all. Lokmanya now declares this '*yoga*' as the science of *Karma Yoga*; and in as much as, the circumstances in which Arjuna found himself were not unique, in worldly life, it is necessary that all should profit by the exposition of the *Karma Yoga* science which has been made in the *Bhagavad-Gita.*

Lokmanya further writes, "Whichever science is taken, it is necessary to properly define the important words occurring in its exposition so that their meanings are properly understood. Otherwise, many misunderstandings or difficulties subsequently arise." Therefore, the examination of the three basic terms *Karma*, *Yoga*, and *Dharma* are now taken up.

Starting with *Karma*, it is indeed a very disseminated term and is seen differently by different people. In the most simplistic terms however, it is a cause and effect chain. Good actions, good words and good ideas lead the doer to beneficial effects. Conversely, bad actions, bad words and wicked thoughts eventually bring harm to the person who indulges in them. To overcome the normal failure of such a 'good lead to good and bad lead to bad' pattern showing up, a gestation period is added to the equation. And it is believed that the fructification of deeds transcends one or even many human lives. The gains of apparent bad people are seen as the reward of their good deeds in earlier lives delivered now. Similarly, failure of good people is also rationalised as late manifestation of a past fallacy.

The 'good lead to good and bad lead to bad' theme is further compounded to include some recuperative actions like penance, worship, pilgrimage and charity. By undertaking these socially benevolent deeds, one could make a mid-course correction of a downward fall of one's soul from harsher life conditions that are even extended to birth in the animal and even microbial and plant forms to a superior existence.

Jaimini took away involvement of gods from the affairs of mankind. He declared the rituals as 'cause and effect', by themselves akin to a chemical process where the compounds involved carry out the reaction by themselves following certain well-laid down principles. For different gains, different rituals were invented. Jaimini indeed reduced ritual parts of the *Vedas* as *Dharma*. Lokmanya writes, "My only reason for explaining this is that the reader should not be confused by the limited and restricted meanings in which this word *karma* has been used in *Mimamsa* philosophy or in other places. Religion prescribes some action or the other for reaching *Ishvara*. According to the ancient Vedic religion, this action was sacrificial ritual; and the *Purva-Mimamsa* of Jaimini has been written with the sole purpose of showing how the various different and sometimes apparently contradictory statements which are to be found in the Vedic treaties regarding the performance of sacrificial rituals can be reconciled with each other."

Lokmanya declares, "The *Samhitas* and the *Brahmanas* contain nothing else but a description of sacrificial rituals... These orthodox ritual masters and pure *karma-vadins* say that only by performing the sacrificial ritual prescribed by the *Vedas* and not otherwise; and that, that is so, whether you perform the *Yajna* ignorantly or after realizing *Brahman*, one can attain heaven. Although the sacrificial rituals are accepted by the *Upanishads*, yet their worth is declared to be lower than that of the Knowledge of the *Brahman*, and the *Upanishads* say that though heaven may be attained by the *Yajnas*, the realisation of *Brahman* (*brahma-jnana*) is necessary for attaining true Release."

Lokmanya now expands the discussion on the rituals. He writes, "All these actions are again sub-divided into everyday (*nitya*), occasional (*naimittika*), and for-a-particular-purpose (*kamya*) actions. Such actions as must be performed every day, such as bathing and offering prayers at twilight, are called *nitya-karma*. By performing these kinds of actions, no special purpose (*artha-siddhi*) is achieved. However, if they are not performed, one incurs sin."

"*Naimittika* (occasional) actions are those that have to be performed because some occasion necessitating them has arisen, such as, the pacification of inauspicious stars, penances, etc. If that occasion for which we perform this pacification or penance had not come into existence, there would be no necessity for performing this action. In addition to these, there are certain other actions which we very often perform because we desire a particular thing and for acquiring that thing, as enjoined by the *Shastras*. These actions are *kamya* (desire-prompted) actions; e.g., sacrificial ritual etc., for causing rain, or for obtaining a child… Actions such as drinking of alcohol etc., have been pronounced to be totally objectionable by the *Shastras* and therefore, they are named *nishiddha* (objectionable) actions."

The *Bhagavad-Gita* indeed raises the issue of how to decide what is right, doable and a superior alternative in a given situation, without any external help. A purely 'do and do not' approach is seen as inadequate. As Lokmanya has already shown in the earlier chapter, the myriad situations of life keep presenting contradictions between what is prescribed as right by the *Shastras*. There are situations in which even *Shastras* are not unanimous on the absolutely right course of action. A warrior must fight, but not always, and certainly not without discretion. So instead of keep creating many and contradictory commandment type of manuals about how to live a good life, raising the human consciousness to a higher level and act from there is considered necessary.

Activities of an energetic and constructive life go much beyond doing what is known, and therefore, no manual of what is to be done can indeed ever be made. The purpose of a human life cannot be to go to heaven and a virtuous way of life therefore cannot be capsuled in to performance of rituals, carrying out obligatory duties, and staying away from the prohibited activities. Lokmanya writes, "It is not necessary for the purpose of this exposition to pay any special attention to the divisions of *Karma*. The word '*Karma*' as used in the exposition made in the *Gita* must not be taken in the restricted meaning of actions prescribed by the *Shrutis* or the *Smrtis*, but in a more comprehensive meaning."

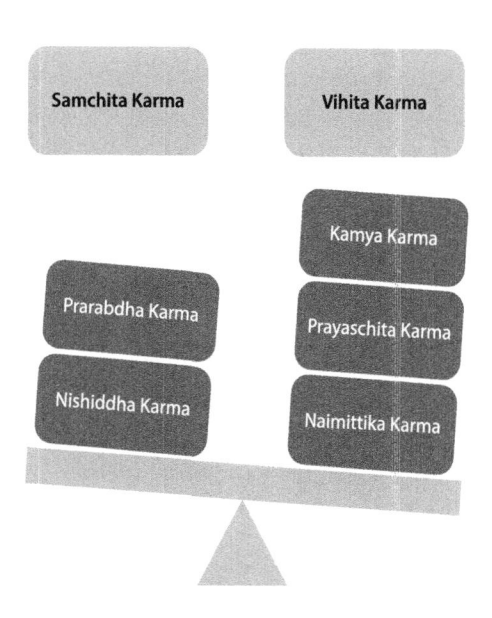

```
Samchita Karma        Vihita Karma

                      Kamya Karma
Prarabdha Karma
                      Prayaschita Karma

Nishiddha Karma       Naimittika Karma
```

British theosophist Annie Besant (1847–1933) famously said, "Karma brings us ever back to rebirth, binds us to the wheel of births and deaths. Good Karma drags us back as relentlessly as bad, and the chain, which is wrought out of our virtues holds as firmly, and as closely as that forged from our vices."[2]

The *Gita* sees actions beyond the apparent performance. Every activity of the body, thought or even speech is seen as action. Therefore, instead of calling activities like fighting, farming, trading, etc. only as actions, acts like breathing, and walking are also called actions. Even sleeping, meditating, completing, desiring, or keeping quiet are actions. All activities of the body and mind are indeed actions– these emerge out of a complex interplay of qualities of nature and carry with them incontrovertible consequences.

---

[2] *Theosophical Review*, Volume 17, p. 139

नैव किञ्चित्करोमीति युक्तो मन्येत तत्त्ववित्।
पश्यञ्शृण्वन्स्पृशञ्जिघ्रन्नश्नन्गच्छन्स्वपञ्श्वसन् ॥८॥
प्रलपन्विसृजन्गृह्णन्नुन्मिषन्निमिषन्नपि ।
इन्द्रियाणीन्द्रियार्थेषु वर्तन्त इति धारयन्॥९॥

Shri Krishna called upon Arjuna to differentiate the engagement of senses with their objects with the soul, overseeing it as a detached witness. The man who is united with the Divine knows this truth and does not confuse the ever-changing flux of sensory activities of seeing, hearing, touching, smelling, tasting, walking, sleeping, breathing, speaking, emitting, grasping, opening and closing the eyes, with his actions.
(Bhagavad-Gita Chapter 5, Verses 8, 9)

Seen this way, remaining alive or dying is a wilful action. A man can choose to live in servitude or die fighting for emancipation. The actions when compounded with this sort of a decision-making become duty-bound (*kartavya-karma*), proper actions (*vihita-karma*) or unfitting actions (*akarma*).

किं कर्म किमकर्मेति कवयोऽप्यत्र मोहिताः।
तत्ते कर्म प्रवक्ष्यामि यज्ज्ञात्वा मोक्ष्यसेऽशुभात्॥१६॥

Even the wise are found bewildered to discern between what is to be done and what should not be done. Shri Krishna tells Arjuna that He would disclose to him this secret so that he would not suffer this indecision and would stay away from committing any sin. (Bhagavad-Gita Chapter 4, Verse 16)

The concept of *Karma* is not restricted to the actions of human beings. It even encompasses the activities of the moveable and immoveable world. But Lokmanya suspends further discussion on this to take it up later in chapter 10.

Lokmanya now examines the term *'Yoga'*. The word *'Yoga'* is even more complicated in its meaning than the word *'Karma'*. The present-day ordinary meaning of this word is 'controlling the mental impulses of the organs with the help of the breath (*Pranayama*) or the *yoga* of mental absorption or meditation as prescribed by the *Patanjali-Sutras*. The word has been used with the same meanings in the *Upanishads* also. Lokmanya also writes, "But it must first be borne in mind that this restricted meaning is not the meaning in which it has been used in the *Bhagavad-Gita*. The word *'Yoga'* comes from the root *'yuj'* which means 'to join', and its root meaning is 'the state of union', 'combination', 'addition' or 'co-existence' or 'staying together', and later on, it has also come to mean the 'means', 'device' or 'method' or 'thing to be done', that is, the *karma* (action) which is necessary for acquiring that state. The *Amarakosha*, a thesaurus of Sanskrit written by the ancient Indian scholar Amarasimha, who wrote during the reign of Chandragupta Vikramaditya (380-415 CE), has given all these meanings of the word in the following sutra (3.3.371):

योगः संहननोपायध्यानसंगतियुक्तिषु ।

In practical astrology, if some planets have become propitious or unpropitious, we say that they are forming a propitious or unpropitious *'yoga'*, and the word *'yoga'* in the phrase *'yoga-kshema'* means 'acquiring such things as one has not got'. Lokmanya writes, "In the *Gita*, the word *yoga*, *yogi*, or other compounds from the word *yoga* have occurred about 80 times. We find the word used almost everywhere more or less in the meaning of 'means', 'skilful device,' 'method', 'the thing to be done', 'union', etc., and it must be said that this is one of the comprehensive words used in the *Gita*-science".

Over a period of time, *yoga* has turned in to a market of lemons. There are so many definitions of *yoga*, and so many *yogis* now float in the world that the term has indeed lost its original meaning. Mindful of this, Lokmanya linked the root definition of *yoga* to the proprietary of the action involved. Take for example the activity of acquiring money. It can be done by earning it through effort, by borrowing, or by stealing it or snatching it away from those who have it. The *'yoga'* of acquiring money (*dravya-prapti-yoga*) in this example is, 'earning money by one's own effort without sacrificing one's independence.' This simple and yet profound perspective exposes in an instant so many millionaires of the modern world as exploiters, fraudsters and defaulters of banks, unfit for the status and respect they command in society.

Lokmanya argues, "If the Blessed Lord Himself has intentionally and specifically defined the word *yoga* in the *Gita* itself as *yogah karmasu kaushalam*, that is *yoga* means a special device of performing actions, then, there should strictly speaking remain no doubt whatsoever about the primary meaning of this word in the *Gita*. But, as several commentators have extracted various hidden meanings from the *Gita* by twisting the meaning of this word, disregarding this definition of the word given by the Blessed Lord Himself, it is necessary here to go deeper into the meaning of the word *'yoga'* in order to clear that misinterpretation."

When the word *yoga* is first mentioned in the *Gita*, in the second chapter, the Blessed Lord has linked it with the intellect and defined it in the clearest way. Shri Krishna first justifies the war against Kauravas on the authority of the *Samkhya* philosophy, and then provides justification for Arjuna, an accomplished warrior, to fight the war on the authority of the *yoga* (one's own effort without sacrificing one's independence).

एषा तेऽभिहिता साङ्ख्ये बुद्धियोगे त्विमां शृणु ।
बुद्ध्या युक्तो यया पार्थ कर्मबन्धं प्रहास्यसि ॥३९॥

Having explained Samkhya with a standpoint of body and soul as two distinct entities (esha tebhihita samkhye), Shri Krishna now explains to Arjuna the yoga of buddhi (buddhiryoga) wherein the mind should be guided by the buddhi rather than united to the senses. Work with such understanding is freed from the bondage of karma (karmabandham prahasyasi).
(Bhagavad-Gita Chapter 2, Verse 39)

The Blessed Lord explains that desire propelled worship and rituals are not only futile, but also even harm the minds of those who seek favours from the gods and in that process disregard the irrefutable law of *karma*. The eulogies sung and sacrifices made to please gods can't alter even by a miniscule, the inevitable consequences of the past deeds. The future is already created in the past. The repentance and right action is what is needed to mitigate the destruction that is already set in motion.

यामिमां पुष्पितां वाचं प्रवदन्त्यविपश्चितः ।
वेदवादरताः पार्थ नान्यदस्तीति वादिनः ॥४२॥
कामात्मानः स्वर्गपरा जन्मकर्मफलप्रदाम् ।
क्रियाविशेषबहुलां भोगैश्वर्यगतिं प्रति ॥४३॥

Shri Krishna distinguishes true action from ritualistic piety. The Vedic sacrifices are seen as reward-seeking offerings made to the heavenly gods. Devising arduous and complex rites to secure their own pleasure and their own power, such people construct their own heaven. These fools come back to the mortal world after having happiness in heaven (svargapara) as quid pro quo (janma karmaphala pradam).
(Bhagavad-Gita Chapter 2, Verse 42, 43)

Repentance and right action is the product of a steadfast mind. The Blessed Lord asks Arjuna not to allow his mind to run after desires and wither its energy, but anchor it in an emotional state that is unaffected by aversions and attachments and then act out his duty.

योगस्थः कुरु कर्माणि सङ्गं त्यक्त्वा धनञ्जय ।
सिद्ध्यसिद्ध्योः समो भूत्वा समत्वं योग उच्यते ॥४८॥

Steadfast in inner composure (yogasthah) do your work. Once attachments are abandoned and the mind takes success and failure with an inner poise, the action becomes yoga (samatvam yoga uchyate). It is self-mastery. It is conquest of anger, sensitivities, pride and ambition.
(Bhagavad-Gita Chapter 2, Verse 48)

The Blessed Lord thus defines yoga as imperturbability. One need not be anxious or unsettled either by success or failure. The actions carried out in such a mental state are always superior, wholesome and beneficial than the ones, which are promoted out of personal desires and afflictions like pride and prejudice.

दूरेण ह्यवरं कर्म बुद्धियोगाद्धनञ्जय ।
बुद्धौ शरणमन्विच्छ कृपणाः फलहेतवः ॥४९॥

Seek refuge in divine knowledge and insight, O Arjuna, and discard reward-seeking actions that are certainly inferior to works performed with the intellect established in Divine knowledge. Miserly are those who seek to enjoy the fruits of their works. (Bhagavad-Gita Chapter 2, Verse 49)

The Blessed Lord conclusively declares that actions carried out by an unperturbed mind, unaffected by any personal motive of profit, revenge or appeasement add to the good order of the world and neither cause harm to the doer nor create any karmic consequences. The nature of *yoga* is concisely defined as *yogah karmasu kaushalam*, leaving no doubt about it being a skilful act carried out with an unperturbed state of mind.

Lokmanya writes, "There are two ways in which the Self-Realised man should live in this world which have been prescribed by the Vedic religion in existence long before the date of Shri Shankaracharya. One of these ways is the literal abandonment (*samnyasa*) or giving up (*tyaga*) of all action after Self–Realisation. The other way is of not giving up actions even after Self-Realisation, but going on performing them while life lasts, in such a way that one does not thereby incur either sin or merit."

Samnyasa means to 'give up' and *yoga* means 'stick to'; therefore, these are two independent paths of the giving up or the sticking to action. The two words *Samkhya* and *yoga* (*Samkhya-yogau*) are two abbreviated terms, which are used later on with reference to these two paths:

साङ्ख्ययोगौ पृथग्बालाः प्रवदन्ति न पण्डिताः ।
एकमप्यास्थितः सम्यगुभयोर्विन्दते फलम् ॥४॥

Only the ignorant speak of Samkhya (renunciation of actions, or karma samnyasa) and karma yoga (work in devotion) as different. Those who are truly learned say that by applying ourselves to any one of these paths, we can achieve the results of both. (Bhagavad-Gita Chapter 5, Verse 4)

The Science of Right Action

An equable mind works like a skilful device, our Body-Mind-Soul will cooperate with our hands carrying out work with full concentration, dedication, and abilities. It was a common practice to test eligible grooms for a bride for their prowess. For the marriage of his daughter Draupadi, the king of Panchala (modern day Central Uttar Pradesh), set a difficult test for the eligible groom to penetrate the eye of a rotating fish by looking at its reflection in the water below.

Concluding his exposition of the term *yoga*, Lokmanya clarifies, "It is true that the sixth chapter of the *Gita* contains a description of the postures (*asanas*) of the *Patanjala Yoga* necessary for steadying the 'Mind'." He then asks, "But for whom has that description been given?" and answers, "Not for the ascetic, but for the *Karma Yogi*, for the person who continues skilfully performing actions, and, in order that he might thereby acquire an equable frame of 'Mind'." The advice given to Arjuna is cited as a concluding proof:

तपस्विभ्योऽधिको योगी ज्ञानिभ्योऽपि मतोऽधिकः ।
कर्मिभ्यश्चाधिको योगी तस्माद्योगी भवार्जुन ॥४६॥

A yogi is superior to the tapasvi (ascetic), superior to the jnani (a person of learning), and even superior to the karmi (ritualistic performer). Therefore, O Arjuna, strive to be a yogi.
(Bhagavad-Gita Chapter 6, Verse 46)

When the Blessed Lord asks Arjuna to become a *yogi*, the instructions are to have equanimity of mind and excellence of skills and thereby perform without the burden of a desire upon the action. Lokmanya settles any confusion here about Arjuna advised to follow *Patanjali* Yoga, which would be ludicrous a command in that situation of warring armies staring at each other to commence the fight. Hereafter, 'yoga' is seen as an abbreviated term for '*Karma Yoga*', which means the integration of unperturbed emotional state, equanimity of mind, and the most skilled action.

Lokmanya wrapped this discussion on *Yoga* as *Karma Yoga* with the shining example of Raja Janaka. In spite of being a king of great authority and power, he lived as a *yogi* and was thus revered as the philosopher-king, a term the Greek philosopher Plato (428-348 BCE) would later use in his political theory to describe the ruling elite who seeks to apply philosophy in the exercise of power. Raja Janaka held regular conferences of scholars and engaged them in debates about the true path of human life and the nature of enlightenment. Scholars following different traditions and schools would argue for days, weeks and even months and yet, the king failed to find an answer that could satisfy him. The story of 'Ashtavakra' slips into the narration here, who would eventually become Janaka's spiritual master.

As goes the legend, there was a Brahmin called Kahoda, who used to discuss spiritual matters with his equally learned wife. During such discussions when she was pregnant, the extraordinary foetus used to capture the teachings. On one occasion, he interrupted his father's discourse when he was making a mistake, by creating a sound from inside the mother's womb. This infuriated Kahoda and he cursed the foetus to be born with deformities. Of course, in spite of living with a body deformed in eight limbs, therefore named as 'Ashtavakra', the child excelled in his studies.

In one of the customary assemblies of scholars at Raja Janaka's court, Kahoda was invited and the child Ashtavakra accompanied his father. Midway during the animated debate on if there is an absolute reality that pervades all that exists, the child Ashtavakra suddenly got up, rather bored with the unending arguments and pedantic fault-finding between scholars gathered there and said, "All this is empty talk. All the people assembled here, are talking their heads out without any clue to the real nature of the *Atman*."

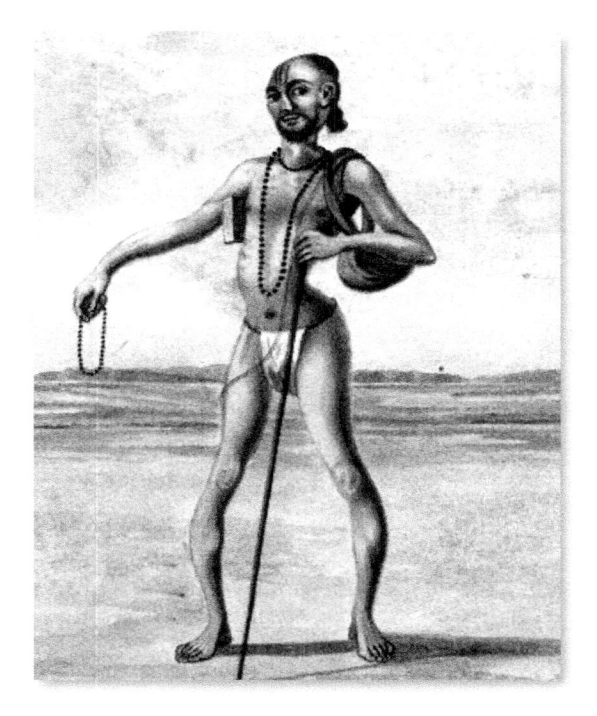

Ashtavakra is greatly revered. In Valmiki Ramayana he is even compared to Shri Rama as a son's ideal. When Raja Dasharatha descends from the heavens to bless Shri Rama after his victory over Ravana, he described him as redeemed by his virtuous son similar to how Ashtavakra redeemed his father.
(Book 6 (Yuddha Kanda), Chapter (Sarga) 119, Shloka 17)

Shell-shocked with the audacity of a young child with deformed limbs to declare the debate between learned scholars meaningless, Raja Janaka asked if Ashtavakra could explain the *Atman*. Ashtavakra boldly said, "Yes, I can." Surprised but respectful to the child, Raja Janaka asked him to explain. Ashtavakra said that it was not the right place and time for Raja Janaka to receive the answer. The king must come to the forest alone where Ashtavakra lived, to know the answer. Ashtavakra then left the assembly.

After a few weeks, the perplexed Raja Janaka went in search of Ashtavakra in the forest and found him meditating under a tree. When Raja Janaka started dismounting from his horse, Ashtavakra asked him to be instantly still like a statue. Raja Janaka somehow held himself still in the awkward position of one leg up in the air and another on the saddle. Raja Janaka felt as if time had stopped. He could not know if it was a minute, an hour, a day, a week, or a year, he was there still and the stillness was long enough. He indeed became a realised being.

An enlightened Janaka, after getting off his horse, fell at the feet of Ashtavakra and said, "I have nothing to do with my kingdom and other activities of this world as they do not make any sense to me anymore." He expressed his desire to live in the forest with Ashtavakra. But Ashtavakra declined his request and said, "Real enlightenment is to know that life is not about living according to your likes and dislikes. It is not about your needs and desires either. So, whether you like it or not, whether you need it or not, the good people of your kingdom deserve to be ruled by an enlightened king and therefore, you must go back and be their king."

The Blessed Lord gave the example of Raja Janaka as a perfect king and *Karma Yogi* in the *Gita*. He ruled over his kingdom as a duty and not for any personal gain or pleasure. He lived in this world to perform without desires, taking events in his stride with a deep sense of equanimity. Readers of the Ramayana know well his measured conduct and immaculate response to the ordeal his daughter Sita went through.

कर्मणैव हि संसिद्धिमास्थिता जनकादयः ।
लोकसंग्रहमेवापि सम्पश्यन्कर्तुमर्हसि ॥२०॥
यद्यदाचरति श्रेष्ठस्तत्तदेवेतरो जनः ।
स यत्प्रमाणं कुरुते लोकस्तदनुवर्तते ॥२१॥

It was by carrying out their duties that King Janaka (the king of Mithila and father of Sita, the wife of Shri Rama) and others like him perfected their lives. They worked for the good of the world (lokasmgraha). The actions of such perfect people are imitated by the common people. Whatever standards they set, the entire world follows (lokas tad anuvartate).
(Bhagavad-Gita Chapter 3, Verse 20, 21)

Our outward reactions mean little in comparison to our inward response to what happens to us. This life is more about working on oneself, rather than correcting others around you. Even when a teacher is teaching the students, he is indeed improving his own understanding of the subject. When a woman is cooking food for the family, she is performing the divine act of nourishing the people around her. More than the outward expression of your activities, the inner intent, the motivation behind what you are doing decides the merit of the act. Life is indeed a pilgrimage and how far one moves towards the divine inside, defines the progress of the journey.

Lokmanya writes, "It is our great fortune that this work of preaching the *Karma Yoga* was taken on His own shoulders by Shri Krishna Bhagwan, who was the promulgator of this path of *Yoga* and who was the personified *Ishvara* of all *yogas* (His name *Yogeshvara*– *Yoga* plus *Ishvara*), and He has explained the esoteric import of it to Arjuna for the benefit of the whole world."

Here onwards, Lokmanya referred to the word '*yoga*' as a science '*Karma-yoga-shastra*.' As with any other science, there are principles and methods involved in '*Karma-yoga-shastra*.' It involves all theories, validations, and ways to deduce the truth like any other science. There are no commandments and revelations offered here, but processes are established by which one can know whether a particular action can always be performed, or there are exceptions possible; and even how these exceptions may arise. Instead of calling a path or course of action merely good or bad, a framework is put in place that helps decide what is bad, and on the strength of this, decisions of carrying out an act or otherwise are indeed based.

Lokmanya writes, "'Good' or 'bad' are words in ordinary use

and the following other words like: propitious and unpropitious, or beneficial and harmful, or meritorious and non-meritorious, or sin and virtue, or righteous and unrighteous, are used in the same sense. The meaning conveyed is the same by the word-couples doable and not-doable (*karya* and *akarya*), duty and non-duty (*kartavya* and *akartavya*), just and unjust (*nyayya* and *anyayya*). Nevertheless, as various persons who have used these words have different ideas about the formation of the universe, there have also come into existence, different ways in which the *Karma Yoga* science has been expounded."

Lokmanya now takes up a detailed explanation of the *Karma Yoga* science. "Whatever science is taken, the subject-matter of it can be discussed ordinarily in three ways: the *Adhi-bhautika* (Materialistic) way of considering them; the *Adhi-daivika* (Theological) examination of the object; and an *Adhyatmika* (Metaphysical) examination of the object. These three ways of examining any subject matter have been in existence since time immemorial and they seem to have been followed even in the *Upanishads*."

The materialistic way is to consider the various objects in the physical world as our sensory organs perceive them, and there is no inquiry made beyond that. For instance, when you look up at the Sun it is seen as a huge fireball with various properties such as its heat, light, weight, and distance. Even properties like its weight and power of attraction are determined. Similarly a tree is seen as a trunk, branches and leaves with some assumption of roots and photosynthesis. Lokmanya writes, "The examination of the subject matter in chemistry or physics or the science of electricity or other modern sciences is of this kind. Indeed, materialists imagine that when they have examined in this way the visible properties of any object that is all they need to do and that it is useless to further examine the objects in the world."

The next level of inquiry transcends the materialistic form of the objects and looks for the power or principle behind their existence, then one has to transcend the material examination of the object. The fireball Sun now becomes a manifestation of the Sun' (*Surya Deva*) which dwells within it and carries on the activities of the material Sun. Lokmanya writes, "Such examination is called the *Adhi-Daivika* (Theological) examination of the object. According to this point of view, there are in the trees, the water, the air, etc., innumerable deities, which are distinct from those objects, and which activate those objects."

The inquiry now reaches a higher level where an overabundance of independent deities operating in all the various objects in the gross world, energy is assumed as the prime mover or the root cause of all the phenomenon. Lokmanya writes, "This Spiritual Force, i.e., factor of consciousness (*Chitta Shakti*) is imperceptible to the organs, but it carries on all the activities of the external world, the belief is that the Spiritual Force exists in the human body in the shape of an *Atman* and acquaints the human being with the entire creation; and that this cosmos is kept going by that force. Such consideration of the object is called an *Adhyatmika* (Metaphysical) examination of the object."

Lokmanya concludes, "Out of these three methods, our religious writers attach a higher importance to the metaphysical (*adhyatmika*) method of consideration than to others, relying on the authority *Adhyatma-vidya vidyanam* (the metaphysical science is the highest of all sciences) declared in the *Bhagavad-Gita*":

सर्गाणामादिरन्तश्च मध्यं चैवाहमर्जुन ।
अध्यात्मविद्या विद्यानां वादः प्रवदतामहम् ॥३२॥

The Blessed Lord tells Arjuna to know Him as the beginning, middle, and end of all creation. Of the sciences, I am the science of the self (adhyatmavidya vidyanam), and of those who debate I am the dialectic (vadah pravadatam aham).
(Bhagavad-Gita Chapter 10, Verse 32)

Lokmanya now draws the attention of the readers to how Western philosophers looked at the phenomenon. Lokmanya mentioned French philosopher Auguste Comte (1798-1857), who is considered the pioneer of the social sciences. Comte emphasised on the apparent materialistic nature of the world and interaction between people rather than the unseen dynamics. When the early man tried to comprehend the natural phenomena– animals, trees, water, sky, winds and storms– these were taken as deities. Comte called it the Theological consideration of the universe. But as time passed and human intelligence grew, man started looking for the underlying reasons.

The Theological understanding of the phenomenon replaced the metaphysical reasoning. While attempting to understand that what is happening around is not a random game of deities but a well-organised interaction of unseen forces, which are as real as the seen objects and indeed control them, man himself learned to control these forces. The invention of electricity, steam engine, the telegraph, were possible by the rise of understanding to a higher level. The mysteries of the phenomena are now used to create a better and more convenient world. In the final stage of understanding, what Comte called the sociological basis of human life, is the concern for the entire humanity and pursuit of making our planet more liveable.

It is akin to attributing death to recall by Yama (the God of Death) to a verifiable cause of an illness such as a heart attack or a cancer and gradually understand it as death of a living tissue in the absence of oxygen. For example, deposition of a plaque is formed by undigested cholesterol that gradually narrows the arteries in the heart, and a day arrives when the flow of the blood completely stops and the heart tissue starved of oxygen dies. The visit of Yama is now seen as stopping of the blood supply to the heart muscle. Lokmanya writes, "These three systems have been respectively given by me the ancient names of *Adhidaivika, Adhyatmika*, and *Adhibhautika* in this book." Of course, questions like why it happens to the one and not to the other and why it happens sooner or later, are still investigated and hypothesised. But this entire exercise changes nothing. The day of the death arrives, for this or that reason; cells do not get oxygen and die.

Lokmanya now presents a succinct examination of the term '*Dharma*'. The word '*dharma*' is in ordinary practice very often used to imply only the path leading to the next-world happiness. When we ask someone, "What is your *dharma* (religion)?", our intention is to ask him by what path he goes - whether Vedic, Buddhist, Jain, Christian, Muslim or Parsi - for acquiring happiness in the next world; and the reply which he gives is also from the same point of view.

Looking at *Dharma* this way, a plethora of definitions have sprung up. So the process of carrying out rituals becomes *dharmicanushthan*. The dutiful way of a ruler becomes *raja dharma*, and the duty of people becomes *praja dharma*, of lay people– *desh dharma*, members of a caste– *jati dharma*, in a family– *kula dharma* and bonhomie between friends– *mitra dharma*. Even *svadharma* is discussed. Extending logic to the afterlife, we have *moksha dharma*. Modern writer Wayne Dyer (1940-2015) summarised it best– "I know that I came into the world with what I call 'big *dharma*'– with a blueprint to teach self-reliance and a positive loving approach to large numbers of people all over the globe. I am ever so grateful for the circumstances of my life that allowed me to be pretty much left alone and to develop as I was so intended in this incarnation."[3]

Vardhamana Mahavira (600-528 BCE) declared *dharma* the nature of things. *Dharma* is also seen as the order that holds the society together. The purpose of life is not seen as emancipation (*moksha*) anymore, but as one of the many, and that too the final one. The four ideals of manhood (*purushartha*) puts the order as morality of conduct, acquisition of wealth, fulfilling of desires and finally, release. In this way, *dharma* has turned in to a set of ethics. Dr. B. R. Ambedkar (1891–1956) said, "A people and their religion must be judged by social standards based on social ethics. No other standard would have any meaning if religion is held to be necessary good for the well-being of the people."[4]

At this point, Lokmanya clarified a widespread commotion about the caste system in Hindu society. The word *dharma* has been used on many occasions and in many places citing the duties of the four castes– *brahmin, kshatriya, vaishya*, and *shudra* as well as their specific duties and positions in the society. In the *Bhagavad-Gita* the word *dharma* has been used as meaning 'the duties of the

---

[3] http://www.awaken.com/2017/01/divine-love-is-the-answer-to-your-true-purpose/
[4] Dr. B. R. Ambedkar, *A Reply to the Mahatma*, http://ccnmtl.columbia.edu/projects/mmt/ambedkar/web/appendix_2.html

four castes in this world'. The Blessed Lord is telling Arjuna to fight, having regard for what his *dharma* is.

स्वधर्মमपि चावेक्ष्य न विकम्पितुमर्हसि ।
धर्म्याद्धि युद्धाच्छ्रेयोऽन्यत्क्षत्रियस्य न विद्यते ।३१॥

The Blessed Lord tells Arjuna that having regard for his own duty (svadharmam) he should not falter. No other option indeed exists for a warrior (chreyo 'nyat ksatriyasya na vidyate). (Bhagavad-Gita Chapter 2, Verse 31)

Lokmanya writes, "In the expression '*svadharme nidhanam shreyah paradharmo bhayavahah*', i.e., it is better to die performing one's caste duties; following the duties enjoined to another caste is dangerous", the ancient *rishis* had created the institution of four castes– which was in the nature of a division of labour in that all the affairs of society go without a hitch, and that society should be protected and maintained on all sides, without any particular person or group of persons having to bear the whole burden." This concept of division of labour also existed in the Bronze Age Mycenaean civilisation on mainland Greece around 1600-1100 BCE. Plato said so beautifully, "All men are by nature equal, made all of the same earth by one Workman; and however we deceive ourselves, as dear unto God is the poor peasant as the mighty prince."[5]

श्रेयान्स्वधर्मो विगुणः परधर्मात्स्वनुष्ठितात् ।
स्वधर्मे निधनं श्रेयः परधर्मो भयावहः ॥३५॥

Carrying out one's own duty, even though faulty (vigunah), is more virtuous (shreyan) than performing the duty of others (para-dharmah). Death in the line of one's own duty (nidhanam) is glorious, while dying while doing others' work is perilous (bhaya-avahah). (Bhagavad-Gita Chapter 3, Verse 35)

Dr. S. Radhakrishnan writes in the commentary of this *shloka*, "We have not all the same gifts, but what is vital is not whether

---

5 Plato was a philosopher in Classical Greece and the founder of the Academy in Athens

we are endowed with five talents or only one but how faithfully we have employed the trust committed to us. We must play our part, manfully, be it great or small. Goodness denotes perfection of quality. However distasteful one's duty may be, one must be faithful to it even unto death."[6]

Lokmanya observes, "Later on, people belonging to this society became *jatimatropajivi* (persons, who forgetting their respective caste duties, belonged to a particular caste merely by reason of birth) and became mere nominal *Brahmins, Kshatriyas, Vaishyas,* or *Shudras*. Originally, this institution had been made for the maintenance of society and it is quite clear that if any one of the four castes had given up the *dharma,* the duties allocated to it, or if any particular caste had totally ceased to exist and its place had not been taken by some other persons, the entire society would to that extent have been disabled and would later on have either been gradually destroyed or would have at least sunk to a very low stage."

Lokmanya now explains *dharma* as the binding force of the society. He writes, "The word *Dharma* comes from the root *dhr,* to hold or uphold, and all human beings are held together by *dharma*. That by which the holding together (of all human beings) takes place is *dharma*. Therefore, when this *dharma* ceases to be observed, the binding-ropes of society may be said to have become loose, and when these binding ropes are loosened, society will be in the same position as the planetary system consisting of the Sun and the planets would be in the sky without the binding force of gravitation or as a ship would be on the ocean without a rudder."

The Vedic concept of *Rta* is now introduced. This word has no exact equivalent in English, as this concept itself is alien to the Western thought. However, it is akin to the Chinese concept of the Tao, which explains an existential order in the phenomenon, including the fate of humanity. This idea can be expanded to include the cosmic order of the universe, or seen as the Divine order balancing out the good and the evil, or even taken as a Gnostic unfolding. In Vedic culture, *Rta* is the Supreme force, like the unifying force that holds the myriad entities and their operative

---

6 S. Radhakrishnan, *The Bhagavad Gita*, HarperCollins Publishers, Noida, India, 2014, p. 168.

forces together as one entity in a great balancing act. Even God is not allowed to violate it. Shri Rama realised this when he wanted to dry out the sea, which declined Him passage to Lanka.

> "At that moment the King of Ocean rose serenely above the weltering billows in all his splendour, attended by shining water snakes. He addressed Rama with great reverence, reminding him that according to ancient laws he must remain unfordable, but counselling him the while to seek the aid of the Vanar chief Nala, son of Vishwakarma, the divine artisan, so that a bridge might be constructed to enable the armies to cross the deep." [7]

This clearly establishes that the *Rta* holds the *dharma*, which settles on the conduct of the people. Here again, there is this unique concept of *Rna* (ऋण), a deep sense of indebtedness to the order of the universe. Food, health, and life itself, are all taken with gratitude and as a primordial debt. A morsel of food carries with it salt from the ocean, grain from the fields and oil from the seeds. No one pays for the oxygen that keeps one alive. It is given free and therefore, one must be grateful for life itself.

Dharma seen this way, is seen as the guiding principle not only of all human interactions but also balancing the life overall that includes conservation of the environment and nurturing other forms of life on the planet. There is a plethora of writings covering every possible aspect of human life vis-a-vis the world around man. The tenets of *Dharma* not only establish every little detail of self-care, family-care, community care and jurisprudence, but also duties for kings and even for mendicants. Morality is not seen with the limited view of what is right between two people, but what is right for the whole existential order.

Albeit Lokmanya cautions, "Although we accept maintenance of society as being the chief outward use of *dharma*, yet we never lose sight of the Redemption of the *atman* (*atma-kalyana*) or 'Release' (*moksha*) which is the highest ideal according to the Vedic or all other religions and which is the special feature of our viewpoint. Whether it is maintenance of society or the general material welfare

---

[7] Donald Alexander Mackenzie, *Indian Myth and Legend*, Gresham, 1913, p. 417

of everybody, if these externally useful principles obstruct the Redemption of the *atman*, we do not want them." Lokmanya further writes, "Even the ancient Greek philosophers were of the opinion that one has to take 'the greatest benefit' or 'the climax of virtue' as the highest ideal of mankind and deal with the question of the doable and the not-doable from that point of view."

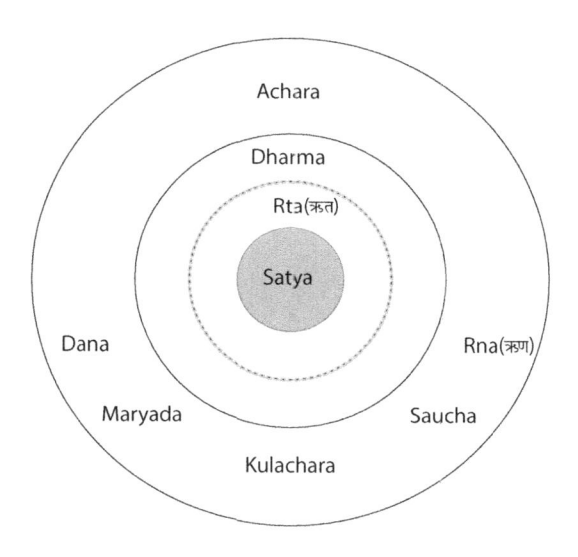

```
        Achara
        Dharma
        Rta (ऋत)
        Satya
Dana                    Rna (ऋण)
    Maryada      Saucha
        Kulachara
```

Satya is the Law, Rta is the Order, which implements the law, and Dharma is the upholding of the law. Dharma itself is one of the angles of the Dharma-Artha-Kama triangle which guides one's life. Manu says Dharma is supreme, whereas Chanakya Kautilya says Artha, and Rishi Vatsayana says all three are equal in most cases.[8]

Lokmanya concludes this chapter by saying, "Call *dharma* born of custom, or call it something that upholds or keeps together (*Rta*), or call it some percept which has been dictated (*Achara*), whichever definition of worldly morality is accepted, none of them is much useful for coming to a definite conclusion."

Setting the theme of the next chapter, Lokmanya writes, "But in order that all these various, difficulties should be solved, one has

---

8   http://dharmalaw.blogspot.in/2008/12/dharma-rajya-rule-of-dharma.html

first to see what these difficulties are. And, therefore, ancient as well as modern writers, before dealing with the subject matter to be proved by a science, first enumerate all the other existing aspects of the same subject-matter, and show the faults, or inefficiencies in them."

Lokmanya clarifies, "It is true that these other devices were not very much in vogue in India but were promulgated principally by Western philosophers. But it cannot, on that account, be said that I should not consider them in this book; because, it is necessary to be acquainted with these other devices, if even to a small extent, not only for the purpose of comparison, but also in order to understand the true importance of the Metaphysical (*adhyatmika*) *Karma Yoga* expounded in the *Gita*."

ॐ

4

Pursuit of Happiness

> Man falls from the pursuit of the ideal of plain living and high thinking the moment he wants to multiply his daily wants. Man's happiness really lies in contentment.
>
> *Mahatma Gandhi*

> What is right is not always popular and what is popular is not always right.
>
> *Albert Einstein*

Although the pursuit of happiness has always been present in the hearts and minds of people, it was formally expressed as an undeniable right in the United States Declaration of Independence, along with the right of life and right of liberty. It is no surprise that an increasing number of people in the modern world apply considerable time, energy and money in pursuing happiness, confusing it with pleasure and entertainment and therefore, living a life of indulgence and hedonism. The quest starts with earning money for the necessities of life, but almost invariably and compulsively, necessities are replaced with desires. And in some cases, desires become fantasies and the pursuit of happiness becomes a free fall in to a bottomless pit of despair. In Buddhist parlance, such people become 'hungry ghosts' driven by intense emotional needs like animals. It is a well-established anthropological fact that increase in material goods and sensory pleasures are never met with corresponding increase in happiness, and often end in pain and suffering. As stated earlier in the Preface, the message of the *Bhagavad-Gita* has assumed even more relevance in the modern world which is revolving on the axis of more production and more consumption, and an ever-eluding sense of satisfaction and fulfilment.

The question that haunts people, particularly those youth who have enough money and are yet unhappy, is whether there might be a simple, empirically grounded prescription for allocating discretionary resources in the pursuit of happiness. There is definitely something missing between the apparent cycle of consumption, consumer aspirations, and well-being. Lokmanya establishes in this chapter that life is about *giving* by carrying out dutiful action and not about *taking* under various pretexts of power, prestige or pleasure. True happiness springs out from this way of living using the discretionary power bestowed upon human beings by God, and not by indiscriminately indulging in sensory pleasures and mental obsessions. This chapter, supported by numerous examples from our scriptures, denotes that dispositional materialism is negatively associated with subjective well-being and psychological health. It forewarns young readers against the pervading culture emphasising on 'having', (which indeed prevents self-actualisation and happiness), versus 'being'.

Materialism is not new to India. Before the arrival of various invaders in to India, the people of India were living in abundance and were most advanced as compared to people living in other parts of the world at the time. India produced a quarter of the world's GDP and consequently, some of the richest people of the world were Indians. It is a fact that ancient India had many different forms of business organisations, right from around 800 BCE. A corporation of traders namely the *Sreni* used to procure raw materials, control the quality of manufactured goods and their prices, and also locate markets for their sale. This predates the earliest Roman proto-corporations by centuries.[1] Around 600 BCE, the *Mahajanapadas*, which were essentially the people's republics, minted punch-marked silver coins and were engaged in intensive trade activity as well as

---

1   Vikramaditya Khanna, *The Economic History of the Corporate Form in Ancient India*, (http://www.law.harvard.edu/programs/corp_gov/papers/2006sp-Speakers_Paper03_02-21_Khanna.pdf)

urban development.[2] After they settled down through agriculture and shunned away the earlier hunter-gathering mode of living, human beings needed the goods and services of each other. The initial transactions were based on offering what one had, to get from the other what he had, based on the mutual meeting of the needs of both the parties. Indians and Greeks were the first civilisations to replace the barter system with coins. In fact, Chanakya laid down the first tenets of doing business in writing for the Mauryan Empire in 4th century BCE.

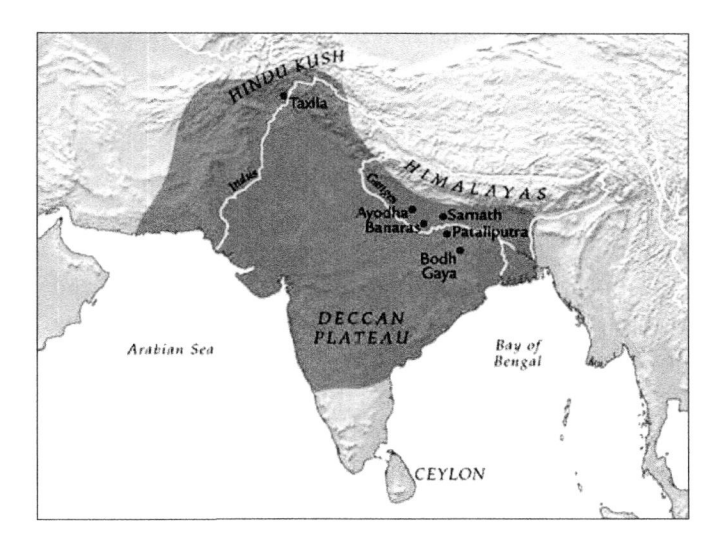

Established by Chandragupta Maurya in 322 BCE, the Maurya Empire was a principal world power of its time. Later, his grandson Ashoka expanded it to 5 million square kilometres and made it even bigger than the Roman Empire.

Common economic system is the hallmark of an empire. India's recent 'one country one tax' campaign is a good attempt to strengthen the Republic. The common economic system put together by the Mauryan Empire lasted its own time. For the next 1500 years, India saw prosperous kingdoms of the Rashtrakutas between the 6th and 10th centuries in the Central or West India; the

---

2   Mahajan Nupur, Balasubramaniam, 'Scanning electron microscopy study of an ancient silver punch-marked coin with central pentagonal mark', *Numinismatic Digest*, 21-2, 153-64.

Hoysalas between the 10th and the 14th centuries in what is modern day Karnataka; and Eastern Ganga, from the 11th century to the early 15th century. The Hoysalas kingdom of Kalinga, once conquered by Ashoka resurrected itself and flourished to rule over present day Odisha, West Bengal, Chhattisgarh and the eastern part of Andhra Pradesh. It is said that by the end of the first millennium, India was the largest economy of the world accounting for about a quarter of all the world's wealth.

Emphasising on the good life that Indian people enjoyed over a long period of time, Lokmanya opens this chapter called 'Materialistic Theory of Happiness'. All religions of the world can be seen as a response to the rationalisation of the formidable natural forces that both, sustained and threatened life on the earth. From what is called as paganism in Western parlance, ancient man developed his consciousness to see natural forces as part of the overall existence and not to be treated as either the divine or the demonic. Extending the logic, some people even rejected the concept of soul and afterlife and considered what is here and now as the only truth. This led to seeking pleasure and avoiding hardships as the right way of leading life and attracted the acceptance of the laity. It is even given the status of a philosophy and called *Lokayata*, the viewpoint of the people. The purpose of life is to make merry and do good to oneself first and foremost, and then to the people around to dispose off the plenty.

Ajita Keshakambali (Ajita with the Hair Blanket) was amongst the first in the Hindu tradition to reject the existence of all non-sensory experience. He is therefore seen as the first Indian atheist who repudiated the existence of the soul and therefore discarded ideas like reincarnation and *karma*. Ajita Keshakambali indeed pioneered the Charvaka School of Indian philosophy. Rejection of the ideas like good and evil, charity and compassion, and ethical conduct propagated by Ajita and his followers was scorned by the learned of that time and the Charvaka School remained on the fringes of mainstream Indian philosophy. Later, with the rise of Buddhism and Jainism in India, the pleasure-seeking lifestyle acquired derogatory connotations and was even called sophistry. With the rise of Shri

Shankaracharya in the 8th century, indulgence with the world was seen as animalistic drives and by the 12th century, The Charvaka School completely withered away.

Lokmanya writes, "The positive physical sciences, which have had an immense growth in modern times have to deal principally with the external or visible properties of tangible objects. Everyone is unwilling to suffer pain and everyone wants happiness." Scientists who have spent their entire lives studying the physical sciences, or those who attach a lot of importance to the critical methods particular to these sciences often get into the habit, of always considering only the external effects of things; their philosophical vision being thereby limited to a certain extent, narrowed too close, in discussing any particular thing, they do not attach much importance to causes which are Metaphysical, or intangible, or invisible, or which have any kind of a reference to the next world. Although on that account, they leave out of consideration, the Metaphysical or the next world point of view. Having said that, as codes of morality are necessary for the satisfactory regulation of the mutual relations of human beings and for public welfare, even those philosophers who are indifferent about life after death or who have no faith in the intangible and who don't really have faith in God, look upon the 'science of proper action' (*Karma Yoga*) as a most important science."

Lokmanya now takes an analytic view at the materialistic theory of happiness. "I shall now precisely and in their proper order, consider the various divisions into which the modern or ancient Materialistic philosophers fall, as a result of differences of opinion between them as to whether the external material happiness which has to be considered for determining the ethical propriety or impropriety of an action is one's own happiness or the happiness of another, and whether of one person or of several persons; and I shall also consider to what extent these opinions are proper or faultless."

The core of the Materialistic philosophy is the idea of nihilism. These are the people who believe that life is meaningless and therefore, reject all religious and moral principles as the basis of living in a society. Such people even project their idea of meaningless upon the others and hold that proponents of religious, ethical and moral conduct are basically selfish people who say what they say to serve their own purposes. To such people, there are no objective moral facts or true propositions. No action is morally good, bad, wrong, right, but based on the situation and the circumstances to promote one's own good and happiness. These people thereby justify slavery, prostitution and hunting expeditions, and even the killing of other people. Best put by the American novelist Cormac McCarthy (*b.* 1933) in *No Country for Old Men*, "The point is there ain't no point."

Lokmanya debunks this philosophy and cites a story from Valmiki's Ramayana, of the Rishi Jaabaali who was an advisor of King Dasharatha. It is said that Rishi Jaabaali unsuccessfully tried to persuade Rama to give up his exile, using rational arguments but was rebutted by the Blessed Lord himself.

When Bharata returned to know of the horrendous event, that his elder brother Shri Ram was sent in to exile as schemed by his mother Kakaiyee, and that his father Dasharatha died in grief, he decided to salvage the situation. After conducting the funeral of his father, he went to the forest to bring his brother back and hand over the throne of Ayodhya to him. Bharata argued that this would be in the best interest of the people of the kingdom. Jaabaali, a priest and member of Dasharatha's council of ministers, who declared that Shri Rama would be performing *Kshatriya Dharma* by returning to the throne and ruling, supported Bharata. However, Shri Rama rebuked Jaabaali for his misplaced knowledge of *Dharma*.

निन्दाम्यहं कर्म कृतं पितुस्त द्यस्त्वामगुह्राद्विषमस्थबुद्धिम् ।
बुद्ध्यानयैवंविधया चरन्तं
सुनास्तिकं धर्मपथादपेतम् ॥
यथा हि चोरः स तथा हि बुद्धस्तथागतं नास्तिकमत्र विद्धि ।
तस्माद्धि यः शक्यतमः प्रजानाम् ।
स नास्तिकेनाभिमुखो बुधः स्यात् ॥

I accuse the act done by my father in taking you into his service, you with your misleading intelligence, a firm atheist fallen from the true path. It is an exact state of the case that a mere thought

deserves to be punished as it were a thief and know an atheist to be on par with a mere intellectual. Therefore, he is the most suspect, and should be punished in the interest of the people. In no case should a wise man consort with an atheist.[3]
(Ramayana, Ayodhya Kanda Chapter, 109, Verse 33, 34)

After nihilism comes ego-centredness. American writer Wayne Dyer (1940–2015) put it so elegantly, "The ego is only an illusion, but a very influential one. Letting the ego-illusion become your identity can prevent you from knowing your true self. Ego, the false idea of believing that you are what you have or what you do, is a backwards way of assessing and living life."[4] People centre their lives on the ego. Whatever happens, whoever comes across them, they remain the protagonists of the phenomena. Instead of saying I am traveling by such and such airline, they say, "I am flying." Instead of saying, "I have bought certain shares of a company in the market," they say, "I am a part-owner of that company." For these people, this world, this life, is the only existence. Consequences of their deeds for others beyond their lives are not their concern. Their religious conduct is also an activity for the gratification of their self-identity and status. They will donate to build a toilet in a school on the condition that a plaque is fixed on the wall announcing not only their names, but also of their parents and even grandparents. Go around and see the vulgarity of such charitable and religious people on display everywhere– schools, bus shelters, temples, parks, even benches constructed on the roadside for elderly people to steady themselves while walking, carry the names of their donors. Such people have reduced their lives to these plaques and memorials. The *Bhagavad-Gita* very bluntly describes such charities as godless endowment (*asurisampatti*).

इदमद्य मया लब्धमिमं प्राप्स्ये मनोरथम्।
इदमस्तीदमपि मे भविष्यति पुनर्धनम् ॥१३॥

---

3 Valmiki, *Book II: Ayodhya Kanda– Book Of Ayodhya*, Chapter [Sarga] 109. Valmiki's Ramayana, Translated by Desiraju Hanumanta Rao & K. M. K. Murthy.
4 https://www.drwaynedyer.com/blog/the-ego-illusion/

असौ मया हतः शत्रुर्हनिष्ये चापरानपि ।
ईश्वरोऽहमहं भोगी सिद्धोऽहं बलवान्सुखी ॥१४॥
आढ्योऽभिजनवानस्मि कोऽन्योऽस्ति सदृशो मया ।
यक्ष्ये दास्यामि मोदिष्य इत्यज्ञानविमोहिताः ॥१५॥

In these three shlokas, the Blessed Lord described the claim of deluded people to be the master of their actions: This day is the day of my life, so that I can attain my desires and create my wealth. I will annihilate my enemies and enjoy my might. I am wealthy and highborn and no one can be equal to me. I shall perform Yajna, offer assistances to the needy and thus live in my abundance and generosity." (Bhagavad-Gita Chapter 16, Verse 13, 14, 15)

Eknath Easwaran, in his commentary on *shlokas* 16.14 and 16.15 writes, "These two verses of the *Gita* convey something very interesting about the arrogance of power: with one hand power glorifies in its capacity to destroy others; with the other hand, power takes pride in the lavishness of its own generosity by not harming others."[5]

Lokmanya warns, "Pure and naked selfishness or self-centredness never succeeds in the world; because, although physical and material pleasures may be desirable to everyone, yet, as is a matter of actual experience, if our happiness interferes with the happiness of others, those others will certainly do us harm." Although one's happiness or selfish purposes may be one's goal, yet, in as much as it is not possible for one to acquire such happiness unless one makes some sacrifices for other people that is similar to those one wants for oneself from them, one must long-sightedly take into account the happiness of others in order to obtain one's own happiness.

Nihilism and ego-centredness is followed by fear. People carry out charity out of fear. American author Napoleon Hill (1883-1970), in his book *Think and Grow Rich*, writes, "There are six basic fears, with some combination of which every human suffers at one time or another. Most people are fortunate if they do not suffer from the

---

5 Eknath Easwaran, *The Bhagavad-Gita for Daily Living*, Jaico Publishing House, Mumbai, India, 2007, Vol. III, p. 277.

entire six. Named in the order of their most common appearance, they are: fear of poverty, fear of criticism and fear of ill health. These three fears are almost always operating at the bottom of most of one's worries. Then there are the fears of loss of love of someone, the fear of old age, and above all the fear of death."[6] Instead of going the Charvaka way, the edifice of cooperation and self-preservation is constructed. The nagging force of fear motivates a lot of good work, charity, and even sacrifice. This fear-driven morality is indeed bogus and such people turn ruthless and cruel the moment their fears are allayed.

Lokmanya writes, "Because of the fear that we, in our turn may have to suffer the same pain, we are plagued by the thought of our possible future unhappiness. Charity, generosity, pity, love, gratefulness, humbleness, friendship, and other qualities, which at first sight appear to be for the benefit of others are, if we trace them to their origin, nothing but means of acquiring our own happiness or warding off our own unhappiness in another form. Everybody helps others or gives in charity but with the internal motive that if he ever found himself in the same position, other people should also help him similarly. We also love others, only in order that others should love us."

To be seen as good by others is a huge motivator. Lokmanya rejects the idea of man as a bundle of selfish desires or a fear-driven animal trying to act good in a circus. Citing the English philosopher Joseph Butler (1692-1752), Lokmanya declared man as an amalgamation of good and the bad. Like a mix of multiple seeds put in the soil, some germinate while others do not. Then there are aspects like availability of water and the season that decides which seed will germinate and which will not. It is erroneous to view a person as good or bad. He is almost always a product of the circumstances and the inner conflict between different tendencies is never absent. Swami Vivekananda explained it so succinctly: "There is evil and there is good; and the apex, the centre, is the Reality. He is neither evil nor good; he is the best. The best can be only one,

---

6   Napoleon Hill, *Think and Grow Rich,* Amazing Reads, India Book Distributors (Bombay) Limited, Mumbai, India, 2014.

the good can be many and the evil many. There will be degrees of variation between the good and the evil, but the best is only one, and that best, when seen through thin coverings, we call different sorts of good, and when through thick covers, we call evil. Good and evil are different forms of superstition."[7]

Lokmanya now brings up the story of Yajnavalkya and his wife Maitreyi mentioned in the *Brihadaranyaka Upanishad*. Following the tradition of renouncing the world after attaining a certain age, Yajnavalkya, who lived in Videha, a kingdom in the region which is now called the north Bihar, in the seventh century BCE, discussed with his two wives, Maitreyi and Katyayani, the issue of partitioning his wealth between them. Maitreyi asked her husband to give her that which made her permanently happy. Flabbergasted with the demand, Yajnavalkya told his wife that no amount of wealth in this world, no power, no authority could make anyone permanently happy or immortal. Each person who is born must die. What is gained will eventually be lost. Maitreyi then questioned of what use was this wealth, which Yajnavalkya was trying to divide?

Maitreyi further confronted her scholar husband ready to shun the householder life asking, if not wealth, then what else could be done to attain immortal bliss. The answer to this question of Maitreyi's by Yajnavalkya is indeed considered the jewel of Indian philosophy. Yajnavalkya explained to Maitreyi that everything that exists is indeed unreal and impermanent and a manifestation of *Atman*, which is only real and permanent. Each one of us is an aspect of *Atman* and all relations, transactions, interactions, feelings of love, hatred, attraction and aversion are the interplay of subjects and objects both, unreal in and by themselves. Yajnavalkya even described his relationship with Maitreyi, and for that matter between any couple, a condition of mutual fulfilment by two minds. Neither does a man really love his wife and nor does she love her husband. They both live a mental construct of each other and as both are unreal, fulfilment can never be achieved.

Sage Yajnavalkya is deeply revered. In the introduction to *Ramcharitmanas*, the Saint-poet Goswami Tulsidas declared

---

7   http://www.vivekananda.net/PDFBooks/PracticalVedanta.pdf. Last accessed on 9 August 2017.

that he would be merely restating the story of Shri Ramachandra narrated by Yajnavalkya to Bharadwaja Rishi, the father of his wife Katyayani with the purpose of filling the hearts of the righteous with happiness.

जागबलिक जो कथा सुहाई । भरद्वाज मुनिबरहि सुनाई ॥
कहिहउँ सोइ संबाद बखानी । सुनहुँ सकल सज्जन सुखु मानी ॥

Through the Yajnavalkya-Maitreyi dialogue, a very subtle difference is presented here between the Supreme Self, and the person self. Both are indeed same and yet different. Akin to the shadow of the moon in a placid pond, the Supreme Self is reflected in the personal self. The presence of mud in the water or stirring disturbs the reflection. In the same manner, the personal self appears wavering, confused, and even wrong and evil due to the quality of the water, or better still to say, in the presence of the mud and stirring in the water. The love between two people is indeed the omnipresent love that flows through and binds the entire creation seen through the mud of relations and stirring of interactions. Those who free their personal selves of the dirt and stirring of the worldly affairs become a true reflection of the Supreme Self.

Swami Vivekananda explained, "As to all water, the one goal is the ocean; as to all touch, the skin is the one centre; as of all smell, the nose is the one centre; as of all taste, the tongue is the one goal; as of all form, the eyes are the one goal; as of all sounds, the ears are the one goal; as of all thought, the mind is the one goal; as of all knowledge, the heart is the one goal; as of all work, the hands are the one goal; as a morsel of salt put into the sea water melts away, and we cannot take it back, so is this Universal Being eternally infinite; all knowledge is in Him. The whole universe rises from Him, and again goes down into Him. No more is there any knowledge, dying, or death."[8]

Lokmanya now writes, "Having thus proved that human nature is not purely selfish and is not governed wholly by the *tamas* quality, nor totally ungodly, and that a benevolent (*sattvik*) mental

---

8 http://www.vivekananda.net/PDFBooks/PracticalVedanta.pdf. Last accessed on 9 August 2017.

impulse forms part of human nature from birth along with the selfish impulse, and that doing good to others is not long-sighted selfishness, one has to give equal importance to the two principles of *svartha*, i.e., one's own happiness and *parartha*, i.e., the happiness of others, in building up the science of the doable and the not-doable (*karyakarya-vyavasthiti*)." The discussion is concluded with the words of *Bharthruhari* (450-510 CE), who is considered one of the most original philosophers of language and religion in ancient India.

एते सत्पुरुषाः परार्थघटकाः स्वार्थान् परित्यज्य ये ।
सामान्यास्तु परार्थमुद्यमभृतः स्वार्थाऽविरोधेन ये ॥
तेऽमी मानुषराक्षसाः परहितं स्वार्थाय निघ्नन्ति ये ।
ये तु घ्नन्ति निरर्थकं परहितं ते के न जानीमहे ॥

Truly good people do not hesitate in foregoing their own interests to help others. Then there are ordinary people who help others but only if their interests are not compromised. People who harm others for their own interests are not good people and must be looked upon as beings bereft of divinity. Difficult to describe are those people who are even worse than these people for they needlessly harm the interests of others. (Neeti Shatakam of Bharthruhari, Praise of helping others (paropakaarastuti), Verse 74).

Lokmanya further expands the inquiry, "There is a great deal of difference between the meanings of the two words 'happiness' (*sukha*) and 'benefit' (*hita*); but, although for the moment that difference is not taken into consideration and the word *sarvabhutahita* is taken as meaning 'the greatest happiness of the greatest number', yet it will be seen, that numerous important difficulties arise, if we rely only on this principle for distinguishing the doable from the not-doable."

The concept of morality remained arguable. Some considered it as a universal constant, a timeless value system, while others saw it as an evolutionary variable, which is shaped by socio-political dynamics. Religion as source of morality is also disputed, or rather fiercely fought about. There is wide variation on what is considered right in one religion than in the other. The situation becomes extremely complicated with the right of one religion becoming the wrong of another. Hindus worship the cow but it is slaughtered for food by the people of many other religions. Dr. A. P. J. Abdul Kalam declared, "No religion has mandated killing others as a requirement for its sustenance or promotion." Who would then decide which religion is right?

Lokmanya writes, "Numbers have no fixed bearing on morality. It must also be borne in mind that something which is ordinarily considered as productive of happiness by all persons, is, by a far-sighted person, seen to be disadvantageous to all. Take for example the cases of Socrates and Jesus Christ. Both of them were preaching to their countrymen what, in their respective opinions, was ultimately beneficial. But their countrymen denounced them as 'enemies of society', and put them to death." Mahatma Gandhi summed it up so well, "Jesus is ideal and wonderful, but you Christians– you are not like him."

What is good remained an enigma and the conflict between what is good for an individual and what is for the people around him is indeed perennial. The Greek philosopher Aristotle (384–322 BC) used the idea of 'the common interest' to separate out the interests of the powerful and the rulers from being called good. To reign the power of the rulers by a moral fence, the Italian mendicant, Saint Thomas Aquinas (1225-1274) elevated 'the common good' (*bonum commune*, in Latin) as the basis and purpose of any government. English philosopher John Locke (1632–1704) saw 'the peace, safety, and public good of the people' as the ultimate purpose for which a political society exists, and even declared the well-being of the people as the supreme law.

As for the moral standards of the people themselves, the Scottish philosopher David Hume (1711-1776) contended that 'social conventions' are made to serve common interests of the people. The American statesman and Founding Father, James Madison (1751-1836) declared justice as the touchstone to declare an act as good for the people. French-Swiss philosopher Jean-Jacques Rousseau

(1712-1778) understood 'the common good' (*le biencommun*, in French) to be the object of a society's general will which should be pursued by the government and delivered to the people it governs. Abraham Lincoln said it best, "Government of the people, by the people, for the people, shall not perish from the Earth."[9]

It is indeed never easy to conclude that an action is good. The dynamics of the external factors notwithstanding, there is such great variation in human internal drives. Human beings have always been unpredictable and their responses can never be relied upon unlike machine output. Human beings also differ in the level of their consciousness– from carnal to divine– and the laity almost never understands what the saints realise. Lokmanya writes, "There is no sense in repartee: Our ethical principle is correct; what can we do if ignorant persons have wrongly applied it?" Because, although the principle may be correct, one must at the same time explain who are the proper persons to give effect to it, and when and how these persons do so, and other similar limitations of the principle."

Lokmanya cites an example here. There was once an occasion to construct a tramway for the benefit and happiness of all the citizens of a big city in America. But there were delays in obtaining the requisite sanction from the proper authorities. Thereupon, the directors of the tramway company gave a bribe to the persons in authority, and the necessary sanction was immediately obtained; and the construction of the tramway being complete soon afterwards, all the people in the city were in consequence considerably benefited to great convenience. Sometime after that, the bribery was found out, and the manager of the tramway was criminally prosecuted and convicted. The principle of the greatest good of the greatest number is useless by itself. The external effect of the bribery, namely, that the tramway came to be constructed because the bribe was given, was the greatest good of the greatest number yet, on that account, the fact that the bribe was given does not make it legal.

In another example, of the act of giving charity is cited. People

---

[9] Gettysburg Address– a speech by U.S. President Abraham Lincoln. Delivered by Lincoln during the American Civil War, on the afternoon of Thursday, November 19, 1863, at the dedication of the Soldiers' National Cemetery in Gettysburg, Pennsylvania.

give charity to not only help the needy but also for their own name and fame. Though the external effects of the two acts of giving in charity– one desireless in the belief that it is one's duty to do so (*datavyam*), and the other for the sake of reputation or for some other purpose are the same, yet, even the *Bhagavad-Gita* distinguishes between the two by saying that the first gift is *sattvik* (benevolent) and that the second gift is *rajasa* (desire-prompted); and the same gift, if made to an unworthy person is said to be *tamasa* (ignorant) and objectionable.

दातव्यमिति यद्दानं दीयतेऽनुपकारिणे ।
देशे काले च पात्रे च तद्दानं सात्त्विकं स्मृतम् ॥२०॥

Gifts without any expectation in return and with a sense of duty at a proper place, at right time, and to a deserving person are only held good. (Bhagavad-Gita Chapter 17, Verse 20)

Dr. S. Radhakrishnan adds in his commentary of this *shloka*, the ideal of *atmasamarpana*, a gift as described by the Blessed Lord here, leads to giving one's own self to the society. He writes, "Gifts to the poor not only help the poor but help the givers. He who gives receives."[10]

यत्तु प्रत्युपकारार्थं फलमुद्दिश्य वा पुनः ।
दीयते च परिक्लिष्टं तद्दानं राजसं स्मृतम् ॥२१॥

Gifts given with the expectation of receiving favours, or gifts that hurt the giver are not held good as these are smacked with desire. (Bhagavad-Gita Chapter 17, Verse 21)

अदेशकाले यद्दानमपात्रेभ्यश्च दीयते ।
असत्कृतमवज्ञातं तत्तामसमुदाहृतम् ॥२२॥

Gifts given at wrong time to unworthy persons, without even showing respect, or with contempt, are held as dull and unwise. (Bhagavad-Gita Chapter 17, Verse 22)

---

10 S. Radhakrishnan, *The Bhagavad Gita*, HarperCollins Publishers, Noida, India, 2014, p. 413.

Having established through various examples the inadequacy of any ethical percept to guide human beings, Lokmanya now inquires in to the possibility of an internal mechanism to decide on what is right action. The problem such a mechanism would face is whether it could be a definite and faultless system to guide its subject on the right path of the universal good. Right in the beginning of the *Gita*, the Blessed Lord declares Reason (*buddhi*) to be of greater importance than action, this could then be the inner mechanism of deciding about right action.

दूरेण ह्यवरं कर्म बुद्धियोगाद्धनञ्जय ।
बुद्धौ शरणमन्विच्छ कृपणाः फलहेतवः ॥४९॥

The Blessed Lord advises Arjuna to anchor in Buddhi. This is the only way to get rid of reward-seeking actions that are certainly inferior to selfless effort. Those who perform merely to fulfil their desires are indeed pitiable. (Bhagavad-Gita Chapter 2, Verse 49)

Purity of mind is fundamental for the inner mechanism to function properly. Just like a driver high on alcohol is prone to accidents on the road, how can a mind afflicted with destructive emotions like greed, lust and anger guide one on the right course of action? A pure mind is by default connected to God. There are instances, and indeed a large number of them, when people with pure minds, survived great dangers and emerged out of the most perilous situations. Purity of mind is also seen as an amplifier with the gift of three fistfuls of boiled dried rice given by Sudama to Shri Krishna, which the Blessed Lord considered equal to the value of the three worlds. Mahatma Gandhi said, "Always aim at complete harmony of thought and word and deed. Always aim at purifying your thoughts and everything will be well."

Lokmanya now goes beyond philanthropy and presents other aspects of humanness. He poses a question, "When we consider the scale of life gradually rising from the most minute organisms to the human race, the question arises: Is the virtue of philanthropy the only virtue which has been fully developed in the human race, or have other benevolent (*sattvik*) virtues, such as justice, kindness, wisdom, farsightedness, logic, courage, perseverance, forgiveness, control of the organs, etc., also been developed in man?" He articulates the answer as: "When one thinks of this, one has to say that all virtues have been more fully developed in the human race than in any other living being. We will for the present refer to this aggregate of *sattvik* qualities as 'humanness'. When in this way 'humanness' is seen to be superior to philanthropy, one has, in determining the propriety or impropriety or the morality of any particular action, to examine that action from the point of view of its 'humanness'– that is, from the point of view of all those various qualities which are seen to be more developed in the human race than in other living beings– rather than from the point of view of its philanthropic value."

Lokmanya concludes, "It is better to call that action alone virtuous, or to say that that alone is morality, which will enhance the state of being human or the 'humanness', of all human beings, or which will be consistent with the dignity of such 'humanness', instead of merely relying on the virtue of philanthropy." When one considers minutely what is 'humanness', or 'the state of being human', we return to the question of Yajnavalkya that the *Atman* should be seen as the true state of a human being.

Further emphasising the point, Lokmanya brings in the story of Nachiketa from the *Katha Upanishad*. A part of Indian folklore, the child Nachiketa had an encounter with Yama, the god of death. Nachiketa asked Yama what happens to a person after death. Unwilling to share the secret, Yama offered Nachiketa attractive gifts instead, but Nachiketa remained steadfast to his query. Eventually, Yama taught Nachiketa the knowledge of *Atman*, the immortal true identity of a mortal person. The story provides the most iconic presentation of the body as a chariot driven by five horses. Yama tells Nachiketa that the mortal body is like a chariot driven by five horses that are the five senses– hearing, seeing, tasting, smelling, and touching. Virtuous people maintain strict control over their senses. They eat what is good for them and not what tastes good. They are not played upon by their senses; rather, they command their senses to what they feel and think is right action for them. Uncontrolled senses take human mortals towards death following the path of pleasures (*preyas*). The path of sensory restraints, guided by the *Buddhi* leads one to a virtuous life (*shreyas*).

Nachiketa has been one of the most influential characters in Hinduism. Swami Vivekananda famously said: "If I get ten or twelve boys with the faith of Nachiketa, I can turn the thoughts and pursuits of this country in a new channel."[11]

The modern world runs on *preyas* and not *shreyas*. There is a paradigm shift in the lifestyles of people right from eating nutritious food, doing physical exercise, spending some quiet time in worship, to home-delivered food, sedentary habits of sitting before the computer or television and not a minute without a message on the phone, the increasing prevalence of promiscuity, alcohol and smoking. People have taken to the path of self-destruction. Dr. Kalam once told me after returning from a hospital where he saw several young patients in an ICU ward, "I see a vicious spiral rolling out. The lifestyle of our youth is getting out of control and dangerous and reckless and thoughtless. It scares me, because people are getting hurt." There is an immediate need to engage our young people in voluntary work, social service, and thinking.

---

11 http://www.nachiketatapovan.org/about-nachiketa-in-swami-vivekananada-s-words-.html

Pursuit of Happiness

श्रेयश्च प्रेयश्च मनुष्यमेतस्तौ संपरीत्य विविनक्ति धीरः ।
श्रेयो हि धीरोऽभिप्रेयसो वृणीते प्रेयो मन्दा योगक्षेमाद् वृणीते ॥२॥

Man in entangled with both, good and bad. The wise hold on to the meritorious (shreyas) and escape away from the corporeal (preyas). Conversely, the ignorant man willingly gets himself caught in the corporeal web and cuts out all that is good for him.
(Katha Upanishad Part 1, Canto 2, Shloka 2)

Since we are born as humans, we can make choices. No other creature here on this earth or anywhere else in the universe has been given this ability. The reverse side of this great endowment is that no human being can escape out of this. Every moment, whether we realise it or not, we are making choices between several alternatives in whatever we think, say, or do. Every choice has consequences. If we choose *preyas* over *shreyas* in our thoughts, speech and actions, we create a future of disease, disability and despair for ourselves.

Preyas gives instantaneous pleasure, delight, enjoyment, a feeling of elation and fulfilment. Eating a sweet dish, drinking a pint of beer, quiet time with the beloved…, the feel good is spontaneous and apparent. But the hitch with it is that *preyas* is so very ephemeral. It does not and cannot last long. The sweetness on the tongue lasts for a minute, the effect of the beer, for an hour, and time with the beloved converts itself in to pangs of separation as soon as it is over. All too soon, the feel-good of *preyas* is gone and we are begging for it and craving it again. The good, the meritorious, the wholesome *Shreyas*, on the other hand is unpleasant and cumbersome at the beginning, be it learning, exercising, eating salads and millets, or chastity, but it brings long-lasting benefits and glorious results.

Lokmanya writes, "Not only is internal happiness obtainable through reason, or metaphysical happiness of greater worth than the external happiness obtained through the medium of the organs, but the physical pleasure is transient, it exists today comes to an end tomorrow. The same is not the case with rules of ethics. Non-violence, veracity and other moral principles are looked upon by people as independent of external circumstances, that is, of external happiness or unhappiness and as being constant in their application at all times and in all circumstances, that is to say, they are looked upon as permanent by everybody."

Winding up the argument against materialism as a philosophy of life, whether selfish, familial, communal, or 'for the greatest happiness of the greatest number,' which keeps changing with time, places and situations, Lokmanya points out that the unshaken moral edifice in the world cannot be based on such fleeting ideas.

Lokmanya cites the *Mahabharata*:

न जातु कामान्न भयान्न लोभाद्धर्मं त्यजेज्जीवितस्यापि हेतोः ।
धर्मो नित्यः सुखदुःखे त्वनित्ये जीवो नित्यो हेतुरस्य त्वनित्यः ॥५०॥

Moral principles can only be abandoned at our own peril when faced with the drives of lust, fear and greed. The laws of living a good life are embedded in the human soul. The survival involves decoding, understanding, and applying these precepts in managing the affairs of one's life.
(Mahabharata, Svargarohana Parva, Adhyaya 5, Shloka 50)

Lokmanya so eloquently freed the concept of morality from all religious, philosophical, and legal fetters. A virtuous life is indeed the destiny of every human who has been bestowed with guidance in the psycho-spiritual organ called soul that controls and even overrides all physical functions and drives. This is the default architecture. Now the human being has to choose to shut this option off and switch over to the sense-driven commands. These commands are mostly alluring, gratifying and give a good feeling and heighten the spirit, but in the long run, they set off a self-destructing mechanism, which is unfortunately irreversible.

The crux is the choice to opt for *shreyas* over *preyas*. No one in this universe is given this power except human beings but this same power turns into a condemning curse if used improperly. The senses that indeed are the instruments of the soul to progress on its evolutionary journey in this world, are turned in to snares by the ignorant. Caught in the play set up by sensory pleasures, man first surrenders his mind to the senses, and gets swayed by them, rather than controlling them. People turn into alcoholics, smokers, gamblers, thieves and murderers and waste away their lives. There are also those who do succeed in controlling their senses by their strong minds but the same strong mind now becomes a menacing ego. Like a deer is swallowed live and digested by a python, the mind loses its vitality. Instead of taking instructions from the intellect that is coupled with the soul by design, the ego starts giving instructions of its own to the mind and through it, to the senses. That is how Yudhishthira could gamble away his wife Draupadi in a game of dice. Debunking the external edifice of moral injections and introducing the reader to the soul embedded with all necessary guidance in this chapter, Lokmanya sets the theme of the next chapter with the words, "We have now to consider the true nature of happiness and unhappiness and to see what permanent happiness is."

ॐ

5

An Inside Job

> It is not God's will merely that we should be happy, but that we should make ourselves happy.
>
> *Immanuel Kant*

> Happiness is not something readymade. It comes from your own actions.
>
> *Dalai Lama*

Does happiness lie inside or outside of a human body? This simple question has many and complex answers. If happiness is inside, is it a feeling, sensation, sentiment? And if so, can it be deduced to biochemical interplay in the brain? This way, happiness becomes pleasures. But then arises the question as to how much of it is good enough? If happiness is outside and lies in the objects then it becomes a matter of competition and those who are affluent, strong and strive hard will always be happy as they would achieve the objects and others would unhappy with their failures. If happiness is neither outside nor inside but arises out of a connection between inside of the body to the objects outside through senses, then are the senses the agents of happiness? And if so, can the efficient use of senses bring happiness? Can activities like smoking, eating sweets, drinking alcohol, inhaling perfumes, which bring pleasure to the senses become the actions of happiness?

Is happiness a tendency or an activity? Once again, this simple question has many and complex answers. If happiness is a tendency, is it innate, a quality from birth, or is it acquired during nurturing and by conditioning when one grows up? If it is an activity, can it be timed, regulated, maximised or sustained over longer periods of time? And what is the absence of happiness? Is unhappiness like that darkness that has no existence of its own except that it is merely the absence of light? Or does unhappiness exist on its own in the form of feelings of anxiety and fears, like the other side of the happiness coin? What if my happy time ends, and worse still, ends abruptly, sooner rather than later? Cynicism and despondency soon follow. As English author T.H. White (1906-1964) wrote in *Ghostly, Grim and Gruesome*, "Life is such unutterable hell, solely because it is sometimes beautiful. If we could only be miserable all the time, if there could be no such things as love or beauty or faith or hope, if I could be absolutely certain that my love would never be returned: how much more simple life would be."

The Buddha called *Anitya* (impermanence), *Anatman* (no self), and *Dukkha* (suffering) as three marks of existence (*Tri Lakshna*). Everything is therefore impermanent. Suffering is an essential part of existence, and nothing exists by itself without dependence upon the others, both for its origin and sustenance. It gives a sense of ever-changing flux where the world around us is ever-changing. When we are walking on a road, there are so many others moving– people walking, travelling in buses or cars and riding motorcycles. Where we are staying there are others, houses inhabited by other people, their guests, and visitors. At the workplace there are so many co-workers, superiors, juniors and customers. Each one carries his own ever-changing existence with him. At each and every moment, a new connection is being made between inside and outside and the old one is being broken. What is near now will be far later and *vice versa*. In such a situation, is it really possible to know what gains make one happy and even if it can be comprehended, then why does all that is gained turn into unhappiness when inevitably it is eventually lost? German physiologist Eduard Friedrich Wilhelm Pflüger (1829-1910) was most accurate when he laid down the dictum, "The cause of every need of a living being is also the cause of satisfaction of the need."[1]

Lokmanya opens this chapter he titled as the consideration of happiness and unhappiness (*sukha-dukha-viveka*) with these words: "Our philosophers have accepted the position that every

---

[1] Walter B. Cannon, *The Wisdom of the Body*, New York: The Norton Library, 1967, p. 21.

human being in this world is continually struggling in order to obtain happiness, or to increase the existing amount of happiness, which he has obtained, or to obviate or reduce his unhappiness."

Nobody has as yet found a tangible approach to be happy in life. A strategy for happiness for a population is therefore an impossibility. Every life is a cycle of happiness and unhappiness and their frequency of arriving and the duration of their spells vary. Happiness and unhappiness can be seen as the presence and absence of each other. Although human beings are enormously adaptable in dealing with life events, their response to any event is generally a good or bad feeling. Good feelings, more frequent and intense, come together to create what is called happiness. Conversely, clustering of too many bad feelings too, quickly creates unhappiness.

People in the East consider life a suffering. Buddha even called it a Noble Truth. People in the West consider life as an opportunity of merry making. Founders of the United States of America called 'pursuit of happiness' as a national goal and placed it at par with the life and liberty. Whichever position we take, human beings, whether in the East or the West, endeavour to avoid unhappiness and seek happiness whichever way they can in total disregard for the feeling of others. British philosopher and Nobel laureate Bertrand Russell (1872-1970) summed it up neatly saying, "If there were in the world today any large number of people who desired their own happiness more than they desired the unhappiness of others, we could have a paradise in a few years."

God has bestowed upon humans a large prefrontal cortex in the brain that allows us to make rational decisions and even plan the future. We can imagine possibilities that have yet to occur and make choices. Upon this capacity to make choices indeed depends the course of human life. Choices seeking happiness are obviously not always good. Lokmanya writes, "The words *hitam* (advantage), or *shreyas* (merit), or *kalyanam* (benefit) are ordinarily more often used than the word *sukham* (happiness); and I shall explain later on, what the difference between them is. Yet, if one takes for granted that the word 'happiness' includes all kinds of benefits, then the proposition that ordinarily every human being strives to obtain happiness is generally accepted."

An Inside Job

In the *Parashar Gita*, embedded in the *Shanti Parva* of the *Mahabharata*, it is written:

यदिष्टं तत्सुखं प्राहुर्द्वेष्यं दुःखमिहोच्यते ।
कृताकृतस्य तपसः फलं पश्यस्व यादृशम् ॥२७॥

We feel happy to get what we seek (ishta) and become unhappy when it is lost. We feed sad when our efforts end in unfavourable results. Happiness and unhappiness are the illusions of one's mind. (Mahabharata, Shanti Parva, Adhyaya 284, Shloka 27).

All that is desirable and favourable is indeed the goal of a human endeavour. It is indeed true that by default, our conscious and unconscious minds are pre-set to seek desirable things or objects. But what is not true is that once the desirable things and objects are acquired, we would become happy. Whenever we are thirsty we seek water, and desperation to drink it increases by the hour, but no one has ever called water as happiness. So how can, money, jewellery, love, bungalow or even a beloved be 'happiness'? While it is true that satisfaction of the organs leads to happiness, that does not make all desirable objects the products of happiness.

Lokmanya elaborates, "The *Nyaya* school has given the two definitions: *anukulavedaniyamsukham* (desirable suffering is happiness), and *pratikulavedaniyamduhkham* (undesirable suffering is unhappiness), and it has treated both pain and happiness as some kind of suffering."

In Hindu philosophy, happiness and unhappiness is not limited to the cause and effect of human enterprise. Heavenly forces, gods and demons are all seen involved in the drama of this world. Anger of the deities is deeply feared and seen as the cause of most of the infectious diseases and especially mental disorders. Lokmanya writes, "In treaties of *Vedanta*, the pain and happiness is usually divided into *adhi-daivika* (God-given), *adhi-bhautika* (physical) and *adhyatmika* (metaphysical)."

Modern science has established the fact that while pathogens, bacteria and viruses, affect human bodies, the innate immunity of the body must crumble for them to succeed. There is a well-established science of Immunology also but it stops at a certain point and why some people show resistant to pathogen and others do not, has not yet been established. The finger is pointed towards expression of certain genes, but who controls the switch that expresses or inhibits a gene is unclear. So a lot of physical happiness and unhappiness is indeed metaphysical. Lokmanya writes, "As it is clear, the pain or happiness which arises as a result of the blessings or the anger of the deities, has ultimately to be borne by man through his body or through his mind... I have adopted only the two divisions, external or bodily (*bahya* or *sharir*), and internal or mental (*abhyantra* or *manasika*)."

A cascade of emotions emerges. It all starts with a thirst, a feeling of dissatisfaction, inadequacy, and incompleteness. We act to satiate the thirst, fill the vacuum, bridge the gap, and grab the object of our liking. Once it is done, the thirst goes away only to return– for another gap, another object and most doggedly for more of the same. Man is caught in to thousands of addictions– some are apparent and physical like smoking or chewing tobacco, consuming alcohol or gambling, but others are subtle like infatuation, lust, greed and thousand varieties of obsessive-compulsive behaviour from tea, television and idle chatter to social events, religious rituals and participation in cults. Millions of men become composts of meaningless lives. It is not the action of renunciation or giving away that brings peace to man but the uprooting of the thirst along with its infinite forms, and to continue working with an equable frame of mind. *Ashtavakra Gita* says:

अलमर्थेन कामेन सुकृतेनापि कर्मणा ।
एभ्यः संसारकान्तारे न विश्रान्तमभून् मनः ॥१०-७॥
कृतं न कति जन्मानि कायेन मनसा गिरा ।
दुःखमायासदं कर्म तदद्याप्युपरम्यताम् ॥१०-८॥

The mind keeps wandering in the dense forest of prosperity,
pleasure, pious deeds incessantly and without rest (10.7)
This painful loop of seeking with body, mind and speech is going
on for countless lifetimes. It must now stop. (10.8)

Lokmanya declares, "The Jain and the Buddhist religions copied the Vedic path of Renunciation and therefore in the religious treatises of both these religions, the evil effects of 'Thirst' (*Trishna*) have been described as above, and even in more forcible terms... It is not that the *Bhagavad-Gita* has not acknowledged the evil effects of 'Thirst'. But since the doctrine of the *Gita* is that the total abandonment of action is not the proper course for obviating those evil effects, it is necessary therefore, to consider the above explanation of the nature of pain and happiness."

Lokmanya writes, "We cannot, in the first place, accept as totally correct the dictum of the *Samnyasa School* that all happiness arises from the preventing of pain, such as thirst etc. Wishing to experience again something, which one has once experienced (seen, heard, etc.) is known as desire (*kama, vasana,* or *iccha*). When this desire becomes stronger as a result of the pain due to one's not obtaining soon enough the desired object, or when the obtained happiness being felt to be insufficient, one wants more and more of it, this desire becomes a 'Thirst'. But if desire is satisfied before it has grown into 'Thirst', we cannot say that the resulting happiness arises from the removal of the unhappiness of 'Thirst'."

The concept of Thirst as cause of pain is indeed faulty. Thirst is indeed a force that drives the very life. French novelist Honoré de Balzac (1799-1850) explained it best by saying, "Small natures require despotism to exercise their sinews, as great souls thirst for equality to give play to their heart." The thirst is inevitable but desires are optional. There is a fine line where thirst gets quenched, needs get met, adequacies are completed, gaps are filled, and indulgence starts. The crossing is so subtle that even the most attentive gets deceived. The Buddhist characterisation of "Hungry Ghosts" (*preta* in Sanskrit) as one of the six modes of existence, summed this eventuality best. "Hungry ghosts are pitiable creatures with huge, empty stomachs. They have pinhole mouths, and their necks are so thin they cannot swallow, so they remain hungry. Beings are reborn as hungry ghosts because of their greed, envy and jealousy. Hungry ghosts are also associated with addiction, obsession, and compulsion."[2]

---
2   https://www.thoughtco.com/hungry-ghosts-449825

Lokmanya writes, "We have to abandon the definition of happiness of the *Samnyasa* school, and say that our organs have an inherent capacity for feeding on good or bad objects, and that when they are in that way carrying on their various activities, they come into contact sometimes with a desirable and sometimes, an undesirable object, and we, thereupon, experience either pain or happiness." It is all a matter of scale. Every sensory contact with an object– physical for the touch, sight for the eye, auditory for the ear, smell for the nose, taste for the tongue, and even the thoughts of lust, greed and anger in the mind– creates feeling and in a most subject manner creates happiness or sadness of the experiencer. The *Gita* called it *matrasparsha*.

मात्रास्पर्शास्तु कौन्तेय शीतोष्णसुखदुःखदाः ।
आगमापायिनोऽनित्यास्तांस्तितिक्षस्व भारत ॥१४॥

The Blessed Lord calls the opposites of cold and heat, pleasure and pain, mere fleeting sensations, a matter of degree only (matra-sparsastu). Arjuna is advised to endure these non-permanent changes with patience and without getting disturbed (titiksasva). (Bhagavad-Gita Chapter 2, Verse 14)

There is no explanation for why the audible limit of sound is 70 dB + 1.5 dB and in the frequency range of 20 Hz to 20,000 Hz. Anything beyond this, a human ear can't hear and sound louder than 71.5 dB hurts the eardrum. It is the same with seeing. The human eye can see light with wavelengths between 400– 700 nano meters in a colour range of violet through red. All music is nothing but a play of these frequencies. There are six tastes, namely, sweet, sour, salty, pungent, bitter and astringent, and everyone has a unique tolerance for their excess. The heat pain threshold for skin is around 45°C. Skin gets numb at 7°C and frostbite is risked at 0°C. The human nose can smell ten basic smells. These are figuratively described as Flowery, Fruity (all non-citrus fruits), Citrus (lemon, lime, orange), Woody and resinous (pine or fresh cut grass), Chemical (ammonia, bleach), Sweet (chocolate, vanilla, caramel), Minty (peppermint, camphor), Toasted and nutty (popcorn, almonds), Pungent (sour curd, cigar smoke), and Decayed (rotten vegetables, sour milk). The pungent and decayed are indeed called 'sickening'. As for the mind, four chemicals in the brain, namely, Dopamine, Oxytocin, Serotonin, and Endorphins create the feelings of happiness or sadness. It is with this apparatus that human beings contact the world. The *Gita* says:

इन्द्रियस्येन्द्रियस्यार्थे रागद्वेषौ व्यवस्थितौ ।
तयोर्न वशमागच्छेत्तौ ह्यस्य परिपन्थिनौ ॥३४॥

The senses are coupled with their objects and thus in bind with them. The influence of such attachments is the major stumbling block (paripanthinau) for the evolution of the soul.
(Bhagavad-Gita Chapter 3, Verse 34)

Dr. S. Radhakrishnan adds in his commentary of this *shloka*, "Men should act according to *buddhi* or understanding. If we are victims of our impulses, our life is as aimless as that of animals. If we do not interfere, attachments and aversions will determine our acts. So long as we act in certain ways because we like them and abstain from others because we dislike them, we will be bound by our actions. But if we overcome these impulses and act from a sense of duty, we are not victims of the play of *prakrti*. The exercise of human freedom is conditioned and not cancelled by the necessities of nature."[3]

What is called domain theory in the modern mathematical parlance had been visualised in the *Gita* as an interaction of senses with their objects. Like in the domain theory framework that defines the data values and primitive operations of a programming language, the objects engaged with the five body senses have been included in the field of human activities although they exist outside the body. A critical feature of domain theory is the fact that program operations are also data values and are therefore considered as elements of computational domains. In exactly the same manner, the gross objects outside the human body also exist in their subtle forms inside the human mind. Not only do they participate in the cognitive process, but they are also capable of affecting the physiology. We all know well that when we see a certain object in

---

3 S. Radhakrishnan, *The Bhagavad Gita*, HarperCollins Publishers, Noida, India, 2014, p. 168.

our dream it creates powerful emotions– anxiety, fear, even lust– and elicits corresponding body responses.

The term *vyavasthi* is used to describe this object-sense-mind-body dynamics. The senses are outwardly entangled with the objects through forces of attraction and repulsion, though unseen but very powerful indeed. Inwards, the senses extend this connectivity to the *buddhi*, which decides how these activities will become beneficial or can be made beneficial by us and then communicate it to the *Atman*. It is indeed foolish to wish away the existence of object-sense forces and expect the mind to destroy these forces. It is an impossibility and therefore, such an effort is futile. The focus is not on annihilation of these forces, but steering them in a way that they are beneficial to us and not harmful. In any case, these forces cannot be left unchecked for their destructive power is indeed immense. In a very significant break from the doctrine of sense control and renunciation from the world and its object, the *Gita* calls for the management of object-sense-mind-body system with the benefit of the world as the criterion and cancelling out the attraction/aversion noise out if it as is done to operate an efficient engineering system.

An examination of whether pain and happiness are two independent experiential states or whether one of them is merely the absence of the other is undertaken based on the *Samkhya Yoga* theory of existence. The existence is seen as comprised of 24 elements. There is gross existence surrounding us– the earth, trees, mountains, rivers, sky, celestial bodies– that is explained as created by five gross elements, namely earth, water, fire, air, and space and are collectively called as the *pancha-mahabhuta* (the five great elements). A man contacts the surrounding existence through the sensory apparatus of the five senses. Each sensory apparatus consists of three parts: the physical parts– ears, eyes, tongue, skin, and nose; the executive parts– voice, hands, legs, genitals, and anus; and the operational parts– taste, touch, smell, sight, and sound. The five operational senses are called *pancha-tanmatras*. The *Gita* used a collective term *dashaikam* (ten plus one) for the five physical, five executive parts along with the mind. Of the remaining four elements, *Samkhya* philosophers named *Purusha* (consciousness), *Prakrti* (primordial matter, yet to manifest), *Mahat-Buddhi* (systemic and individualised intelligence) and *Ahamkara* (individual self identity).

महाभूतान्यहङ्कारो बुद्धिरव्यक्तमेव च
इन्द्रियाणि दशैकं च पञ्च चेन्द्रियगोचराः ॥५॥

The Blessed Lord describes in this shloka the existential experience as constituted by the five gross elements, ego (ahamkara), the intellect (buddhi), the unmanifest primordial matter, the eleven senses (five knowledge senses, five working senses, and mind), and the objects of these senses. (Bhagavad-Gita Chapter 13, Verse 5)

Happiness and unhappiness are therefore systemic activities and not some pick and choose kind of situations.

Within this matrix of 24 elements where is thirst, happiness and unhappiness? Lokmanya writes, "Even if we believe that happiness does not consist of the destruction of thirst, or of the absence of unhappiness, and that happiness and unhappiness are two independent things, yet, in as much as both these sufferings are mutually opposite or contrary to each other, we are next faced with the question whether it is possible for a man to experience the pleasure of happiness, if he has never suffered unhappiness." Happiness has therefore emerged as a matter of sensory conditioning. The English poet John Milton (1608-1674) said it so aptly in Paradise Lost, "The mind is its own place, and in itself can make a heaven of hell, a hell of heaven. What matter where, if I be still the same..."[4] A verse from the *Mahabharata* is cited here in this context:

प्रायेण श्रीमतां लोके भोक्तुं शक्तिर्न विद्यते ।
काष्ठान्यपि हि जीर्यन्ते दरिद्राणां नराधिप ॥२९॥

Happiness is a matter of conditioning. The digestive system of rich people, conditioned by eating the best food eventually loses appetite for it. But poor people can appreciate and digest even wood-like coarse and tasteless food. (Shanti Parva, 28.29)

---

[4] John Milton, *Paradise Lost*, Book I, Lines 233-235

It is indeed useless to consider whether it is possible to enjoy continual happiness without unhappiness. Stephan Covey (1932–2012) in his book *The 7 Habits of Highly Effective People*, called happiness and unhappiness proactive choices. Recent scientific breakthroughs established that the brain can actually change as a result of the conscious selection of thoughts and therefore, happiness is attainable and can be called as subjective well-being. Each of us is unique. We are born with a genetically coded happiness set point and what happens to us indeed becomes pleasant or painful depending upon it. There are people who are naturally cheerful most of the time, while many others are always gloomy. That the brain's structure can be modified through practice is an established truth. We have to learn the kinds of things we can do, day by day and bubble our set point up. Conversely, we must avoid the things that drag the set point down. But to an untrained person, unhappiness follows on the steps of happiness, and similarly happiness comes in the wake of unhappiness. A verse of Kalidasa from his great work *Meghaduta* is cited:

कस्यैकान्तं सुखमुपनतं दुःखमेकान्ततो वा ।
नीचैर्गच्छत्युपरि च दशा चक्रनेमिक्रमेण ॥

Life, like a wheel's revolving orb turns around,
Now whirled in air, now dragged along the ground.
(Meghaduta, Translation: H.H. Wilson, 109)

Lokmanya writes, "No one experiences continual happiness or continual unhappiness; pain and happiness always move alternatively up and down like the points on the circumference of a wheel." The story of king Yayati is cited. Yayati is a popular king in the ancient world. He rules over the earth like Indra rules over the heavens. He had two wives– Sarmishta and Devayani. He has a son from each of them. Sarmishta's son is Puru and Devayani's son is Yadu. Yayati is not equal in his affection to them. He favours Sarmishta and ignores Devayani and the partiality is extended even to the sons. An upset Devayani complains to her powerful father Shukracharya who curses Yayati to lose his youth, which he felt was responsible for the neglect of his Devayani. In an instant, Yayati turns into a decrepit old man. Shukracharya told a repentant Yayati that he could regain his youth only if someone offers his youth to him and is willing to suffer his worn out body. But why someone would do that?

"Know this for certain... not all the food, wealth and women of the world can appease the lust of a single man of uncontrolled senses. Craving for sense-pleasures is not removed but aggravated by indulgence even as ghee poured into fire increases it....One who aspires to peace and happiness should instantly renounce craving and seek instead that which neither grows old, nor ceases– no matter how old the body may become.[5]

Puru, the wise son of the beloved wife of Yayati comes to his father's rescue and exchanges his youth with his father so that he goes on loving his mother for time immemorial. But then comes a day of reckoning when Yayati realises that in spite of the thousand years of lust and sensory pleasures that he enjoyed, he remains insatiate and as thirsty and inadequate as ever before. This story

---

5 Swami Venkatesananda, *The Concise Srimad Bhagavatam*, State University of New York Press, p. 227–229.

is included in the *Mahabharata* and the conclusion of Yayati is recorded as:

न जातु कामः कामानामुपभोगेन शाम्यति ।
हविषा कृष्णवर्त्मेव भूय एवाभिवर्धते ॥५०॥

No object can ever satiate the desire for pleasure; the more one gets, the more one seeks. Like the fire in a Yajna gets fierce every time a sacrifice is made, pleasure feeds on itself in a perpetual cycle of self-destruction. (Mahabharata, AdiParva, 75.50)

This story stands as a blunt reminder to all those who consider going for sensory pleasures as the purpose of their life. The world is full of stories of very rich, powerful and famous people, who deep in to the pleasures of their senses and obsessed with the objects of their desires ended their lives in great pain and despair. In Buddhist parlance, King Yayati is called Mandhata. He says at the time of his death.

न कहापणवस्सेन तित्ति कामेसु विज्जति ।
अपि दिब्बेसु कामेसु रतिं सो नाधिगच्छति ॥

"Not though a rain of coins fall from the sky! Could anything be found to satisfy? Pain is desire, and sorrow is unrest: He that knows this is wise, and he is blest." [6]

Lokmanya now takes another line to explain thirst/desire in a positive way. It need not be said that a society divided into four castes will soon go to rack and ruin if the *Brahmins* give up the desire for knowledge, the *Kshatriyas* for worldly prosperity, and the *Vaishyas* for property. Lokmanya writes, "There ought to be liking or desire, but that should be for success; and one must also have a vice, but that should be of learning; that vice is not prohibited. Desire can be an internal powering, rather than external force acting with intent to influence us. Just as in a car, the power is generated in the internal combustion engine; our internal desire process drives our life. Just as driving the car without a planned and fixed destination does not make any sense, our aimless desires turn our life in to a futile sojourn.

---

6   http://www.sacred-texts.com/bud/j2/j2111.htm. Last accessed on 15 August 2017.

An Inside Job

Dalai Lama says, "When you are discontent, you always want more, more, more. Your desire can never be satisfied. But when you practice contentment, you can say to yourself, 'Oh yes– I already have everything that I really need.'"[7] Desire is seen as an endowment (*sampatti*). The beast-like thirst for sensory gumption turns this endowment in to a self-destruction mechanism, but the absence of thirst leads to wastage of one's endowment. Giving up desires and thereby escaping from actions is not the right way to live in this world. Thirsts and desires are not only natural but necessary, as these are the instruments of the evolution of the soul for which human birth takes place. By understanding our soul and listening to its voice, we can indeed free ourselves from hurry, obsession, unfulfilled desires, and persistent discontent.

Thirst or discontent are indeed natural in any sentinel being and generate energy for effort, enterprise and progress in this world. Just as it is stupid to kill a stranger moving in the dark out of the fear of him being a robber or a terrorist, destroying the thirst and living with content is defeating the purpose of life– that is to work. It is not thirst and discontent but their wrong motives and objects that create unhappiness. A skilful course of moving away from a particular hope, thirst or discontent which produces unhappiness, and harbouring aspirations for the betterment and welfare of every one is the message of the *Gita*. *Karma Yoga* is not becoming free from discontent and the renunciation of all action out of fear, but the courage and skill of taking up wholesome actions. Mahatma Gandhi even called healthy discontent the prelude to progress.

The sensory organs and the activities performed by them get meaning from the mind (*manas*). Whether the mind is driven by the senses or the senses are controlled by the mind are two very different scenarios. A man hears by his ears, feels by his skin, sees by his eyes, tastes by his tongue, and smells by his nose; but that does not make him happy or unhappy. It is what he wants to hear, wants to touch, wants to see, wants to taste and wants to smell, and whether it is happening or not that decides his happiness or unhappiness. It means that his natural tendencies are at the root

---

7 http://www.oprah.com/omagazine/oprah-interviews-the-dalai-lama/2

of the happiness-unhappiness phenomenon. Forgetting this and running away from the organs contacting objects is indeed foolish. Human beings are unique creatures, not yet found elsewhere in the universe that examine, comprehend, think, imagine and reflect upon the reality around them. Serbian-American inventor Nikola Tesla (1856–1943) puts it succinctly, "It is paradoxical, yet true, to say, that the more we know, the more ignorant we become in the absolute sense, for it is only through enlightenment that we become conscious of our limitations. Precisely one of the most gratifying results of intellectual evolution is the continuous opening up of new and greater prospects."

Lokmanya writes, "In order to experience Material pain or happiness, the organs are not sufficient by themselves, but they require the assistance of the 'Mind'; and as regards Metaphysical pain or happiness, it is purely mental. It therefore follows that all experience of pain or happiness ultimately depends on the 'Mind'; and if this is true, it naturally follows that it is not impossible to control the experience of pain or happiness if one controls the mind."

Lokmanya challenges the understanding of unhappiness–*asvedana* (suffering) given by the *Nyaya* philosophy of four *pramanas*, namely, perception, inference, analogical reasoning, and testimony. The *Nyaya* School sees unhappiness as physical and mental suffering, and places the actual nature of pain and happiness external to the human body and mind. Lokmanya cites Manu and defines happiness as one's ability to control what is happening to him in a particular situation.

सर्वं परवशं दुःखं सर्वमात्मवशं सुखम् ।
एतद्विद्यात्समासेन लक्षणं सुखदुःखयोः॥

Pain and happiness is a matter of control over phenomenon. When others control our affairs we feel unhappy. We are happy only when we are in control of our lives. (Manusmiriti 4.160)

In direct contrast to the *Nyaya* School that shows the actual external nature of pain and happiness, Manu is emphasizing the internal experience of pain and happiness. It is concluded that we do not make the experience of pain or happiness depend on the organs. Contemporary teacher Swami Sitaramananda elaborates, "Objects appear to give you happiness because of the conditioning of your mind to like this and dislike that, but truly objects cannot bring you lasting happiness. All objects are external things, but happiness comes from within you; it is your true nature… It is possible to see the true happiness of your own nature using your mind; you just have to make the mind calm and un-wavy (devoid of thoughts). When the mind is wavy, you can only see a distorted picture of what constitutes happiness, what constitutes yourself. Therefore, it is important to keep the mind calm and transparent– like a mirror or a calm lake– so you can see yourself."[8]

दुर्लभा वेदविद्वांसो वेदोक्तेषु व्यवस्थिताः ।
प्रयोजनमतस्त्वत्र मार्गमिच्छन्ति संस्तुतम् ॥२॥

The most potent method of dealing with unhappiness is not to deal with it so that it can wither.
(Mahabharata, Shanti Parva, Adhyaya 205, Shloka 2)

After proving that happiness and unhappiness do not exist outside the mind, the external objects get excluded from the equation. From the habit of the mind to seek only favourable outcomes of the actions taken, and getting perturbed if that does not happen, emerges the root of unhappiness. Any action which is undertaken with the mind in firm control and without expectation of results does not create any unhappiness. So, abandoning actions for the fear of unhappiness is indeed nihilism and against the basic principle of life. Lokmanya writes, "The concept of giving up the desire for the result does not mean giving up the resulting benefit, if it has been acquired; nor does it mean entertaining a desire that no one should ever get the benefit of. In the same way, there is a world of difference between the desire for the result and the desire, hope, or motive for a performing action, or employing a particular means for obtaining a particular result."

---

[8] Swami Sitaramananda, *20 Notes on Lasting Happiness*, cited at– http://joythruyoga.com/20-notes-on-lasting-happiness-by-swami-sitaramananda/

What does it mean? Most of the actions are actually entangled with the desires of favourable results and made with intent. The two wheels of *ahamkara* (the I-ness) and the *mamatva* (mine-ness) drive the mind, which in turn command the body into action. The intended result is the propelling force behind most of the human enterprise. Here enters the aspect of quality of mind. A mind afflicted by anger, attachment, ignorance, jealousy and pride leads the doer to unwholesome actions. And when such actions do not achieve their intended results a cascade of misery sets in affecting not only the individual but also people around him. If the obstruction is seen as caused by other people, hate, violence and destruction follow. But if the obstruction is inevitable and seen as fate, despair, gloom and despondency follow.

The desires for results follow a deed like a shadow moves with the body. Greek philosopher Epicurus (341-270 BCE) was exactly on target when he said, "Do not spoil what you have by desiring what you have not; remember that what you now have was once among the things you only hoped for."

Lokmanya writes, "This attachment, in the shape of mine-ness, for the result of the action, is also known as *phalasha* (hope of benefit), *sarnga* (fondness), *ahamkara-buddhi* (egoism), and *kama* (desire). The chain of unhappiness in life really starts at this point. The *Gita* declares that Desire springs from Attachment for objects of pleasure, Anger (*krodha*) from Desire, Mental Confusion (*moha*) from Anger, and ultimately, the man himself is destroyed."

ध्यायतो विषयान्पुंसः सङ्गस्तेषूपजायते ।
सङ्गात्सञ्जायते कामः कामात्क्रोधोऽभिजायते ॥६२॥

Objects of the senses create attachment in the mind through their contact with the senses. From attachment spring desires. Any hindrance or obstacle to the fulfilment of these desires creates anger. (Bhagavad-Gita Chapter 2, Verse 62)

क्रोधाद्भवति सम्मोहः सम्मोहात्स्मृतिविभ्रमः ।
स्मृतिभ्रंशाद् बुद्धिनाशो बुद्धिनाशात्प्रणश्यति ॥६३॥

Anger clouds judgment and leads to disorientation and even loss of memory. When the memory is disconcerted, the intellect gets wrecked. No more able to discriminate between right and wrong, one is eventually ruined. (Bhagavad-Gita Chapter 2, Verse 63)

The hope for result, desire, or attachment with which man performs those actions is established as the true root of unhappiness. It implies that unhappiness can be effectively handled by controlling the mind so as to give up the attachments with the favourable results. It is indeed not necessary to give up all objects of pleasure, or actions, or desires but what is important is not to be affected by the failure of these pursuits.

रागद्वेषवियुक्तैस्तु विषयानिन्द्रियैश्चरन् ।
आत्मवश्यैर्विधेयात्मा प्रसादमधिगच्छति ॥६४॥

But one whose has disciplined his mind can remain free from the bondage with the objects of the senses. Without attachment and aversion towards anyone, he attains purity of spirit. As he has no desires, he performs his work as duty and accepts results as fruits of his action. (Bhagavad-Gita Chapter 2, Verse 64)

The much-celebrated concept of *sthitaprajna* enters here. *Prakrti* cares least about man. Its forces of *sattva, rajas* and *tamas* are most objective and do not discriminate between people by their gender, social status or age. It is indeed foolish for a man to look for subjectivity in the activities of *Prakrti*, harbour desires and hope to receive favours. Such expectations are futile and bring only pain and happiness. Activities carried out in alignment with the forces of *Prakrti* are bound to happen and the doer must take any suffering or the pain which they may cause with equanimity. Dada Bhagwan (1908-1988), the preceptor of the *Akram Vignan* movement that emerged out of Jainism in Gujarat, said so cogently, "When attachment does not occur when someone gives flowers and no abhorrence occurs when someone throws stones; that is considered equanimity." The *Bhagavad-Gita* describes *'yah sarvatranabhsnehas tat tat prapya shubhashubham'* as the characteristic feature of the *sthitaprajna*.

यः सर्वत्रानभिस्नेहस्तत्तत्प्राप्य शुभाशुभम् ।
नाभिनन्दति न द्वेष्टि तस्य प्रज्ञा प्रतिष्ठिता ॥५७॥

One who is without affection on any side, remains unattached under all conditions. He does not rejoice upon flourishing nor laments the depravation. Such a person is indeed anchored in wisdom. (Bhagavad-Gita Chapter 2, Verse 57)

Eknath Easwaran elaborates on *sarvatranabhisnehas* in his commentary on this *shloka*. "His wisdom is unshaken, he is deeply rooted in himself, who has no trace of selfish attachment on any level."[9]

न प्रहृष्येत्प्रियं प्राप्य नोद्विजेत्प्राप्य चाप्रियम् ।
स्थिरबुद्धिरसम्मूढो ब्रह्मविद् ब्रह्मणि स्थितः ॥२०॥

One should not rejoice in getting something pleasant, nor grieve in confronting the unpleasant. A man with such an understanding is indeed a knower of God and is established in God. (Brahmanisthitah) (Bhagavad-Gita Chapter 5, Verse 20)

Lokmanya writes, "Just as Moon never comes within the grasp of the little children who spread out their little hands towards the heavens in order to catch hold of it, so also those persons, who run after Material Happiness in the hope of reaching the highest form of happiness, will in any case find it very difficult to reach the highest form of happiness. But as Material Happiness is not the only kind of happiness, it is possible to find out the way of acquiring the highest and the constant form of happiness, even in this difficult position."

The control of the mind so that it guards the senses and does not sway either with joy or sorrow is what actually matters the most. Lokmanya cites English philosopher John Stuart Mill (1806-1873) who said, "It is better to be a human being dissatisfied than a pig

---

9 Eknath Easwaran, *The Bhagavad-Gita for Daily Living*, Jaico Publishing House, Mumbai, India, 2007, Vol. I, p. 111.

satisfied; better to be Socrates dissatisfied than a fool satisfied. And if the fool, or the pig, is of a different opinion, it is only because they only know their own side of the question."

Human beings are superior to the other animals due to the endowment of a vast inner space wherein they can process their sensory inputs and imagine the future that does not even exists. B.K.S. Iyengar called it the 'Sky of Consciousness' (*Chidakasha*). He writes, "Here, even attention dies and evaporates into the space of consciousness (*chidakasha*)... All the dynamics of doing, of action, is extinguished... In the outer aim, any object whatsoever can be used: the blue of the sky, a sound, the sun, the moon, a flowing river, and so on. The outer aim gathers the diversity of phenomena (*vikalpa*) toward an undifferentiated perception.... The internal aim relies on the various parts of the internal geography, organic and subtle... The organic aim will open into a bridge of space (*adhara*), a place of contemplation where the *pancha vyomana* (five firmaments) unfold."[10]

Without this inner space, this vast canvas of consciousness where the five realms that separate the 'above' of the earth from the 'below' of the earth get painted, a man is no more than the beast– dogs, pigs, oxen, etc. who live for the happiness of the organs. Lokmanya writes, "In as much as nobody is willing to become a beast, notwithstanding that he can thereby obtain all the physical happiness which can be got by beasts, it is clear that there is something more in a human being than in a beast... and when one has begun to think of this matter, one naturally comes to the conclusion that, that happiness which is to be found in the extremely noble activities and in the purest state of the 'Mind' and of the 'Reason' is the highest, or the most ideal state of happiness of mankind, as compared with the happiness of the enjoyment of objects of pleasure, which is common to both man and beast. This kind of happiness is self-controlled, that is, it can be acquired without depending on external objects, and without reducing the happiness of others, and by one's own exertions; and as a man becomes better and better, the nature of this happiness becomes more and more pure and unalloyed."

---

10 Kofi Busia, Iyengar, *The Yoga Master*, Shambala Publications, Boston, USA, 2007, p. 199.

Lokmanya writes, "In short, our philosophers have been looking upon that 'Reason-born' happiness or Metaphysical beatitude, which results from the Realisation of the *Atman*, as the most superior happiness and their advice is that this happiness is such as can be obtained by everybody, in as much as it is self-controlled, and that everybody should try to acquire it. That wonderful and special happiness which belongs to mankind in addition to its beastly qualities is this happiness; and this happiness of the *Atman* (*atmananda*) is the most constant, the most independent and the most excellent of all happiness, in as much as it is independent of external circumstances."

The peace of the *Atman* is the most excellent of all happiness. Since it emanates out of a controlled mind, it is actually doable. Anybody can acquire it with earnest effort. Although gold is the most valuable of all metals, iron and other metals have their own role and importance. Therefore, happiness (*sukha*) of the body and the peace (*shanti*) of the *Atman* are not exclusive and can co-exist. Lokmanya writes, "At any rate, it cannot be disputed that material objects are necessary for the protection of the body, along with this Peace; and therefore, in the phrases used for blessing, one does not say simply: *shantirastu* (May there be Peace), but says: *shantihpushtistustischastu* (May there also be Material Happiness and contentedness along with peace)… What is the 'right action', and what is the 'wrong action' or 'non-action' must be determined by the metaphysical tests of beatific happiness and not by the materialistic methods of determining questions of Morality."

It is not what surrounds you but your response to it that makes you happy or sad. It is indeed a matter of choice if you react to what happens to you with a negative mindset or respond to it with a positive mindset. While pain is inevitable, suffering is optional. Every one indeed has a mental and emotional attitude. There are people who focus on the bright side of life and expect positive results. There are others, and more in number, whose gaze is always fixed on the negative side of life and they emphasise on what is lacking, rather than what is there. For them, a half-filled glass is always half empty and never half-filled.

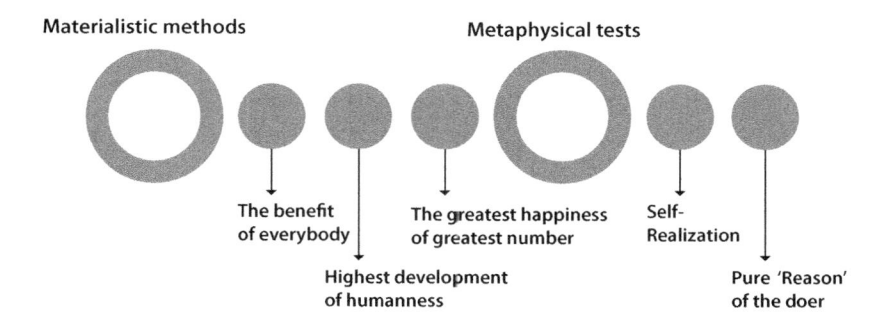

```
Materialistic methods          Metaphysical tests

        The benefit      The greatest happiness    Self-
        of everybody     of greatest number        Realization
                   Highest development         Pure 'Reason'
                   of humanness                of the doer
```

Metaphysical tests supersede materialistic concerns. One must decide what is right through self-realisation and by Reason and not based upon what is materialistically beneficial, happy or superior.

Happiness is explained by Lokmanya as a mental disposition, an anticipation of health and success, a belief that any obstacle and difficulty can be overcome. You need to train your mind to be happy and adopt a positive outlook towards life. One must be steadfast in action and never lose faith in God. There is this beautiful hymn:

God has not promised skies always blue,
Flower-strewn pathways all our lives through;
God has not promised sun without rain,
Joy without sorrow, peace without pain.
But God has promised strength for the day,
Rest for the labour, light for the way,
Grace for the trials, help from above,
Unfailing sympathy, undying love.[11]

Strength for the day, rest for the labour, light for the day, grace for the trials, unfailing sympathy and undying love of God are there for everyone but these must be seen, felt, and taking help of. Life's greatest lessons are mastered through learning to make something good out of the seemingly bad. African-American poetess and social activist *Maya* Angelou (1928–2014) said so eloquently, "If you

---
11   https://www.hymnal.net/en/hymn/nt/720

don't like something, change it. If you can't change it, change your attitude."

Lokmanya writes, "Therefore, our philosophy of *Karma Yoga* has ultimately come to the conclusion that the doctrines of 'the benefit of everybody', or 'the greatest happiness of the greatest number', or the 'highest development of humanness' or other such external tests or Materialistic methods of determining questions of Morality are inferior tests, and that what is the 'right action', and what is the 'wrong action' or 'non-action' must be determined by the Metaphysical tests of beatific happiness in the shape of Self-Realisation, and the attendant 'Pure Reason' of the doer."

People who imprison themselves in the apparent world around them and fail to see the larger dynamics, the superior forces that can be attracted and operated upon by the *Atman* inside them are indeed handicapped and living incapacitated lives. Such people also include those who run away from the world and waste away their lives enchanted in their glorified delusion of *Brahma Maya*. Lokmanya writes, "As the various works on *Vedanta*, which can ordinarily be read now-a-days have been written principally by followers of the Path of Renunciation, and as in the Path of Renunciation, worldly life in the shape of Thirst is looked upon as totally insipid, it is true that the science of *Karma Yoga* has not been properly expounded in their works. Indeed, these writers, who are intolerant of rival cults, have foisted the arguments of the Path of Renunciation on the *Karma Yoga*, and attempted to create the belief that *Samnyasa* (Renunciation) and *Karma Yoga* are not two independent paths for obtaining Release (*moksha*), but that *Samnyasa* is the only correct Path according to the *Shastras*."

The *Gita* system of expounding the science of the 'doable' and the 'not doable' from the metaphysical point of view has been adopted in the West also. German philosophers Immanuel Kant (1724-1804), Arthur Schopenhauer (1788-1860), von Schelling (1775-1854), Johann Gottlieb Fichte (1762-1814) and Georg Wilhelm Friedrich Hegel (1770-1831) and later, English philosopher Thomas Hill Green (1836-1882) followed this point of view. Without knowing who it is inside, seeing and experiencing the phenomenon around, living through this world is a meaningless exercise. Like walking on a treadmill, such people never make any progress and pass through their life-times as passive spectators of a grand drama–occasionally happy but sad most of the time. The advice of Yajnavalkya: *atmava are drashtavyahshrotavyomantavyonididhyasitavyah*, is indeed timeless and is applicable to the modern man even more. Contemporary American spiritual teacher Marianne Williamson phrases it well, "If you're trained in metaphysics, you don't see the world as distinct from yourself. You are one with the world."

Indian philosophy is indeed a vast treasure of dialectics, logic and reasoning to mankind. Nothing is taken for granted and accepted without exhaustive examination of all possible aspects. A format involving two concepts, namely *purva paksha* and *apara paksha*, raising a point and refuting it, is used. Each debater tries to support his point by citing various writings, instances and examples. The Blessed Lord indeed called Himself as *vadahpravadatam* in the *Bhagavad-Gita*:

सर्गाणामादिरन्तश्च मध्यं चैवाहमर्जुन ।
अध्यात्मविद्या विद्यानां वादः प्रवदतामहम् ॥१०.३२॥

I am the creator (adih), sustainer (madhyam) and destroyer (antah) of all beings (sarganam). Of all the debates (pravadatam), I am the conclusion (vadah).
(Bhagavad-Gita Chapter 10, Verse 32)

Lokmanya declares, "Our philosophers have extended their sight far beyond Materialistic philosophers, and have fully justified the science of *Karma Yoga* on the basis of Metaphysics. But, in as much as it is necessary to consider another contrary view (*purva paksha*), which deals with the subject of 'right action' and 'wrong action' or 'non-action,' this discussion will continue in the next chapter.

ॐ

6

The Seed and the Soil

> Somebody is moving across the headlands
> Talking to himself–
> A grey thinker.
> The clay is whitening in the windy light
> Where the sparrows are bathing.
> To-morrow surely
> The seed will go under the harrow
> Nothing must hinder
> The wooing of grain and clay.[1]

Lokmanya introduces in this chapter a different method than the materialistic one that is in vogue in the Western world. As he explained in the earlier chapter that it is indeed foolish to call an action good just because it is creating momentary happiness, in this chapter he states that the decision whether an action is wholesome, unwholesome, or not doing anything at all is a superior option, is based not on thinking or reasoning but on one's ability to understand something instinctively. Lokmanya writes, "Whatever arguments may be advanced by materialistic philosophers, if one considers minutely for a moment what the state of mind of a person is in determining the righteous or unrighteous of any particular action, it will be seen that there are inherent and noble mental impulses like pity, kindness, philanthropy etc., which impel us to do any particular act on the spot."

Not every human action emerges out of a mental analysis. There are drives, impulses and instincts which erupt in an instant and lead a person to actions, which at times are not even imagined possible. It is very common to see abrupt emotional outbursts and sudden

---
1 Irish poet and novelist Patrick Kavanagh (1904–1967).

and unexpected temperamental flare-ups during discussions in families and even between long-standing friends. There is no thinking involved here and most of the time such incidences when rationalised are regretted. Similarly, kind acts like helping someone in crossing a road or climbing stairs, or giving alms, or even smiling at a stranger happen instantly. Most spontaneous actions spring out from the depth of our being. These are almost never created as simulation, imitation nor echoing of someone else. These actions just happen. Of course there is an involvement of certain precursors and a pre-existing build-up, a critical mass, is almost always present. What could this be?

Lokmanya declares, "Therefore, the true foundations of the science of *Karma Yoga* are these noble mental impulses. These mental impulses have not been given to us by anybody; they are Nature-born or inherent traits. As when a judge is seated in his judicial chair, the deity of Justice inspires him when he administers justice, the inherent mental impulses of kindness, pity, philanthropy, gratitude, love for one's duty, courage and other virtues, are the deities just like the deity of Justice." Are there metaphysical aspects of mental impulses? Can they be considered as deities?

No one needs proof of a human being's self-awareness being an aspect of existence. Somewhere inside, there is an audience room for the voice that is not his. Even the layperson is aware of an inner witness that oversees all actions and pokes and prods whenever a transgression is happening from what is just and right. As expressed in a famous Hindi song '*Tora man darpan kahlaye, bhale bure sare karmoko, dekhe aur dikhaye*[2] (your consciousness is like a mirror, it sees and shows you all your actions). This mirror however is not always clean; there is a covering of dust and even greasy muck that interfere in this process. The reflective process is never without struggle and there are almost insurmountable difficulties to communicate with the inner self leading to mental anguish and feelings of guilt when we violate the values we hold dear but fail to apply in our daily lives.

---

2 Written by Sahir Ludhiyanvi, sung by Asha Bhosle on the composition of Ravi for the film Kajal (1965)

The imagery of an inner deity is very helpful to comprehend this phenomenon better. Like the gods and goddesses who reside in heaven, there are deities that exist within the human body. The five viscera, namely the heart, lungs, liver, kidneys, and spleen are seen as deities. We can even add brain, gall bladder, eyes, nose, ears, tongue, and teeth to the list of deities installed in the temple of the human body. These deities fulfil various functions and are related to one another. They act as managers and administrators in a business enterprise and support the balance of the body's functions. Through meditation, one can visualise them in their proper locations and worship them with one's inner breaths and essences and seek protection and sustenance for one's health and longevity. It is even possible to invoke the inner deities to protect one from calamities caused by various external and one's own internal injurious entities. As one advances on the spiritual path, one's visualisation practices become advanced. First, the deities in the mental screen are replaced by the sensation of internal drives and awareness of the mind. Continuous practice gives one focus on the refining of one's inner essence, breath, and eventually the *Atman*. Lokmanya writes, "Everyone by nature knows what the true forms of these deities are. If he defies the inspirations of these deities on account of avarice, hate, or jealousy, or for some other such reason, what can these deities do? Now, it is true that there is sometimes a conflict between these deities themselves and in such cases we are then in doubt as to the inspiration of which deity should we consider as predominant in doing a particular action; and then it becomes necessary for us to consider some other power besides the deities of Justice, Kindness, etc. in order to satisfy this doubt."

While the Latin philosophers called the mind of a newborn child *Tabula Rasa*, a clean slate with nothing written over it, Indians included the experiences the foetus had during its stay in the womb, exemplified by Abhimanyu and Ashtavakra. Then there is a carried forward account of what happened in the earlier lives. Therefore, we could just as well say that a child is born not with a *Tabula Rasa* but with an active Conscience akin to a Mental Deity. Lokmanya writes, "(Without entering) into the intricacies of metaphysical consideration, or of the weighing of pain or happiness, but only consulting our Mental Deity (*mano devata*), that is our Conscience, that deity immediately shows us which path is a more meritorious one; and therefore, Conscience is superior to all deities."

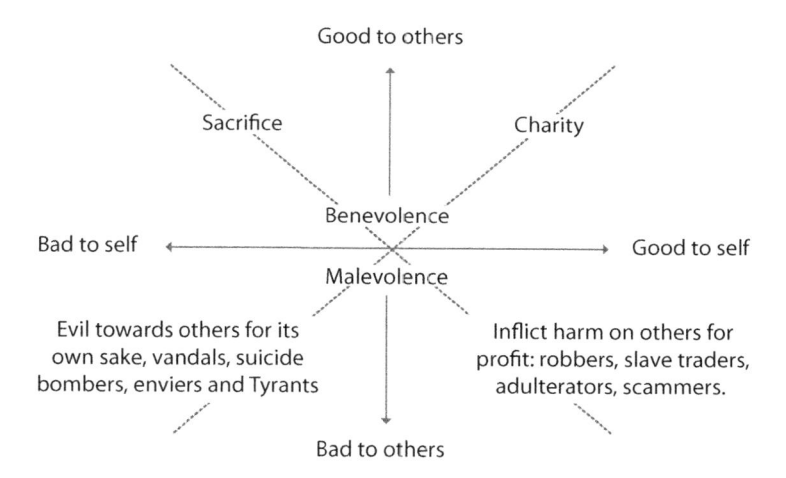

```
                        Good to others
                              ↑
         Sacrifice            |            Charity
                              |
                        Benevolence
  Bad to self  ←───────────────×───────────────→  Good to self
                        Malevolence
                              |
  Evil towards others for its |   Inflict harm on others for
    own sake, vandals, suicide|   profit: robbers, slave traders,
    bombers, enviers and Tyrants|  adulterators, scammers.
                              ↓
                        Bad to others
```

Conscience (viveka) is that kind of deliberation where there is a conscious endeavour to decide in favour of shreyas (benevolence) when confronted with the two opposing ideas of shreyas and preyas (malevolence).[3] The two voices keep buzzing in the mind.

Where from does the conscience arrive? The conception of a child seemingly is merely a biological matter. The recent mushrooming of fertility clinics in every city makes it so obvious. Even films are made on the subject of donation of sperms and surrogate mothers. The visualisation of how sperms move at a fast speed surviving dangerous liquids that they come across on their way to the ovary and only few manage to reach the ovary and take a siege round it in order to impregnate it is indeed publically shown on television. Usually, about 100-300 million sperm are delivered at one time. Only about 15% of these millions of sperm are sound enough to fertilise an egg, which is positioned for fertilisation for only 12 hours each month. Till such time a sperm enters an ovary, there is

---

3   Shrii Shrii Anandamurti, *Adorning the Dawn: Discourses on Neohumanist Education*, Anandamarga Publication, New York, p. 213

no intelligence either in the sperm or in the ovary. But once they unite, an independent life begins and all the intelligence necessary to create a human being gets created in a flash. It is on this first nucleus that conscience and the inner world is eventually cultivated and developed. The beginning of the production of sperms is found in the pituitary gland; it is here that a lot of secrets are concealed.

The process begins in the area of the brain called the hypothalamus-pituitary axis. It is a system of glands, hormones, and chemical messengers called neurotransmitters. The life cycle of a sperm is about 74 days. The pineal gland in the brain secretes the hormone melatonin, which controls the timing and release of female reproductive hormones, and the creation and positioning of the egg cell, called ovum. As of 2017, science knows nothing further than this. But what is not scientifically known can't be called unknown. There are metaphysical considerations. The marriage between the Pineal and the Pituitary is indeed an ancient concept. We connect with the Divine through these glands and our consciousness gets flourished in the process.

Metaphysically, the pineal gland connects us to the ground of our existence, what is called *Prakrti*. It is the egg from which we emerge. The pituitary gland is the channel through which the Divine energy expresses through our physical body and into this world– this is called *Purusha*. In this way, the pituitary is the link of the divine into the earth and its seed in the physical world. Between them, tremendously great and complex potentialities are hidden including the innate moral law. This law cannot be anything else but divine. There can be no other source of it but here.

Lokmanya clarifies, "The word 'Conscience' (*mano devata*) is not to be understood as meaning and including desire, anger, avarice, or other such emotions, which inhabit the mind, but as... the God-given or, the inherent power, which every one possesses in making a choice between the good and the bad... If a person, on doubt, thinks for a moment quietly and with a peaceful mind, this deity, which discriminates between the right and the wrong (*sad-asad-vivechana-devata*) will never fail him."

What importance is to be attached to which virtue seems to be 'prior-listed' with this sovereign deity that immediately gives us her decision on any matter in accordance with this list, as the occasion arises.

Although different people in different times have attempted it, for example, the ten Commandments, a list of the actions which are righteous and which are not has remained elusive. The world is so vast and people so diverse, that what is right and beneficial in one place and situation can become wrong and even harmful in another. Irish philosopher James Martineau (1805-1900) attempted to understand religion on the basis of reason and conscience. He famously said, "Religion is the belief in an ever-living God, that is, in a Divine Mind and Will ruling the Universe and holding moral relations with mankind." Lokmanya mentions 'a list of the relative virtues of righteous and unrighteous actions by the deity of Conscience' published by James Martineau. Lokmanya writes, "In this list, the highest place is given to the feeling of Reverence combined with Humility. On the other hand, Kindness, Gratitude, Generosity and Affection etc., are given consecutively lower grades… when there is a conflict between a virtue of a lower order, and a virtue of a higher order, one must attach higher importance to the virtue of the higher order."

Is there any other proper way of determining the doability or non-doability or the righteousness or unrighteousness of an action? The best of the human reflection, reason, or evaluation, the question 'whether or not one should do' had failed in going beyond 'the greatest good for greatest number'. Human intelligence ends there. Similar is the fate of a pain and happiness based analysis of what is doable and what is not. Being a matter of scale, happiness and unhappiness can be thoroughly misleading as the basis of discerning doable actions from the non-doable. Lokmanya writes, "The decision of the doability or non-doability of an action arrived at after a far-sighted consideration of pain and happiness will meet the same fate as that of a decision, which may have been given by a judge who has not received proper authority from the king."

Someone who is fallen in a well cannot lift himself up. He needs someone outside the well to pull him out. No one can lift himself by pulling his shoelaces. French philosopher Pierre Teilhard de Chardin (1881-1955) convincingly said, "We are not human beings having a spiritual experience. We are spiritual beings having a human experience."[4] Lokmanya reasons, "There must be someone else having a higher authority than ourselves who gives the command; and this function can be satisfactorily discharged only by this God-given conscience, which is superior to man, and therefore, in a position to exercise authority over man."

Deceitful and pretentious people may justify their unwholesome actions by claiming that they are doing it according to the command of their conscience. Our politicians do so regularly at the time of crossing over to the opposition party for the sake of money and power. Lokmanya cautions that by attributing unethical actions to the conscience one can't run away from the consequences of one's folly. He writes, "The fact that when a man has committed a sinful action, he is subsequently ashamed of it, and if his inner consciousness bites him, then it is to be understood that it is nothing else but the punishment of this Mental Deity which thereby proves the existence of this independent Mental Deity as otherwise, we cannot, according to this school of thought, explain why our conscience pricks only ourselves."

The concept of conscience as a seat of divine in a human being is not unique to the Indians. Several religious symbols in the West, like the Star of David and the Greek cross of early Christianity, testified in a way a divine centre inside human being radiating energy outwards. Swiss psychiatrist Carl Jung (1875-1961) described it as, "I began to understand that the goal of psychic development is the self. There is no linear evolution; there is only a circumambulation of the self. Vocation: an irrational factor that destines a man to emancipate himself from the herd and from its well-worn paths... Anyone with a vocation hears the voice of the inner man: he is called."[5]

After establishing the divine credentials of conscience, "An inward capacity that humans possess in order to critique themselves because the Creator provided this process as a means of moral restraint for His creation," Lokmanya now digs deeper in

---

4   Robert J. Furey, *The Joy of Kindness* (1993), p. 138
5   Carl Jung, *Memories, Dreams, Reflections* (1962), p. 222; *Development of Personality* (1954)

to the concept of conscience. He writes, "Conscience is a servant of the value system. A weak conscience is one without any adequate knowledge base and therefore, suffers feelings of guilt. The strong have a proper knowledge and are therefore free of guilt." As an aspect of self-awareness, conscience indeed creates the feeling of pain and pleasure depending upon what is seen and judged as right or wrong. These various feelings are visualised as a multiple source system of mental impulses that guides and drives a human life no different than the celestial deities, whom the ancient man, both in India and in the Greece, saw as governing the affairs of this world.

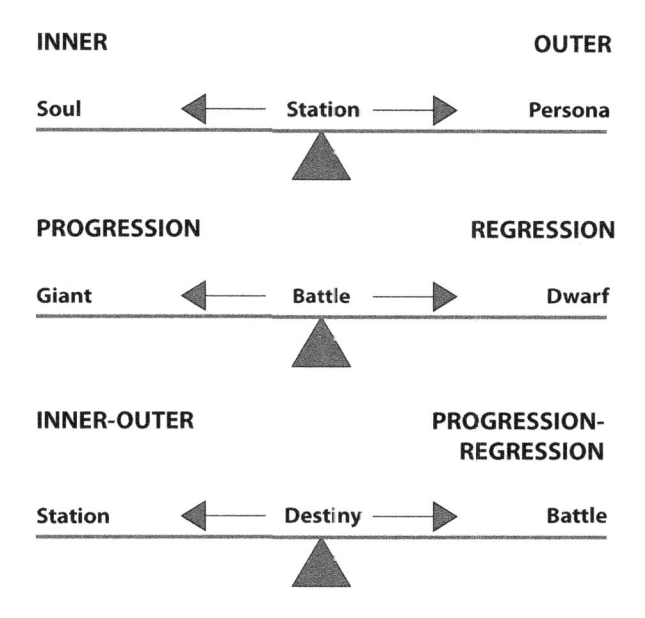

```
INNER                              OUTER

Soul        ◀── Station ──▶        Persona
                  ▲


PROGRESSION                        REGRESSION

Giant       ◀── Battle  ──▶        Dwarf
                  ▲


INNER-OUTER                        PROGRESSION-
                                   REGRESSION

Station     ◀── Destiny ──▶        Battle
                  ▲
```

'Station' represents the balance or tension between the inner and outer tendencies of Soul and Persona. 'Battle' represents the balance of tension between the progressive and regressive tendencies of feeling like a Giant or a Dwarf. 'Destiny' represents final resolution. Specifically, it is the balance or tension between the form of Station and the force of Battle.[6]

Lokmanya writes, "In the *Bhagavad-Gita*, Fame (*kirti*), Opulence (*shri*), Speech (*vak*), Memory (*smriti*), Acumen (*medha*),

---

6 http://www.watchwordtest.com/wdynamics.aspx

Perseverance (*dhriti*), and Forgiveness (*kshama*) are called deities; and out of these, memory, acumen, perseverance, and forgiveness are said to be the qualities of the mind."

मृत्युः सर्वहरश्चाहमुद्भवश्च भविष्यताम् ।
कीर्तिः श्रीर्वाक्च नारीणां स्मृतिर्मेधा धृतिः क्षमा ॥३४॥

The Blessed Lord is driving home to Arjuna that he is not only life and creation, but also death and destruction (mrityuhsarvarah). The feminine qualities of God are enumerated here– radiance of inner beauty (sri), loyalty (dhriti), and forgiveness (kshama). (Bhagavad-Gita Chapter 10, Verse 34)

Eknath Easwaran explains, "The Lord waits patiently while we experiment for a number of years, but finally, if we still have not learned that the purpose of the life is to go beyond death, He takes us back for rest and recuperation. Then, when the right circumstances develop, for us to take up where we left off, He gives us a strong, new body and sends us forth to try again."[7] The feminine qualities mentioned are a particular perspective of this *shloka*. The love of the Lord for us is presented as the selfless love of a mother for her child.

A Deity springs out of the desire of man to be devoted to one that is 'other than oneself', which is considered as a god capable of bestowing all boons. But it does not go beyond that and remains a mental construct without any power, which is sourced from God, and from God alone. Devotion to deities can at best be seen as a satisfaction device. Just as eating food, drinking a beverage, smelling a flower, restful sleep and listening to good music gives satisfaction and these things do not become deities; so are the pursuits seeking glory, praise and status in society. It is our desire for pleasures and status that are construed as deities, mental as well as physical, and worshipping these deities is nothing more than the enterprise of the small minds. Having settled thus, the issue of mental deities as the self-creation of a man, Lokmanya now digs deeper for the truth.

Purity of mind is placed central to differentiate right from what

---

[7] Eknath Easwaran, *The Bhagavad-Gita for Daily Living*, Jaico Publishing House, Mumbai, India, 2007, Vol. II, p. 254.

is not right. The Pure Mind is defined as a state of consciousness without aberrations. The consciousness is still, powerful and clear as a placid lake reflecting all the stars of the night sky and appearing as a starry sky on the ground itself. Pure Mind is not a passive state of consciousness; it does not mean that you are not thinking. Pure Mind is the way to reflect so that your thoughts radiate the divine light. Our *Rishis* wrote prayers in the beginning of their writings for this purity of mind so that what they wrote would reflect divinity and not their mental constructs, judgements, inferences and even biases. Goswami Tulsidas invokes Shri Ganesha to bestow upon him a Pure Mind so that Shri Rama and Sita can forever stay there.

Evolution of a mind by education and its purity by pious conduct is therefore a bridge to connect with the conscience. A man comes to a decision about what is right depending upon his education and purity of mind. Without this, the conscience, though God-given, remains inaccessible and remote, a computer switched off or not booted properly. Lokmanya writes, "The 'Mind' arrives at a correct or incorrect decision as it has been educated. Therefore, our *Rishis* say that everybody must make an effort to develop his 'Mind'; and they have also given rules explaining what this development is and how it is to be made. But they do not accept the position that the power of discrimination between the good and bad (*sad-asad-vivechana-shakti*) is some independent heavenly gift, which is different from the ordinary reason of a man." Developing the awareness of a distinction between 'Mind' that is this field of decision–making (*khetra*) and a witness of this 'Mind' that is eternal, indestructible, and not swayed by what happens in the field, the 'knower of the field' (*kshetrajna*) is the issue. What needs to be addressed is therefore the gaps, obstacles, din and clutter, between the knower of the field (*kshetrajna*) that the field (*kshetra*). The awareness of these barriers between *kshetra* and *kshetrajna* is now elucidated.

Lokmanya writes, "*Kshetra* means the field or body and *kshetrajna* means the *Atman*. This *kshetra-kshetrajna-vichara* is the foundation of Metaphysics... I shall, therefore, in this place briefly consider the science of the Body and the *Atman* to help my readers to properly understand the correct meanings of many of the doctrines of the *Bhagavad-Gita*."

The body is seen as a 'field' (*kshetra*) wherein not only the actions are undertaken but their results are also sown, grown and harvested. On one plane, the body is an efficient factory of material transformation. It takes in the raw material from outside– food, water, oxygen, and sunlight and processes them to gain energy and the wasteful is exhaled and excreted. On another plane, the body is a great action machine.

The body works in conformity with the environment and follows universal biological processes. The body acts upon its surroundings through two types of organs– the organs of action (*karmendriya*) and organs of perception (*jnanendriya*). We act upon our surroundings using five action organs. We move with our feet, work with our hands, speak in our voice, excrete the digestive waste and give birth to children. We connect with our surroundings and feel it by using five perception organs. We smell the surrounding air with our nose, look around with our eyes, hear sounds with our ears, taste food with our tongue and feel the contact with our skin. These ten organs are our connection with the outside world.

The inputs received by the organs of perception are processed by the mind. Without this processing, the sensory inputs remain undifferentiated and meaningless. Sound waves vibrate the eardrums but unless the auditory vestibular nerve transmits it from the inner ear to the brain, we hear nothing. Light waves fall on the retina of the eye but unless visual information is relayed to the visual cortex of the brain, nothing is seen. Lokmanya writes, "When at noon the clock strikes twelve, it is not the ears, which understand what o'clock it is. Just as each stroke falls, aerial vibrations come and strike the ears, and when each of these strokes has in the first place created a distinct effect on the mind, we mentally calculate the sum of all these phenomena and decide what o'clock it is. Even beasts have got the organs of perception, and as each stroke of the clock falls, it causes an effect on their mind through their ears. But their mind is not sufficiently developed to be able to total up the number of strokes and to understand that it is twelve o'clock."

The eighth chapter of *Charaka Samhita Sutrasthana*, titled

The Seed and the Soil

Indriyopakramaneeya Adhyaya, explains in detail the functioning of the mind and its dynamics with the senses.

अतीन्द्रियं पुनर्मनः सत्त्वसंज्ञकं, चेतः इत्याहुरेके,
तदर्थात्मसंपदायत्तचेष्टं चेष्टाप्रत्ययभूतमिन्द्रियाणाम् ॥४॥

The mind transcends sense organs (atindriya), it connects sense organs with the intellect (satvasankamchetah), the quality of Atman (soul) determines mind's action, the mind acts as the driving force for all the sense faculties. (Chapter 8, Shloka 4).

स्वार्थेन्द्रियार्थसङ्कल्पव्यभिचरणात्च्चा अनेकमेकस्मिन्
पुरुषे सत्त्वं रजस्तमःसत्त्वगुणयोगाच्च न चानेकत्वं,
नह्येकं ह्येककालमनेकेषु प्रवर्तते तस्मात् न्नैककाला
सर्वेन्द्रियप्रवृत्तिः ॥५॥

With the entanglement of the senses with the outside objects, the degree of its analytical ability, and the affliction it undergoes by the qualities of nature, namely Sattva, Rajas, and Tamas, the mind in a person emerges as a multifaceted-entity. But mind is indeed one, it cannot attend to more than one sense at a time, and for that reason, there is never an activity of all the sense organs simultaneously. (Chapter 8, Shloka 5)

In the *Bhagavad-Gita*, this is explained by saying *indriyani paranyahurindriyebhyah param manah*:

इन्द्रियाणि पराण्याहुरिन्द्रियेभ्यः परं मनः ।
मनसस्तु परा बुद्धियों बुद्धेः परतस्तु सः ॥४२॥

In this shloka, the Blessed Lord tells Arjuna about the hierarchy of consciousness. The gross body is governed by the senses; the mind operates over the senses. Intellect (buddhi) is beyond the mind and can be accessed only if the mind is not swayed by the senses. The soul is even beyond the intellect and is superior to all.
(Bhagavad-Gita Chapter 3, Verse 42)

Mahatma Gandhi, in his commentary of this *shloka* adds an important insight, "The senses, the mind, and the intellect, these are the dwelling places of desire and anger. But the *Atman* in you is higher than all of them. If we seize the house in which the enemy lodges, we should kill him, else he will leave the place and run away. Occasionally, one may forget Him who is the Lord over these three but that need not worry us, since the moment we think about the Lord, we shall be able to overcome all of them."[8]

The degree of analytical ability is an important aspect here. Their sensory range limits the ability of the action senses. They can see, hear, smell, touch, feel and taste within a certain spectrum. Outside this spectrum, senses are of no use. The perception-senses are superior to the action senses in their analytical ability as they define what is pleasant, favourable and what is not. Mind transcends the senses and can override their inputs. The intellect is even superior to the mind for it can accept or reject the mental constructs. The *Atman* as the real knower, and of divine origin, is even beyond and superior to the intellect. Understanding of this gradation is essential in deciding about the doability and merit of an action.

Lokmanya elaborates, "Just as in ordinary parlance, the word 'mango' is applied both to the mango-tree and the mango-fruit, so also ordinary people very often use the single word *buddhi* for signifying the 'Pure Reason' (*vyavasayatmika buddhi*), as also the fruits of that 'Reason' in the shape of desire etc. (*vasanatmika buddhi*). In order to properly understand the exposition of the *Karma Yoga*, both these meanings of the word *buddhi* have to be continually placed before the mind."

In the mind-intellect tango, it is important to know who the handler is. If the mind is overriding the intellect by overriding senses, as it happens in the case of people suffering addictions, unwholesome acts are always the outcome. But if the intellect is in command, it can overrule the mental-sensory drives by Reason, like a mahout controls the elephant with the goad (*ankusha*). Without the goad in the hand of mahout, the elephant can go berserk and even trample the mahout to death. Lokmanya declares, "The

---

[8] Mahatma Gandhi, *The Bhagavad-Gita*, Jaico Publishing House, Mumbai, 2010, p. 123.

first theorem of the *Karma Yoga* preached in the *Gita* is that the *vyavasayatmika buddhi* must be made pure and steady."

तस्मात्त्वमिन्द्रियाण्यादौ नियम्य भरतर्षभ ।
पाप्मानं प्रजहि ह्येनं ज्ञानविज्ञाननाशनम् ॥४१॥

The Blessed Lord contrasts the discursive mind with a resolute intelligence and establishes bringing the senses under control and avoids irresolute thoughts, which are many-branched (bahushakha) and endless (hyanantahscha).
(Bhagavad-Gita Chapter 3, Verse 41)

Reason is in direct opposition to bodily sensations, perceptions, feeling, and desires, and that way counterbalances the mental impulses. Only with the mind in control can one intuitively apprehend the fundamental truths. After differentiating between 'Mind' and 'Pure Reason' in this way, Lokmanya returns to the idea of conscience as a deity. Just as electricity cannot be part of an appliance that it powers, consciousness cannot be a part of the 'Mind'. Then what is that which overrides the mind? Lokmanya writes, "There may be numerous matters on which one has to think, discriminate, and come to a conclusion. In commerce, war, civil or criminal legal proceedings, money lending, agriculture, and other trades, there arise any number of occasions when one has to discriminate. But, on that account, the *vyavasayatmika buddhi* in each case does not become different. The function of discrimination is common to all these cases; and therefore, the *buddhi* (Reason), which makes that discrimination or decision, must also be one only."

Buddhi by itself is not 'Pure Reason'. Being a human faculty, *buddhi* is shaped and coloured by hereditary, social conditioning, education and several other factors. No two persons can be said to have the same *buddhi*. But there cannot be as many shades of *buddhi* as there are people. Seeing 'Pure Reason' that operates through the *buddhi* solves this problem. But then the question arises when and how does it happen?

Reason has been seen by philosophers as deductive–understanding a part from a whole, and inductive–understanding a whole from its parts. Reason is a braid of integrating and differentiating observation. British writer Clive Staples Lewis (1898-1963) said so poetically, "Reason is the natural organ of truth; but imagination is the organ of meaning."

Lokmanya writes, "That same *buddhi* which differentiates between rice and wheat, or between a stone and a diamond, or which distinguishes between black and white, or sweet and bitter, also discriminates between what is to be feared and what is not to be feared. Moreover, it also differentiates between what is good and what is evil, what is profitable and what is disadvantageous, what is righteous and what is unrighteous, or what is doable and what is not doable, and then comes to a final decision in the matter."

In the *Bhagavad-Gita*, the *buddhi* is seen as one and the same, which is affected by the *sattvik, rajasik,* and *tamasik* qualities of *Prakrti* functions differently. The Blessed Lord says to Arjuna:

प्रवृत्तिं च निवृत्तिं च कार्याकार्ये भयाभये ।
बन्धं मोक्षं च या वेत्ति बुद्धिः सा पार्थ सात्त्विकी ॥३०॥

The Blessed Lord defines goodness here as an understanding about when to act and when not to (pravrttim–nivrttim), between what ought to be done and what is to be avoided (karya–akarya), between what is to be feared and what is not to be feared (bhaya–abhaye) and what binds the soul to this world and what liberates it (bandham–moksam).
(Bhagavad-Gita Chapter 18, Verse 30)

And then He goes on to say:

यया धर्ममधर्मं च कार्यं चाकार्यमेव च ।
अयथावत्प्रजानाति बुद्धिः सा पार्थ राजसी ॥३१॥

The discrimination power of the buddhi to choose right from the wrong (dharmam–adharmam), and deeds to be done from the deeds to be avoided (karyam–akaryam) can be corrupted by the passions (rajas). (Bhagavad-Gita Chapter 18, Verse 31)

Concluding finally that:

अधर्मं धर्ममिति या मन्यते तमसावृता ।
सर्वार्थान्विपरीतांश्च बुद्धिः सा पार्थ तामसी ॥३२॥

The intellect, when shrouded in darkness (manyatetamasavrta), considers irreligion to be religion (adharmam–dharmam), and perceives all things from the wrong end (sarva-arthanviparitan). (Bhagavad-Gita Chapter 18, Verse 32)

Lokmanya writes, "From this explanation, it is clear as crystal that the *Gita* does not accept the theory that there is an independent and a distinct deity of whom the function is *sad-asad-viveka* (discrimination between good and evil)... The *buddhi* is one and the same, but the *sattvik* quality of choosing only the right thing is acquired by it by previous impressions, or by education, or by control of the organs, or by the nature of the food which a man eats etc. In the absence of such factors as previous impressions etc., that same *buddhi* becomes *rajasik* or *tamasik*, not only in the matter of the discrimination between the doable and the not-doable but also in all other matters."

Different qualities of *Prakrti* operating upon one universal *buddhi* explains the difference in the thinking of different people– lawyers, doctors, soldiers, politicians; and people of different regions– mountain people, people living near sea, villagers and city dwellers; and people of different natures– active and energetic, contemplative and reflective, lazy and slothful. On the question of transforming *buddhi* into 'Pure Reason', Lokmanya writes, "So long as the *vyavasayatmika buddhi* acts only according to the dictates of the organs, without discriminating between or examining what promotes one's true benefit, it cannot be called Pure. Therefore, one must not allow the *buddhi* to become the slave of the 'Mind' and the organs, but one must on the other hand, arrange it in such a way so that the 'Mind' and the organs are under its control."

The *Katha Upanishad* gives a powerful analogy in this regard. The senses are depicted as horses which pull that chariot which is the body. The horses must be reined and guided with skill by the charioteer, who is the *buddhi*, so as to keep the chariot keep moving on the right path.

आत्मानं रथिनं विद्धि शरीरं रथमेव तु ।
बुद्धिं तु सारथिं विद्धि मनः प्रग्रहमेव च ॥

One must understand the Atman as the rider (soul in the worldly state) and the body like a chariot (ratham). The Intellect is the charioteer (sarathim) which must rein the mind characterised by violation, doubts etc. (pragraham).
(Katha Upanishad Part 1, Canto 3, Sholka 3)

Dr. S. Radhakrishnan writes in his commentary of this *shloka*, "The teacher distinguishes, as modern psychologists do, two main types of seekers, introverts whose natural tendency is to explore the inner life of spirit and extroverts whose natural bias is towards work in the outer world. Answering to these, we have the *yoga* of knowledge, for those whose inner being is bent towards flights of deep spiritual contemplation, and the *yoga* of action for energetic personalities with love of action. But this distinction is not ultimate, for all men are in different degrees introverts and extroverts." [9]

इन्द्रियाणि हयानाहुर्विषयांस्तेषु गोचरान् ।
आत्मेन्द्रियमनोयुक्तं भोक्तेत्याहुर्मनीषिणः ॥

The sense organs (indriyani) are the horses (hayan) and the road is imagined as the road (goacharan). The Atman associated with the body, organs and mind (the transmigrating soul) is the enjoyer (bhokta).
(Katha Upanishad Part 1, Canto 3, Sholka 4)

विज्ञानसारथिर्यस्तु मनःप्रग्रहवान्नरः ।
सोऽध्वनः पारमाप्नोति तद्विष्णोः परमं पदम् ॥

The man with the discriminating intellect (vijnana sarathih)

---

[9] S. Radhakrishnan, *The Bhagavad Gita*, HarperCollins Publishers, Noida, India, 2014, p. 150.

controlling the vagaries of the mind (manah pragrahavan) reaches the ultimate destination (adhavanah param), the supreme abode of the all-pervading (tad vishnoh paramam padam). (Katha Upanishad Part 1, Canto 3, Sholka 9)

*"Know the self as a rider in a chariot,
and the body, as simply the chariot.
Know the intellect as the charioteer,
and the mind, as simply the reins.
The senses, they say, are the horses,
and sense objects are the paths around them....
When a man lacks understanding,
and his mind is never controlled;
His senses do not obey him,
as bad horses, a charioteer."* [10]

Ancient Greek philosophers also thought in the similar fashion. They saw life as the journey of the soul through this phenomenal world. Plato (428-348 BCE) in his book *Phoedrus* independently uses the same metaphor of a chariot with a little difference. The chariot has two winged steeds instead of five in the *Katha Upanishad*. One horse is white representing aspirations, audacity, boldness and another is black representing thirst, greed, and sloth. With ascend to divine heights as the purpose of the journey; while

---
10 Patrick Olivelle (Translator), *Upanisads*, Oxford University Press, 1996, p. 238-239

the white horse takes one forward, the black horse poses problems. Plato writes, "The divine is beauty, wisdom, goodness, and the like; and by these the wing of the soul is nourished, and grows apace; but when fed upon evil and foulness and the opposite of good, wastes and falls away."[11]

How can life's journey be successful without the involvement of and synergy amidst the body, the senses, the mind, the *buddhi*, and the *Atman*? Each of these must play its own part in this journey– the body must have vigour and strength, senses must be sharp and in control of the mind, the mind must draw directions from the *buddhi* and not be frenzied by the unrestrained senses. The art of living lies in the skill that the *buddhi* and the mind are trained and disciplined into their true forms and initiative and control passes from the senses to the *buddhi* through the mind.

What is the true form of the mind? A pure mind is aligned with the *buddhi*, and not enchanted by the senses. Without this anchoring, it cannot stand the turbulence of the ever-changing world. The true form of the *buddhi* is the state of 'Pure Reason', when it is not the dumping ground of scrutinised sensory data allowed to reach it by an inept mind. Only in its 'Pure Reason' state can the *buddhi* reflect the awareness of the *Atman* supporting the entire cognitive system. The *buddhi*, without a trained mind guarding it from the vagaries and fancies of the senses loses its 'Pure Reason' state. Ego and its weapons of pride and prejudices can also incapacitate the *buddhi*. Such persons descend to the level of their senses and wither away their lives in the mundane and profane. A sense-dominated journey is like walking on a treadmill– life remains at the gross worldly stage and people die at the mental age of ten or fifteen years, even after reaching the sixties and seventies of their physical ages.

A life governed by the senses is devoted to the flesh– wining, dining, dresses and jewellery, perfumes and cosmetics. Titillations of the nerves and subsistence of the body are considered achievements and such people measure those others around them in their family, community, and work place in terms of these superficialities. On the other hand, *buddhi* free from these aberrations becomes become

---

11 Plato, *Phaedrus*, Chariot Allegory (Jowett, 1892), [246e]

splendid and serene, steady and sure. Such a *buddhi* is the best guide in life's journey. The fusion of intelligence, imagination and will is like elixir that nourishes life to its full blossom.

Lokmanya writes, "I have for the time being only to show how it is necessary to consider the question of *Atman* when one wishes to find out how the Reason is to be purified. This question of the *Atman* has to be considered from two points of view: (1) the first method of exposition is to examine one's own body as also the activities of one's mind, and... admit the existence of the *Atman* in the shape of a *kshetrajna*, or an owner of the body. (2) Whether the elementary principle which is arrived at by such examination, and the principle which is arrived at by the examination of the *brahmanda* or the visible world around us, are the same or are different."

The two-stage examination carried out by Lokmanya brings out the existence of two realms of creation. There is the immediate, here and now, and visible realm. All that exists in this realm is mutable, perceptible, and apparent. The other realm is neither here, nor in the future and is concealed. This realm is immutable, imperceptible, and invisible. Both realms are not exclusive, but co-exist concurrently. All things have an internal extension, an inherent directive nature. This is the mind aspect of an entity that is not constrained to time and space. Then there is an external extension. It is born out of the inherent directive nature when it interacts with the surroundings– what is poetically called in the beginning of this chapter 'wooing of the grain and the clay.' The *Bhagavad-Gita* declares most unequivocally:

द्वाविमौ पुरुषौ लोके क्षरश्चाक्षर एव च ।
क्षरः सर्वाणि भूतानि कूटस्थोऽक्षर उच्यते ॥१६॥

There are two kinds of beings (dvaupurusau) in creation, the kshar (perishable) and the akshar (imperishable). In the material world everything perishes. The spiritual world is infallible. (Bhagavad-Gita Chapter 15, Verse 16)

Both the realms however, evolve out of a Root Element that is beyond both, aptly called the Super Soul (*Paramatman*). Clear understanding of the material nature, which is mutable; the immutable individual soul that accompanies the mutable body; and the Super Soul, leads one to liberation in to the spiritual realm, never to return in the material realm. This can be a personal endeavour or in association with saintly persons (*Satsang*), or guided by a Spiritual Master (*guru*).

$$\text{परस्तस्मात्तु भावोऽन्योऽव्यक्तोऽव्यक्तात्सनातनः ।}$$
$$\text{यः स सर्वेषु भूतेषु नश्यत्सु न विनश्यति ॥२०॥}$$

Beyond the unmanifested creation, there is yet another unmanifested dimension, which is changeless and eternal (vyaktovyaktatsanatanah). In the midst of all changes, it does not die when all existences perishes (nasyatsunavinasyati).
(Bhagavad-Gita Chapter 8, Verse 20)

The *Karma Yoga* of the *Gita* is indeed the 'science of proper action' to purify the *buddhi* to export one from this material realm (*kshar*) to the immutable reality (*akshar*) which is the abode *(dham)* of the God. The Akshardham Mandirs constructed by Shri Bochasanwasi Akshar Purushottam Sanstha (BAPS) follow this principle.

$$\text{अव्यक्तोऽक्षर इत्युक्तस्तमाहुः परमां गतिम् ।}$$
$$\text{यं प्राप्य न निवर्तन्ते तद्धाम परमं मम ॥२१॥}$$

That unmanifest dimension is called the Imperishable and My supreme abode (akshardham). One who reaches this ultimate destination (paramamgatim) never returns into this world.
(Bhagavad-Gita Chapter 8, Verse 21)

Mahatma Gandhi, in his commentary of this *shloka* clarifies that persons of little intelligence do not know the unmanifest state of the God. They mistake the manifest universe for the invisible reality behind. Gandhiji writes, "If, for instance, we worship the Sun, which gives light and heat, we divide the divine power of God into several aspects and worship one of them, we should try to know the highest, the invisible state of God. The visible universe is ever taking new shades. The gods change their forms but God is ever the same."[12]

The rest of this chapter deals with the body-soul (*pinda-atman*) interdependence. The *Prashna Upanishad* written in the second half of the first millennium BCE contains six questions and their answers dealing with creation. Logically arranged, these questions have an embedded structure; beginning with macrocosmic aspects, how universe and celestial bodies are created, and then proceeding to increasing details of microcosmic aspects, for example, how the human body works.

With the answer to the first question, it is established that when God desired to create many for the one, he created two forces, namely *Prana* or the life principle, and *Rayi* or matter, in a manner such that *Prana* acts on *Rayi* and manifests in various forms. The intermingling of *Prana* and *Rayi* can be seen everywhere and in every creation. *Prana* is the sun, day, *Amurta* (formless), life, spirit, northern path and invisibility, belong to the life side. *Rayi* is the moon, the night, *Murta* (with form), matter, visibility and the southern side. The other questions refer to how divine energy constitutes and supports the body, the nature and origin of the *Prana*, about sleep and dreams, eternity and time.

Life has no material reality and is a projection of God. What is seen as real– the body, animals, plants, and so many names and forms around are indeed the invisible *Prana* operating over the visible *Riya*. It is *Prana* that guides the body and sustains the life in the body through senses and various other organs. Without *Prana*, the limbs and organs will dry up and waste away. *Prana* originates in the *Atman* and always remains with it just as shadow remains with man. It however, enters into the body and operates upon it through the mind.

Like a king rules through ministers and executives, *Prana* governs the different areas of the body and carries out activities through the five *vayus* (winds)– *Pranavayu* (different from the undivided master *Prana*), *Apanavayu*, *Samanavayu*, *Udanavayu*, and *Vyanavayu*. The *Prana vayu* in the region of the lungs and the heart is the inward moving vital energy. It governs the inhaling of breath, eating and also all sensory inputs reaching the mind. The *Apanavayu* in the

---

[12] Mahatma Gandhi, *The Bhagavad-Gita*, Jaico Publishing House, Mumbai, 2010, p. 225.

pelvis region involves the outward flow of energy, exhaling of breath and digestive elimination. The *Samanavayu* located at the navel, balances the *prana* and *apana* energies together and acts as the fire, for both digestion and purification. The *Udanavayu* meaning the ascending, emanating between the heart and the head opens up the dormant energies and leads consciousness from lower to the upper levels. The *Vyanavayu*, meaning all-pervading air integrates all *vayus*. The *Vyanavayu* helps to balance the other four *vayus*, and is present throughout the body.

The example of the sun is given to answer the question– What are they that sleep in man and what again are they that awake in him? As the rays of the sun appear as if they withdraw in to the sun when it sets below the horizon and comes forth again when the sun rises next morning, so also, all the senses turn dormant in the mind during sleep and become one with the mind. In what precedes the celebrated theories of mind by psychologists in the West by a millennium, the Prashna *Upanishad* so succinctly explains, "In dream the mind creates a world of its own out of the impressions received in the waking state and enjoys the vision. The mind itself is the perceiver (subject) and the perceived (object). The mind itself assumes the forms of mountains, rivers, trees, flowers etc. then."[13]

Opening up of the mind to a wider understanding on a perspective of life and the Universe, and transcending the consciousness beyond what has been previously acquainted is the crux of spiritual practice. It is indeed possible to expand our awareness by spiritual practice. All through the ages, spiritual practitioners have demonstrated the capacity to express several different levels of consciousness. For the lay people different levels of consciousness can be said to contain their different concerns. For someone who is only concerned with personal issues and his own physical well-being, the physical body will outline the outer limits of his concerns. For someone whose concerns extend to emotional interactions with others, we can say that such a person has an emotional level. And for one whose concerns include the world of ideas, that person can be credited with having a mental level as well.

---

13 Swami Sivananda, *Essence of the Prasnopanishad*, para 113, cited at http://sivanandaonline.org/public_html/?cmd=displaysection&section_id=583

Lokmanya now explains how consciousness indeed functions. He writes, "The 'Mind' and 'Reason' are the means or the organs for thought. If the gross Body does not possess movement (*chetana*) in the form of Vitality (*prana*) in addition to these, it will be just the same whether the 'Mind' and the 'Reason' exist or not. Therefore, it is necessary to include one more element in the Body, namely, Movement (*chetana*). The word *chetana* is sometimes also used as meaning the same thing as *chaitanyam* (total field of consciousness). But one must bear in mind that the word *chetana* has not been used in the sense of *chaitanyam* in the present context."

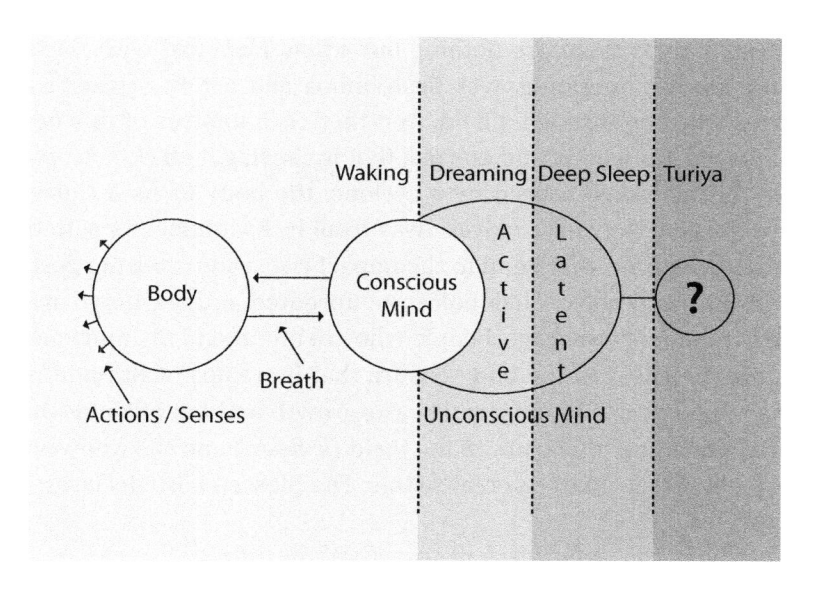

When we are sleeping, the consciousness recedes from the waking in to the inner space, like a tortoise withdrawing its limbs. The samskaras and antahkarna create dreams. Deeper still, the consciousness can recede into seedform. The potential is still there, but everything is non-active. Can we make choices here and wake up as a new person?[14]

The *Chetana* principle is a beautiful concept that captures the movement of the life forces in the gross body as energy in continuous motion within itself. Like a vortex, it keeps whirling with lot of

---

14 'Nidra in Yoga Meditation', http://tripurashakti.com/nidra/

motion at the periphery but stillness at the core. Though it passes through everything that comes its way, and imparts energy to those objects (*chaitanyam*), it is still by itself. The imparted energy is transient; it comes, hits, and moves on. The induced consciousness is therefore *nashvara*, exists now and decays the next moment; the still core is *Ishvara*, the eternal and never decaying. *Chetana* is thus seen as a connection of the divine with the gross. The uniqueness of the Hindu idea of life is awareness of the ephemeral nature of presence of consciousness in the gross. The destiny of ephemeral life is dedicating, devoting, and surrendering itself to the eternal and non-decaying existence of *Ishvara* (*Ishvara pranidhana*).[15]

The body is therefore nothing but a field (*kshetra*) with senses, mind, nerves, operating over flesh, limbs and action organs, as a vortex whirling through a field. And there is a knower of this field, unaffected, unmoving and eternal, that is causing it all (*kshetrajna*). Like the wreckage caused by a cyclone, the body turns a cadaver once the consciousness moves away from it. As it happens with the cyclone, the trees that bend to the impact rise again after the gust is gone, but rigid objects like poles are uprooted and are flown away and turned into wreckage. People who are mindful of the movement of consciousness in the body ensure that it creates health and not illness, nourishment and not disease, growth and not atrophy. Only those who know this truth of the Field (*kshetra*) and the Knower of the Field (*kshetrajna*) can realise this. The Blessed Lord declares:

ऋषिभिर्बहुधा गीतं छन्दोभिर्विविधैः पृथक् ।
ब्रह्मसूत्रपदैश्चैव हेतुमद्भिर्विनिश्चितैः॥५॥

The Blessed Lord describes in this shloka the existential experience as constituted by the five gross elements, ego (ahamkara), the intellect (buddhi), the unmanifest primordial matter, the eleven senses (five knowledge senses, five working senses, and mind), and the objects of these senses.
(Bhagavad-Gita Chapter 13, Verse 5)

---

15 *Patanjali Yoga Sutra* 1.23

Contemporary American theoretical physicist Michio Kaku explains the consciousness phenomenon so deftly, "It is sometimes helpful to differentiate between the God of Miracles and the God of Order. When scientists use the word God, they usually mean the God of Order. ...The God of Miracles intervenes in our affairs, performs miracles, destroys wicked cities, smites enemy armies, drowns the Pharaoh's troops, and avenges the pure and noble. ...This is not to say that miracles cannot happen, only that they are outside what is commonly called science."[16]

With a sense of pride, Lokmanya concludes this chapter with these words: "And when we realise that this kind of examination has been made even in the Western countries, and that the doctrines advanced by Western philosophers like the German philosopher Immanuel Kant and others, are very much akin to the doctrines of *Vedanta* philosophy, we cannot but feel a wonder about the super manly mental powers of those persons, who laid down these doctrines of *Vedanta* by mere introspection, in an age when the material sciences were not so advanced as they are in the present day. But we must not stop with feeling wonder about this matter - we must feel proud of it."

ॐ

---

[16] Michio Kaku, *Hyperspace: A Scientific Odyssey Through Parallel Universes, Time Warps, and the 10th Dimension*, Oxford University Press (1995), p. 331

7
The Riddle of the Universe

> I want to know how God created this world. I'm not interested in this or that phenomenon, in the spectrum of this or that element. I want to know His thoughts, the rest are details.
>
> *Albert Einstein*

In this chapter, the concept of the human body as a field (*kshetra*) upon which an eternal knower of the field (*kshetrajna*) operates is expanded. Envisioning the body as a field opens up several dimensions beyond its physical form of the flesh and organs supported by skeletons and covered by the skin. There is the soul body, our truest self, the spiritual speck, migrated from earlier lives in to the physical body, and at least two other forms of bodies between the physical and the spiritual, called the astral, and the ethereal bodies. The astral body is closer to the physical body minus its form. It is impervious to aging and disease. The ethereal is closer to the mind minus the brain. It is like a powerful receiver that can draw information from the vast sea of consciousness beyond this world and even planet earth. These four bodies are seen as superimposed and do not exist separate from one another till the time of death.

Ancient Greeks believed that the human race came into being not out of evolution from animals, as is now believed by scientists, but as an expansion of heavenly spirits who wanted to spread their order into the material realm. Greek mythology is full of stories when these spirits interfered with the affairs of the early human lives and kingdoms. According to Plato, "Atlantis was a great island (larger than Libya and Asia combined) in the Atlantic Ocean, but its control extended beyond the 'Pillars of Heracles' into the Mediterranean as far as Egypt and Tyrrhenia (Italy). Its powerful and remarkable dynasty of kings arose directly from Poseidon, the god of the sea and of earthquakes, though this divine and heroic lineage gradually became diluted by mixing with mortal stock."[1] Thoth was one such god-mortal hybrid who lived in Egypt. He is depicted in his human form with the head of the long-legged wading bird Ibis found in Africa. In later times, the civilisation of Greece made him one of their gods and renamed him Hermes. The Hermetic teachings with the famous aphorism, *'As above, so below; as below, so above'*, withstood the passage of time and survived as seven spiritual principles namely, Mentalism, Correspondence, Vibration, Polarity, Rhythm, Cause and effect and Gender.[2] Everything in the universe can be understood as governed by these seven principles.

The Law of Mentalism sees all things as the manifestation of God's Mind. The Law of Correspondence defines the Creation existing in accordance with harmony, agreement and correspondence between the physical, mental and spiritual realms. The Vedic concept of *Rta* also makes the same point. The Law of Vibration describes the entire Creation as vibration. Modern physics indeed establishes this. Of course, science has not been able to validate or refute the Law of Mentalism.

The Law of Polarity sees everything as dual, implying a pair of opposites and two sides to everything that exists. The Law of Rhythm describes all movements as oscillatory and cyclic. The Law of Cause and Effect sees every effect with its cause as tells the Buddhist law of dependent origination. The Law of Gender sees gender in everything. There is nothing without its opposite gender quality as seen by the Chinese principle of Yin and Yang. Together, these seven laws form the framework that holds the universe together.

The Vedic seers visualised Bhagwan Vishnu, the Creator of the universe, sleeping on a giant snake Ananta and floating over the formless and infinite sea of all causes (*kshirasagara*). A lotus sprouts out of His navel on which manifests Brahma, representing the

---
1 Dr. Iain Stewart, 'Echoes of Plato's Atlantis', http://www.bbc.co.uk, Last updated 2011-02-17
2 The Three Initiates, *The Kybalion* [1912], is a book claiming to be the essence of, Hermeticism–a religious, philosophical, and esoteric tradition based primarily upon writings attributed to Hermes Trismegistus.

universe that can be seen. Brahma then creates all other forms. Just as the lotus blossoms and falls every season, so also, the universe is created and annihilated so that it can be created once again; of course, this season lasts for billions of years." Now this universe represented by Brahma is not a permanent universe, it is temporary, Brahma lives for 100 years, says the *Vedas*, and then dies and then a new universe (Brahma) is born. So as per the *Vedas*, our universe lives for 100 years. Talking of time measurements– Brahma lives for hundred years say the *Vedas* and we are in the first day of the 51st year of Brahma. A universe endures for about 4,320,000,000 years (one day of Brahma, the creator or *Kalpa*) and is then destroyed by fire or water elements. At this point, Brahma rests for one night, just as long as the day. This process, named *Pralaya*, repeats for 100 Brahma years (311 trillion, 40 billion human years) that represents Brahma's lifespan. Brahma is regarded as a manifestation of *Brahman* as the creator."

When I asked Dr. Kalam about the beginning of the Universe he said, "It is generally considered proven that the Universe began about 14 billion years ago with the Big Bang... God is a unique force which caused the Big Bang and created the Universe for some purpose... I rest my belief in Albert Einstein's theory that the Universe is following an eternal series of oscillations, each beginning with a Big Bang and ending with a big crunch, till such time a consensus emerges on this issue. According to this theory, the Universe will continue to expand till such time that the gravitational attraction of matter causes it to collapse inwards and bounce back again."[3]

Inferred from the age of 4.3 billion-year-old zircon crystals, the earth is a little over 4.5 billion years old. It suffered unremitting rain of meteorites before it started cooling. The surface then got solidified to a crust and then the atmosphere got formed around it ushering the creation of water followed by life. Initially, single-celled prokaryotic cells such as bacteria got created. Then multicellular life evolved over a billion years. Fishes came 530 million years ago–

---

[3] A. P. J. Abdul Kalam and Arun Tiwari, *Squaring the Circle: Seven Steps to Indian Renaissance*, University Press, Hyderabad, India, 20

what the Vedic seers called the *Matsya Avatar*. Mammals didn't evolve until 200 million years ago (*Varaha Avatar*) and our own species, Homosapiens, only 200,000 years ago. The homosapiens will exist for 24 millenniums, called a *Manvantara*, before extinction. Each cycle starts with the *Satya Yuga*, goes on to the *Treta Yuga*, followed by *Dvapara Yuga* and finally into a *Kalyuga*, with decreasing duration. Our present time is a *Kalyuga*, which started at 3102 BCE with the end of the *Mahabharata* war.

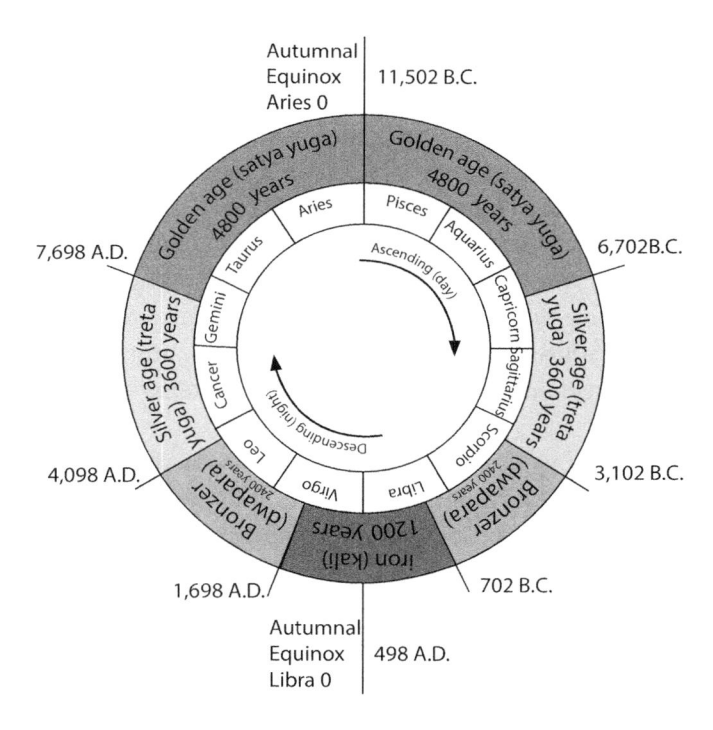

The 24,000 year cycle (the Yuga Cycle) is made up of 4 different Ages that some refer to as the Iron, Bronze, Silver, and Golden Ages. The Ages are similar to seasons, where each has a different characteristic, but in this instance feature varying levels of human consciousness that consequently reflect different trends in human society.[4]

---

4   Walter Cruttenden, *Lost Star of Myth And Time*, St. Lynn's Press (2005), cited at–http://www.everythingology.com/lost-star-of-myth-and-time/

Having established in the last chapter the live connection between the human body and the universe by the *kshetra-kshetrajna* code, Lokmanya takes up the examination of the visible world and the fundamental principle in it– the *kshara* (mutable) and the *akshara* (immutable), and goes on to the determination of the nature of the *Atman*. Just to recap, as per the *kshetra-kshetrajna* code, the human body, which is called the *kshetra*, is an active dynamic field reflecting *Prakrti* (Nature). Whatever exists in the Universe is immanent in the human body. Conversely speaking, the Universe itself is a reflection of the Inner Being– the *kshetrajna*, who oversees the entire creation. Ancient Greeks called it macrocosm and microcosm– the part (microcosm) reflects the whole (macrocosm) and vice versa.

Lokmanya begins the examination of the *kshara* (mutable) and the *akshara* (immutable) with a long view of the Indian philosophical systems. He writes, "There are three systems of thought, which scientifically consider the mutable and the immutable world. The first of these is the *Nyaya* School and the second one is the *Kapila Samkhya* School. But the *Vedanta* philosophy has expounded the form of the *Brahman* in a third way altogether, after proving that the propositions laid down by both of those systems of thought are incomplete."

To put things in to perspective, the six main schools of Hindu Philosophy were formalised over a millennium before the commencement of the Common Era, starting with the *Samkhya* philosophical systems given by Rishi Kapila. The *Yoga* school, expounded by Patanjali, and the *Nyaya* school of Aksapada Gautama, and the *Vaisheshika* School founded by Kanada followed it. The two later schools, namely, *Purva Mimamsa* and the *Uttara Mimamsa*, also called the *Vedanta* interpreted and established the authority of the *Vedas* and the *Upanishads*, respectively.

Dr. S. Radhakrishnan writes, "From the beginning the Indian felt that truth was many-sided, and different views contained different aspects of truth which no one could fully express… *Samkhya* is the oldest school. Next came *Yoga*, next *Mimamsa* and *Vedanta*, and the last of all *Vaisheshika* and *Nyaya*."[5]

---

5 S. Radhakrishnan, *Indian Philosophy, Vol. 1*, Oxford University Press, 2008, p. 25, 34.

The *Samkhya Sutra* written by Rishi Kapila has been referred to in the *Bhagavad-Gita* several times. The *Samkhya* in Sanskrit means the number and the *Samkhya* school got its name as it took upon itself the enumeration of the true principles that are the basis of the creation of the human world (*Tattvas*). *Prakrti* is the field (*kshetra*) and *Purusha* is the farmer (*kshetrajna*). So it is with the body, which is the field of the soul. They are characteristically quite different from each other. Dr. S. Radhakrishnan writes, "The dualistic metaphysics of the *Samkhya* is the logical development of the conception of *Hiranyagarbha* floating on the waters. The description of the ecstatic conditions caused by the performance of sacrifice or the singing of hymns or the effects of the *Soma* juice when we see the glories of the heavenly world remind us of yogic states of divine blessedness where voices are heard and visions are seen."[6]

The 24 elements described by the *Samkhya* School are as follows: There are five basic structural elements (*bhootas*), five subtle elements (*tanmatras/vishayas/pranas*), five executive organ systems (*Karma Indriyas*), five sensory organ systems (*Jnana Indriyas*) and four intellectual systems collectively called *Antahkarna* (inner operative or executive instruments namely, the mind (*Manas*), the intellect (*Buddhi*), the ego (*Ahamkara*), and the consciousness (*Chitta*). The consciousness (*Chitta*) is divine and comes from the God (*Purusha*).

The pre-eminent worth of Rishi Kapila becomes clear from the following words of the Blessed Lord in the *Gita*:

अश्वत्थः सर्ववृक्षाणां देवर्षीणां च नारदः ।
गन्धर्वाणां चित्ररथः सिद्धानां कपिलो मुनिः ॥२६॥

Amongst trees I am the sacred tree (asvatthah, Pipal tree); of the heavenly advisors (devarsinam) I am Narada. Amongst the singers of the gods (gandharvas) I am Chitraratha, and amongst the perfected ones (siddhas) I am the learned Kapila (the preceptor of the Samkhya philosophy).
(Bhagavad-Gita Chapter 10, Verse 26)

---

6 S. Radhakrishnan, *Indian Philosophy*, Vol. 1, Oxford University Press, 2008, p. 86.

Prakrti and its Evolutes

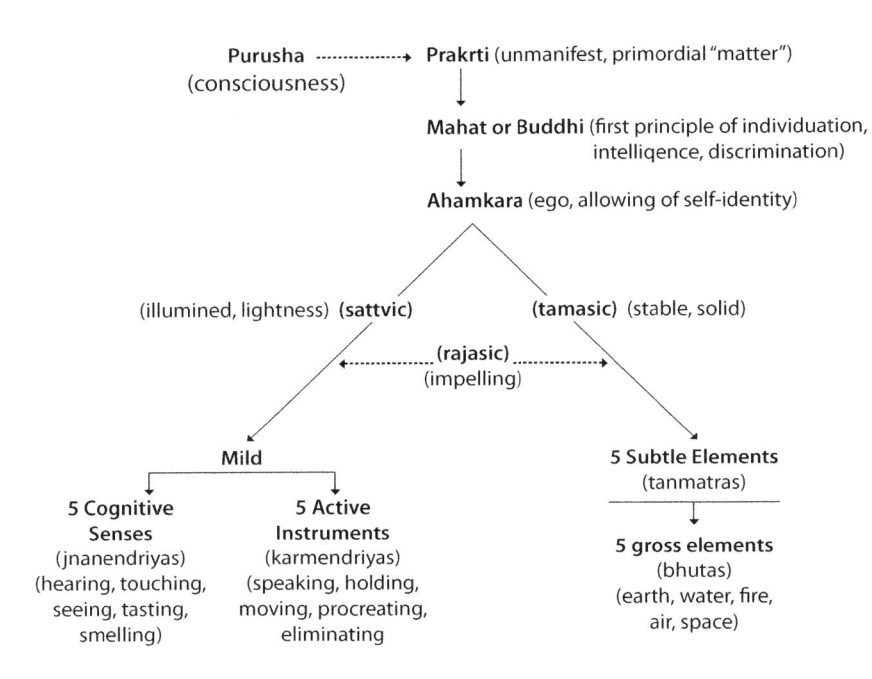

Purusha ┈┈┈→ **Prakrti** (unmanifest, primordial "matter")
(consciousness)
↓
Mahat or Buddhi (first principle of individuation, intelligence, discrimination)
↓
Ahamkara (ego, allowing of self-identity)

(illumined, lightness) **(sattvic)**　　　**(tamasic)** (stable, solid)

←┈┈┈ **(rajasic)** ┈┈┈→
(impelling)

Mild

5 Cognitive Senses
(jnanendriyas)
(hearing, touching, seeing, tasting, smelling)

5 Active Instruments
(karmendriyas)
(speaking, holding, moving, procreating, eliminating)

5 Subtle Elements
(tanmatras)
↓
5 gross elements
(bhutas)
(earth, water, fire, air, space)

Samkhya philosophy views anything that is subject to change, death, decay or decomposition as being "unreal" rather than "real." This does not mean that the objects are not there in front of you. Rather, they are not ultimately "real" in that their form keeps morphing from this to that to the other. What is considered "real" is that final substratum which never changes, cannot die, and cannot possibly decay or decompose. It is the direct experience of that "absolute reality" which is being sought.[7]

Astounded by the profoundness of *Samkhya*, Russian-German spiritualist, author and co-founder of the Theosophical Society in 1875, Helena Petrovna Blavatsky (1831–1891) considered Rishi Kapila not as one person but a series of sages who together developed the *Samkhya Yoga*. She writes, "The *Samkhya* philosophy may have been brought down and taught by the first, and written out by the last Kapila… the Kapila who slew King Sagara's progeny– 60,000 men strong– was undeniably Kapila, the founder of the *Samkhya* philosophy, since it is so stated in the *Puranas*… the

---

[7] http://www.swamij.com/prakriti-purusha-sankhya.htm

60,000 sons, brutal, vicious, and impious, are the personification of the human passions that a "mere glance of the sage"– the self who represents the highest state of purity that can be reached on earth– reduces to ashes."[8]

Lokmanya explained the crux of the *Samkhya* philosophy with these words– "The *Samkhya* philosophers have laid down the proposition that whatever product you may take, its present concomitants and qualities must in some form or the other have been in existence in its original cause." This proposition is known by a self-explanatory term *satkaryavada* that establishes the principle that all qualities of a product (*sat*) are essentially present in the inputs from which the product is created (*karya*). Lokmanya writes, "The seed is not destroyed when the sprout comes into existence, the sprout is not destroyed when the tree comes into existence; they are transformed. They absorb other elements into themselves from the earth and from the air, and thereby the seed takes the new form of a sprout. Similarly, even if wood is burnt, it is only transformed into smoke, ashes etc. It's not that the elements in the wood are totally destroyed and a new thing in the form of smoke comes into existence. Curds can be made only out of milk, and not from water; oil comes out of *til* (sesame), not out of sand; from these and other actual experiences, one must draw the same conclusion."

Samkhya-karika (Verses on *Samkhya*) is an authoritative text on the *Samkhya* philosophy. Ishvarakrishna wrote it in the 2nd century CE. The *Samkhya-karika* declares the pursuit of happiness as the basic need of all human beings but happiness is almost always elusive and impermanent even if it arrives, and most people suffer mental torments of various kinds. The aim of this book is to share with the people the means of counteracting suffering.

दुःखत्रयाभिघाताज्जिज्ञासा तदपघातके हेतौ ।
दृष्टे साऽपार्था चेन्नैकान्तात्यन्ततोऽभावात् ॥१॥

Because of the torment of the three-fold suffering arises this inquiry to know the means of counteracting it. If it is said that

---

8 H. P. Blavatsky, *The Secret Doctrine: The Synthesis of Science, Religion, and Philosophy*, Cambridge University Press (2011), p. 571

> *such inquiry is useless because perceptible means of removal exist, we say no because these means are neither lasting nor effective. (1)*[9]

Dr. S. Radhakrishna observed that the *Gita* does not recognise any ultimate distinctness of individual souls. He quotes from *Samkhya-karika*, "The character of the individual soul and its relation to nature as given in the *Bhagavad-Gita* show the influence of the *Samkhya* theory. *Purusha* is the spectator, and not the actor. *Prakrti* does everything. He who thinks, 'I act' is mistaken. To realise the separateness of *Purusha* from *Prakrti*, soul from nature, is the end of life. The theory of *gunas* or qualities is accepted. There is no entity on earth or in heaven among the *devas* that is free from the three qualities born out of *Prakrti*. The *gunas* constitute the triple chord of bondage. So long as we are subject to them we have to wander in the circuit of existence."[10]

The allegory of one blind and one lame person left in the forest from *Samkhya-karika* (verse 21) is cited to explain the relationship of *Purusha* with *Prakrti*. These two persons inspire mutual trust and confidence and share their duties. The blind person does the walking and the lame person does the seeing. This way, the lame person sitting over the shoulders of the blind person, pass through the forest.

पुरुषस्य दर्शनार्थं कैवल्यार्थं तथा प्रधानस्य ।
पङ्ग्वन्धवदुभयोरपि संयोगस्तत्कृतः सर्गः ॥२१॥

There is conjunction (Samyoga) between the Spirit (Purushasya) and the Nature (Pradhanasya) enabling exhibition (Darshnartham) of (the Prakrti) by the Purusha and emancipation (Kaivalartham) of the Purusha by the Prakrti, like the lame and the blind (pangu-andhavat). The creation proceeds from this conjunction (tat krtah sargah). (21)

Lokmanya rejects Ishvarakrishna's understanding that the act of union of *Purusha* and *Prakrti* itself brings about the evolution

---

9 https://en.wikipedia.org/wiki/Samkhyakarika. Last accessed on 10 September 2017.
10 Radhakrishnan, *Indian Philosophy, Vol. 1*, Oxford University Press, 2008, p. 450-451.

for the sake of enjoyment and liberation of the one by the other as fallacy. He writes, "When once the *Satkaryavada* is taken as proved, then, the theory that the visible universe came into existence out of *shunya*, there having been nothing whatsoever in existence before, naturally falls to the ground. Because *shunya* means non-existing (and) that which exists can never come into existence out of that which, does not exist. Therefore, it becomes absolutely clear that the universe must have come into existence out of some substance or the other, and that all those constituents (*gunas*) which we now see in the universe must have also been in this original substance."

Dr. S. Radhakrishnan explains it so succinctly, "In the Narayaniya section of the *Mahabharata* is found the story of Narada's visit to Badrikashrama to see Nara and Narayana. Finding there Narayana performing some religious rites, Narada with a perplexed mind asked whether there was anything the Supreme Lord had Himself to worship. Narayana answered that He worshipped the eternal spirit, his original substance. Eager to see it, Narada goes to Shvetadvipa (island in the ocean of milk, the White Land) where the great Being (Vishnu) tells him that he is not to be seen by one who is not absolutely devoted to Him. (No one can enter into this island of Shvetadvipa, but they can stand on the shore of the ocean of milk and transmit their message to Lord Vishnu). The religion of Vasudeva is explained to Narada. Vasudeva is the supreme soul, the internal ruler of all. Living beings are represented by Samkarshna, who is a form of Vasudeva. From Samkarshna springs Pradyumna or mind, and from Pradyumna, Aniruddha or self-consciousness arises. These four are forms of the Supreme."[11]

Many sacred scriptures described quadruple expansions of God in the consciousness. Shri Ramanuja (1017–1137) bridged the ideas of the *Pancharatra* movement with the monistic ideas of God. He visualised four forms of the God with whom the embodied souls (*Jiva Atman*) can interact depending upon their state of consciousness– the waking state (*Aniruddha*), the dream state (*Pradyumna*), the state of deep sleep (*Samkarshna*), and the fourth state which is beyond them and is none of these (*Vasudeva*).

---
11 Radhakrishnan, *Indian Philosophy, Vol. 1*, Oxford University Press, 2008, p. 415.

The invisible, formless, eternal supreme form is *Para* (beyond) *Brahman* (creation). The invisible, impermanent supreme in form is called as *Vyuha* (formation). "Whereas in a *vyuha* an army re-sets its different able warriors and weaponry into a specific arrangement as per battle demands, the Supreme Being re-sets the contents of consciousness through *Yoga Maya* with each formation concealing yet another formation."[12]

"*Para Brahman* is fountainhead of the *Chaturvyuha*, i.e., *Vasudeva, Samkarshna, Pradyumna* and *Aniruddha*, each succeeding *Vyuha* emanating from its immediate predecessor... from *Vasudeva* originates the individual soul called *Samkarshna*; from *Samkarshna* the internal organ called *Pradyumna*; and from *Pradyumna*, the principle of egoity called *Aniruddha* originate."[13] At the commencement of their worship of God, AUM (or OM) is chanted. By this chanting, the worshipper first invokes *Aniruddha* (A), then *Pradyumna* (U) and finally, *Samkarshna* (M).

Lokmanya writes, "Now, if you look at the universe, many objects in it, such as trees, animals, men, stones, gold, silver, diamonds, water, air etc., are perceptible to our organs, and their forms and qualities are all different. The *Samkhya* doctrine is that this diversity or difference is neither permanent, nor fundamental and that the fundamental substance in all things, or Matter, is only one... this original or fundamental substance at the root of all the things in the universe is known in *Samkhya* philosophy as *Prakrti*. The *Prakrti* is fundamental and all things, which subsequently arise out of *Prakrti* are called *vikrti*, or *vikaras* (transformations) of the fundamental substance."

The question now arises that if there is only one fundamental substance in all things and if this substance had also only one constituent quality, then how do we find abundant qualities of the matter? A dynamic and transformative picture emerges. Everything that exists is worked upon by– inertia (no movement), activity (movement) and Transcendence (beyond movement). There can be

---

[12] Dennis Hudson, D., *The Body of God: An Emperor's Palace for Krishna in Eighth-Century Kanchipuram*, Noida: Oxford University Press, 2008, p. 40.

[13] Janmajit Roy, *Theory of Avatara and Divinity of Chaitanya*, Atlantic Publishers and Distributors, 2002, p. 28.

no physical entity that exists outside this three-dimensional force field. Not a single atom exists without a certain static nature, of energy, and of vibrancy. In yogic parlance, Inertia is called *tamas*. Activity is called *rajas*. Transcendence is called *sattva*.

Lokmanya writes, "Though the Matter is gross, yet it carries out all this activity of its own accord. Out of these three constituents, knowledge or intelligence is the sign of the *sattva*, and the *rajas* constituent has an inspirational tendency, that is to say, it inspires a person to do some good or maybe an evil act. These three constituents can never exist by themselves independently. In everything, there is a mixture of all the three constituents; and in as much as the mutual ratio of the three constituents in this mixture always varies, the fundamental Matter though is originally one and assumes the various forms of gold, earth, iron, water, sky, the human body etc. as a result of this diversity in constituents."

It is indeed astonishing how Lokmanya analysed the interplay of *gunas* more than a hundred years ago. Contemporary writer Stephen Lovatt echoes Lokmanya's words when he writes, "At a lower level of complexity, the Severn Bore (a tidal bore in the River Severn in South Western England, that behaves differently in different stretches of the river) is also alive– but hardly so that it matters, as such, is nothing more than emergent self-organisation. This is potentially, a property of any complex non-linear system. The degree to which something is alive should be evaluated in terms of the complexity of its persistent pattern and of its robustness... the patterns' ability to evade or withstand external perturbations that would tend to its destruction. According to such a measure a squirrel is much more alive than a shock wave."[14]

It is worth noting the precedence and a priori of the idea of *Samkhya* that qualities as forces are acting upon inert matter, energising it. Also incredible is the brilliant visualisation of consciousness, space and time as abstract derivatives of God by Shri Ramanuja much before such concepts were developed anywhere in the world. As recently as Newton (1642-1727), science saw matter

---

14 Stephen Lovatt, *New Skins for Old Wine: Plato's Wisdom for Today's World*, Universal-Publishers, USA, 2007, p. 66

as the basis of physical existence. But as scientific understanding improved, the curiosity to learn about the building blocks of the universe led Hermann Minkowski (1864–1909) and Albert Einstein (1879–1955) to shorn matter of its characteristic as solid stuff. They accorded matter a somewhat subordinate and derivative status of energy.

British biologist and science writer Sir John Royden Maddox (1925–2009), who was editor of one of the world's most acclaimed multidisciplinary scientific journals, 'Nature' for 22 years wrote rather prophetically in 1990, "If only it were possible to make materials in which electromagnetically waves cannot propagate at certain frequencies, all kinds of almost-magical things would happen."[15] The more inward inquiry in to the molecules, and within them the atoms, and within the atoms into sub-atomic particles, into quarks, and strings got culminated in to the finding of the Higgs boson as an elementary particle, on 4 July, 2012 at The European Organisation for Nuclear Research (CERN's) Large Hadron Collider, aptly called 'the God particle'.

With modern understanding of how sub-atomic particles behave and photonics works, Lokmanya's words sound so incredible, "As the intensity or proportion of the *sattva* constituent is higher than that of the *rajas* and *tamas* constituents in the object which we consider as *sattvik*, all that happens is that these (the other) constituents are merely latent and are not noticed by us. But strictly speaking, it must be understood that the three constituents– *sattva, rajas* and *tamas* are to be found even in those objects, which are *sattvik* by nature. There does not exist a single object, which is purely *sattvik*, or purely *rajasik*, or purely *tamasik*. In each object, there is an internal engagement going on between the three constituents, and we describe a particular object as *sattvik, rajasa,* or *tamasa* according to one of those three constituents, which becomes predominant."

As understood well in the beginning of the 21st century, one of the greatest truths about existence is that our consciousness creates a reality first in our thoughts, beliefs and emotions before it manifests in the real world and indeed comes into being. Our

---

15   John Maddox, *Nature*, 348, 481 (Issue dated: 6 December 1990)

thoughts, emotions and beliefs are activated and deeply affected by the energies not only outside us but also in different time-space. Our minds and the cells of our body are all open to this multidimensional energy field all the time. As lay people ignorant of this knowledge, we are conditioned to experience only what is here and now and the rest remains beyond our grasp though existing and operating upon us at all times. It appears that all this was known as understood by Lokmanya in his investigation of the *Gita Rahasya*.

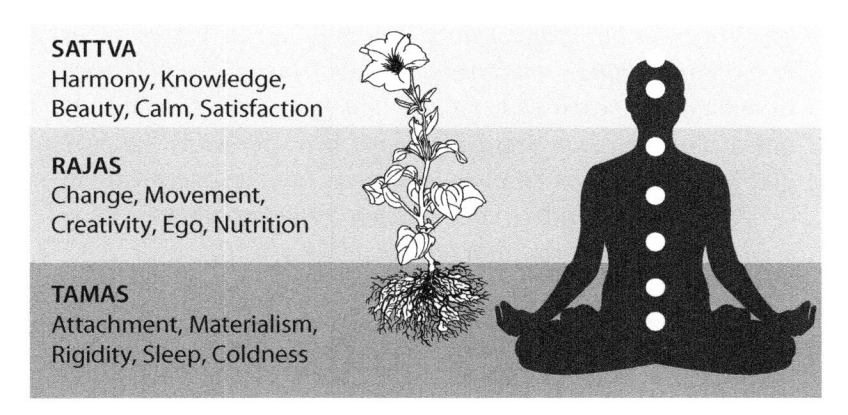

SATTVA
Harmony, Knowledge, Beauty, Calm, Satisfaction

RAJAS
Change, Movement, Creativity, Ego, Nutrition

TAMAS
Attachment, Materialism, Rigidity, Sleep, Coldness

All the qualities of the world have been identified as three basic gunas– tamas, rajas, and sattva. Inertia is called tamas. Activity is called rajas. Transcendence is called sattva. There is no physical entity without all these three dimensions. Not a single atom is free of these three dimensions of a certain static nature, of energy, and of vibrance.[16]

Lokmanya writes, "For instance, when in one's own body the *sattva* constituent assumes preponderance over the *rajas* and *tamas* constituents, knowledge comes into being in our body and we begin to realise the truth about things and our mind becomes peaceful. It is not that in this mental condition, the *rajas* and the *tamas* constituents cease to exist in the body; but as they are repressed, they do not produce any effect. If instead of the *sattva* constituent, the *rajas* constituent assumes preponderance, then avarice arises in the human heart, and the man is filled with ambition and he is

---

16 http://isha.sadhguru.org/blog/yoga-meditation/demystifying-yoga/the-three-gunas-tamas-rajas-and-sattva/

inspired to do various actions. In the same way, when the *tamas* constituent assumes preponderance over the *sattva* and the *rajas* constituents, faults like sleep, idleness, confused memory etc. arise in the body."

The Blessed Lord declares in the *Bhagavad-Gita*:

रजस्तमश्चाभिभूय सत्त्वं भवति भारत ।
रजः सत्त्वं तमश्चैव तमः सत्त्वं रजस्तथा ॥१०॥

The incessant interplay of three modes of nature is present in all human beings. Sometimes goodness (sattva) prevails over (abhibhuya), the passion (rajas) and ignorance (tamas). At other times, passion (rajas) prevails over goodness (sattva) and ignorance (tamas). Even ignorance (tamas) prevails over goodness (sattva) and passion (rajas) at times.
(Bhagavad-Gita Chapter 14, Verse 10)

Dr. S. Radhakrishna explains in his commentary of this *shloka*, "When the theory of the 'humours' of the body dominated physiology, men were divided into sanguine, the bilious, the lymphatic and the nervous, according to the predominance of one or the other of the four humours. In the Hindu classification, the psychic characteristics are taken into account. The *sattvik* nature aims at light and knowledge; the *rajasik* nature is restless, full of desires for things outward. While the activities of a *sattvik* temperament are free, calm, and selfless, the *rajasik* nature wishes to be always active and cannot sit still and its activities are tainted by selfish desires. The *tamasik* nature is dull and inert, its mind dark and confused and its whole life is one continuous submission to environment."[17]

There is a timeless domain where everything and everyone is connected and there is no separation. At the most basic level, we are all made of energy. The separation is only in the physical realm. When this separation is taken to the energy realm where we are all one, and attempts are made to dominate and control other beings,

---
17 S. Radhakrishnan, *The Bhagavad Gita*, HarperCollins Publishers, India, 2014, p. 377.

we create serious disturbances in the energy system and disruptive energy explodes in to our physical plane as spiteful quarrels and even violent conflicts. This concept of what is present, seen and felt (*vyakta*) and what is not here and not now but imminent (*avyakta*) is indeed a cornerstone for understanding life. Swedish diplomat and the second Secretary-General of the United Nations Dag Hammarskjöld (1905-1961) said it rather bluntly, "Your body must become familiar with its death– in all its possible forms and degrees– as a self-evident, imminent, and emotionally neutral step on the way towards the goal you have found worthy of your life."[18]

The ability to put what is apparent in the context of the larger non-apparent picture, is indeed a great skill and art. There have been great visionaries who mastered this art and they could see the shades of the future in the present and place the invisible forces outside the here and now boundary acting upon the present moment. British writer Horace Gundry Alexander (1889–1989) says in a matter-of-fact manner, "It is indeed a matter of great difficulty to discover, and effectively to distinguish, the true motions of particular bodies from the apparent; because the parts of that immovable space, in which those motions are performed, do by no means come under the observations of our senses. Yet the thing is not altogether desperate; for we have some arguments to guide us, partly from the apparent motions, which are the differences of the true motions; partly from the forces, which are the causes and effects of the true motions."[19]

Lokmanya writes, "This fundamental Matter, which is in an equable state, is *avyakta*, that is, not perceptible to the organs; and all the various objects which come into existence as a result of the mutual internal warfare of its *sattva*, *rajas* and *tamas* constituents, and become perceptible to the organs, that is to say, all which we see or hear or taste or smell, or touch, goes under the name of *vyakta*... (that) means all the objects which are definitely perceptible to the organs, whether they become perceptible on account of their

---

18 Expressed by Dag Hammarskjöld in a series of *Markings* from 1957, when he was serving as Secretary-General of the United Nations.
19 Winterbourne, A., *The Ideal and the Real: An Outline of Kant's Theory of Space, Time and Mathematical Construction*, Springer Science & Business Media, 2012, p. 4.

form, colour, smell, or any other quality." Perceptible objects are numerous, and out of them, trees, stones, etc., are gross (*sthula*); whereas others like the Mind, Reason, Ether, etc., though perceptible to the organs, are subtle (*sukshma*). The word *sukshma* does not here have its ordinary meaning of 'small'; because, though ether is *sukshma*, it has enveloped the entire universe."

American philosopher William James (1842-1910) in *The Varieties of Religious Experience* called it 'a perception of something there'. He writes, "It is as if there were in the human consciousness a sense of reality, a feeling of objective presence, a perception of what we may call something there, more deep and more general than any of the special and particular senses by which current psychology supposes existent realities to be originally revealed."

The law of causality does not turn invalid if the cause of something in a scientific experiment is not established. As every doctor and many patients know, failure to record the presence does not become its absence. An undetected cancer does not stop from spreading or lose its fatalness.

There are so many unseen forces operating around us. Take for example, electricity. We are all aware of it as modern life runs on it. But no person dealing with electrical tools and appliances could ever see electricity itself or feel and touch its weight or softness. The passage of electricity through a wire cannot be perceived through the senses. Similarly, electromagnetic waves are present everywhere and yet no one can see them. Our mobile phones are connected to transmission towers we but cannot see the connection. Even light cannot be seen unless it illuminates a surface.

Lokmanya writes, "Here a question arises, namely: if *prakrti* is not perceptible to any organ, then, what is the evidence that it exists? To this the reply of the *Samkhya* philosophers is that by considering the various objects, it is proved by inference by the law of *satkaryavada* that the root of all of them, though not actually perceptible to the organs, must nevertheless be in existence in a subtle form. The *Vedanta* philosophers have accepted the same line of argument in order to prove the existence of the *Brahman*."

No one becomes unselfish just by merely saying that he is for the people. For selfishness to go, one has to get rid of the lust and desires. This never occurs without the worship of the God. Therefore, a man who wants to be an unselfish organiser of the people should be under the umbrella of the God. One shouldn't ever forget that the God is nothing but the Atman, which resides in everything.[20]

Lokmanya introduces the 17th century saint and spiritual poet Shri Samarth Ramdas Swami (1608-1681) here. This was the time when India was suffering the double whammy of foreign rule and moral deprivation. Discarding the life of a monk in solitude, Shri Samarth Ramdas took up the challenge of rescuing people out of a condemned future for their progeny and took up service to alleviate their miseries compounded by turpitude, poverty and addictions. Shri Samarth Ramdas accepted Shivaji Maharaj as his disciple and guided him in state affairs. After a gap of over 1000 years, the trend of taking the renunciation path by the brightest and the best of

---

20 Sadguru Shree Samarth Ramdas Swami Maharaj, *The Dasbodha*, http://www.sadgurubhagwanshreedharswamimaharaj.com/dasbodh.pdf.
Samarth Ramdas was a noted 17th-century saint and spiritual poet of Maharashtra. He is most remembered for his *Advaita Vedantist* text, the *Dasbodh*.

Indian people was finally reversed and India got a just rule for its people, what if over a small area! Shri Samarth Ramdas saw God in people and served them as a devotee. He says in the *Dasbodh*:

जिकडे पाहावें तिकडे अपार । कोणेकडे नाहीं पार ।
येकजिनसी स्वतंत्र । दुसरें नाही ॥३॥

> *In whichever direction we see, the existence appears endless. There seems no other side beyond this creation. One Creator who is independent created everything. There is no other than this One Creator. (20. 2. 3)*

Expanding the example of Shri Samarth Ramdas, Lokmanya explained the irrefutable link between what is here and now (*vyakta*) and what would emerge out in future, based on the actualisation of the potentiality of this (*avyakta*). Shri Samarth Ramdas could see the imminent destruction of the Hindu civilisation in the deprivation and social dilapidation that its people were going through and decided not to preach from a higher pedestal but to serve people in their miserable living conditions utilising the mechanism and capacity of the state administration. Lokmanya writes, "When the words *sukshma, vyakta, sthula,* and *avyakta* have been defined as above, one comes to the inevitable conclusion that in the beginning of the universe, every object is in the form of subtle and imperceptible *prakrti* and that it afterwards becomes *vyakta* (perceptible to the organs), whether it is subtle or gross; and that at the time of *pralaya* (total destruction of the universe), when its perceptible form is destroyed, it again merges into imperceptible Matter and becomes imperceptible."

The entire concept of *avyakta* (imperceptible Matter) is summarised by the Blessed Lord Himself in the *Bhagavad-Gita*:

अव्यक्तादीनि भूतानि व्यक्तमध्यानि भारत ।
अव्यक्तनिधनान्येव तत्र का परिदेवना ॥२८॥

> *The Blessed Lord tells Arjuna about the perpetual transformation of material in all created beings. These are not apparent before*

creation *(avyaktadini)*, become apparent upon creation, and again turn unmanifest after they are dismantled or decayed. It is therefore futile to lament *(paridevana)* upon the end of something *(nidhanani)*. *(Bhagavad-Gita Chapter 2, Verse 28)*

Eknath Easwaran explains, "The mystics tell us we should be concerned less about these details of packaging and concerned more with the contents. When I look at people, I like to look into their eyes. These are the windows into the content, which is the Lord. Gradually, as we become more and more conscious of the *Atman*, we will be looking straight at people through their eyes and deep into the Lord of Love who is within."[21]

अव्यक्ता व्यक्तयः सर्वाः प्रभवन्त्यहरागमे ।
रात्र्यागमे प्रलीयन्ते तत्रैवाव्यक्तसंज्ञके ॥१८॥

At the advent of Brahma's day, all living beings emanate from the formless prakrti *(avyaktat)*. And when the night of Brahma comes *(praliyante)*, all embodied beings merge into the Formless again. *(Bhagavad-Gita Chapter 8, Verse 18)*

Eknath Easwaran explains, "It is a very personal conception. The Lord wakes up and the world of name and form comes in to play, very much as it does when we wake up out of deep sleep. Creation starts; matter and energy, time and space, all come in to existence; the great chain of evolution begins. The Hindu scriptures tell us, after a while, the Lord becomes tired of all this cosmic play and wants to take a nap. When you or I take a nap there is no awareness of the world outside us; it drops out of our consciousness completely. So here the Lord curls up on his endless serpent *Ananta*, and the whole creation is withdrawn into a state of latency, with no more reality than the tree, which will sprout from the seed. This state of primordial equilibrium is the night of Brahma, in which everything is dissolved and all creation returns to the unmanifest."[22]

---

21 Eknath Easwaran, *The Bhagavad-Gita for Daily Living–Vol. I*, Jaico Publishing House, India, 2007, p. 79.

22 Eknath Easwaran, *The Bhagavad-Gita for Daily Living–Vol. II*, Jaico Publishing House, India, 2007, p. 117-118.

After explaining the umbilical connection of the here and now existence (*vyakta*) with the future (*avyakta*), the differentiation between what is changeable or mutable is made with the immutable and neither can the God undergo any change in any respect, nor can anything external affect the God. What is termed as the Doctrine of Divine Immutability (DDI) in Western philosophy, was explained by Lokmanya as, "In the *Samkhya* philosophy, this imperceptible Matter is also known as *akshara* (Immutable) and all things, which are formed out of it, are known as *kshara* (Mutable). The *kshara* is not to be understood as meaning something, which is totally destroyed, but only the destruction of the perceptible form is meant here. It is also true that *prakrti* has other names too such as, *pradhana* (fundamental), *gunakshobhini* (stirrer up of the constituents), *bahudhanaka* (many seeded), and *prasava-dharmini* (generative)."

Our experience is not confined to the phenomena but transcends the boundaries of the material world and also time. Human perceptions of shapes and figures, motions and sizes, hot and cold, do not necessarily depend on the properties of the real objects. Whatever is mutable is nothing but the transformation of immutable from one form to another– the cocoon dies and the butterfly is born. Whatever is transient is nothing but the passage of the eternal. This concept of an unseen reality, the seen governed by the unseen, the present as a product of the past that is out of sight now and a precursor to a future that has not yet arrived is therefore, not a complex idea but a simple truth. The Immutable, and impassable God is indeed existing everywhere and yet, is seen nowhere. The manifestations of the imperceptible Matter have an objective existence and all the phenomena of nature declare the power of that wise Essence. Austrian born Israeli-Jewish philosopher Martin Buber (1878-1965) so strikingly says, "A person cannot approach the divine by reaching beyond the human. To become human, is what this individual person, has been created for."[23]

Human beings are uniquely blessed with the power to imagine, to comprehend the imperceptible, to reach the divine penetrating the *Prakrti*. Lokmanya writes, "Prakrti has also other names, such as

---

23 Maurice Friedman, *Martin Buber and the Human Sciences*, State University of New York Press, New York, USA, 1996, p. 97

pradhana (fundamental), *gunakshobhini* (stirrer up of constituents), *bahudhanaka* (many-seeded), and *prasava-dharmini* (generative). It is *pradhana* because it is the fundamental root of all objects in the universe; it is *gunakshobhini* because, it of its own accord breaks up the equable state of its three constituents (*gunas*); it is *bahudhanaka*, because, it contains the germs of differentiation between various objects in the shape of the three constituents; and it is *prasava-dharmini*, because, all things are born or come into existence out of it. That is the reason why these different names are given to Matter. This *prakrti* is known in *Vedanta* philosophy as *Maya*, an illusory appearance."

What is the evidence that psycho-spiritual organs like *Manas, Chitta, Ahamkara* and especially the *Atman*, exist? Swami Jnaneshvara Bharati explains, "The four functions of the mind are like four spokes that drive the wheel to operate in the external road of life. While the wheel turns, the centre hub remains still, like the centre of consciousness, the Self, which remains still. While the hub is the source of the energy driving the wheel of life, the very centre of the hub does not itself move. To know the centre or hub (the Self), one must go through the spokes. The only vantage point from which one may fully be witness to the spokes is the Self. One who knows that centre hub through *Yoga* and meditation knows the Self."[24] So, while on the one hand, it is something that can always be experienced and verified through a process even by a layperson, on the other, even the most intelligent person, by his knowledge cannot grasp it.

Lokmanya presents the view of his contemporary German biologist Ernst Haeckel (1834–1919) that, "the Mind, Intelligence, Individuation and the *Atman* are all faculties of the body", and dwells upon his logic. "We see that when the brain in a man's head is deranged, he loses memory and even becomes mad. Similarly, if any part of the brain is deadened on account of a blow on the head, the mental faculty of that part is seen to come to an end. In short, mental faculties are only faculties of gross Matter and they can never be separated from gross Matter. Therefore, the mental faculties and

---

24 http://www.swamij.com/fourfunctionsmind.htm#chitta

the *Atman* must be classified along with the brain in the category of the perceptible. When you have made this classification, the imperceptible and the gross Matter is ultimately the only thing which remains to be disposed off, because all perceptible objects have sprung out of this fundamental imperceptible."

Lokmanya, who sees the absorption of consciousness in to the gross matter as a process, refutes this definition of *Atman* and the other psycho-spiritual organs as part of the *Prakrti*. He describes the observation of materialistic philosophers as a delusion and declares the interplay of consciousness with the material as the mind, body and world as a perpetual process. The *Manas*, *Buddhi* and Chitta, all emanate from consciousness, and never for a moment, are they separate from it.

Mental processes such as thinking, sensing and perceiving are indeed orchestrations of the mind, body and the world. Though the mind, the body and the worldly phenomenon appear outside and separate of the mind and body, the worldly affairs are never anything other than the consciousness that already eternally is. German theologian, Meister Eckhart (1260–1328) said so beautifully, "The eye through which I see God is the same eye through which God sees me; my eye and God's eye are one eye, one seeing, one knowing, one love."[25]

Lokmanya wonders, "(If) there is no other creator or generator of the world except *Prakrti*, when the Energy of the fundamental Matter (*Prakrti*) gradually increases, it acquires the form of *Chaitanya* (consciousness) or of the *Atman*. This fundamental *Prakrti* is governed by fixed laws or rules like the *satkaryavada*, and in accordance with those laws, the entire universe, as also man, is acting like a prisoner... then, where is the room for salvation?"

Just as we cannot penetrate through the enigma of worldly phenomenon by merely using our sensory organs, the same is the limitation with the empirical sciences, which cannot acquire knowledge beyond the boundaries of the supra sensory, and the ordinary scientific thinking is mostly limited around what is seen, tested and recorded. Of course, there are exceptions like Albert

---

[25] https://cac.org/meister-eckhart-part-ii-2015-07-16/

Einstein, who dared to explore beyond the contingent and the rational. Einstein puts it straight, "A knowledge of the existence of something we cannot penetrate, of the manifestations of the profoundest reason and the most radiant beauty– it is this knowledge and this emotion that constitute the truly religious attitude; in this sense, and in this alone, I am a deeply religious man."[26] Martin Buber, putting it differently, writes, "All journeys have secret destinations of which the traveller is unaware."

Lokmanya now presents his conclusion. "But in as much as this *advaita* doctrine is based on something, which is gross, and as it incorporates everything within gross Matter, I have named it *jadadvaita* (Gross Non-dualism) or Non-dualism based on the Natural sciences." Since consciousness is divine, and it is always the subject witnessing the phenomenal world, it can never be objectified. Also, the subject and the object can never be the same. This means, all objects belong to the realm of the unconscious, *jada*. Lokmanya rejects the assertion of the *Samkhya* philosophy that "the 'Mind', 'Reason' and 'Individuation' are qualities of Gross Matter, and consequently, it is stated in the *Samkhya* philosophy that 'Reason', 'Individuation', and other qualities gradually spring out of the fundamental imperceptible Matter." Lokmanya highlights the contradiction in the *Samkhya* philosophy that while the *Samkhya* asserts that, "It is impossible that consciousness (*chaitanya*) should spring out of gross Matter and not only that, but the words, "I know a particular thing", cannot come to be used unless the one who knows, understands, or sees Matter, is different from Matter. No one can sit on his own shoulders, looking at the affairs of the world. It is the experience of every one that whatever he knows or sees is different from himself."

The *Bhagavad-Gita* declares: '*Prakrtim purushamchaiva viddhyanadi ubhavapi*' which means that, *prakrti* and *purusha* are both without a beginning and are eternal.

प्रकृतिं पुरुषं चैव विद्ध्यनादी उभावपि ।
विकारांश्च गुणांश्चैव विद्धि प्रकृतिसम्भवान् ॥२०॥

---

26 http://www.spaceandmotion.com/albert-einstein-god-religion-theology.htm

The Blessed Lord tells Arjuna that both, Prakrti (material nature) and Purusha (the living entity) are eternal. It is the material energy that keeps on transforming itself through the three modes of nature causing pain or pleasure to the living entities. (Bhagavad-Gita Chapter 13, Verse 20)

In the *Gita*, the Blessed Lord has referred to Matter as His creation.

दैवी ह्येषा गुणमयी मम माया दुरत्यया ।
मामेव ये प्रपद्यन्ते मायामेतां तरन्ति ते ॥१४॥

The Blessed Lord reveals to Arjuna that He created Maya, consisting of the three modes of material nature (gunamayi). It is supernatural (daivi) and therefore very difficult to overcome by the mortals (duratyaya). Only those who surrender unto me (mam eva ye prapadyante) can cross over it (taranti). (Bhagavad-Gita Chapter 7, Verse 14)

मम योनिर्महद् ब्रह्म तस्मिन्गर्भं दधाम्यहम् ।
सम्भवः सर्वभूतानां ततो भवति भारत ॥३॥

The total material substance, Prakrti, is My womb in which, I cast the seed (tasmingarbham dadhamy aham) and thus, all living beings are born (sarva-bhutanam tato bhavati). (Bhagavad-Gita Chapter 14, Verse 3)

Dr. S. Radhakrishnan explains, "This verse affirms that all existence is a manifestation of the Divine. He is the cosmic seed. With reference to this world, He becomes *Hiranyagarbha*, the cosmic soul. The forms of all things, which arise out of the abysmal void, are derived from God. They are seeds He casts into non-being."[27]

As regards the Spirit, Shri Krishna has said: *mamaivansho jiva-loke*, i.e., it is a part of me. Therefore, the *Gita* has gone further than the *Samkhya* philosophy.

---

[27] Radhakrishnan, *The Bhagavad Gita*, HarperCollins Publishers, India, 2014, p. 372.

ममैवांशो जीवलोके जीवभूतः सनातनः ।
मनःषष्ठानीन्द्रियाणि प्रकृतिस्थानि कर्षति ॥७॥

The Blessed Lord clearly declared the identity of the living beings as His own innumerable expansions. They are all eternal, not temporary manifestations and struggling or grappling hard trapped in the nature (prakrti-sthani karsati) by their six senses (shasthaniindriyani, of which mind is the sixth one).
(Bhagavad-Gita Chapter 15, Verse 7)

The *Bhagavad-Gita* decisively establishes the ideal of, "the *siddha* or released man who, having escaped the meshes of *Maya* (Illusion) with its three constituents, has realised the *Paramatman* (Supreme Spirit) which is beyond both Matter and Spirit, and not of a *Samkhya* philosopher, who looks upon Matter and Spirit as two distinct principles and who looks upon the isolation of the Spirit as the state of transcending the three constituents of Matter." *Samkhya* by itself has been shown as logically flawed and does not survive the philosophical scrutiny of Lokmanya.

Lokmanya now declares, "As the Blessed Lord has in many places in the *Gita* used the *Samkhya* terminology and arguments, one is likely to get the wrong idea that the *Gita* accepts as correct the pure *Samkhya* philosophy. Therefore, I have repeated here this difference between the *Samkhya* philosophy and the propositions similar to it in the *Gita*."

Lokmanya asserts, "Release is not an independent state which results to the spirit from some outside agency; nor it is a state which is different from the fundamental and inherent state; just as the outer skin of a stick of grass is different from the internal stock, or as the fish in the water is different from the water, so are Matter and Spirit relational towards each other. Ordinary persons, being steeped in ignorance, as a result of the constituents of Matter, do not realise this distinction and remained tied up within the periphery of family affairs. But he who realises this distinction may well be said as released."

The Supreme Creator is established as the source of both, the matter and the consciousness. Creation is an act of a creative energy.

The Big Bang is not a material process, but an event created by God. The expansion and contraction of the universe is not a material property but a cosmic activity and a creation of God's mind. This difference would be made clearer in Chapter 9 of this book that would deal with the philosophy of the Absolute Self.

Lokmanya, in a rational manner establishes that the *advaita* principle of the *Vedanta* philosophy is a more logical and consistent version of *Samkhya* philosophy. It is proved that the *Samkhya* is absorbed into *Bhagavad-Gita*. Lokmanya writes, "Shri Shankaracharya has stated in the *Vedanta Sutra-Bhashya*, that he is prepared to accept all the propositions of the *Samkhya* philosophy but not to give up the *Advaita* theory of the *Upanishads* that there is only one fundamental principle in the world, namely, *Parabrahman* (Supreme Spirit), which is beyond both, Matter and Spirit and from it the entire creation, including Matter and Spirit, has sprung."

Lokmanya established in this chapter that the *Gita* departed from the *Samkhya* by the assertion that Matter too, is the Divine. Spirit is presented as the soul of Matter and soul is shown as the body of the Spirit. The layperson's mind may question– Why all this'? What is the purpose of all this? What did the Creator achieve by this? The answer is indeed simple and yet astonishing– nothing. Hindu seers called it *Lila* (God's play). There is no purpose assigned to the God for the creation of the universe. The physical existence is an outflow of divine energy and its manifestation in the material form.

Sri Aurobindo declared, "If the world is a manifestation of the Force of *Satchitananda*, the deployment of its existence and consciousness, its purpose, can be nothing but delight. This is the meaning of *Lila*– Lila the play, the child's joy, the poet's joy, the actor's joy, the mechanic's joy of the soul of things eternally young, perpetually inexhaustible, creating and recreating Himself in Himself for the sheer bliss of that self-creation, of that self-representation, Himself the play, Himself the player, Himself the playground."[28]

ॐ

---

[28] Ram Nath Sharma, *Shri Aurobindo's Philosophy Of Social Development*, New Delhi, Atlantic Publishers and Distributors, 1991, p. 39-40

8

The Mint of the Matter

> Nature always wears the colours of the spirit.
> *Ralph Waldo Emerson*

> Death is not extinguishing the light; it is only putting out the lamp because the dawn has come.
> *Rabindranath Tagore*

More than seven billion people inhabit the earth. These people are divided as different races and live together in different social formations and cultures. Indeed, each human being is different from the other. People have different personalities, different world views and even experience the same reality differently. The separateness between 'I' and 'you' between 'we' and 'they' are existential truths. A person identifies with a group, ascribes to one or the other viewpoint, and belongs to a culture. This truth co-exists with another truth that people belonging to different cultures, and different societies, have different manners, attitudes and lifestyles.

Each person has his unique needs, follows his own agendas, and is responsible for his actions. So there are 'my actions' and 'your actions'. An attempt has been made in Germany to understand how, in an apparently chaotic world, meaningful perceptions are possible. Kurt Koffka (1886–1941), Max Wertheimer (1880–1943) and Wolfgang Köhler (1887–1967) developed a unique philosophy of mind and called it the *'Gestalt* psychology'. The German word *'gestalt'* means formation. When the human mind forms a percept, it has a reality of its own, independent of the parts out of which it is formed, and is called a *'Gestalt'*, which is essentially bigger and richer than the parts that form it. Later, Friedrich Perls (1893–1970) established a school of psychotherapy based on the *Gestalt* concept and used an assertion that he called the '*Gestalt* prayer' as a therapy tool.

> "I do my thing and you do your thing.
> I am not in this world to live up to your expectations,
> And you are not in this world to live up to mine.
> You are you, and I am I;
> And if by chance we find each other, it's beautiful.
> If not, it can't be helped."[1]

The prayer underlined a striking paradox of human nature– in the experience of difference there is sameness. The assertion– 'You are you, and I am I'– underlines the same struggle, the same suffering, that makes a life. It is through this 'I' and 'you' realisation that we can appreciate the– 'If by chance we find each other, it's beautiful'– reality of this world.

A child, at the time of its birth is not a personality. At the time of its birth, the infant arrives in the simplicity and completeness of the present moment. American psychologist Louise Janet Kaplan (1929-2012) explains brilliantly, "As he moves out of the limbo of newbornness and into oneness with his mother, the infant moulds his body to hers. From the infant's point of view there are no boundaries between himself and the mother. They are one. This is how we first discovered merging bliss and inner harmony."[2] It is only when the child grows, that it starts to identify with a separate little self inside and begins to become a personality.

Dr. T. Glenn Pait describes personality as, "The combination of thoughts, emotions and behaviours that makes you unique. It's the way you view, understand and relate to the outside world, as well as how you see yourself. A person's personality forms during their childhood and is shaped through an interaction of two factors, their inherited tendencies and their environment. Inherited tendencies are aspects of your personality passed on to you by your parents, such as shyness or having a happy outlook. Your environment,

---

1   http://www.gestalt.lv/gestalt-prayer/. Last accessed on 15 September 2017.
2   Louise Kaplan, *Oneness and Separateness: From Infant to Individual*, Simon and Schuster, New York,1978, p. 28.

meanwhile, is the surroundings you grew up in, events that occurred, and relationships with family members and others. It includes such things as the type of parenting you had, whether loving or abusive."[3]

As a child grows in to adolescence and finally turns in to an adult, the competitive force with the others around drives his personality growth. Not merely the presence but also the strength and intensity of these forces puts a child on the trajectory to become a strong or weak personality later in the adult life, or using the terminology of Carl Jung, the completion or halt of the individuation process. Jung writes, "What is it, in the end, that induces a man to go his own way and to rise out of unconscious identity with the mass as out of a swathing mist? It is what is commonly called vocation: an irrational factor that destines a man to emancipate himself from the herd and from its well-worn paths. ... Anyone with a vocation hears the voice of the inner man: he is called."[4]

There is a real and incessant conflict between the 'inner self' and the 'outer forces' of society, government, religion, education, and of course, the media. The 'outer forces' try to enforce upon people the illusion of separateness, entitlements, rights and privileges by clouding the self inside. French Renaissance philosopher Michel de Montaigne (1533–1592) said so stunningly, "Every one rushes elsewhere and into the future, because no one wants to face one's own inner self." Gradually, a disconnect sets in with our existential reality at a great cost of internal suffering and mental anguish. It is the inner self that experiences the outer world and not the other way round. The deeper we go in to the inner self, the vision of an eternal power that creates and maintains all life becomes clear. A feeling of empathy arrives and we are able to see oneness in the myriad forms outside. In this chapter, Lokmanya positions the inner self in the vast existence outside and quotes Shri Jnaneshwar Maharaj (1275–1296), who called the materialistic drama of this world as, 'the Mint of the Matter' and articulated the way to deal with it and to not get lost in it and lose our reality in the process.

As we grow up, we are indeed shaped by our surroundings.

---

[3] T. Glenn Pait, M.D., of UAMS and the host of the program– 'Here's to Your Health', Transcript of September 14 Broadcast– 'How is your personality formed?'

[4] C. G. Jung, *The Development of Personality*, Vol. 17, p. 175

The people who live around us– siblings, parents, teachers, and neighbours– shape our personality. Even the village, locality where we reside, town or the city makes their mark on us. Noble laureate in Medicine and celebrated author of *Man the Unknown*, Alexis Carrel (1873–1944) writes, "Man is literally made from the dust of the earth. For this reason, his physiological and mental activities are profoundly influenced by the geological constitution of the country where he lives, by the nature of the animals and plants on which he generally feeds. His structure and his functions depend also on the selection he makes of certain elements among the vegetal and animal foods at his disposal."[5] Even our patterns of thought are influenced by what we are exposed to. Seen in this manner, the uniqueness of man emerges out as a heroic action of preventing homogenisation of his inner self by the external forces. However, it has a dangerous other dimension too. There are people who, instead of stamping their uniqueness on the environment, take the easier route of altering the reality in their minds and creating fantasies of conditions that do not even exist.

Lokmanya extends in this chapter, the difference between the *Samkhya* philosophy and the propositions similar to it in the *Gita*. He writes, "According to the *Bhagavad-Gita*, the Matter does not carry on its activities independently, but has to do so according to the will of the *Parameshvara*… but according to the *Samkhya* philosophy, its (matter's) union with Spirit is a sufficient proximate cause for its diffusion to commence… as soon as Matter is united with Spirit, its minting starts. Just as in the spring, trees get foliage and after that, leaves, flowers, and fruits follow one after the other, so also is the fundamental equable state of Matter disrupted, and its constituents begin to spread out. On the other hand, in the *Veda-Samhitas*, the *Upanishads*, and the *Smriti* texts, the *Parabrahman* is looked upon as fundamental instead of Matter… from *Parabrahman* the Golden Egg first came into existence, and from this Golden Egg, the whole world was created (*hiranyagarbhah samavartatagre bhuttasya jatah patirekaasit*)."

The Creation vs. Evolution debate indeed hinges on this question

---

5   Alexis Carrel, *Man the Unknown*, Wilco Publishing House, Delhi, 2010

of origin. Are we the product of purposeful intelligence (Golden Egg) or are we merely the end result of countless transformations of Matter? Over a period of time since English naturalist Charles Darwin (1809–1882) first propagated it, the Creation vs. Evolution debate got regressed in to Science vs. Religion counter positions. Creation is called religious and evolution is seen as scientific. Lokmanya offers deep insights here and explains how the evolution model of origin is not beyond a reasonable doubt and those who subscribe to the theory of evolution do so by faith.

Lokmanya writes, "According to this theory (Theory of Evolution), there was originally one subtle, homogeneous substance in the Solar system, and as the original motion or heat of that substance gradually became less and less, it got more and more condensed, and the Earth and, the other planets gradually came into existence, and the Sun was the final portion of it which remained. The Earth was originally a very hot ball, the same as the Sun, but as it gradually lost its heat, some portion of the original substance remained in the liquid form, while other portions became solidified, and the air and water which surround the earth and the gross material earth under them, gradually came into existence and later on, all the living and non-living creations came into existence as the result of the union of the three. On the line of this argument, Darwin and the other philosophers maintained that even man had in this way gradually come into existence through evolution from microorganisms."

Why is the creation vs. evolution debate important? What difference does it make whether we humans are created or whether we have evolved? Or whether we have evolved out of animals of lesser brains or have been created in the image of the God? These questions are important because the way human origin is seen constructs human behavioural patterns. The views on morality, justice, purpose, self-worth, humanity, obligation, and destination turn meaningless when seen from the evolution perspective. Seen this way, the brute forces of nature like famine, floods and germs create the most exalted objects and we humans are merely a species of animal without any intrinsic value and nothing more than the fodder of the nature beast.

But that is not the case. Throughout its existence, mankind asserted its dominance over other species on planet earth. Charles Darwin writes, "Man does not actually produce variability; he only unintentionally exposes organic beings to new conditions of life, and then nature acts on the organisation, and causes variability. But man can and does select the variations given to him by nature, and thus accumulates them in any desired manner. He thus adapts animals and plants for his own benefit or pleasure. He may do this methodically, or he may do it unconsciously..."[6] Whether this is due to man created specially by God to dominate over planet earth, or evolved to have physical, mental, and even genetic superiority over animals cannot be proved or disproved scientifically. The fact is, man has farms and slaughterhouses to produce food and dams, furnaces and even nuclear energy to alter, if not overpower the course of the nature.

Lokmanya writes, "...there is still a great deal of difference of opinion between the materialists and the meta-physicians as to whether or not the Soul (*Atman*) should be considered as an independent fundamental principle. The German naturalist and philosopher Ernst Haeckel and some others like him maintained that the Soul and Vitality have gradually come into existence out of Gross Matter. On the other hand, metaphysicians like the German philosopher Immanuel Kant say that in as much as all the knowledge we get of the cosmos is the result of the synthetic activity of the Soul, the Soul must be looked upon as an independent entity. Therefore, saying that the Soul which perceives the external world is a part of the world which is perceived by it, or that it has come into existence out of the world, is logically as meaningless as saying that one can sit on one's own shoulders."

Contemporary Hungarian philosopher of science and system theorist Ervin László (b. 1932) says, "We are– as far as we know– the only creatures able to contemplate who we are, why we are here and how we fit into the universe. This coherence also allows evolution to happen and that has enabled us to evolve from a microscopic bacterium right through to the complex beings that we are with all

---

[6] Charles Darwin, *On The Origin of Species by Means of Natural Selection...*, D. Appleton Co. New York, USA, p. 405

our mental, physical, emotional and spiritual capabilities."[7] If we hold the theory of the Golden Egg and Big Bang together and go by the scientific observation that the universe is expanding, there would be a time when the universe will stop expanding and start contracting to eventually crunch and become the Golden Egg again and then bounce to start the next cycle. Any cyclic phenomenon is marked by the fact of a perpetual intelligence rolling over through time and again when the cycle repeats itself. The precise numbers for gravity and electromagnetism are so exact that these numbers cannot be seen as randomly evolved but transferred from previous universes.

EVOLUTION OF CONSCIOUSNESS

Universal	0.72	?
Galactic	12.8 yrs	? (2012)
Planetary	256 yrs cycle	Industrialism (1769)
National	5.125 years cycle	Written Language (3100 BC)
Regional	102.000 years cycle	Spoken Language (100.000 yrs)
Tribal	2 million years cycle	First humans (2 million yrs)
Familial	41 million years cycle	First monkeys (40 million yrs)
Mammalian	820 million years cycle	First animals (850 million yrs)
Cellular	16.4 billion years cycle	First matter / "Big Bang" (14-16 billion yrs)

Human evolution, at first, seems extraordinary. How could the process that gave rise to slugs and oak trees and fish produce a creature that can fly to the moon and invent the Internet and cross the ocean in boats?[8] According to contemporary American social philosopher William Irwin Thompson (b. 1938), "For the first time in human evolution, the individual life is long enough, and the cultural transformation swift enough, that the individual mind is now a constituent player in the global transformation of human culture."[9]

---

7   Ervin Laszlo, *Science and the Akashic Field*, cited at https://www.scienceandnonduality.com/akashic-field-and-consciousness/

8   Dr. Steven Pinker, transcript of the interview *Evolution: The Mind's Big Bang*, WGBH Educational Foundation. Dr. Pinker is a professor of psychology in the Department of Brain and Cognitive Sciences at MIT.

9   William Irwin Thompson, *Self and Society: Studies in the Evolution of Culture*, Imprint Academic, UK

Putting together the concept to the human life that is again seen as cycle of birth and rebirth and the unity of our consciousness with the conscience of the universe, it can be understood that the same force that is moving the stars and galaxies is giving us the ability to develop our consciousness in the material matrix that is *prakrti*. This can explain life after death and immortality of the soul and the past is ever present in everything we do. Activities such as controlling our mind to extract our consciousness from the material matrix a little and plug our minds to the universal consciousness can help us become much more than we are at present. Science and spirituality are not set against each other but are talking the same thing, in perhaps different language and using different terms.

It is indeed amazing how Lokmanya wrote more than a hundred years ago, "It is even now being maintained by many learned scholars in the Western countries that however much the Materialistic knowledge of the universe may grow, the consideration of the form of the Root Principle of the Cosmos must always be made from a different point of view. But my readers will see that as regards the question of the order in which all perceptible things came to be created from one Gross Matter, there is not much difference of opinion between the Western Theory of Evolution, and the Diffusion out of Matter described in the *Samkhya* philosophy."

The principle *'guna guneshu vartante'* given in the *Bhagavad-Gita* is indeed a great truth told when the Western civilisations were not even in existence.

तत्त्ववित्तु महाबाहो गुणकर्मविभागयोः ।
गुणा गुणेषु वर्तन्त इति मत्वा न सज्जते ॥२८॥

Knower of the Absolute truth (tattvavit) that the soul is distinct from gunas (vibhagayoh) never indulges (nasajjate) in sense gratification (guneshu). (Bhagavad-Gita Chapter 3, Verse 28)

Dr. S. Radhakrishnan comments on this *shloka*, "*Prakrti* and its modes represent the limits of human freedom such as the force of heredity and the pressure of environment. The empirical self is the

The Mint of the Matter

product of works even as the whole cosmic process is the result of the operation of causes."[10]

Swami Prabhupada clarifies, "The knower of the Absolute Truth is convinced of his awkward position in material association. He knows that he is part and parcel of the Supreme... that his position should not be in the material creation. He knows his real identity as part and parcel of the Supreme, who is eternal bliss and knowledge, and he realises that somehow or other he is entrapped in the material conception of life."[11]

Lokmanya explains, "...the principle: *guna guneshu vartante*, i.e., 'constituents come out of constituents,' which is the principle of the diffusion or expansion of constituent qualities and is common to both (the *Samkhya* philosophers and the *Gita*). *Samkhya* philosophers say that as a folding-fan is gradually opened out, so also, when the folds of Matter in its equable state (in which its *sattva*, *rajas*, and *tamas* constituent qualities are equal) are opened out, the whole perceptible universe begins to come into existence. Therefore, there is no real difference between this conception and the Theory of Evolution.

Nevertheless, the fact that the *Gita*, and partly also the *Upanishads* and other Vedic texts have, without demur accepted the theory of the growth of the *gunas* (constituents) side by side with the Monistic *Vedanta* doctrines, instead of rejecting it as is done by the Christian religion, is a difference which ought to be kept in mind from the point of view of the Philosophy of Religion."

Taking a scholarly stand, Lokmanya does not feel that spirituality undermines science, but rather, sees it illuminating science. As a reliable eyewitness testimony enables a detective to correctly interpret how an incident could have happened, the Vedic concept *gunotkarsavada* (the theory of the unfolding of constituent qualities), or *gunapmrjamavada* (the theory of the development of qualities) gave insights to scientists like Isaac Newton (1642-1727), William Herschel (1738-1822), John Dalton (1766-1844), James Joule (1818-1889), and James Clerk Maxwell (1831-1879).

---

10 S. Radhakrishnan, *The Bhagavad Gita*, HarperCollins Publishers, India, 2014, p. 165.
11 A. C. Bhaktivedanta Swami Prabhupada, *Bhagavad-Gita As It Is*, The Bhaktivedanta Book Trust, Mumbai, 2006, p. 174.

Albert Einstein put it so beautifully, "A human being is part of the whole called by us as universe, a part limited in time and space. We experience thoughts, our feelings and ourselves as something separate from the rest; a kind of optical delusion of consciousness. This delusion is a kind of prison for us, restricting us to our personal desires and to affection for a few persons nearest to us. Our task must be to free ourselves from the prison by widening our circle of compassion to embrace all living creatures and the whole of nature in its beauty. The true value of a human being is determined by the measure and the sense in which they have obtained liberation from the self. We shall require a substantially new manner of thinking if humanity is to survive."[12]

Lokmanya writes, "It need not be said that every man comes to a decision according to his own intelligence to perform an act or that he must first get the inspiration to do an act... there are statements even in the *Upanishads,* which state that the universe came to be created after the one fundamental *Paramatman* was inspired with the desire to multiply (*bahusyamprajayeya*)."

Patrick Olivelle, Professor of Sanskrit and Indian Religions at the University of Texas, Austin explains '*bahusyamprajayeya*' mentioned in the *Chandogya Upanishad* (Chapter 6, Part 2, Shloka 3), "And it (*Parabrahman*) though to itself: 'Let me become many. Let me propagate myself.' It emitted heat. The heat thought to itself: 'Let me become many. Let me propagate myself.' It emitted water. The water thought to itself: "Let me become many. Let me propagate myself.' It emitted food. Wherever it rains, therefore food becomes abundant; and thus it is from water that food stuffs are produced." [13]

Ekanath Easwaran translates this *shloka*, a conversation between Uddalaka and his son Shvetketu as:

तदैक्षत बहु स्यां प्रजायेयेति । तत्तेजोऽसृजते । तत्तेज ऐक्षत । बहु ।
स्यां प्रजायेयेति । तदपोऽसृजत
तस्माद्यत्र क्व च शोचति स्वेदते वा पुरुषस्तेजस एव तदध्यापो जायन्ते ॥३॥

---

12 http://www.spaceandmotion.com/albert-einstein-god-religion-theology.htm
13 Patrick Olivelle, *Upanishads, Translated from the Original Sanskrit,* Oxford University Press, United Kingdom, 1998, p. 149.

Out of himself he (the God) brought forth the cosmos
And entered into everything in it.
There is nothing that does not come from him.
Of everything he is the Self Supreme.
You are that (Shvetketu), you are that."[14]

The universe came to be created after the one fundamental *Paramatman* was inspired with the desire to multiply.

सोऽकामयत । बहु स्यां प्रजायेयेति । स तपोऽतप्यत ।
स तपस्तप्त्वा । इदं सर्वमसृजत । यदिदं किञ्च ।
तत्सृष्ट्वा । तदेवानुप्राविशत् ।

Dr. S. Radhakrishnan explained this *shloka* (*Taittiriya Upanishad* 2.6) as, "He (the supreme soul) desired. Let me become many let me be born. He performed austerity (*tapas*). Having performed austerity he created all this, whatever is here. Having created it, into it, indeed, he entered. Having entered it, he became both: the actual and the beyond, the defined and the undefined, the founded and the non-founded, the intelligent and the non-intelligent, the true and the untrue. As the real, he became whatever there is here. That is what they call the real. As to that, there is also this verse."[15]

The rest of the chapter deals with extensive discussion on understanding of the existence of the human existence and experience according to *Samkhya* philosophy, where *Vedanta* philosophers differed from the *Samkhya* and what is the position of the *Bhagavad-Gita* on this. Why such an inquiry is indeed necessary? The best answer comes from English orientalist Horace Hayman Wilson (1786–1860), who writes in the Preface of his translation of *Samkhya Karika* that the purpose of all philosophical inquiry is, "ascertainment of the means by which the pain of corporeal existence may be finally and absolutely remedied and the soul freed for ever from body."[16] Wilson explains that this alone led to the

---

14 Eknath Easwaran, *The Upanishads,* Jaico Publishing House, Mumbai, 2010, p.133
15 S. Radhakrishnan, *The Principal Upanishads*, HarperCollins Publishers India, 2010, p, 548.
16 H. H. Wilson, *The Sankhya Karika; Or, Memorial Verses on the Samkhya Philosophy* by Íswara Krishna; Translated from the Sanskrit by H. T. Colebrooke, Valpy, 1837

inquiry of the real nature of the human existence in the *Samkhya* enumeration of things. These things are twenty-five and their relative character, as producing or produced indeed uncovers all the secrets of corporeal existence.

Indians, through the ages by and large considered life as a condition of pain and suffering. Happiness and pleasures are always seen as ephemeral and unreal. Bodily existence, with its pain in heat and cold, thirst and hunger and sickness and aging are seen as bondage and even evil. Escape from this bondage was considered as the ultimate purpose of life that can be achieved through life itself. All infirmities of the mind, imperfections of the flesh, and awkwardness of the situations are seen as opportunities for correction and spiritual work in progress.

Is it really necessary to wrestle our minds with esoteric concepts like the twenty-five elements of *Samkhya* philosophy to find a solution to our sufferings? If one can find relief by taking an alcoholic drink why to do *tapas* and sit in meditation? Is it not much easier to seek the objects of happiness rather than taking up the unnecessary trouble of going through what people have written and discussed in the good old world? Are not the pleasures of the senses, luxuries, dresses, ornaments, and massage parlours better and faster means of fixing mental distress? The answer is a firm no! After observing the recurrence of pain that has been supressed, sages have concluded that the obvious means of alleviating the pains of life are neither absolute nor final and inquiry in to other means is not only essential but also inevitable.

लौकिकादुपायाद्धनादेरत्यन्तदुःखनिवृत्तिसिद्धिर्नास्ति । कुतः ।
धनादिना दुःखनिवृत्तेः पश्चाद्धनक्षये पुनरपि दुःखानुवृत्तिदर्शनात् ।

Worldly means and measures such as wealth and the like cannot accomplish the cessation of life's pain. Why is this? It is because the pain, which ceases upon the arrival of wealth, returns immediately after the wealth is spent.
(The Samkhya Karika, Commentary by H. H. Wilson p. 12)

H.H. Wilson writes, "This discriminative wisdom is the accurate discrimination of those principles in to which all that exists is distributed by the *Samkhya* philosophy. *Vyakta,* 'that which is perceived, sensible, discrete; *Avyakta,* that which is unperceived, indiscrete; and the *Jna,* that which knows or discriminates: the first is matter, in its perceptible modifications; the second is crude, unmodified matter; and the third is soul. The object of the *Samkhya Karika* is to define and explain these three things, the correct knowledge of which is of itself release from worldly bondage, and exemption from exposure to human ills, by the final separation of soul from the body."[17]

S. S. Suryanarayana Sastri sums up, "Permanence and change, subject and object, unity and multiplicity might well appear to be such fundamental concepts (confirming to the law of parsimony) whereon... an adequate scheme of the universe (can indeed be erected). By sticking to these concepts and hypostatising their opposed aspects, we get the two notions of *Purusha* and *Prakrti.* It is a scientifically justifiable and intellectually honest method to seek to explain the universe with the help of these two notions." [18]

Lokmanya now picks up 'Occam's razor' and writes, "Modern materialistic natural scientists have now begun to admit that unless one credits Matter with some Energy which, though non-self-intelligible (*asvayamvedya*), is yet of the same nature as human intelligence, one cannot reasonably explain the mutual attraction or repulsion seen in the material world in the shape of gravitation, magnetic attraction repulsion, or other chemical actions. Also, one need not be surprised about the proposition of the *Samkhya* philosophy that 'Reason' is the first quality, which is acquired by Matter. One may give this quality which first arises on the matter, the name of Reason, which is non-vitalised, or non-self perceptive (*asvayamvedya*). But it is clear that the desire, which a man gets, and the desire which inspires Matter belong originally to one and the same class; and, therefore, both are defined in the same way in both the places. This 'Reason' has also such other names as *mahat,*

---

[17] Ibid. p. 16.
[18] P. Koslowski, *The Concept of God, the Origin of the World, and the Image of the Human in the World Religions,* Springer Science & Business Media, New York, 2012, p. 20.

jnana, mati, asuri, prajna, khyati, etc. Out of these, the name *mahat* (first person singular masculine, *mahan*, i.e., 'big') must have been given because Matter now begins to be enlarged, or on account of the importance of this quality."

At the cosmic level, *Mahat* can be seen as supreme intelligence that triggered the gross matter in to a never-ending cascade of transformation in to different forms. *Mahat* is therefore, the first principle for the manifestation of the *Avyakta*. It is also called 'Pure Reason' or 'Reason' depending upon the context. Lokmanya writes, "In as much as this quality of *Mahat* is the result of the admixture of the three constituent qualities of *sattva, rajas*, and *tamas*, this quality of Matter can later on take diverse forms, though apparently it is singular. This is so because though the *sattva, rajas* and *tamas* constituents are apparently only three in number, yet, in as much as the mutual ratio of these three can be infinitely different in each mixture and so the varieties of 'Reason' which result from the infinitely different ratios of each constituent in each mixture can also be infinite." In a human body, from *Mahat* comes *Ahamkara*. From *Sattvik Ahamkara* comes mind; from *Rajasik Ahamkara* comes *Prana*; from *Tamasik Ahamkara, Tanmatras*. Finally, *Tanmatras* keep the gross elements of the body alive.

The operability of *Mahat* over matter through the dynamics of three qualities inherent in all that exists gives rise to the principle of individualisation. As the energy gets enmeshed in the material, after a while, it cannot step out of the circumscribed individuality it only creates. The gross material becomes molecules with precise configurations and specific properties and human beings become self-hypnotised and feel separate from other individuals and the world becomes the playground of manifold separateness composed of countless individuals with their respective minds and bodies which all came in to existence from one and the same *Mahat* principle.

Lokmanya writes, "The Individuation in man, and the Individuation by Reason (*Mahat*) of which trees, stones, water, or other fundamental atoms spring out of homogeneous Matter are of the same kind and the only difference is that as the stone is not self-conscious, it does not have the knowledge of *aham* ('I'), and as it does not have a mouth, it cannot by self-consciousness say, 'I am different from you'. Otherwise, the elementary principle of remaining separate individually from others, that is, of consciousness or of Individuation is the same everywhere."

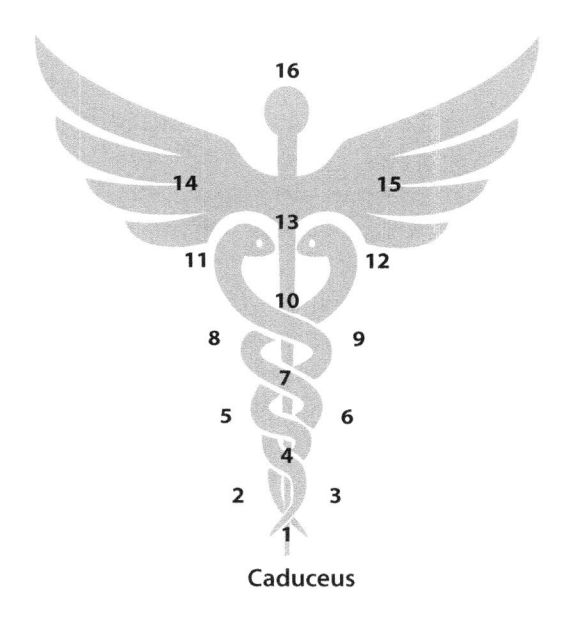

Caduceus

Individuation is about how the individual develops out of having a one-sided perspective into being a more whole and balanced individual. From the original state of undifferentiated unconsciousness, (1) a typological function is differentiated (2) and the opposite is projected onto other people. When those projections are withdrawn and owned (3), and the person refrains from exercising preference, it allows a new dominant function to emerge from the unconscious.[19] Carl Jung famously said, "The right way to wholeness is... snakelike, a path that unites the opposites in the manner of the guiding caduceus."

There is great similarity in the mind-blowing diversity of life forms on earth. The intelligence that makes and operates us all is more inside than outside. Modern science has established the intelligence present in each of the cells of any living entity, human, animals and even plants and insects as genes in the nucleus. The genes are made of DNA. Deoxyribonucleic Acid (DNA) is the

---

19 Steve Meyers, 'Can Psychological Type be a Barrier to Individuation?', *Typeface*, the quarterly magazine of the British Association for Psychological Type (BAPT), Vol. 25(4), 14-18

hereditary material in humans and almost all other organisms. It is made of four base pairs, namely, adenine (A), guanine (G), cytosine (C), and thymine (T) configured in unique formations that make an entity grow and age, live and die. There are about 3 billion bases and it is surprising that 99 per cent of these bases are the same in all the people who live on this earth. Even higher animals like mammals, have more than 90 per cent DNA similar to the human. It is the difference in the configuration of the few that makes all the difference in the life forms.

Going further back in time, even before the evolution of life on earth, it is interesting to know how life arrived here. How the organic molecules– chains of carbon, hydrogen and nitrogen– covered in energy from sunlight from the above and from geothermal heat from below did not get charred and become asphalt? From where came what or who made the organic materials escape their asphaltic fate to not only survive but also multiply? The closest answer science has reached is that life began 3.9 billion years ago; but how, remains a mystery. There is a Panspermia theory that claims that the DNA materials needed to kick start life on earth were brought in from outer space by comets and meteorites.

As for the human body, modern science has established that it works as an intricate system based on complex communication between cells. There are various kinds of cells with innumerable sensors and hormones transmitting and receiving information that holds the key for the wellness and the diseases. No organ is independent of another and the most outer and obvious skin carries millions of exteroceptors and mechanoreceptors, sensing stimuli originating from outside of the body, such as touch, vibration, pain, vision, and sound; and responding to these external mechanical stimuli. It is an established medical fact that the skin, the nervous system and immunity are interdependent systems. They work together using the same language of cytokines and neurotransmitters.

As for the mind, contemporary neuro-psychiatrist E. S. Krishnamoorthy explains the working of the mind in computer terms. He writes, "The mind... is a virtual entity, one that reflects the workings of the neural networks, chemical and hormonal systems in our brain. The mind cannot be localised to particular areas within the brain, though the entire cerebral cortex and deep grey matter form important components. Consciousness, perception, behaviour, intelligence, language, motivation, drive, the urge to excel and reasoning of the most complex kind are the product of the extensive and complex linkages between the different parts of the brain. Likewise, abnormalities attributed to the mind, such as the spectrum of disorders dealt with by psychiatrists and psychologists, are consequences of widespread abnormalities, often in the chemical processes within different parts of the brain."[20]

It is indeed interesting to read what Lokmanya wrote much before all this scientific knowledge arrived. "According to the *Samkhya* philosophy, after the eleven organic faculties or qualities, which are the basis of the organic world, and the five subtle elementary essences (*tanmatras*) which are the basis of the inorganic world have thus come into existence as a result of the *sattvik* and *tamasa* Individuation respectively, the five gross primordial elements (which are also called *Vishesas*), as also gross inorganic substances, came into existence out of the five fundamental subtle essences (*tanmatras*). When these inorganic substances, come into contact with the eleven subtle organs, the organic universe comes in to existence."

The order in which the various Elements come out of fundamental matter has been discussed in the earlier chapter. Lokmanya shares here the following description of the *Brahma Vrksha* (Tree of Life), which has occurred twice in the *Anu-Gita* in the *Mahabharata*:

अव्यक्तबीजप्रभवो बुद्धिस्कन्धमयो महान् ।
महाहंकारविटपः इन्द्रियान्तरकोटरः ॥१२॥
महाभूतविशाखश्च विशेषप्रतिशाखवान् ।
सदापर्णः सदापुष्पः शुभाशुभफलोदयः ॥१३॥
आजीवः सर्वभूतानां ब्रह्मवृक्षः सनातनः ॥१३॥
एतच्छित्वा च भित्त्वा च ज्ञानेन परमासिना ।
हित्वा चामरतां प्राप्य जह्याद्वै मृत्युजन्मनी ॥१४॥

---

20 https://www.ncbi.nlm.nih.gov/pmc/articles/PMC3115284/

> *The imperceptible (avyakta) is its seed, Reason (mahan) is its trunk, Individuation (Ahamkara) is its principle foliage, the mind and the ten organs reside inside the trunk. The five primordial elements in their subtle forms (tanmatras) and in their gross forms are its five large and five sub-branches. The branches are always covered with leaves and flowers, and fruits, both auspicious and inauspicious (shubh-ashubhphala). It is the fundamental support of all living entities– such is the ancient gigantic tree of life (Brahma Vrksha Sanatana). Only by a philosophical sword (jnana parama sina) a scient can destroy its bonds, which cause life, old age and death.*
> (Mahabharata, Ashvamedhika Parva, Adhyaya 48, Shloka 12-14)

The tradition of visualising existence as a 'tree' is very ancient and dates from the time of the *Rig-Veda* where it has been has been called *Sanatana ashvatthavrksha*. In the Katha *Upanishad*, Yama used the metaphor of the reversed inverted tree, with roots in the heaven and branches, leaves and fruits in this world while discussing the secret of death with Nachiketa.

ऊर्ध्वमूलोऽवाक्शाख एषोऽश्वत्थः सनातनः ।
तदेव शुक्रंतद् ब्रह्म तदेवामृतमुच्यते ।
तस्मिँल्लोकाः श्रिताः सर्वे तदु नात्येति कश्चन ।
एतद्वै तत् ॥१॥

Its roots above, its branches below,
This is the eternal banyan tree.
That alone is bright! That is Brahman!
That alone is called immortal!
On it the entire world rests;
Beyond it no one can pass.[21]

The metaphor of the inverted tree is also included in the *Bhagavad-Gita*.

---

21 Patrick Olivelle, **Upanishads**, Oxford University Press, United Kingdom, 1996, p.244

The Mint of the Matter

अधश्चोर्ध्वं प्रसृतास्तस्य शाखा
गुणप्रवृद्धा विषयप्रवालाः ।
अधश्च मूलान्यनुसन्ततानि
कर्मानुबन्धीनि मनुष्यलोके ॥२॥

The branches of the tree extend downward and upwards (adhah cha urdhvam), nourished by the three modes of material nature (gunapravrddhah). The roots of the tree hang downward, with senses objects hanging on them (visayapravalah). A person gets bound in the world of human society (manusya-loke) according to his actions (karmanubandhini)
(Bhagavad-Gita Chapter 15, Verse 2)

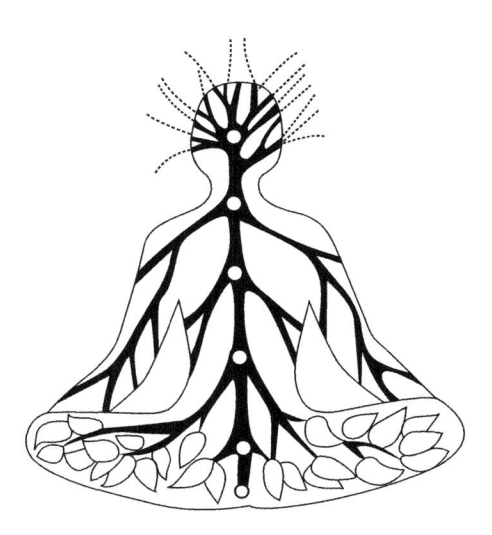

The allegory of a tree with its roots descending from above the trunk and branches spreading below strikingly convey the illusionary nature of the world, which is rooted in the Divine. As we move away from the root, the greater is the crumbliness, the loss of the substance and existence not lasting beyond a season.

Eknath Easwaran adds, "The more we try to put our senses out to enjoy the world, the more we are sticking out our necks... People who are highly taste oriented, for example, are extruding their palate farther and farther and farther. Obsessed with food, always thinking about what to eat and when and where and how often, they squeeze all their consciousness into their taste buds; they are feeling the world through the palate... Overeating is one of the most familiar illustrations of how consciousness can be concentrated on a particular sense organ, which really lives it out on a limb."[22]

A closer examination of the twenty-five elements of existence– the *purusha* and the fundamental (*mula*) *prakrti* with its 23 evolutes are grouped into four divisions: (1) fundamental *prakrti*, (2) *prakrti-vikrti*, (3) *vikrti* and (4) neither *prakrti* nor *vikrti*. The *Mahat*, being the first evolute of the *Prakrti* is called *prakrti-vikrti*. In the same way, Individuation (*ahamkara*), and the five *tanmatras* are also classified under the heading of *prakrti-vikrti*. But as the five organs of Perception, the five organs of action, the 'Mind', and the five Gross primordial elements, do not procreate any further, these sixteen elements are called *vikrti* (evolutes). The Spirit (*Purusha*) is neither *prakrtin* or *vikrti*. Ishvarakrishna, explains it as:

मूलप्रकृतिरविकृतिः महदाद्याः प्रकृतिविकृतयः सप्त ।
षोडशकस्तु विकारो न प्रकृतिर्न विकृतिः पुरुषः ॥३॥

The fundamental Prakrti is evolved of no other substance but gets differentiated in to seven evolutes (prakrti-vikriti). There are sixteen variants of these seven evolutes (vikara). The Purusha is neither a prakrti nor a vikriti. (Samkhya Karika, Verse 3)

Departing from the *Samkhya* philosophy, the *Vedanta* school does not give *Prakrti* an independent status. *Prakrti* is seen as also created along with the *Purusha*– both emerge out of the *Parameshvara* (Supreme God). The *Vedanta* therefore negates the distinction made by the *Samkhya* philosophers between the fundamental *Prakrti* and the *prakrti-vikrti*. According to *Vedanta*, both, the *Purusha*, which is called the Soul (*Jiva*), and the *eight-fold Prakrti* are eternal, indestructible realities. The other sixteen elements out of twenty-five are left untouched. The *Bhagavad-Gita* accepts the *Vedanta* classification with a small distinction. The *Jiva* is described as the most sublime form of the Ishvara (*para*), and the

---

22 Eknath Easwaran, *The Bhagavad-Gita for Daily Living*, Jaico Publishing House, Mumbai, 2007, Vol. III, p. 176-177.

Prakrti is referred to the inferior form of the Ishvara (*apara*).

भूमिरापोऽनलो वायुः खं मनो बुद्धिरेव च ।
अहङ्कार इतीयं मे भिन्ना प्रकृतिरष्टधा ॥४॥

Earth, water, fire, air, space, mind, intellect, and ego (ahankarah)– these are My eight (astadha) separated material energies (bhinnaprakrti). These eight are the forms which unmanifested nature (prakrti), takes when it becomes manifested. (Bhagavad-Gita Chapter 7, Verse 4)

The Blessed Lord further clarifies:

अपरेयमितस्त्वन्यां प्रकृतिं विद्धि मे पराम् ।
जीवभूतां महाबाहो ययेदं धार्यते जगत् ॥५॥

This is my lower nature. Know now My higher nature which is the soul (paramjiva-bhutam) by which this world is upheld (yayedam dharyate jagat). (Bhagavad-Gita Chapter 7, Verse 5)

Dr. S. Radhakrishnan adds, "The Supreme is *Ishvara*... who contains conscious souls (*kshetrajna*) and unconscious nature (*kshetra*). The two are regarded as His (God's) higher (*para*) and lower (*apara*) aspects. He is the life and form of every being... The integral undivided reality of the Supreme appears divided into multiplicity of souls. The unity is the truth and multiplicity is an expression of it..."[23]

Lokmanya thus concluded the description of how the homogeneous, inorganic, imperceptible and gross Matter, which was fundamentally equable, acquires organic heterogeneity as a result of Individuation after it has become inspired by the non-self-perceptible *buddhi* (desire) of creating the visible universe. Also how, later, as a result of the principle of the Development of Constituents (*guna parinama*), namely that, "Qualities spring out of qualities," (*guna guneshu jayante*), the eleven *sattvik* subtle elements, which are the fundamental elements of the organic

---

[23] S. Radhakrishnan, *The Bhagavad Gita*, HarperCollins Publishers India, 2014, p. 251-252.

world come into existence on the one hand, and the five subtle fine elements (*tanmatras*), which are the fundamental elements of the *tamasa* world come into existence on the other hand.

After making clear the fundamental difference between *Samkhya* philosophy and the *Vedanta* wherein *Prakrti* is not energised by *Purusha* created prior, but concurrently emerged from the *Parameshvara*, and how the *Gita* looked at *Purusha* as the *Jiva* (as *amsha* of *Parmeshavara*), Lokmanya now explains the order of the subsequent creation and cites from the *Taittiriya Upanishad* (Chapter 2, Verse 1).

ओं: ब्रह्मविदाप्नोति परम् । तदेषाऽभ्युक्ता ।
सत्यं ज्ञानमनन्तं ब्रह्म । यो वेद निहितं गुहायां परमे व्योमन् ।
सोऽश्नुते सर्वान्कामान्सह । ब्रह्मणा विपश्चितेति ।
तस्माद्वा एतस्मादात्मन आकाशः संभूतः । आकाशाद्वायुः ।
वायोरग्निः । अग्नेरापः । अद्भ्यः पृथिवी ।
पृथिव्या औषधयः । औषधीभ्योऽन्नम् । अन्नात्पुरुषः

"Aum. The knower of Brahman reaches the Supreme. As to this, the following has been said: He who knows Brahman as real, as knowledge and as the infinite, placed in the secret place of the heart and in the highest heaven realises all desires along with Brahman, the intelligent. From this Self, emerge (sambhutah, emanated and not created) ether (akasha) arose; from ether air; from air fire; from fire water; from water the earth; from the earth herbs; from herbs food; from food the person." [24]

Lokmanya writes, "This subsequent creation is the result of the mixture of the five primordial elements, and the process of that mixture is called *Panchikarana* in the *Vedanta* treatises. *Panchikarana* is based on the assumed quintuplicating of the basic/primordial five subtle elements (*panchbhootas*). Shri Shankaracharya wrote a treatise on this theory, which is titled as *Panchikaranam*. The *panchikarana* means the coming into existence of a new substance by the mixture of different qualities of each of

---
24 S. Radhakrishnan, *The Principal Upanishads*, HarperCollins Publishers India, 2010, p. 541-542.

the five primordial elements. This union of the five *panchikarana* can necessarily take place in an indefinite number of ways."

Swami Sivananda Saraswati (1887–1963) famously said, "A mountain is composed of tiny grains of earth. The ocean is made up of tiny drops of water. Even so, life is but an endless series of little details, actions, speeches, and thoughts. And the consequences whether good or bad of even the least of them are far-reaching." He provides a lucid explanation of three bodies in every individual (*Jiva*)." The physical body is composed of five elements, viz., earth (*Prithivi*), water (*Apah*), fire (*Tejas*), air (*Vayu*) and space (*Akahsa*). There are seven primary essences (*Sapta-Dhatus*) of the physical body, namely, Chyle (*Rasa*), blood (*Asra*), flesh (*Mamsa*), fat (*Medas*), bone (*Asthi*), marrow (*Majja*) and semen (*Sukla*). There are six modifications of the body (*Shad-bhava-vikaras*, namely, *Asti* (existence), *Jayate* (birth), *Vardhate* (growth), *Viparinamate* (change), *Apaksheeyate* (decay), and *Vinashyate* (death)... Because the body decays (*Sheeryate*) on account of old age, it is called *Sharira*. Because it is cremated or burnt (*Dahyate*) it is called *Deha*."[25]

Brilliantly placing the human life in the world, Swami Sivananda expounds, "The body (*Deha*), action (*Karma*), love and hate (*Raga-dvesha*), egoism (*Ahamkara*), non-discrimination (*Aviveka*) and ignorance (*Ajnana*) are the seven links of the chain of *Samsara* (*world-experience*). From *Ajnana* (that you are immortal *jiva*, currently in this body), *Aviveka* (non-discrimination between the real and the unreal) is born. From *Aviveka* is born *Ahamkara* or egoism; from egoism is born *Raga-dvesha* (like and dislike); from *Raga-dvesha, Karma* (action) arises; from *Karma* the body or the *Deha* is produced. If you want to free yourself from (this endless loop of) the pain of birth and death, destroy *Ajnana*... (and) all the other links will be broken by themselves. This physical body of yours is the result of your past actions and is the seat of your enjoyment of pleasure and pain."[26]

It is necessary now to consider the question of what happens to a man after he dies. Lokmanya writes, "It is quite clear that the *Atman*

---

[25] Sri Swami Sivananda, *Vedanta for Beginners*, A Divine Life Society Publication, India, World Wide Web (WWW) Edition: 1999, http://www.dlshq.org
[26] ibid

of the man who dies without having acquired Self-Realisation does not escape entirely from the meshes of Matter; because, if such were the case, the difference between sin and virtue will lose its importance. Likewise, if we say that after death, the *Atman* or the Spirit alone survives, and that it, of its own accord, performs the action of taking new births, then the fundamental theorem that the Spirit is inactive and apathetic, and that all the activity is of Matter is contradicted. Besides, by acknowledging that the *Atman* takes new births of its own accord, you admit that to be its property and fall into the impossible position that it will never escape from the cycle of birth and death. Therefore, it follows that though a man may have died without having acquired Self-Realisation, his *Atman* must remain united with Matter, in order that Matter should give it new births."

The concept of multiple bodies enters here. Gross body *(sthula sharira)* is what is seen as the presence of a person in this world. The subtle body *(sukshma sharira)* is made up of five elements in their nascent forms *(apanchikrta-pancamahabhutaih)*. The *Taittiriya Upanishad* (*Brahmanda Valli*, II, III, IV, and V) describes five bodies, starting from the physical body formed by food *(anna-Maya)* and proceeds through subtler bodies made of vital breath *(prana-Maya)*, self-made by the mind *(mano-Maya)*, the self-body made of intellect *(vijnana-Maya)*, and the body of bliss *(ananda-Maya)*. Together, these four bodies beneath the physical body constitute the subtle body.

अन्नाद्वै प्रजाः प्रजायन्ते । याः काश्च पृथिवीं श्रिताः ।
अथो अन्नेनैव जीवन्ति । अथैनदपि यन्त्यन्ततः ।
तस्माद्वा एतस्मादन्नरसमयात् । अन्योऽन्तर आत्मा प्राणमयः ।
तस्माद्वा एतस्मात्प्राणमयात् । अन्योऽन्तर आत्मा मनोमयः ।
तस्माद्वा एतस्मान्मनोमयात् । अन्योऽन्तर आत्मा विज्ञानमयः ॥

(The gross body of) all beings whatever exists on earth are born of food, sustained by food, and go back to become food. (The annamaya kosha, the physical sheath). And apart from this, constituted upon the essence of food, there is another separate

self made of Prana. (The pranamaya kosha, the energy sheath). And so apart from the pranamaya, there is another separate self consisting of the mind. (The manomaya kosha, the lower mind sheath). Then that and differenrt from this (which is formed by the mind) is the inner self formed by Vijnana. (The vijnanamaya kosha, the higher mind sheath).[27]

The third one is the causal body (*karanasharira*). It is the innermost body covering the *Atman* and storing impressions of the subconscious mind. It is annihilated once the *Atman* realises its true identity as the *amsha* of *Parameshvara*. But till such time, it keeps covering the *Atman*. At the time of death, when the *Atman* leaves the body, the causal body also leaves the body along with the *Atman* carrying along the impressions of the subconscious mind and one's karmic account to be settled in the new life that the *Atman* will now take with a new body.

In the *Bhagavad-Gita*, the Subtle Body is described as consisting of *manah-shashthaniindriyani* that is, of 'the Mind and the five organs of Perception':

ममैवांशो जीवलोके जीवभूतः सनातनः ।
मनःषष्ठानीन्द्रियाणि प्रकृतिस्थानि कर्षति ॥७॥

The Blessed Lord clearly declared the identity of the living being as His own innumerable expansion. They are all eternal, not temporary manifestations and struggling or grappling hard trapped in the nature (prakrti-sthanikarsati) by their six senses (sasthaniindriyani, of which the mind is the sixth one).
(*Bhagavad-Gita* Chapter 15, Verse 7)

Dr. S. Radhakrishnan adds, "*Mamaivanshah*, a fragment of myself... does not mean that the Supreme is capable of division or partition into fragments. The individual is the movement of the Supreme, a focus of the one great Life. The self is the nucleus, which can enlarge itself and embrace the whole world... Each individual has eternal significance in the cosmos. When he rises above his

---
27 Swami Sarvanand, *Taittiriya Upanishad*, The Ramakrishna Math, TN, 1921, p. 58-68

limitations, he is not dissolved... but lives in the Supreme and enters into a co-partnership with God in the cosmic activity. Shri Shankaracharya makes out that the self is a part of the Supreme in the same way as the space in an earthen jar or a house is part of the universal space. For Shri Ramanujacharya, the soul is an actual fragment (*amsha*) of God. It becomes a substantial individual soul in the world and suffers by entering the service of the sense objects." [28]

The causal body according to the *Gita*, leaves the gross body at the time of death in the same way as the breeze carries scent from the flowers– *vayurgandhanivashayat*:

शरीरं यदवाप्नोति यच्चाप्युत्क्रामतीश्वरः ।
गृहीत्वैतानि संयाति वायुर्गन्धानिवाशयात् ॥८॥

Like the air carries fragrance (vayurgandhanivasayat) from place to place, in the same manner, the soul carries the psycho-spiritual constituents of living beings (grhitvaitani) with it while leaving the body at the time of death in to the new body. The subtle body (mind, intelligence and ego, which controls the gross physical body) accompanies the soul in its wanderings through cosmic existence. (Bhagavad-Gita Chapter 15, Verse 8)

The causal body even causes the soul to inhibit bodies other than human, such as, animals, birds, etc. Since *Jiva* is inherently apathetic and inactive; it does not assume the responsibility of creating different bodies. *Samkhya* philosophy and *Vedanta* differ again on this issue. According to the *Vedanta* philosophy, the causal body is indeed an active agent and is comprised in the well-known term, *Karma*.

But the *Samkhya* philosophy does not accept *Karma* as a third fundamental principle. The *Samkhya* philosophers see the incarnation phenomenon as the activity, property, or manifestation of *Mahat* resulting from the varying intensity of the *sattva*, *rajas* and *tamas* constituents. The casual body is seen as the property or propensity of the *Mahat* and is called the *Bhava*. The varying intensity of the *sattva*, *rajas* and *tamas* constituents by the natural

---

28 S. Radhakrishnan, *The Bhagavad Gita*, HarperCollins Publishers India, 2014, p. 388.

process of permutation and combination creates innumerable *bhavas* and adheres to the subtle body in the same way as scent adheres to a flower or colour to a cloth.

Lokmanya writes, "The different categories of gods or men or animals or trees, are the results of the combination of these *bhavas*. When the *sattvik* constituent becomes absolute and pre-eminent in these *bhavas*, man acquires Self-Realisation and apathy towards the world, and begins to see the difference between Matter and Spirit. The Spirit then reaches its original state of Isolation (*kaivalya*), and the subtle body being discarded, the pain of man is absolutely eradicated. But if this difference between Matter and Spirit has not been realised, and merely the *sattva* constituent has become predominant, the subtle body is re-born, among gods, i.e., in heaven and if the *rajas* quality has become predominant, it is re-born amongst men, on earth. Also, if the *tamas* quality has become predominant, it is re-born in the lower (*tiryak*) sphere."

This chapter is concluded providing a clear understanding that all the living and non-living observable things in the universe have come into existence from one single source. There is an underlying existential unity in the myriad expositional diversity seen in the cosmic phenomenon. Lokmanya logically established the difference between the earlier *Samkhya* philosophy and the later *Vedanta* philosophy.

In the *Samkhya* tradition, the *Purusha* is spirit, pure and distant. It is beyond subject and object. No one can understand it for that would make it an object. *The Purusha* cannot know or understand anything either, for that would make it a subject. The *Prakrti*, the Matter, is composed of three *gunas*– *sattva, rajas*, and *tamas*. When the *Purusha* unites with the *Prakrti* the equilibrium of the *gunas* is disturbed and the world order must evolve. The *Samkhya* philosophy does not have any philosophical place for the creator God. The *Purusha* gets attracted to the *Prakrti* in the way a man is attracted when he watches a beautiful woman dancing. Then they come closer and the *Purusha* becomes trapped inside the *Prakrti*.

After rejecting the *Purusha-Prakrti* dualism of the *Samkhya* philosophy and establishing that both, *Prakrti* and *Purusha* are manifestations of one eternal and quality-less (*Paramatman*), Lokmanya cautions, "Although the *Bhagavad-Gita* accepts the principle of devotion to a personal God Vasudeva and the theory of Action (*Pravrtti*) propounded in the *Naraniya* or *Bhagavata* religion, it does not accept the further doctrine of that religion that *Samkarshna* (*Jiva*) was first created out of Vasudeva and *Pradyumna* (Mind) out of *Samkarshna*, and *Aniruddha* (Individuation) out of *Pradyumna*. The words *Samkarshna, Pradyumna* and *Aniruddha* nowhere come across in the *Gita*." He writes, "Let us now consider whether or not there is some element or principle... which is beyond the *Prakrti* and *Purusha* mentioned in the *Samkhya* philosophy (and rejected by the *Bhagavad-Gita*)."

ॐ

9
Thing-in-itself

> God, who is eternally complete, who directs the stars, who is the master of fates, who elevates man from his lowliness to Himself, who speaks from the cosmos to every single human soul, is the most brilliant manifestation of the goal of perfection.
>
> *Alfred Adler[1]*

By far, in the book, Lokmanya brought out the prominence of the *Samkhya* philosophy and how *Purusha* (spirit) & *Prakrti* (material) are seen as two eternal entities. *Purusha* is indivisible, not destructive and numerous. *Prakrti* is one, divisible and even mutable by the interplay of its three *gunas– sattva, rajas* and *tamas–* producing the diversity of the world. *Purusha* impregnates *Prakrti* as happens between a man and a woman, and the world of forms keeps expanding and getting crowded.

The *Bhagavad-Gita* takes a different philosophical stance. *Purusha* and *Prakrti* are taken at par and both created by the God (*Ishvara*). *Prakrti* is divided into eight forms; five perceptible, namely, earth, water, fire, air, space, and three imperceptible, namely, mind, intellect (*buddhi*) and egoism (*ahamkara*). The idea of the union of *Purusha* and *Prakrti* is not accepted. The God (*Ishvara*) is both, the cause and support of all that exists. The universe is the manifestation of God's mind and God's energy is pervaded in everything, holding it together into this world-pattern, just as a string keeps the pearls together in a necklace– *mayi sarvamidam protam sutre manigana iva (Bhagavad-Gita Chapter 7, Verse 7)*

Lokmanya writes, "The *Bhagavad-Gita* does not accept the *Samkhya* dualism of Matter and Spirit, and the first doctrine of the

---

1 Alfred Adler (1870–1937) was an Austrian medical doctor and founder of the school of individual psychology.

philosophy of the Absolute Self in the *Gita*, as also in the *Vedanta*, is that there is at the root of the moveable and immoveable world, a third Principle which is all-pervading, imperceptible and imperishable, and which is beyond both, the Matter and the Spirit."

परस्तस्मात्तु भावोऽन्योऽव्यक्तोऽव्यक्तात्सनातनः ।
यः स सर्वेषु भूतेषु नश्यत्सु न विनश्यति ॥२०॥

Beyond the unmanifested creation, there is yet another unmanifested dimension, which is changeless and eternal (vyaktovyaktatsanatanah). In the midst of all changes, it does not die when all existence perishes (nashyatsu na vinashyati).
(Bhagavad-Gita Chapter 8, Verse 20)

The Indian mind, over the ages, paid enormous attention to the philosophical enquiry of divine reality. Seers and sages avoided assuming that God existed and laboured to find out whether this was truly so. In the *Mahabharata*, on the tenth day of the war, when Bhishma, the grandfather of the warring Pandavas and Kauravas, siding with the Kauravas, fell to the ground, pierced all over his body with arrows by Arjuna, his body did not touch the ground and instead rested on a 'bed of arrows'. Bhishma, bestowed with a boon to choose the time of his death, decided to wait for the sun to complete its southern solstice, which was a few days away.

Shri Krishna advised Yudhishthira to approach Bhishma during this period and absorb his peerless knowledge about the world. Bhishma graciously agreed when Yudhishthira approached him and answered all his questions. During one such session, Yudhishthira asked Bhishma, by whom the universe had been created, how life entered a creature and where it went after death. Bhishma cited the old narrative of the sacred words that Rishi Bhrigu narrated to Rishi Bharadwaja.

मानसो नाम विख्यातः श्रुतपूर्वो महर्षिभिः ।
अनादिनिधनो देवस्तथाभेद्योऽजरामरः ॥११॥
अव्यक्त इति विख्यातः शाश्वतोऽथाक्षरोऽव्ययः।
यतः सृष्टानि भूतानि जायन्ते च म्रियन्ति च ॥१२॥

सोऽसृजत्प्रथमं देवो महान्तं नाम नामतः ।
आकाशमिति विख्यातं सर्वभूतधरः प्रभुः ॥१३॥

"There is a Primeval Being, known to the great Rishis, of the name of Manasa. He is without beginning and without end. That Divine Being is incapable of being penetrated by weapons. He is without decay and is Immortal. He is said to be Unmanifest. He is Eternal and Unchangeable. He first created a Divine Being known by the name of Mahat. From Mahat emerged Consciousness, which created Space. That puissant Being is the holder of all created objects." [2]
(Mahabharata, Shanti Parva, Adhyaya 175, Shloka 11-13)

Lokmanya writes, "One is likely to think that these two definitions of the Creator (*Paramatman*) are different from each other. However, realistically speaking, they are not so. As there is only one *Paramatman*, how can a two-fold characteristic or definition of one and the same *Paramatman* be given, by saying once that it is beyond the Mutable and then again by saying that it is Immutable and beyond *Jiva* (Soul) or the *Purusha*." Lokmanya cites Kalidasa, who has described best the *Parameshvara* in the *Kumarasambhavam*, in the following words:

त्वामामनन्ति प्रकृतिं पुरुषार्थप्रवर्तिनीम् ।
तद्दर्शिनमुदासीनं त्वामेव पुरुषं विदुः ॥२.१३॥

"You are the matter, which exerts itself for the benefit of the Spirit, and You are also the Spirit which, apathetic itself, observes that matter. (Kumarasambhavam, Chapter (Sarga) 2, Verse 13)."

So also, the Blessed Lord has said in the *Gita*:

मम योनिर्महद् ब्रह्म तस्मिन्गर्भं दधाम्यहम् ।
सम्भवः सर्वभूतानां ततो भवति भारत ॥३॥
सर्वयोनिषु कौन्तेय मूर्तयः सम्भवन्ति याः ।
तासां ब्रह्म महद्योनिरहं बीजप्रदः पिता ॥४॥

---

2 http://www.sacred-texts.com/hin/m12/m12b009.htm. Last accessed on 20 September 2017.

The total material substance, Prakrti, is My womb in which, I cast the seed (tasmingarbham dadhamyaham) and thus all living beings are born (sarva-bhutanam tato bhavati).
(Bhagavad-Gita Chapter 14, Verse 3)
All species of life (sarva-yonisu) are born out of the material matrix of the universe (brahma mahadyonir) and I am the seed-giving father (aham bija-pradah pita).
(Bhagavad-Gita Chapter 14, Verse 4)

Dr. S. Radhakrishna explains, "*Prakrti* is the mother and God is the father of all living forms. As *Prakrti* is also of the nature of God, the God is the father and mother of the universe. He is the seed and womb of the universe. This conception is utilised in certain forms of worship...."[3]

ममैवांशो जीवलोके जीवभूतः सनातनः ।
मनःषष्ठानीन्द्रियाणि प्रकृतिस्थानि कर्षति ॥७॥

The Blessed Lord clearly declared the identity of the living being as His own innumerable expansions. They are all eternal, not temporary manifestations and struggling or grappling, hard-trapped in the nature (prakrti-sthani karshati) by their six senses (Shasasthani indriyani), of which the mind is the sixth one).
(Bhagavad-Gita Chapter 15, Verse 7)

भूमिरापोऽनलो वायुः खं मनो बुद्धिरेव च ।
अहङ्कार इतीयं मे भिन्ना प्रकृतिरष्टधा ॥४॥

Earth, water, fire, air, space, mind, intellect and ego (ahamkara)– these are My eight (astadha) separated material energies (bhinna prakrti). These eight are the forms, which unmanifested nature (prakrti) takes when it becomes manifested. (Bhagavad-Gita Chapter 7, Verse 4)

The twenty-five *Samkhya* elements have been referred to in many places in the *Mahabharata*. Giving a quick recap, there are

---

3 S. Radhakrishnan, *The Bhagavad Gita*, HarperCollins Publishers India, 2014, p. 373.

five gross elements, namely earth, water, fire, air, and space; five subtle elements, namely, sound, touch, form, taste, odour; five action instruments, namely, speaking, holding, moving, procreating, eliminating; five cognitive instruments, namely, hearing, touching, seeing, tasting, smelling; the mind, the *ahamkara*, the cosmic intelligence (*Mahat, buddhi* in individualised form), *Prakrti* and *Purusha*.

Lokmanya writes, "Nevertheless, it is stated that in each place, there is beyond these twenty-five elements an Absolute Element (*param tattva*), which is the twenty-sixth (*shadvimshatihim*) Element, and that a man does not become a *buddha* (enlightened) unless he has realised It. Our world is nothing but that knowledge which we get of all the objects in the world by means of our organs of Perception, which is why Matter or Creation is sometimes referred to as *jnana* (Knowledge), and from this point of view, the Spirit becomes *jnata* (the Knower). But the real *To Be Known* (*jneya*) is beyond both, the Matter and the Spirit, i.e. beyond both, the Knowledge and the Knower, and that is what is known as the Absolute Spirit (*param purusha*) in the *Gita*."

अध्यात्मज्ञाननित्यत्वं तत्त्वज्ञानार्थदर्शनम् ।
एतज्ज्ञानमितिप्रोक्तमज्ञानं यदतोऽन्यथा ॥१२॥

Constant pursuit of spiritual knowledge (adhyatma); and philosophical pursuit of the Absolute Truth (tattva-jnana)– these I declare as the knowledge, and all the knowledge other than this (atoanyatha), I call ignorance (ajnanam).
(Bhagavad-Gita Chapter 13, Verse 12)

A. C. Bhaktivedanta Swami Prabhupada, in his Introduction to the *Shrimad-Bhagavatam*, gives a wonderful explanation of the Absolute that is beyond this existence and the ultimate source of all energy. He writes, "The conception of God and the conception of Absolute Truth are not on the same level. The *Shrimad-Bhagavatam* hits on the target of the Absolute Truth. The conception of God indicates the controller, whereas the conception of the Absolute Truth indicates the *summum bonum* or the ultimate source of all energies... So without a doubt, whenever we refer to control over others, we must admit the existence of a personal feature. Because there are different controllers for different managerial positions, there may be many small gods. According to the *Bhagavad-Gita*, any controller who has some specific extraordinary power is called a *vibhutimat sattva,* or controller empowered by the Lord. There are many *vibhutimat sattvas,* controllers or gods with various specific powers, but the Absolute Truth is one without a second. This *Shrimad-Bhagavatam* designates the Absolute Truth or the *summum bonum* as the *param satyam.*"[4]

Lokmanya now takes up the task "to determine the exact nature of, and the mutual relationship between, these three substances (*Jiva, Prakrti* and *Parameshvara*) and one finds this subject-matter discussed everywhere in the *Upanishads.*" Lokmanya declares, "There is no unanimity of opinion amongst Vedantists on this point; some of them say that these three substances are fundamentally one, while others say that the *Jiva* (personal Self) and the Cosmos are fundamentally different from the *Parameshvara*, whether to a small or a large extent; and on that account, the Vedantists are divided into *Advaitins* (Monists), *Visistadvaitins* (Qualified-Monists), and *Dvaitins* (Dualists)."

There is no confusion on the Absolute being the ultimate source of all energies, the creator and the controller of all the activities of the *Jiva* and of the *Prakrti*. The *Hiranyagarbha-Sutra* of the *Rig-Veda* declares that God manifested Himself in the beginning as the Creator of the Universe, animating it as the Supreme Intelligence.

हिरण्यगर्भः समवर्तताग्रे भूतस्य जातः पतिरेकआसीत् ।

Hiranyagarbha was present at the beginning; when born, he was the sole lord of created beings; he upheld this earth and heaven.

Nonetheless, there are differences of understanding as to how the creation progressed thereafter. Some believe that the three substances, namely Matter, Spirit, and the Absolute, are fundamentally homogenous and intact, just as the unity of a

---

4 http://www.vedabase.com/en/sb/1/introduction

pomegranate is not destroyed on account of the numerous grains in it. Contemporary British philosopher and theologian Keith Ward (b. 1938) expressively put the perception variances in his book, 'Religion and Creation'. He writes, "Three models are suggested in the *Brihadaranyaka Upanishad*. They are, the web of a spider, the spoke of a wheel, and the sparks from the fire. 'As a spider emerges by threads, as small sparks rise from a fire, so from this Self do... all contingent beings rise up'. 'Just as the spokes of a wheel are together fixed onto the hub and felly, so are all contingent beings... fixed in this Self'. These suggest a natural or even inevitable tendency to produce finite beings rather than some freely intended creation of the universe. The *Mundaka Upanishad* adds further models which are similarly naturalistic, the growing of plants on earth and the growth of hair on the head... in failing to give a very clear or positive reason for the generation of the universe, parts of the *Upanishads* decrease the importance of individual, finite life and activity."[5]

Lokmanya writes, "Before considering this matter further, let us see what the Blessed Lord has Himself said in the *Gita* about the mutual relationship between the Cosmos (*Prakrti*), *Jiva* (*Atman* or *Purusha*), and *Parabrahman* (*Paramatman* or *Purushottam*, i.e., Absolute *Atman* or Absolute Spirit). My readers will see from what follows that there is unanimity on this matter between the *Gita* and the *Upanishads*, and all the ideas in the *Gita* are to be found in the *Upanishads*, which were earlier in point of time."

Shri Shankaracharya emphatically said, "Nothing that is unconscious is ever found capable, independently and unaided, of giving rise to anything to meet the very distinctive requirement of a person, the enjoyer. It is unconceivable then, that the alleged unconscious '*pradhana*' has, of itself and without being guided and controlled, and therefore, without being regulated by some conscious principle, produced this wonderful world-order, distinguished into the order of enjoyers having diverse formations of bodies and organs suiting their deserts and also into the external realm of objects having diverse composition, and requisite for being enjoyed in some settled ways... If the evolute of '*pradhana*'

---

5 Keith Ward, *Religion and Creation*, Clarendon Press, Oxford, United Kingdom, 1996, p. 82.

have formed themselves into this wonderful order of enjoy and the enjoyed, as the *Samkhya* holds, *'pradhana'* will have to be conceived as having been sustained and regulated by a conscious principle." [6]

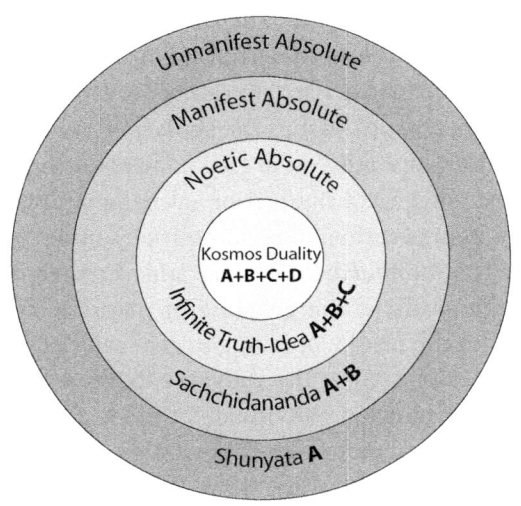

```
Unmanifest Absolute
  Manifest Absolute
    Noetic Absolute
      Kosmos Duality
         A+B+C+D
      Infinite Truth-Idea A+B+C
    Sachchidananda A+B
  Shunyata A
```

A = Unmanifest Absolute
B = Manifest Absolute
C = Noetic Absolute
D = Finite Existence

There is an Ultimate Absolute from which everything manifests. Universes manifest, live out their huge, cosmic but ultimately finite cycles and then reintegrate with the Absolute. Once manifested, there are three categories: Spirit, Consciousness and Matter, all interconnected and undergoing cycles of evolution. The universe and all within it evolves including souls, which go from a small low state to a high godlike state beyond qualities (gunateet), free of karma.[7]

Lokmanya writes, "As the Blessed Lord Sri Krishna, who was a living incarnation of the *Parameshvara*, was personally standing in front of Arjuna to advise him, indicated towards himself in the first person by referring to His perceptible form, in the following phrases in various places in the *Gita*: *Prakrtim svamavashtabhya* (*Prakrti* is My form, 9.8); *mamaivansho jiva-loke jiva-bhutah sanatanah* (The

---
6   S.K. Chattopadhyaya, *The Philosophy of Sankar's Advaita Vedanta*, Sarup & Sons, 2000, p. 234
7   https://steampunkopera.wordpress.com/2011/12/29/theosophy-so-whats-it-all-about-anyway/

embodied souls in this material world are my eternal fragmental parts, 15. 7); *'aham atma gudakesha sarva-bhutashaya-sthitah'* (I am the *Atman* inhabiting the heart of all created things, 10. 20); *'yadyadvibhutimatsattvam shrimadurjitamevava tat tad evavagachchhatvam mama tejonsha-sambhavam'* (Whatever you see as beautiful, glorious, or powerful, know it to spring from but a spark of my splendour, 10. 41); *'man-manabhava mad-bhakto mad-yaji mam namaskuru'* (Keep your mind fixed on Me and become My devotee, 9. 34); and *'man-mana bhava mad-bhakto mad-yaji mam namaskuru mam evaishyasi satyam te pratijane priyosi me'* (Always think of me, be devoted to me, worship me, and offer obeisance to me. Doing so, you will certainly come to me. This is my pledge to you, for you are very dear to me, 18. 65); and after having satisfied Arjuna by showing him His Cosmic Form... that He was the fundamental repository of the *Brahman*... one may safely say that the *Gita* from beginning to end describes only the perceptible form of the Blessed Lord."

The important question now arises: How can an imperceptible God be dealt with? Is the destiny of man like that of a puppet, where The God has all the control over him, but he has no access to his controller? Is it possible for any mortal to see the God as manifest before his eyes? Shri Swaminarayan (1781– 1830) answered this question succinctly in the *Vachnamru* (*Gadhada* 1.78), "God...who is beyond mind and speech, and who is imperceptible– himself, out of compassion, resolves: 'May all the enlightened and unenlightened people on earth behold me.' Having resolved in this manner, God– whose will always prevails– becomes perceivable to all people on earth, out of compassion."[8]

Lokmanya cautions, "But one cannot, on that account, look upon as correct the opinion of some followers of the Path of Devotion or of some commentators, that a perceptible *Parameshvara* is considered to be the ultimate object of attainment in the *Gita*; because, side by side with the descriptions referred above, of His perceptible form, the Blessed Lord has Himself stated that it is illusory, and that His imperceptible form, which is beyond (*para*) that perceptible form,

---

8 Swamin Paramtattvadas, *An Introduction to Swaminarayan Hindu Theology*, Cambridge University Press, United Kingdom, 2017, p. 148.

and which is not cognisable by the organs, is His principal form."

The Blessed Lord declared most categorically in the *Bhagavad-Gita*:

अव्यक्तं व्यक्तिमापन्नं मन्यन्ते मामबुद्धयः ।
परं भावमजानन्तो ममाव्ययमनुत्तमम् ॥२४॥

People of less intelligence (abuddhayah) think of Me (the Supreme Lord) as a personality (vyaktim, Shri Krishna). They do not understand My higher nature (param bhavam), My imperishable (avyayam) and finest (anuttamam) form.
(Bhagavad-Gita Chapter 7, Verse 24)

Farther on, in the next verse, The Blessed Lord has said:

नाहं प्रकाशः सर्वस्य योगमायासमावृतः ।
मूढोऽयं नाभिजानाति लोको मामजमव्ययम् ॥२५॥

Veiled by My creative power (Yoga Maya), I am not visible to everyone (sarvasya). My unborn and inexhaustible form (mam ajamavyayam) cannot be comprehended (abhijanati) by the fools (mudhah). (Bhagavad-Gita Chapter 7, Verse 25)

He has ultimately, in the concluding eighteenth chapter of the *Bhagavad-Gita*, advised Arjuna as follows:

ईश्वरः सर्वभूतानां हृद्देशेऽर्जुन तिष्ठति ।
भ्रामयन्सर्वभूतानि यन्त्रारूढानि मायया ॥६१॥

The Supreme Lord dwells in the hearts of all living entities (sarva-bhutanam hrddese). All that exists (sarva-bhutani) moves (bhramayan) as a machine (yantra) placed under the force field of the material energy (arudhani mayaya).
(Bhagavad-Gita Chapter 18, Verse 61)

Swami Vivekananda explains this *shloka* as, "The Lord dwells in the heart of all beings... by his illusive power, causing all beings to revolve as though (a chunk of clay) mounted on a potter's wheel...

the wheel goes on and the same combination comes up; the pitcher and the glass have stood there before, so too, that onion and potato. What can we do... He has us on the wheel of life."[9] The individual is always under God's control.

सर्वभूतानि कौन्तेय प्रकृतिं यान्ति मामिकाम् ।
कल्पक्षये पुनस्तानि कल्पादौ विसृजाम्यहम् ॥७॥
प्रकृतिं स्वामवष्टभ्य विसृजामि पुनः पुनः ।
भूतग्राममिमं कृत्स्नमवशं प्रकृतेर्वशात् ॥८॥

The Blessed Lord says that the entire existence (sarva-bhutani) returns to me after the end of their time (kalpa kshaye) and then again (punah) I create them (aham visrjami) and send them forth (kalpa-adau). (This is a cycle).
(Bhagavad-Gita Chapter 9, Verse 7)
The whole cosmic order (prakrtim) is my personal Self (avastabhya). All the cosmic manifestation (ksrsnam bhuta-gramam) I create (visrami) again and again (punah punah), is under my obligation (vasat).
(Bhagavad-Gita Chapter 9, Verse 8)

Dr. S. Radhakrishnan explains, "Human souls are not lords of their action. While they are subject to nature, the Supreme controls nature. In the divine embodiment, it is *Yoga Maya, Atman Maya, and Prakrti*, which is filled with the light and joy of the Supreme and acts under his control... The human soul is entangled in ignorance and is helplessly bound in its work, through its subjugation to *Prakrti*."[10]

Parameshvara also resides in the heart of everybody and makes them carry on their various activities:

ईश्वरः सर्वभूतानां हृद्देशेऽर्जुन तिष्ठति ।
भ्रामयन्सर्वभूतानि यन्त्रारूढानि मायया ॥६१॥

The Blessed Lord tells Arjuna that He, as the Supreme Lord

---

9 Swami Vivekananda, *Complete Works*, 9.406, In: Swami Madhurananda (Compiler), 'Bhagavad-Gita as viewed by Swami Vivekananda', Kolkata: Advaita Ashrama, Seventh Reprint, 2016, p. 146.
10 S. Radhakrishnan, *The Bhagavad Gita*, HarperCollins Publishers India, 2014, p. 285.

of all living entities (Ishvara sarva-bhutanam), resides in everyone's heart and directs their wanderings (bhramayan), who are nothing but the machines made of the material energy (yantrarudhani mayaya).
(Bhagavad-Gita Chapter 18, Verse 61)

A. C. Bhaktivedanta Swami Prabhupada explains, "...(every) living entity gets what it deserves... under the direction of the Supersoul (*Paramatman*). As soon as a living entity is placed in a particular type of body, it has to work under the spell of that bodily situation (a machine made out of material energy). (As) a person seated in a high-speed motor car goes faster than one seated in a slower car... Similarly, by the order of the Supreme Soul, material nature fashions a particular type of body to a particular type of living entity to work according to his past desires. The living entity is not independent."[11]

Lokmanya writes, "Although it is thus clear that the superior form of the *Parameshvara* is not perceptible, but is imperceptible, yet, it is necessary to consider whether this imperceptible form has qualities or is quality-less because, we have before ourselves the example of a quality-full imperceptible substance in the form of the *Samhkhya Prakrti* which, being imperceptible, is at the same time possessed of qualities, i.e., which possesses the *sattva, rajas*, and the *tamas* qualities; and according to some persons, the imperceptible and superior form of the *Parameshvara* must also be considered quality-full in the same way... The forms of the *Parameshvara* who is imperceptible (that is, imperceptible to the organs) have thus been described as only two, namely, quality-full (*saguna*) and quality-less (*nirguna*); but in some places, both the forms are mixed up in describing the imperceptible *Parameshvara*." Lokmanya cites the following *shloka*:

न च मां तानि कर्माणि निबध्नन्ति धनञ्जय ।
उदासीनवदासीनमसक्तं तेषु कर्मसु ॥९॥

The Blessed Lord tells Arjuna that none of the activities (tani

---

11 A. C. Bhaktivedanta Swami Prabhupada, *Bhagavad-Gita As It Is*, The Bhaktivedanta Book Trust, Mumbai, 2006, p. 745.

karmani) bind Him. He remains like a neutral observer (udasina), without any attraction towards these actions (asaktam tesu karmasu). (Bhagavad-Gita Chapter 9, Verse 9)

Dr. S. Radhakrishna explains, "Though the Supreme controls creation and dissolution, as their spirit and guide, He is not involved in them, for He is above the procession of cosmic events... God is thus unweariedly active in the play of the universe and yet, above the universe and free from its laws."[12]

Contemporary scholar Francis Xavier Clooney (b. 1950), Professor of Comparative Theology at the Harvard Divinity School observes, "Shri Ramanujacharya offers a sophisticated model of the God-world relationship that seems almost an ideal Hindu version of panentheism. This world exists within the reality of God, in a unity that is 'not two'. God is transcendent and beyond all imperfection, yet includes within the divine reality all the material and spiritual realities that are subject to change and imperfection; God's knowledge is pure self-conscious yet, also a knowledge of all individual things as they truly are."[13]

The opening of Shri Ramanujacharya's '*Gita* Bhashya' says:

परं ब्रह्म पुरुषोत्तमो नारायणो ब्रह्मादिस्थावरान्तम्
अखिलं जगत् सृष्ट्वा स्वेन रूपेण अवस्थित:, ब्रह्मादिदेवमनुष्याणां
ध्यानाराधनाद्यगोचर: अपि अपारकारुण्यसौशील्यवात्सल्यौदार्यमहोदधि:,
स्वमेव रूपं तत्तत्सजातीयसंस्थानं स्वस्वभावम् अजहद् एव कुर्वन्
तेषु तेषु लोकेषु अवतीर्य अवतीर्य तै: तै: आराधित:, तत्तदिष्टानुरूपं
धर्मार्थकाममोक्षाख्यं फलं प्रयच्छन्

"The highest Brahman, the highest person, Narayana, emitted the entire universe, beginning with Brahma, all the way down to immovable objects, while yet remaining in His form. He was inaccessible in meditation, worship, etc., to Brahma and the other gods, and to humans. Yet, since He was also a vast ocean of boundless mercy, affability, affection and generosity, He

---

12 S. Radhakrishnan, *The Bhagavad Gita*, HarperCollins Publishers, Noida, India, 2014, p. 285-286
13 Loriliai Biernacki, Philip Clayton (ed.), *Panentheism Across the World's Traditions*, Oxford University Press, United Kingdom, 2014, p. 123-124.

emitted His own form in a configuration appropriate to each kind of being, yet without giving up His own proper nature. Thus, He descended again and again into each world, was worshipped in each world, and bestowed the results known as righteousness, wealth, enjoyment, and liberation, according to the desires of each." [14]

The Blessed Lord declares:

यदा भूतपृथग्भावमेकस्थमनुपश्यति ।
तत एव च विस्तारं ब्रह्म सम्पद्यते तदा ॥३१॥

When a sensible man starts visualising the diverse variety of living beings (bhuta prthagbhavam) situated in one material nature (eka-stham), and understands all of them to be born from it (vistaram), he captures the concept of the Brahman.
(Bhagavad-Gita Chapter 13, Verse 31)

Swami Muktananda (1908– 1982) writes in his commentary of this *shloka*, "The ocean modifies itself in many forms such as the wave, froth, tide, ripples, etc. (The person) who is shown all these individually for the first time may conclude that they are all different. But the person who has knowledge of the ocean sees the inherent unity in all of these elements. Similarly, there are numerous forms of life in existence, from the tiniest amoeba to the most powerful celestial gods. All of them are rooted in the same reality– the soul, which is a part of God, seated in a body, which is made from the material energy. The distinctions between the forms are not due to the soul, but due to the different bodies manifested by the material energy... When we see the variety of living beings all rooted in the same material nature, we realise the unity behind the diversity. And since material nature is the energy of God, such an understanding makes us see the same spiritual substratum pervading all existence..."[15]

---

14 Swami Adidevananda (Translator), Sri Ramanuja Gita Bhasya, Sri Ramakrishna Math, Chennai, p. 41
15 http://www.holy-bhagavad-gita.org/chapter/13/verse/31

Lokmanya concludes, "To express the same thing in short, we have to now consider how that which was 'One', acquired diversity; how that which was non-dual, acquired duality; how that which was untouched by opposite doubles (*dvamdva*), became affected by these opposite doubles; or, how that which was unattached (*asamga*), acquired attachment (*samga*)."

In the *Brihadaranyaka Upanishad* (3.9), a beautiful story sums this issue best. In the assembly hall of Raja Janaka, after the conclusion of a *Yajna*, the question, 'How many gods are there?' came up for discussion. Sage Yajnavalkya said, "It depends. There are thirty-three gods. Six gods. Three gods. Two gods. One-and-a-half gods are there." "What are those 33 gods?" wondered the scholars assembled. Yajnavalkya then elaborated, "The 33 gods are 8 *vasus* (aspects of nature), 11 *rudras* (aspects of energy) and 12 *adityas* (solar deities), Indra (the king) and Prajapati (the creator). These 33 are immanent in us. The six gods are fire, earth, air, space, heaven and the sun. The three gods are the three levels of awareness we live in. The two gods are food and life force energy and matter. The whole universe consists of these two only– energy and matter, nothing else. Outwardly it is matter. Inwardly it is energy." Finally, explaining the 1½ god, Yajnavalkya said, "There is One God that makes all these various gods flourish. 'One Effulgence' that shines in myriad ways. This Effulgence, while shining as all other effulgence's, is also beyond them. It plays the game of hide and seek, making you think it is far away somewhere outside when, in fact, it is the closest to you, present in you, above you, beside you in all places, at all times. Because it appears different from yourself, I said 1½ gods. There is only one God."[16]

The sages of the *Upanishads* have gone beyond *Prakrti* and *Purusha*, and laid down the doctrine that the quality-less (*nirguna*) *Brahman*, which is even higher than the *Satchitananda Brahman*, i.e. the *Brahman* possessed of the qualities of eternal Existence (*sat*), Consciousness (*chit*), and Bliss (*ananda*), and is indeed the root of the world. The essence (*sat*) of all this that we see in the world is *Brahman sarvamkhalvidam brahma* (*Chandogya Upanishad*

---

16 https://callofthevedas.wordpress.com/2015/12/01/how-many-gods-are-there/

3.14.1); *Brahman* is Consciousness (*chit*), *prajnanam brahma* (Aitareya *Upanishad* 3.1.3); and *Brahman* is Bliss, *ananda* (*Taittiriya Upanishad* 3.6.1).

Coming back to the question of how the human mind can feel God, the two concise and crisp words, *nirguna* and *saguna,* indeed embrace many difficult questions about the human-God interaction. How could imperceptible and even incomprehensible *Parabrahman*, acquire qualities which are perceptible to human organs, and remain 'One'? How could the it possess the worldly makings of taste, smell, touch, sound and form? How could it indulge and yet remain a witness concurrently? How could it be the earth and the earthenware pot simultaneously?

German-American philosopher Paul Tillich (1886– 1965), one of the most influential theologians of the twentieth century, explains that the essence of religious attitudes emanates from an ultimate concern in the human heart about connecting with the holy; distinct from his ordinary reality. The child in every human heart yearns for the missing parent throughout life to whom it could surrender, and who, in turn, promises total fulfilment.

Paul Tillich writes, "The form… (this) ultimate concern… varies from one religious community to another. Ultimate concern may take the form of worship, and involve praise, love, gratitude, supplication, confession, petition, and the like. But it can also take the form of a quest for the ultimate good. The object of the quest is an existentially appropriated knowledge of the ultimate good or a union with it that transforms us and overcomes our wrongness… The most striking disagreement is between those who regard the divine reality as personal and those who do not… the two forms of ultimate concern may be combined or exist separately… theistic Hinduism combines both."[17]

Lokmanya writes, "I must now explain how the Quality-full (*saguna*) came out of the Quality-less (*nirguna*); because, it is a doctrine of *Vedanta*, as of *Samkhya* philosophy, that that which is not, is not; and that that which is, can never come into existence out of that which is not…"

---

17 https://plato.stanford.edu/entries/concepts-god/

Advaita Vedanta insists that the ultimate reality (*Brahman*) is without parts or attributes. The God is, therefore, 'one without a second'. It becomes problematic to the heart looking for solace of surrendering to a missing parent and seeking love. If the *Brahman* has no properties, how could it be the God?

Mahatma Gandhi pondered upon Arjuna's question to Shri Krishna, "Some devotees worship you in *saguna* form while others worship you in *nirguna* form. Whom do you like more?" In his discourse, Gandhiji explained, "What answer could the Lord give? It is just like asking a mother having two sons, "Whom do you love more?" The younger son is a little child, deeply attached to his mother. He is happy only in her company and is restive if she is out of sight even for a moment. He cannot bear separation from her even for a moment. Without her, the world is like a big void for him. The elder son, too, is full of love for the mother, but he is grown up and mature. He can stay away from her. He serves her and takes all the burden and responsibility upon himself. Being absorbed in work, he can endure separation from her. He is admired by the world and his reputation pleases his mother. If you tell this mother that she can have only one of these two sons and she will have to choose between them, what could she do? How can she make a choice? The mother replied, "I can bear separation from the elder one, if I cannot help it"... It is more difficult for her to tear away the younger son from her bosom... The Lord has been put in exactly the same predicament. The Lord has replied exactly like that mother. He says, "I love the former– the *saguna bhakta*– and the latter too is Mine." Gandhiji then declared, "In fact, this is the truth. There is absolutely no difference between these two types of devotees. Both have equal merit. To compare the two, is to transgress the limit of propriety."[18]

The concept of the *Saguna Brahman* thus emerges as a useful tool for people to embark on their spiritual journey and find solace in the tribulations of their daily lives. But a seer, a committed traveller on the spiritual path, must cast aside the all powerful, all knowing, all good, the sovereign-lord-of-heaven-and-earth imagery of the God aside, and become fully enlightened to eventually reach

---

18 http://www.mkgandhi.org/talksongita/chap12.htm. Last accessed on 20 September 2017.

and realise joyous empty consciousness– impersonal, inactive, and anonymous, which is the *Nirguna Brahman*.

Lokmanya now refines the question of *Saguna-Nirguna* understanding to the pursuit of self-realisation. Citing from the most acclaimed Yajnavalkya-Maitreyi conversation in the *Brihadaranyaka Upanishad*, Lokmanya writes, "In the same way as it is impossible to quench thirst by a mirage, or to get oil out of sand, so also is it futile to hope that immortality can ever come out of that which is palpably perishable; and, therefore, Yajnavalkya has definitely told Maitreyi that, however much of wealth one may acquire, yet, '*amrtatvasya tu nashasti vittena*' (Do not entertain the hope of obtaining immortality by such wealth). Lokmanya writes, "From where this idea of permanent happiness, beyond the span of one's own life, that is to say, of immortality comes?... Ever since the day when the human being came into this world, he has been continually thinking of what the fundamental immortal principle at the root of this visible and perishable world is and how he will reach it... Indeed, on that day when this ambition of a human being comes to an end, we will have to say of him, *so vai mukto athava pashuh*, that is, "he is either a Released soul, or a brute!"

No philosophers from any other country have yet found an explanation that is more reasonable than the one given in our ancient treatises, about the existence of an Element, which is unbounded by time or place, and is immortal, eternal, independent, homogeneous, sole, immutable, all-pervasive, and quality-less, or as to how the quality-full creation came into existence out of that quality-less Element. The German philosopher, Immanuel Kant, has minutely examined the reasons as to why a man acquires a synthetic knowledge of the heterogeneity of the external universe, and he has given the same explanation as our philosophers, but in a clearer way and according to modern scientific methods. Although Georg Hegel (1770– 1831) has gone beyond Kant, yet his deductions do not go beyond those of the *Vedanta*. The same is the case with Arthur Schopenhauer (1788– 1860). He had read the Latin translation of the *Upanishads*, and he himself has admitted that he has, in his works, borrowed ideas from this "most valuable work in the world's literature."

Lokmanya writes, "It is not possible to consider in a small book like this, these difficult problems and their pros and cons, or the similarity and dissimilarity between the doctrines of *Vedanta* philosophy, and the doctrines laid down by Kant and other Western philosophers, or to consider the minute differences between the *Vedanta* philosophy appearing in ancient treatises like the *Upanishads* and the Vedanta-Sutras, and that expounded in later works. Therefore, I have, in this book, broadly referred to only that portion of them to which it is necessary to refer in order to impress on the minds of my readers the veracity, the importance, and the reasons for the Metaphysical doctrines in the *Gita*, on the authority, principally of the *Upanishads,* and the *Vedanta-Sutras*, and of the *Bhashyas* (commentaries) of Shri Shankaracharya on them."

With this assertion, Lokmanya presents to the reader a simplistic understanding of the *reality*. He writes, "Ordinary people define the word *satya* by saying *chakshurvai satyam*, that is, "that which is seen by the eyes is real"; and if one considers the ordinary course of life, it is needless to say that there is a world of difference between seeing in a dream, that one has got a lakh of rupees, or hearing about a lakh of rupees, and actually getting a lakh of rupees."

Paul Tillich writes, "*Advaitins* and theistic *Vedantins* agree that the proper object of ultimate concern is maximally great; they disagree on just how maximal greatness should be construed. This disagreement, in turn, is rooted in metaphysical and epistemological disagreements, in differences in scriptural interpretation, and in differences in religious practice and aspiration. The most fundamental difference, however, is arguably, a difference in evaluation. Theistic *Vedantins* prize love in a way in which *Advaitins* do not. Since love is a relation between persons, it is not surprising that, the theistic *Vedantic* maximal greatness necessarily includes personhood."[19]

Bhaktisiddhanta Sarasvati (1874– 1937) in *Gaudiya Kanthahara* provides a great synthesis of comprehending the God in Chapter 7, *Krishna Tattva*.[20]

---
19 https://plato.stanford.edu/entries/concepts-god/
20 http://www.iskcondesiretree.com/profiles/blogs/krishna-tattva-must-read-6

वदन्ति तत्तत्त्वविदस्तत्त्वं यज्ज्ञानमद्वयम् ।
ब्रह्मेति परमात्मेति भगवानिति शब्द्यते ॥११॥

The one Absolute Truth is realised in three different ways: Great seers of the truth, who understand the nature of the Absolute Truth, describe that non-dual truth in three ways as Brahman, Paramatma, and Bhagwan.
(Bhagavatam Skandha 1, Adhyaya 2, Shloka 11)

न तत्र सूर्यो भाति न चन्द्रतारकं नेमा विद्युतो भान्ति कुतोऽयमग्निः ।
तमेव भान्तमनुभाति सर्वं तस्य भासा सर्वमिदं विभाति ॥१५॥

The conclusion of the Shrutis about Brahman: In the transcendental abode of the Lord there is no need of sun, moon, or stars for illumination; nor is there any need of energy, what to speak of lamps. All of them get their power of illumination from the Lord's effulgence alone. In fact, the whole universe exists only because of His existence.
(Katha Upanishad Adhyaya 2, Valli 2, Shloka 15)

केचित्स्वदेहान्तर्हृदयावकाशे प्रादेशमात्रं पुरुषं वसन्तम् ।
चतुर्भुजं कञ्जरथाङ्गशङ्खगदाधरं धारणया स्मरन्ति ॥८॥

Paramatma is the partially complete portion (ekamsa) of the Supreme Lord: The God resides within the body in the region of the heart, and (measuring only a fist's size). People conceive the Personality of Godhead with four hands, holding a lotus, wheel, conch, and club. (Bhagavatam 2.2.8)

ऐश्वर्यस्य समग्रस्य वीर्यस्य यशसः श्रियः ।
ज्ञान-वैराग्ययोश्चैव षण्णां भग इतीरणा ॥

The meaning of Bhagwan: The wealth of all kind, power over all others, fame all around, and beauty; the knowledge, and renunciation, The One who is complete in these six-fold opulence is known as Bhagwan. (Vishnu Purana 6.5. 74)

The Greek philosopher, Hermes Trismegistus, famously wrote, "The path to immortality is hard, and only a few find it. The rest await the Great Day when the wheels of the universe shall be stopped and the immortal sparks shall escape from the sheaths of substance. Woe unto those who wait, for they must return again, unconscious and unknowing, to the seed-ground of the stars, and await a new beginning." [21]

Lokmanya writes, "All that has been said before may be summarised by saying that though the human organs cannot actually perceive or know anything except Names and Forms, yet, there must be some invisible i.e., imperceptible, eternal substance which is covered by this cloak of non-permanent Names and Forms. It is on that account that we get a synthetic knowledge of the world. Whatever knowledge is acquired is acquired by the *Atman*; and therefore, the *Atman* is called the *Jnata* (Knower). Whatever knowledge is acquired by this Knower is of the Cosmos, which is defined by the Name and the Form; and, therefore, this external Cosmos, which is defined by Name and Form is called knowledge (*Jnana*) and the Thing-in-itself (*vastu-tattva*), which is at the root of this Named and Formed (*nama-rupa-atmaka*) Cosmos is called To-be-known (*Jneya*)."

Accepting this classification, the *Bhagavad-Gita* says:

ज्योतिषामपि तज्ज्योतिस्तमसः परमुच्यते ।
ज्ञानं ज्ञेयं ज्ञानगम्यं हृदि सर्वस्य विष्ठितम् ॥१८॥

The Blessed Lord described Himself as the creation and the knowledge of this creation. When the devotees understand this, he attains My state. (Bhagavad-Gita Chapter 13, Verse 18)

Dr. S. Radhakrishna describes 'My state' in this *Shloka* as the characteristics of freedom, love and equality.[22]

Lokmanya now takes up the important concept of *jneya*. In matters related to the God, between what is known and what is

---

21 http://gnosticwarrior.com/the-path-to-immortality-is-hard-and-only-a-few-find-it.html. Last accessed on 20 September 2017.
22 S. Radhakrishnan, *The Bhagavad Gita*, HarperCollins Publishers, India, 2014, p. 364.

not known, is the vast field of *jneya*, that which may be known. The *Shrutis* contains statements that the *Brahman* cannot be known, as well as statements that the *Brahman* can be known. How do we reconcile? Lokmanya writes, "To realise *Jneya* is to rest beyond all possibility of manifestation or change… commonly known as birth and death. *Jneya* is not *Sat*, because that is what is already known, *Jneya* is also not *Asat*, because it is the essence and basis of what comes to be recognised as *Sat*. *Jneya*, therefore, is neither *Sat* nor *Asat*, but beyond, while making them both possible."

Lokmanya presents a dynamic perspective. What is known today as *Sat*, may become *Asat* tomorrow. And what is seen as *Asat* today may prove to be *Sat* tomorrow. Lokmanya writes, "*Jnana* is the *Sat* itself rising in view of the ideas of extension and existence. *Ajnana* or *kshetra* is *Asat*, hindering and obscuring the *Jnana* or *Sat* and making all change possible. However, both *Jnana* and *Kshetra*, while as such are not the Jneya, are no more anything outside it or distinct from it." *Jnana* and *Ajnana* are seen as the inside and outside of the circumference of a circle. They both exist on the paper on which they are drawn and the paper is nothing to do with the circle anyway.

Lokmanya writes, "The identification of the *Brahman* with the *Atman* is described in Marathi by saying, 'What is in the *pinda* (Body), is also in the *brahmanda* (Cosmos)'. It logically follows that when, once a man has experienced this identity of the *Brahman* and the *Atman*, there can no more remain any difference between the *jnata*, or observing *Atman*, and the *jneya*, or the subject-matter to be seen."

The question of "the obstruction of the knowable, which may be known" now arises. Lokmanya writes, "In order to see anything (and also in order to hear anything etc.), the eyes (as also the ears etc.) require the help of the 'Mind'. It has been stated before that if the 'Mind' is vacant, objects in front of the eyes are not seen…. (so) if the 'Mind' is taken out of the organs, the dualities in the objects of the senses become non-existent to us, though they might exist in the external world… (therefore by cutting itself from the external objects, the mind will) in this way, become steeped in the *Atman* or in the *Atman*-formed *Brahmanda*, and one will begin to get a visionary experience (*sakshatkara*) of the identity of the *Brahman* and the *Atman*."

Lokmanya seals this idea into finality with these words, "Such a man, who has attained this mental state through meditation, mental isolation, worshipping in solitude, or by intense contemplation of the *Brahman*, will not perceive the dualities or the differences in the visible world, although they may be before his eyes. He then realises the form of the sole (*advaita*) *Brahman*, of his own accord. In this beatific ultimate state, which is the result of the fullest realisation of the *Brahman*... (he) becomes *atmabhuta* or *brahmabhuta*... as, after a lump of salt has been dissolved in water, the difference that one part of the water is salty and another of it is not salty does not remain, so also, once a man has realised the identity of the *Brahman* and the *Atman*, everything merges into the *Brahman*."

Saint Tukaram, about whom it was said, *'jayachi vade nitya vedanta vani'* (one whose voice always uttered *Vedanta*), has been cited as describing the *atmabhuta* or *brahmabhuta* as akin to how a dumb person feels the sweetness of jaggery (without words, that he is unable to speak), or of how a ripple looks at itself (which it can't, as it has no separate identity or existence than the movement of the water at a particular instant).

गोडपणें जैसा गूळ । तैसा देव झाला सकळ ॥
आतां भजो कोणेपरी । देव सबाह्यअंतरीं ॥

God is beyond description, as the taste of jaggery is to the dumb. How can I use my wisdom to discern myself from the God? I am as one with Him as a ripple to the water body.
(Tukaram Gatha, 3637).

The chapter comes to conclusion with a final comment on the Soul-God connection. The Swaminarayan faith describes the human soul (*Jiva*) as free, eternal and functioning under orders from Lord. And yet, the *Maya* binds the *Jiva*. If the *Jiva* is devoted to the Lord, it can be free from *Maya* (worldly desires and entanglement of the senses with external and illusory objects). Through single-minded devotion, one can enjoy the pleasures of serving the Lord (and thereby attain liberation).

According to the Swaminarayan philosophy, "There are three types of *Jivas*, namely, the Bound, the Liberated, and the Eternally liberated. The Bound are those who are caught in the cycle of worldliness; they are called the *Buddhas*. The Liberated are those who, due to their intense devotion to the Lord, leave the body and reside in the abode of the Lord– they are called the *Muktas*. The Eternally Liberated– those who are devotees of *Parabrahman* (highest reality), attain *Akshardham* (the imperishable abode of Lord) and serve the Lord on Par with him (attain the same status as that of the Lord)."[23]

With great humility, Lokmanya writes, "This work of setting out these doctrines in words, can be easily done by anyone who has acquired a little knowledge like me; there is nothing much in that. In order that these doctrines should be impressed on the mind, engraved on the heart and ingrained in one's flesh and bone after they have been understood, and that one should thereby fully realise that there is only one *Parabrahman* which saturates all living things; and in order that by reason of such feeling, one should acquire an immutable mental frame which will enable one to behave with equability towards everybody in times of misfortune, it is necessary to have the continual additional help of impressions acquired during numerous births, control of the organs, persevering practice, meditation, and worship."

Lokmanya declares, "The highest doctrine of the philosophy of the Absolute Self is: only that man may be said to have become fully saturated with the knowledge of the *Brahman*, in whose every action, the principle, "there is only one *Atman* in all created things", has become naturally and clearly visible, even in times of distress; and such a man alone gets Release... that man, in whom such behaviour is not to be seen, is to that extent, imperfectly or insufficiently 'baked' (as an earthen pot) in the fire of the Knowledge of the *Brahman*. This is the difference between real saints and mere *Vedantists*."

Lokmanya writes, "The chapter on the philosophy of the Absolute Self (*Adhyatma*) is now over. Before I go further, I will, following the usual practice of the '*Kesari*' (lion), and look back on the subject matter or road which I have so far traversed; because unless such

---

23 https://www.swaminarayan.faith/read/articles/jiva,-ishwar,-*Maya*,-brahm-and-parbrahm-1

a lion-look has been given, there is a risk of the link between this subject-matter and the next being lost, and of one's going astray."

A book is meaningless unless others read it. Lokmanya now makes the reader take a *'Kesari'* look back, at what has been read so far. After introducing the reader to the subject-matter of the book, i.e., a call for desireless action, Lokmanya writes, "Nothing happens unless something is done, (so) devote yourself to Desireless Action... one should not fail to thoroughly understand this ancient science of the life of a householder, or of worldly life, as early as possible in one's life."

The second and third chapters presented the concepts of Desire for Action (*Karma jijnyasa*) and the science of Proper Action (*Karma Yoga*). In the next three chapters (4, 5 and 6), the question of happiness and unhappiness is dealt with, proving that materialistic happiness is insufficient, and the idea of *Atman* is introduced towards the end of the sixth chapter. In the next two chapters (no. 7 and 8), the Dualistic philosophy of the *Samkhya* School and the shortfall of seeing oneself different from others and God is discussed and the reader is presented with *Atman* as the real identity of a person and its connectivity with all that exists. In this (ninth) chapter, the nature of *Atman* is explained.

Lokmanya writes. "I have explained in this chapter what the nature of the *Atman* is, and in what way ONE, sole, immortal and quality-less *Atman*-Element saturates fully and eternally both, the Body and the Cosmos; and I have finally drawn the conclusion that the Yoga of acquiring an equable frame of 'Mind', which believes that there is only one *Atman* in all created beings, and keeping that frame of 'Mind' perpetually alive, is the climax of Self-Knowledge (*atmajnana*) and of Self-Happiness (*atmananda*); and that the highest humanness of man, that is, the fulfilment of the purpose of human birth, or the highest ideal of a human being, consists in bringing one's mind to this pure Self-Devoted (*atma-nishtha*) state." In the remaining part of the book, Lokmanya takes up the rules relating to Action, and what the effects of Action are, or why this Action must be performed.

ॐ

10

Be Your Own Benefactor

> Man is, as it were, a centre; he draws the whole universe towards him. Good and bad, misery and happiness, all are running towards him and clinging round him; and out of them he fashions the mighty stream of tendency called character and throws it outwards. As he has the power of drawing in anything, so has he the power of throwing it out.
> *Swami Vivekananda*

Lokmanya takes off from where he stopped in the previous chapter– namely, what Action the rationale behind the human birth is, and that the important matter is to know the Science of Action (*Karma Yoga Shastra*). He writes, "Although the *jiva* (embodied soul) belongs fundamentally to the invisible *Brahman* world and is immortal; yet, like other things in the visible world, it is covered by bodily organs in the shape of Names and Forms, in the shape of the bodily organs, which are perishable. Therefore, every human being is naturally desirous of knowing how it is possible to escape from these Names and Forms, and to attain immortality."

The reader has been made aware by this time that we are not our bodies or minds, but the soul, which does not die with the body, but migrates to a new body, carrying along with it certain impressions with certain consequences (causal body), which manifests in the later life. Just like a building with hundreds of rooms, corridors and floors, is nothing but the division of space, created for a purpose, in the same manner, the body, mind, intellect, temperament, aspirations and experiences are all divisions made out of the Self, for a while. When the body dies, the person changes and not the Self, which migrates to another body, or, in some exceptional cases, even unites with the Supreme Soul (*moksha*).

The hallmark of the *Gita* philosophy is the emphasis on Action. It discards the idea of a pre-decided destiny in the lives of human beings, except for the carried-over impressions in the form of the causal body that accompany the soul at the time of conceiving of a new life form. Like a seed, each individual carries inside him the potential of becoming a tree and is capable of producing large quantities of fruits year after year; but like an unsown seed, or a seed sown in barren soil, or a seed eaten away by pests or insects, or not harvested, countless people die or live through suboptimal and even deplorable conditions and die a life wasted. That does not take away a bit from the truth that the seed is complete in itself. The conditions of this world and the efforts involved with sowing, irrigation, protection, harvest, and so on, determine the rest. So is the case with man!

Before we go into the science of Action, it is important to know the general concepts in vogue in the modern world about destiny and free will. Most of the youth, influenced by the businesses marketing their products, and the entertainment industry, consider that the purpose of life is to make merry and consume. They come to believe that the purpose of life is to become bigger, better and happier and it does not matter how one accomplishes this. Fate and destiny are seen more as alibis to cover personal and collective failures. The power of free will is there to choose in favour of what meets the interests of the person. Through this power we can achieve our successes; misusing it, we can create our failures and abusing it, we can even destroy our lives through physical as well as mental wreckage.

The idea of destiny is normally invoked at the time of failures as a psychological defence system. Most people do not accept themselves as responsible for the failures they meet with in life and find it convenient to call them fate. It is very commonplace to ignore bad planning, lack of efforts in the right direction, misjudgement of the situation and outright inadequacy of the effort made, as reasons for one's failures. Of course, destiny is almost always cited as the reason behind why one child is born to rich parents and another to poor ones, failed marriages and untimely deaths. Contemporary Brazilian writer Paulo Coelho (b. 1947) writes very convincingly, "I can control my destiny, but not my fate. Destiny means there are opportunities to turn right or left, but fate is a one-way street. I believe we all have the choice as to whether we fulfil our destiny, but our fate is sealed."

A little moderation of this position is the stance that human beings are free to take the first step, but the 'free will' ends there and what happens thereafter is inevitable and predictable. The laws of life take over and govern the outcome of any human act. Free will is limited merely to the initiative and not to the outcome. The celebrated founder of Apple Inc., Steve Jobs (1955–2011), puts it straight, "You can't connect the dots looking forward; you can only connect them looking backwards. So you have to trust that the dots will somehow connect in your future. You have to trust in something– your gut, destiny, life, (and) *karma,* whatever. This approach has never let me down, and it has made all the difference in my life."

Further moving towards fatalism, a view is taken that there is nothing like 'free will' and human beings are no better than hard-wired machines and are indeed powerless to do anything other than what they actually do. The human mind carries past impressions and bears certain fruits in a strict application of the law of cause and effect. A god, Chitragupta, meticulously keeps complete records of the actions of human beings on earth, so that each individual is made to experience the just consequences of all his actions. No one, whosoever– rich, powerful, influential, religious– is spared! This even includes the potentialities and propensities human beings are born with.

Karma is like a cascade in motion; every action creates an effect and that effect creates another effect and so on. The world in this became a great flux of *karmic* energies flying across, sometimes synergizing and at other times, cancelling each other. Swami Sarvapriyananda of The Vedanta Society of Southern California puts it so eloquently, "When we take a hard look around us, the world doesn't seem to make much sense. If we go by appearances, it would seem that countless people have escaped the noose of fate: many an evil person has died peacefully in bed. Even worse, good and noble people have suffered without apparent cause, their goodness being repaid by hatred and torture. Witness the terrorist attacks killing innocent people; witness child abuse... on the surface, the universe appears absurd at best, and malevolent at worst... (but) when we see a calamity or a triumph, we are seeing only one freeze frame of a very, very long movie. We can see neither the beginning nor the end of the movie. What we do know, however, is that everyone, no matter how depraved, will eventually, through the course of many lifetimes and undoubtedly through much suffering, come to realise his or her own divine nature. That is the inevitable happy ending of the movie."[1] Contemporary writer Deepak Chopra (b. 1946) summarises it as, "*Karma*, when properly understood, is just the mechanics through which consciousness manifests." Gurudev Rabindranath Tagore says it as:

I seem to have loved you in numberless forms, numberless times...

In life after life, in age after age, forever.
My spellbound heart has made and remade the necklace of songs,
That you take as a gift, wear round your neck in your many forms,
In life after life, in age after age, forever.

Karma is the law of 'return', our deeds returns to us.

---

[1] https://vedanta.org/what-is-vedanta/karma-and-reincarnation/

Karma and reincarnation are inseparable. The one cannot be in the absence of the other, as without the concept of rebirth, providing an opportunity to settle the consequences of earlier actions not returned to the doer in one's life, is not possible. Swami Satchidananda (1914– 2002) defined *Karma* and incarnation as a never-ending loop, explaining that *Karma* lives across lifetimes in the form of instincts and defines the innate behaviour of a person. He writes, "Instinct is a trace of an old experience that has been repeated many times and the impressions have sunk down to the bottom of the mental lake. Although they go down, they aren't completely erased. Don't think you ever forget anything. All experiences are stored in the *Chitta*; and, when the proper atmosphere is created, they come to the surface again. When we do something several times, it forms a habit. Continue with that habit for a long time, and it becomes your character. Continue with that character and eventually, perhaps in another life, it comes up as instinct."

To cut the migration of instincts from this life to the future lives, the *Gita* gives the crucial solution of desireless action.

कर्मण्येवाधिकारस्ते मा फलेषु कदाचन ।
मा कर्मफलहेतुर्भूर्मा ते सङ्गोऽस्त्वकर्मणि ॥४७॥

Your right is only to work; you have no entitlement to the results of your work. Do not consider yourself to be the cause of the results of your activities (karma phala) at any time (kadachana), and neither become motivated to receive them as granted, nor become inactive (akarmani) on this account.
(Bhagavad-Gita Chapter 2, Verse 47)

Swami Vivekananda gives the gist of this *shloka* very convincingly, "Work incessantly, but see something behind the work. Even good deeds find a man in great bondage. Therefore, be not bound by good deeds or by desire for name and fame. Those who know this secret pass beyond this round of birth and death and become immortal. Those masterminds producing momentous results in the mankind were content to write their books without even putting their names, and to die quietly, leaving the books to posterity. Who knows the writers of our philosophy, who knows the writers of our *Puranas*? They all pass under the generic name of Vyasa and Kapila, and so on. They have been true children of Shri Krishna. They have been true followers of the *Gita*; they practically carried out the great mandate, "To work you have the right, but not to the fruits thereof.""[2]

Lokmanya, in this chapter, takes the reader through an examination of how the one permanent and independent *Atman*, resides both, in the body and the Cosmos, what separates the two and how the two can reconcile. There is pure spiritual consciousness (*chaitanya*) and there is materially contaminated consciousness (*Chitta*). Lokmanya calls the separation as *Maya*-world and presents it as a flux of names and forms. As soon as the original spiritual consciousness manifests as a living entity, it gets touched by the material nature and eventually gets covered up by matter, in a similar manner as a pure drop of rain falls from the sky and becomes muddy the moment it reaches the ground.

Lokmanya writes, "The covering over the *Atman* is dense in some cases and thin in other cases. According to *Vedanta*, objects in the visible world fall into two classes of *sachetana* (Activated) and *achetana* (Non-Activated). The Activated are again sub-divided into animals, birds, men, gods (superhuman beings or spirits worshipped as having power over nature or human fortunes), *Gandharvas* (distinct heavenly beings), and *daityas* (supernatural malevolent being), etc."

It is very important to understand that *Brahman* is nothing separate out there, but is very much present here and now in this physical world. Contemporary Australian philosopher Ray Morose explains, "There are two distinct forms of life, material energy life that includes biological life and consciousness life. (Material) Energy... regenerates such as trees, plants and flowers, becoming self-sustaining and energy-responsive. Consciousness life is anything that can perceive in some other manner beyond a pure

---

2   *Swami Vivekananda : Complete Works*, 3.275, In: Swami Madhurananda (Compiler), 'Bhagavad-Gita as viewed by Swami Vivekananda', Kolkata: Advaita Ashrama, Seventh Reprint, 2016, p. 51.

energy action or reaction. Both of these forms of life did not appear out of nothing, they were created. You can hold the opinion that energy always existed, and somehow magically interacted to create the physical universe that somehow self-created its self-sustaining directional design that mutated into biological and conscious life, but would that opinion be realistic? How can a design appear from energy without a directional pattern or blueprint allowing it to manifest? Energy requires direction: it simply does not float around doing nothing and then suddenly explode into a physical universe, eventually creating a variety of life forms. Energy has direction and purpose: understanding its direction provides clues to its purpose... it is worth noting, that is all that humans can do with energy, manipulate it. They cannot create it, beyond using pre-existing elements for that creation. Consciousness life is separate from pure energy, but within the human body, they are inextricably linked. Consequently, it is important to have an intellectual appreciation of how and why those two distinct forms of existence can function as one, albeit temporarily."[3]

Lokmanya made this intellectual appreciation a hundred years ago. He writes, "It is true that the *Atman* is the same everywhere; yet, as it is fundamentally quality-less and apathetic, it cannot by itself do anything, without some *Name-d and Form-ed means* like the 'Mind', 'Reason' etc. Moreover, these means are not fully available to the *Atman* except in the human birth, and so such a birth is considered to be the most superior of all. When the *Atman* has got this human birth, its Name-d and Form-ed clothing falls into the two divisions of Gross and Subtle."

The discussion once again returns to how the *Atman* is placed in the body. As Lokmanya explained in the earlier chapter, the *Karma* clings to the *Atman* when it leaves the Gross Body at the time of death. Lokmanya writes, "In considering the difficulty which stands in the way of the embodied *Atman* attaining the *Parabrahman*... escaping the cycle of birth and death... one has to consider both, *Karma* and the Subtle Body. Out of these, the Subtle Body has been dealt with earlier in this book, both, from the point of view of the

---

3   Ray Morose, *The Science of Consciousness*, Ocean View Publications, New South Wales, Australia, 2007, p.358.

Samkhya philosophy and *Vedanta*; and therefore, that explanation is not repeated here. In this chapter, we have considered only the nature of that *Karma* or Action... (whereby) the *Atman* keeps falling into the cycle of birth and death instead of realising the *Brahman*, and also how a man has to live in this world in order that the *Atman* should escape that cycle and acquire immortality (its original state)."

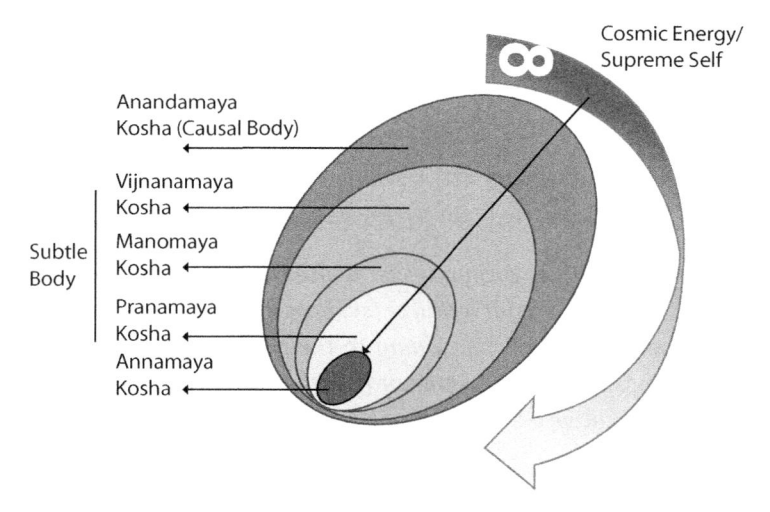

Parabrahman consciousness, smeared with the subtle body of the earlier existence, enters the human body at the time of conception of a human life, caused by the fusion of the nucleus of a sperm and an egg to form a diploid cell, known as zygote. From this instant till a human being dies, the consciousness supports the one zygote cell to eventually become the entire human body inside the womb, and grows it after birth into a powerful adult body and then helps it age till it finally dies. Upon the death of the body, the consciousness fuses another sperm and another egg and the cycle continues life after life, till whatever smears the consciousness regains the purity of the infinite Parabrahman.

In the *Bhagavad-Gita*, the Blessed Lord declares:

अजोऽपि सन्नव्ययात्मा भूतानामीश्वरोऽपि सन् ।
प्रकृतिं स्वामधिष्ठाय सम्भवाम्यात्ममायया ॥६॥

Although I am unborn (ajah), the Lord of all living entities, and have an imperishable nature (avyaya), yet I appear in this world (sambhavami) by virtue of my divine power (atma-mayaya). (Bhagavad-Gita Chapter 4, Verse 6)

Dr. S. Radhakrishnan explains, "*Yoga Maya* refers to the free will of God, His *sveccha*, His incomprehensible power. The assumption of imperfection by perfection, of lowliness by majesty, of weakness by power is the mystery of the universe. It is *Maya* from the logical standpoint."[4]

Later on, in the eighth chapter of the *Gita*, Karma is defined as a process of creation.

अक्षरं ब्रह्म परमं स्वभावोऽध्यात्মमुच्यते ।
भूतभावोद्भवकरो विसर्गः कर्मसञ्ज्ञितः ॥३॥

The Indestructible Brahman is Supreme (aksaram brahma paramam). His eternal nature (svabhavah) is called the Self (adhyatmam). Actions pertaining to the material personality of living beings and its development (bhuta-bhava-udbhava-karah) are called fruitive activities of creation (visargah karma). (8. 3).

Dr. S. Radhakrishnan explains *svabhava* as *Brahman* assuming the form of *jiva*. In his commentary of this *shloka*, he quotes the *Mandukaya Upanishad* to establish the Absolute Supreme and the living God.

नान्तःप्रज्ञं न बहिष्प्रज्ञं नोभयतःप्रज्ञं न प्रज्ञानघनं
न प्रज्ञं नाप्रज्ञम् । अदृष्टमव्यवहार्यमग्राह्यमलक्षणं
अचिन्त्यमव्यपदेश्यमेकात्मप्रत्ययसारं प्रपञ्चोपशमं
शान्तं शिवमद्वैतं चतुर्थं मन्यन्ते स आत्मा स विज्ञेयः ॥७॥

This (Absolute Supreme) is not that which cognises the internal (objects), not that which cognises the external (objects), not what cognises both of them, not a mass of cognition, not cognitive, not non-cognitive. This is unseen, incapable of being spoken of, ungraspable, without any distinctive marks, unthinkable,

---

4 S. Radhakrishnan, *The Bhagavad Gita*, HarperCollins Publishers India, 2014, p. 178.

unnameable, the essence of the knowledge of oneself, that into which the world is resolved, the peaceful, the benign, the non-dual; such, they think, is the fourth quarter (state of spiritual consciousness). He is the Self; He is to be known.[5]

एष सर्वेश्वरः एष सर्वज्ञ एषोऽन्तर्याम्येष योनिः सर्वस्य
प्रभवाप्ययौ हि भूतानाम् ॥६॥

This (the living God, the indwelling soul) is the Lord of all, this is the knower of all, this is the inner controller, this is the source of all, this is the beginning and end of beings.[6]

Ray Morose brilliantly explains the sameness and difference of the embodied and universal consciousness. "The moment conception occurs... the consciousness pattern can be referred to as being 'numbered'... (an) identifiable uniqueness within creation as consciousness can now be personalised. Although there is consciousness equality, no two (embodied) consciousnesses are identical, as being the same consciousness. Consequently, that singular uniqueness is referred to as being 'numbered', or where your individual primordial awareness 'pin' is stuck within Absolute Consciousness, indicates a non-moving location that implies a 'numbered' or unique position that no other can hold. It ensures no one can ever be what you are..."[7]

As a hired taxi car located by the satellite can be seen on your mobile phone screen, moving towards you from its current location, the soul watches the *karma* of a created entity, not only the human beings, but also all the other objects in the world, the animals, the trees, the rocks and oceans, the natural forces, celestial bodies, including even those which are coming into existence and yet to assume their complete form, the seeds, minerals, fetuses, and so on. As the satellite, stationed in the geo-synchronous orbit, 36000 km above the earth, keeps monitoring all the cars moving on the earth, the universal consciousness never changes, watching the movement

---

5   S. Radhakrishnan, *The Principal Upanishads*, HarperCollins Publishers, India, 2010, p. 698.
6   Ibid, p. 697.
7   Ray Morose, *The Science of Consciousness*, Ocean View Publications, New South Wales, Australia, 2007, p.364.

of the pins as a hired taxi moving towards you.

Lokmanya writes, "The Fundamental Substance, which is covered by this Name and Form, never changes and always remains the same. For instance, by the action of weaving, the name 'thread' disappears, and the name of 'cloth' replaces the same substance. By the action of a potter, the name 'pot' takes the place of the name 'clay'. Therefore, in defining *Maya*, *Karma* or Action, these terms are sometimes not mentioned at all, and only Name and Form are included in describing the *Maya*. However, when one has to consider *Karma* by itself, one has to say that the form of *Karma* is the same as the form of the *Maya*. Therefore, it is more convenient to make it clear in the very beginning that *Maya*, Names and Forms, and *Karma* are fundamentally the same in nature."

Going by the Ray Morose allegory of 'numbered consciousness' as just a 'pin' over the universal consciousness, makes us realise the power that we as human beings have over all other species, that, by our thought and action, we can fall apart, align or fuse with the universal consciousness and can indeed become the instrument of the God. This is indeed possible and can be accomplished by wilfully illuminating our embedded universal nature.

Lokmanya writes, "… the Appearance of a *quality-full Maya* is seen in the one, permanent, all-pervading, and quality-less *Parabrahman*, by the feeble human organs." Taking the discussion to the next level, Lokmanya writes, "Here we are faced with a further question, namely, when, in what order, and why did this *quality-full* Appearance, which is seen by human organs, appear in the *quality-less Parabrahman*? Or rather, to explain this in ordinary language, when and why did the eternal and thought-formed *Parameshvara* create the *Name-d and Form-ed perishable*, and gross universe? But, this subject is unknowable, not only to human beings, but also to gods, and to the *Vedas*, as stated in the *Nasadiya-Sutra* in the *Rig-Veda*."

को अद्धा वेद क इह प्र वोचत्कुत आजाता कुत इयं विसृष्टिः ।
अर्वाग्देवा अस्य विसर्जनेनाथा को वेद यत आबभूव ॥६॥

But, after all, who knows, and who can say
Whence it all came, and how creation happened?

The gods themselves are later than creation.
So who knows truly whence it has arisen?8 (Rig-Veda 10. 129. 6)

Lokmanya declares, "One cannot answer that question better than by saying that this is an unknowable pastime (*Lila*) of the ... *Parabrahman*... One has to take it for granted that ever since the commencement of things, *Name-d and Form-ed perishable Karma*, or *quality-full Maya*, has been seen side by side with the *quality-less Brahman*."

In the famous analogy of the snake-rope illusion in spiritual parlance, the world we perceive is not anymore real than a rope that is seen as a live snake curled in a dark corner of a room where we enter. The 'seeing' of the 'snake' (which is a rope) fills us with fear. Our body trembles, our mind gets paralysed, our heartbeats race and we perspire. Then light penetrates; we can now see that the 'snake' is actually a harmless rope. The darkness around superimposed the 'snake' on the rope. The 'snake' never existed. As soon as the light of knowledge of the reality dawns to show us the rope, the illusory snake disappears.

Pure Consciousness in the human body acts as the three phases of electricity in a wire. Three conductors carry alternating current voltages that are offset in time by one-third of the cycle time, say 50 times a second. The loads are distributed between the phases as evenly as is practical. Similarly, there are three ways a human being is conscious. He lives in either the wakeful state, the dream state or the deep sleep state, at any given point of time. When the consciousness is energising the physical body in action, a person is said to be in the wakeful state. When the consciousness is expressing itself through the subtle body, comprised of the sensory inputs collected during waking times and inverted over upon the mind, mixed up with the intellect and the life force movement in the sleeping body, a person becomes a dreamer and when the consciousness even further withdraws inward, now only expressing through the causal body, a person goes into the deep sleep state.

Extending this logic, our real nature, therefore, is divine– the

---

8 http://www.mircea-eliade.com/from-primitives-to-zen/056.html

deep sleep state. We are pure, perfect, and eternally free. We can even say that we do not have to become *Brahman*; we already are *Brahman*. But we do not say that as we are possessed by our ever-wandering mind controlled by the powerful impulses of our body. The concept of *Maya* is helpful here. *Maya* is described as the veil that covers our real nature and it even masks the real nature of the world around us, best exemplified by the character of Dhritarashtra in the *Mahabharata*, who could never see the folly of his sons, and the character of his wife Gandhari, who covered her eyes for life, in self-denial. *Maya* indeed exists and began right at the beginning of creation.

The *Bhagavad-Gita* calls *Maya* the creation of the God. The Blessed Lord declares it as "My *Maya* (*mama maya*)" to entrap human beings in the matrix of *Prakrti*, as a supreme test of their cognition ability bestowed only and uniquely upon them.

दैवी ह्येषा गुणमयी मम माया दुरत्यया ।
मामेव ये प्रपद्यन्ते मायामेतां तरन्ति ते ॥१४॥

The Blessed Lord reveals to Arjuna that He created Maya, consisting of the three modes of material nature (gunamayi). It is supernatural (daivi) and therefore very difficult to overcome by the mortals (duratyaya). Only those who surrender unto me (mam eva ye prapadyante) can cross over it (taranti).
(Bhagavad-Gita Chapter 7, Verse 14)

प्रकृतिं पुरुषं चैव विद्ध्यनादी उभावपि ।
विकारांश्च गुणांश्चैव विद्धि प्रकृतिसम्भवान् ॥१९॥

The Blessed Lord tells Arjuna that both, prakrti (material nature) and purusha (the living entity) are eternal. It is the material energy that keeps on transforming itself through the three modes of nature, causing pain or pleasure to the living entities. (Bhagavad-Gita Chapter 13, Verse 19)

Eknath Easwaran writes, "These are very difficult concepts to understand, because we identify so thoroughly with the field of matter and mind. The *Gita* reminds us over and over that actions occur only within the field; thoughts take place only in the field. Yet the field itself is inert. There is no consciousness in this field of matter and mind, which means that the mind does not really enjoy anything of itself; the intellect can really not analyse; the senses cannot experience. Only the Self, pure consciousness, the same in all, can be said to see, enjoy and understand."[9].

Lokmanya writes, "*Karma* is the activity which is to be seen in the fundamental quality-less *Brahman*, at the time when the visible world began to be created out of the Imperceptible.

Lokmanya cites the *Brihadaranyaka Upanishad*. A debate that happened in the court of Raja Janaka, between Yajnavalkya and Gargi Vachaknavi, a venerated woman seer, on the issue of who is the actual doer behind all the action in this world, is included in the *Upanishad* (third Chapter, eight *Brahmana*). Gargi asked Yajnavalkya two questions. The first question of Gargi was, "What is that on which the things in heaven and on earth and beneath the earth and between earth and heaven that people call past, present and future, are woven like warp and woof?" Yajnavalkya answered that these are all woven on the space. When Gargi asked the second question, "On what is the space woven back and forth?", Yajnavalkya answered, "It is the Imperishable."

एतस्य वा अक्षरस्य प्रशासने गार्गि सूर्याचन्द्रमसौ विधृतौ तिष्ठतः।
द्यावापृथिव्यौ विधृते तिष्ठतः।
निमेषा मुहूर्ता अहोरात्राण्यर्धमासा
मासा ऋतवः संवत्सरा इति विधृतास्तिष्ठन्ति।
प्राच्योऽन्या नद्यः स्यन्दन्ते श्वेतेभ्यः पर्वतेभ्यः
प्रतीच्योऽन्या यां यां च दिशमनु।
ददतो मनुष्याः प्रशंसन्ति

This is the Imperishable, at whose command the sun and the moon stand apart
The earth and the sky stand apart

---

9 Eknath Easwaran, *The Bhagavad Gita for Daily Living*, Jaico Publishing House, Mumbai, India, 2007, Vol. III, p. 93.

The seconds and hours, days and nights, fortnights
Months, seasons and years stand apart
Rivers flow from the snowy mountains
In their respective directions
People flatter donors
Gods are dependent on patrons of sacrifices, and forefathers on ancestral offerings.

Lokmanya writes, "... the energy of *Karma* is never destroyed, and the energy which appears today under one Name and Form, reappears under another Name and Form when the former Name and Form has been destroyed. Moreover, if the sentient cannot escape taking up other Names and Forms after one Name and Form has been destroyed, one cannot definitely say that these various subsequent Names and Forms will be lifeless, and that it is not possible for them to be something different... One has to suffer tomorrow for what one does today, and day after tomorrow, for what one does tomorrow. Rather, one has to suffer in the next birth for what one does in this birth. In this way, the cycle of the universe is continually going on."

Lokmanya returns to the story of Bhishma, shared in the earlier chapter. Pierced all over his body with arrows, Bhishma is waiting on a 'bed of arrows' for the auspicious time of his death and Yudhishthira approaches his learned grandfather, asking him to share his wisdom. During one such session, Yudhishthira asks Bhishma about the realm of the afterlife.

Bhishma tells Yudhishthira:

पापं कर्म कृतं किंचिद्यदि तस्मिन्न दृश्यते ।
नृपते तस्य पुत्रेषु पौत्रेष्वपि च नप्तृषु ॥

Although a particular man may not be seen to suffer the results of his evil actions in his life, the suffering returns in new life forms– as sons, grandsons, great-grandsons and so on.
(Shanti Parva 129.20)

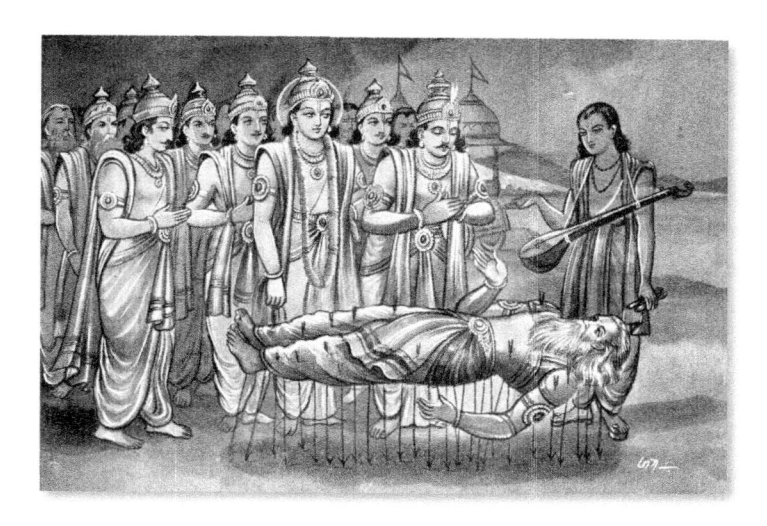

Karma does not die with the body. When the soul enters a new human body, it brings along with it, the list of lessons that one is meant to acquire in that particular lifetime so that the soul can advance to a higher level of consciousness. Each life is, therefore, a course and unless it is mastered and the exam passed, promotion to the next class is indeed ruled out.

In a concept that is unparalleled to any other theosophical doctrine in the world, *Vedanta* fixes the responsibility of one's action upon him and places the God beyond the meanderings of the petty affairs of this world and the pleadings of people made out of their vested interests. Though every thing exists within the God, yet the results depend on the worth of the action, non-action, or bad action taken by the free-willed person. God is in this way unconcerned to what one decides to do with the littleness of his existence. No one is good or bad before the God. The Blessed Lord declares '*samo aham sarva-bhutesu*', I am equally disposed to all living entities.

समोऽहं सर्वभूतेषु न मे द्वेष्योऽस्ति न प्रियः ।
ये भजन्ति तु मां भक्त्या मयि ते तेषु चाप्यहम् ॥२९॥

The Blessed Lord tells Arjuna, "I am equally disposed to all living beings (samo aham sarva-bhutesu). None is hateful (dvesyah) or dear (priyah) to me. But the devotees who worship me (bhajanti mam bhaktya), reside in me and I reside in them (mayite tesu capyaham). (Bhagavad-Gita Chapter 9, Verse 29)

Dr. S. Radhakrishnan writes, "God has no friends or foes. He is impartial. He does not damn any nor elect any by His capricious will. The only way to win His love is by faith and devotion and each must tread the path by himself."[10]

नादत्ते कस्यचित्पापं न चैव सुकृतं विभुः ।
अज्ञानेनावृतं ज्ञानं तेन मुह्यन्ति जन्तवः ॥१५॥

Though present everywhere (vibhuh) the God does not involve himself (naadatte) in the sinful or virtuous deeds of anyone (kasyachitpapam na chaiva sukritam). The living entities are deluded because their inner knowledge is covered by ignorance (ajnanenaavritam). (Bhagavad-Gita Chapter 5, Verse 15)

Swami Mukundananda adds, "God is not responsible either for anyone's virtuous deeds or sinful actions. God's work in this regard is threefold: 1) He provides the soul with the power to act. 2) Once we have performed actions with the power supplied to us, he notes our actions. 3) He gives us the results of our *karmas*."[11]

Lokmanya writes, "The *Parameshvara* does not accept either the sin or the meritorious action of anybody and so the cycle of the inherent effects of *Karma* or *Maya* is continually going on. Each created being has to suffer happiness or unhappiness according to its own Action.

It is not possible for human reason to explain when *Karma* was first started in the world, by the desire of the *Parameshvara*, or when man first came within the clutches of *Karma*. However, inasmuch as the further consequences or fruits of *Karma* are found to result according to the laws of *Karma*, human 'Reason' can come to the definite conclusion, that every living being has been caught in the prison of eternal *Karma* in the shape of Names and Forms, from the very commencement of the world."

---

10 S. Radhakrishnan, The Bhagavad-Gita, HarperCollins Publishers India, 2014, p. 296.
11 http://www.holy-bhagavad-gita.org/chapter/5/verse/15. Last accessed on 30 November 2017.

कर्मणा बध्यते जन्तुर्विद्यया तु प्रमुच्यते ।

Jiva is bound by Karma. Only knowledge can release him.
(Mahabharata, Shanti Prava 240.7)

Shri Shankaracharya, in the *Vivekachudamani*, also emphasised that by nothing but knowledge, can one be freed from the snare of *karma*:

नास्त्रैर्न शस्त्रैरनिलेन वह्निना
छेत्तुं न शक्यो न च कर्मकोटिभिः ।
विवेकविज्ञानमहासिना विना
धातुः प्रसादेन सितेन मञ्जुना ॥१४७॥

This bondage can be destroyed neither by weapons nor by wind, nor by fire, nor by millions of acts– by nothing except the great sword of the knowledge and discrimination sharpened by the grace of the Lord (Paramatman).
(Vivekachudamani, Shloka 147)

Shri Shankaracharya adds the grace of God to this knowledge. Lokmanya mentions the German biologist-philosopher Ernst Haeckel (1834–1919), who declared, "The great harmony in the natural system of coordinated adaptations discovered by the naturalist was "the same as that unity and harmony which men, prior to all scientific research, feel and have sensed– a unity and limitlessness that goes by the name of God.""[12] Jain philosophers saw the relation between *karma* and the soul, to the origin of the soul. "The soul has had this karmic matter bondage since eternity. When karmic matter attaches to the soul, it obscures the soul's essential nature of perfect knowledge, perfect vision, bliss, perfect power, eternal existence, equanimity and non-corporeal nature. The different types of *karma* obscure different qualities or attributes of the soul. This is known as *Prakrtibandha*. There are two aspects of the *Prakrtibandha*: the *Ghati Karma*, which subdues the qualities of the soul, and *Aghati Karma*, which relates to the physical body of

---

[12] http://home.uchicago.edu/~rjr6/articles/Richards.pdf. Last accessed on 24 September 2017.

the living beings. When a person destroys all of his *Ghati Karmas*, he attains *Kevaljnana* (absolute knowledge)… However, he continues to live his human life until all his *Aghati Karmas* are destroyed. He attains liberation only after his death at the time that all his *Aghati Karmas* have been destroyed."[13]

Synthesising the materialistic theories of *karma*, Lokmanya writes and uses it as a precursor to explain the purport of the *Gita* on this matter. Lokmanya writes, "A man must go where the cycle of creation drags him. No human being in this world is a free agent to do any particular act… As whatever the act a man does today is the result of what has been done before by him or by his ancestors, it is also never dependent on his will, whether or not to do a particular thing." Lokmanya now presents Arjuna's question and the answer of the Blessed Lord:

अथ केन प्रयुक्तोऽयं पापं चरति पूरुषः ।
अनिच्छन्नपि वार्ष्णेय बलादिव नियोजितः ॥३६॥

Arjuna asks Shri Krishna: By what is a person impelled to commit sinful acts, even unwillingly, as if by force?
(Bhagavad-Gita Chapter 3, Verse 36)

Dr. S. Radhakrishnan explains, "*Anicchannapi*– even against his will. This is what Arjuna feels, that a man is forced to do things even against his will. But it is not really so. Man is indeed driven by his cravings. Dr. Radhakrishnan cites Shri Shankaracharya, "What we speak of as the *prakrti* or the nature of a person; draws him to its course, only through attachment and aversion."[14]

The Blessed Lord replies:

काम एष क्रोध एष रजोगुणसमुद्भवः ।
महाशनो महापाप्मा विद्ध्येनमिह वैरिणम् ॥३७॥

It is the sensual desires; it is anger, energised by the mode of passion (rajo-guna) that creates a most strong craving (maha-

---

13 http://www.jaina.org/?page=KarmaTattvas. Last accessed on 24 September 2017.
14 S. Radhakrishnan, *The Bhagavad Gita*, HarperCollins Publishers India, 2014, p. 169.

sanah) and great sin (maha-papma). Know the sensual desires, therefore, as the greatest enemy (vairinam) of human life in this world. (Bhagavad-Gita Chapter 3, Verse 37)

Lokmanya now raises a question, "If a man is, in this way, not free to do or not to do a particular action, it becomes futile to say that he should improve his conduct in a particular way, or that he should, in a particular manner, realise the identity of the *Brahman* and the *Atman* and purify his intelligence. Like a log, which has fallen in the stream of a river, one must, without demur, go wherever *Maya, Prakrti,* the laws of Creation, or the Stream of *Karma* drags him, whether that is progress or regress. But, the question in hand is not whether there can be a change in the formation of the universe or in human nature. We have, at the moment, to determine whether or not a man is in a position to control or to yield to the inspiration or desire which he has, to bring about such a change."

The *Gita*'s explanation of *Karma* as *Maya*, goes much beyond the 'man reaps what he sows' kind of logical chain. The idea that man is already 'fallen' by his past sins is also not accepted by the *Gita*. In fact, the Blessed Lord calls the *Prakrti,* His own creation and the qualities of *Prakrti* as the *cause de rationale* of all action. In the *Gita*, *karma* is seen as a process, going beyond an individual decision-making. *Karma* is seen as a socio-ethical vector, a force having direction as well as magnitude driving the future of communities, nations and even the races.

Lokmanya writes, "A family, a community, a nation, or even the whole universe cannot escape suffering the consequences of their actions, in the same way that an individual also cannot escape. Inasmuch as every human being is born into some family, some community, or some country, to some extent, he has to suffer on account of the actions of not only itself, but also of the community or society, such as the family etc. to which it belongs."

Swami Vivekananda declared, "All the actions that we see in the world, all the movements in human society, all the works that we have around us, are simply the display of thought, the manifestation of the will of man. Machines or instruments, cities, ships, or men-of-war, all these are simply the manifestation of the will of man, and this will is caused by character, and character is manufactured by *Karma*. As is *Karma*, so is the manifestation of the will. The men of mighty will that the world has produced have all been tremendous workers– gigantic souls, with wills powerful enough to overturn worlds, wills they got by persistent work, through ages, and ages. Such a gigantic will as that of a Buddha or a Jesus could not be obtained in one life, for we know who their fathers were. It is not known that their fathers ever spoke a word for the good of mankind. Millions and millions of carpenters like Joseph had gone; millions are still living. Millions and millions of petty kings like Buddha's father had been in the world. If it was only a case of hereditary transmission, how do you account for this petty prince, who was not, perhaps, obeyed by his own servants, producing this son, whom half a world worships? How do you explain the gulf between the carpenter and his son, whom millions of human beings worship as God? It cannot be solved by the theory of heredity. The gigantic will, which Buddha and Jesus threw over the world, whence did it come? Whence came this accumulation of power? It must have been there through ages and ages, continually growing bigger and bigger, until it burst on society in a Buddha or a Jesus, even rolling down to the present day."[15]

Seeing oneself as a spirit and not as a body and understanding the concept of causal body that travels with the soul through countless bodies, lifetimes, and even life forms, instils a sense of accountability in living in a way so as to settle the debts of one's earlier existence and not to accrue problems and burdens for one's future lives. In a brilliant manner, this understanding provides immense peace to the children born with birth defects, mental impairments and even diseases and illnesses in the later lives as the soul's work in progress. A soul may choose to be born amidst problems as a penance or as a mission. William Alger (1822-1905), who attended Harvard Divinity School from 1844-1847, puts it very beautifully, "After every storm the sun will smile; for every problem there is a solution, and the soul's indefeasible duty is to be of good cheer."[16]

---

15 http://www.vivekananda.net/PDFBooks/KarmaYoga.pdf
16 https://www.brainyquote.com/quotes/quotes/w/williamra393781.html?src=t_soul

Lokmanya writes, "But the division of *Karma*, which one commonly comes across in the subject of the Effects of Actions, is different... *Karma* is divided into *Samchita* (accumulated), *Prarabdha* (commenced), and *Kriymana* (Being-suffered). Whatever action a man has performed till date; whether he has performed it in this birth or in the previous births, is his *Samchita Karma*, i.e., Accumulated *Karma*. This *Samchita* is also known as *Adrashta* (invisible), or... *Apurva* (strange)... Whatever may be said, the words *Samchita*, *Adrashta* or *Apurva* undoubtedly mean the accumulation of the effects of all the various Actions performed upto the moment of performing the last Action."

अनारब्धकार्ये एव तु पूर्वे तदवधेः ॥१५॥

But only those past (virtues and vices) get destroyed which have not begun to bear fruits, for death is set as the limit of waiting for liberation. Vedanta/Brahma Sutra (4. 1. 15) [17]

Is it possible to cancel the effect of accumulated bad *karma*? Annie Wilson, contemporary writer on *Vedanta*, gives a good analogy. "*Samchita karma* is like arrows in the quiver, the result of all *karmas* accumulated in this life and in all previous lives. *Aagami karma* is the portion of *Samchita karma* that is just taken for sprouting. Gradually, if the conditions and the environment are suitable, *Aagami karma* will be converted into *Prarabdha karmas*. These *karmas* are like an arrow mounted on the bow. *Prarabdha karmas* are part of the *Samchita karma* that are in the process of manifestation and ready to be experienced through this life. *Prarabdha karmas* are like an arrow that has already left the bow; which is flying in the sky and about to hit the target. *Kriymana karma* is the current active *karma*. The arrow has just hit the target. The target is experiencing it. The reaction to these experiences creates new *karma*.[18]

---

17 Shankaracharya, Swami Gambhirananda (Translator), *Brahma Sutra Bhashya*, Advaita Ashrama, Kolkata, 2011, p.839
18 http://www.inner-light-in.com/2015/03/karma-theory-in-hinduism/.

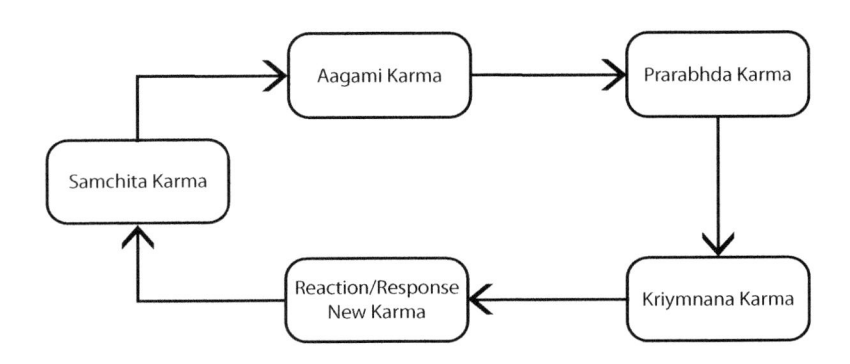

```
                    ┌──────────────┐         ┌──────────────┐
              ┌────▶│ Aagami Karma │────────▶│ Prarabhda Karma│
              │     └──────────────┘         └──────────────┘
    ┌──────────────┐                                  │
    │ Samchita Karma│                                 │
    └──────────────┘                                  ▼
              ▲     ┌──────────────────┐     ┌──────────────┐
              └─────│ Reaction/Response│◀────│Kriymnana Karma│
                    │    New Karma     │     └──────────────┘
                    └──────────────────┘
```

Samchita karma can be mitigated by mindfulness of the Aagami karma. The subconscious mind is the storehouse of Aagami karma. Life provides hundreds of opportunities and challenges. It is up to us how we react to them. If our response is peaceful and humble, the burden of Aagami karma gets lessened. Positive thoughts, determination and will-power can overcome many Aagami karmas.[19]

Lokmanya writes, "*Jnana* (knowledge) is the only way to permanently escape this troublesome cycle, that is to say, to obtain Release. But this *Jnana* does not mean the knowledge of the ordinary things of life, or the knowledge of the creation defined by Names and Forms, but the Realisation of the identity of the *Brahman* and the *Atman*. This is also known as *Vidya (karmanabandhyate januthvidyaya to pramuchate)*… in the same way that a seed, which has been burnt, will not (germinate) take root, so also, when the suffering of (*karma*) has been burnt by *Jnana*, it does not have to be suffered by the *Atman*."

यथैधांसि समिद्धोऽग्निर्भस्मसात्कुरुतेऽर्जुन ।
ज्ञानाग्निः सर्वकर्माणि भस्मसात्कुरुते तथा ॥३७॥

The Blessed Lord tells Arjuna: As the firewood (yatha edhamsi), once kindled, gets reduced to ash (bhasmasat), so does the fire of knowledge (jnana-agnih) burn to ashes all effects of material activities (sarva-karmani). (Bhagavad-Gita Chapter 4, Verse 37)

Lokmanya writes, "*Karma* is, therefore, non-permanent and is

---

19 http://www.inner-light-in.com/2015/03/karma-theory-in-hinduism/

essentially the pastime (*Lila*) of the *Parabrahman*... it can never enslave the *Parabrahman*, (and therefore) the *Atman*, which is fundamentally a part of the *Parabrahman*... gives inspiration to the human mind... Although there is no force in the free vapour, yet, when it is enclosed in a vessel, it begins to exert a pressure on the vessel. In the same way, when the Gross Body is burdened by the previous *Karma*... the *Jiva* (imparts) the desire and inclination to do those actions which can liberate it (the *Jiva*) from this enclosure..."

The Blessed Lord has explained to Arjuna, the *Karma* as a matter of awareness of man about his soul.

उद्धरेदात्मनात्मानं नात्मानमवसादयेत् ।
आत्मैव ह्यात्मनो बन्धुरात्मैव रिपुरात्मनः ॥५॥

Let a man elevate himself by himself and let him not degrade himself. The mind (atmanam, the conditioned soul) can be the friend and also the enemy of the self (bandhuratmaiva ripur).
(Bhagavad-Gita Chapter 6, Verse 5)

This *shloka* clearly brings out the difference between *Atman* (embodied soul of a person) and the *Paramatman* (Universal Self). Dr. S. Radhakrishnan explains, "The Universal Self and the personal self are not antagonistic to each other (They indeed are the same). The Universal Self can be a friend or foe of the personal self. If we subdue our petty cravings and desires, if we do not exert our selfish will, we become the channel of the Universal Self. If our impulses are under control, and if our personal self offers itself to the Universal Self, then the latter becomes our guide and teacher. Every one of us has the freedom to rise or fall and our future is in our own hands."[20]

Lokmanya writes, "One is the owner of oneself and there is no other redeemer for oneself except one's *Atman*... it has in this way been proved that (1) the Realisation of the identity of the *Brahman* and the *Atman* is the most successful method for escaping the bonds of *Karma*, and acquiring the metaphysically perfect state of Realising that there is only one *Atman* in all created beings, and that (2) it is

---

20 S. Radhakrishnan, *The Bhagavad Gita*, HarperCollins Publishers India, 2014, p. 221.

within the control of everybody to acquire that Realisation; yet, we must also remember the second fact, that even this independent *Atman* cannot get rid of this mill-stone of *Prakrti* round its neck in a moment."

Just as a merchant starts business with whatever little capital he has, and gradually acquires vast wealth by such business, so also is the case of the practice of *Karma Yoga* prescribed in the *Gita*. This *Karma Yoga* has got to be started by exercising as much control over the organs as is possible, and thereby, gradually, more and more control over the organs is acquired. At the same time, it is also not proper to sit in a gossiping place... (where) the habit of concentration, which has been acquired by the 'Mind', is likely to be weakened. Therefore, when one is continually practising *Karma Yoga*, it is necessary to spend sometime every day in solitude.

मयि चानन्ययोगेन भक्तिरव्यभिचारिणी ।
विविक्तदेशसेवित्वमरतिर्जनसंसदि ॥१०॥

Shri Krishna is telling Arjuna what is needed for the purification of the inner apparatus of the mind and intellect: Constant and exclusive devotion to Me (mayi chananya-yogena bhaktir) with wholehearted discipline (avyabhicharinī), resort to solitary places (vivikta-desha), aversion for mundane society (jana-sansadi). (Bhagavad-Gita Chapter 13, Verse 10)

Lokmanya writes, "The *Atman* is immortal and the impressions received by it in this life are not destroyed... perfection (comes) after many births... (nevertheless) even a little practice of this method redeems a person of great danger (*svalpamapyasya dharmasya trayate mahato bhayat*). Lokmanya cites this *shloka* from the *Maitryayaniya Upanishad*:

मन एव मनुष्याणां कारणं बन्धमोक्षयोः ।
बन्धाय विषयासङ्गी मोक्षो निर्विषयं स्मृतम् ॥

Mind is the only (eva) cause of both, the bondage and liberation

of a man (bandha-mokshayoh). Till such a time that the mind of a man is enslaved to the objects of pleasure (vishayasangim), he is trapped (in the endless cycle of life and death); freedom from these objects (nirvisaya) is called liberation (moksha).
(Maitryayaniya Upanishad (6.34))

Lokmanya asserts, "*Karma* is not destroyed by becoming homeless (*niragni*), i.e., through Renunciation (*samnyasa*), and by giving up sacrificial ritual to fire etc., nor is it destroyed by remaining action-less (*akriya*) i.e., by remaining idle without performing any action whatsoever. Whether a man desires it or not, the wheel of Matter will go on and therefore, man must also move round and round with it. However, the man who does not dance as a dependent on Matter, like an ignorant person, but keeps his mind steady and pure through control of the organs, and performs all action which befall him in the ordinary course of life, as a duty merely, and calmly, and without allowing his mind to become attached, is the true emotionless (*virakta*) man, the true Steady-in-Mind (*sthitaprajna*), and the one who may be said to be truly merged in the *Brahman*."

The Blessed Lord tells Arjuna:

न कर्मणामनारम्भान्नैष्कर्म्यं पुरुषोऽश्नुते ।
न च संन्यसनादेव सिद्धिं समधिगच्छति ॥४॥

By not doing one's prescribed work, freedom from karmic reactions (naiskarmyam) cannot be achieved. By giving up action, no one can attain perfection (siddhim samadhigacchati).
(Bhagavad-Gita Chapter 3, Verse 4)

Swami Vivekananda explains this *shloka* as: "(Shri) Krishna strikes another note as a teacher of intense activity. Work, work, work (all through the) day and night, says the *Gita*. You may ask, "Then, where is peace? If all through life I am to work like a cart-horse and die in harness, what I am here for?" (Shri) Krishna says, "Yes, you will find peace. Flying from work is never the way to find peace. (Even if you) Throw off your duties… and go to the top of a mountain; even there the mind is going– whirling, whirling, whirling (the mind must be stabilised)."[21]

Lokmanya now takes up a very important point– the ritualistic worship (*puja*) that is so prevalent amongst the Hindus. Uttering the *mantras* with reference to some deity, and offering sesame, rice, or animals into the sacrificial fire is useless. What is important is to offer up animal tendencies like desire, anger etc., which are in everybody's body, by way of sacrifice, into the fire of mental control, in the shape of an equable frame of mind, rather than to (make offerings like) slaughtering animals... Lokmanya writes, "That man alone who has burnt this seed of mine-ness in his ordinary activities, by maintaining an equable frame of mind towards all created things, is Blessed."

Puja and rituals are ways of developing a sense of connection with the divine and nothing more. What could anyone give to God? What is it that the God needs from anyone He himself created? *Puja* and rituals are, therefore, an expression of our desire to connect ourselves to the God. American Yogi Prem Prakash said it nicely, "What is important is not the specific manner in which God is worshipped, but the degree to which the devotee is filled with love... Each soul has its own note to sing in the divine chorus and no voice is more important than another." [22]

Shri Krishna says in the *Bhagavad-Gita*:

पत्रं पुष्पं फलं तोयं यो मे भक्त्या प्रयच्छति ।
तदहं भक्त्युपहृतमश्नामि प्रयतात्मनः ॥२६॥

With devotion, whoever offers to Me a leaf, a flower, a fruit, or water, I delightfully partake of that article offered with love by my devotee (bhakti-upahrtam) in pure consciousness (prayata-atmanah). (Bhagavad-Gita Chapter 9, Verse 26)

Swami Vivekananda narrated the story of the boy Gopala as the example of devotion the God seeks. "So she (Gopala's Mother) bathed and dressed the image (of the God), burned incense before it,

---

21 *Swami Vivekananda: Complete Works*, 4.130, In: Swami Madhurananda (Compiler), 'Bhagavad Gita as viewed by Swami Vivekananda', Advaita Ashrama, Kolkata, Seventh Reprint, 2016, p. 62.
22 Prem Prakash, *The Yoga of Spiritual Devotion A Modern Translation of the Narada Bhakti Sutras*, Inner Tradition, Rochester, Vermont, USA, 1998, p. 48-49, 94.

and for offering?– Oh, she was so poor!– but with tears in her eyes, she remembered her husband reading from the books: "I accept with gladness even leaves and flowers, fruits and water; whatever is offered with love", and she offered: "Thou, for whom the world of flowers bloom, accept my common flowers. You, who feed the universe, accept my poor offering of fruits. I am weak. I am ignorant. I do not know how to approach Thee, how to worship Thee, my God... let my worship be pure, my love for Thee, selfless; and if there is any virtue in worship, let it be Yours, grant me only love, love that never asks for anything– 'never seeks for anything but love'".[23]

Swami Vivekananda says in *Bhakti-Yoga*, "Throughout the history of the world, we find that man is trying to grasp the abstract through thought-forms, or symbols. All the external manifestations of religion– bells, music, rituals, books, and images– come under that head. Anything that appeals to the senses, anything that helps man to form a concrete image of the abstract, is taken hold of, and worshipped. It is vain to preach against the use of symbols, and why should we preach against them? There is no reason why man should not use symbols. They have them in order to represent the ideas signified behind them."[24]

The *Gita* nowhere mentions giving up Action for the sake of 'Release'. The message of the *Gita* is, giving up the reward of action.

काम्यानां कर्मणां न्यासं संन्यासं कवयो विदुः ।
सर्वकर्मफलत्यागं प्राहुस्त्यागं विचक्षणाः ॥२॥

Actions motivated by desires are to be given up (kamyanam karmanam nyasam). Relinquishing the fruits of all actions is what the learned declare to be tyaga.
(Bhagavad-Gita Chapter 18, Verse 2)

A.C. Bhaktivedanta Swami Prabhupada explains, "The performance of activities for results has to be given up. This is the

---
23 *Swami Vivekananda: Complete Works*, 5.168, In: Swami Madhurananda (Compiler), 'Bhagavad Gita as viewed by Swami Vivekananda', Advaita Ashrama, Kolkata, Seventh Reprint, 2016, p. 118.
24 http://www.ramakrishnavivekananda.info/vivekananda/volume_2/bhakti_or_devotion.htm. Last accessed on 24 September 2017.

instruction of the *Bhagavad-Gita*... Sacrifices prompted by desires should be stopped. However, sacrifice for the purification of one's heart or for advancement in the spiritual science (is a different matter and therefore such pursuits) should not be given up."[25]

It is important to take a look at this tri-junction. The path of sensory enjoyment (*Pravrtti-marga*) keeps the *jiva* trapped forever in the cycle of birth and death, suffering and misery. As all material desires create even more desires, a man keeps on sinking in despondency while making his best efforts to achieve material success. Then there is a path of renunciation (*Nivrtti-marga*). It declares Action as an inevitable force that keeps expanding itself, like entropy in a thermodynamic system. Before the *Gita*, *Vedanta* declared *Nivrtti-marga* superior over *Pravrtti-marga* and the best of the people left their prescribed actions to live a life of renunciation, causing decay of the entire Indian civilisation and its helplessness to defend itself from petty invaders and scheming merchants. The third path is that of *Karma Yoga*, which rejects the escape from Action on the *Nivrtti-marga* and the pursuit of materialistic happiness on the *Pravrtti-marga*. The *Gita* starts with the mighty and most skilled Arjuna desperate to take up *Nivrtti-marga* rather than fight his unscrupulous teachers, elder family members and others who wronged not only him, but also his entire clan and the people by their tyranny. The Blessed Lord Shri Krishna then shows Arjuna the path of *Karma Yoga* where *Bhakti* replaces *Pravrtti*. He exhorts him to fight against the tyrants, which is the *Dharma* of a warrior like him, but not in order to gain kingdom or wealth or glory, but as a duty, after surrendering the results of his efforts, and even himself, to the pleasure of the God.

This state of being, the *Karma* with *Bhakti*, is called the Brahmified (*brahma-bhuta*) state. Such an Action does not incur *Karmic* consequences. Shri Shankaracharya writes that this is the most Supreme or the most complete state of the Realisation of the Absolute Self.

---

25 https://asitis.com/18/2.html

न च कार्ये प्रतिपत्त्याभिसंधिः ॥१४॥

Moreover, the firm resolution about attainment is not concerned with what exists (the perceptible Brahman). (But devoted to the Supreme Lord who has created both, the perceptible and the imperceptible Brahman) Vedanta/Brahma Sutra 4. 3. 14.[26]

Lokmanya adds, "In order to acquire this (*brahma-bhuta*) state, a man must be said to have become *Parameshvara* in a way. It need not be said further, that persons who have thus become Brahmified, may be said to have gone beyond the rules of what should be done and what should not be done, in the world of Actions. As the realisation of the *Brahman* is always awake in the case of these people, whatever they do is always inspired by a pure and desireless frame of mind. It is always free from sin or merit. As it is not necessary to go somewhere else or to die in order to attain *Brahman* after this state has been reached, such a Steady-in-Mind devotee of the *Brahman* (*stithaprajnabrahmanihstha*) is known as *jivan-mukta* (birth released)… It is the ultimate ideal of man."

ॐ

---

26 Shankaracharya, Swami Gambhirananda (Translator), Brahma Sutra Bhashya, Kolkata: Advaita Ashrama, 2011, p.882.

11

Good by Choice

> The purpose of life is not to be happy. It is to be useful, to be honourable, to be compassionate, to have it make some difference that you have lived and lived well.
>
> *Ralph Waldo Emerson*

> God is a lawgiver, but he is not a tyrant. God has given freedom to the whole of his creation– not just humanity, but to the whole physical world in some appropriate way.
>
> *John Polkinghorne*[1]

Our life on Earth is short. And if our life is going to end one day, then what are we living for? What is the purpose of life? Is there any real meaning to life? No one is unaware about their mortality. Every day, people die, some of old age and disease. Even young people die in accidents and misadventures. There are calamities taking lives in large numbers. And yet, most of us live with a grand pretention that we are here forever and pick up quarrels and most trivial disagreements and safeguard imaginary territories. Very few people bother to examine if there is a purpose to their lives. Even fewer look for a meaning to their lives. When Socrates declared, "The unexamined life is not worth living for a human being,"[2] he was clear that knowing the purpose of life is the most important thing, not only for philosophers, but also for laypersons. Who is more successful– the rich, the powerful, the famous, the scientist, the philosopher, the enlightened, or the seer? Neither is it possible for anyone to take

---

[1] John Charlton Polkinghorne (b. 1930) is an English theoretical physicist and theologian.
[2] http://www.sjsu.edu/people/james.lindahl/courses/Phil70A/s3/apology.pdf, p. 20, Last accessed on 9 October 2017.

any of the riches beyond one's life, nor can renunciation be the anticlimax of the world which is buzzing with action.

Also, human suffering is one of life's most compelling mysteries. The entire edifice of religion and God as the saviour is created around this question. Why do the innocent suffer? Why does God permit evil? Is God helpless to act, or does he choose not to? Can God be approached and begged for help and redemption? And if God chooses not to act, does that mean God is cruel? Or is God merely indifferent? And are we all condemned to suffer for what we have already done? The feeling of being a mere puppet in the hands of someone we can't even see is too scary and unsettling. This chapter offers a very convincing answer to these troubling questions and brings a feeling of peace and completion.

Lokmanya opens this chapter with these words, "In the last chapter, we have considered in detail the position that there is only one way in which one can escape the toils of eternal *Karma*; by Realising the *Parabrahman*, which exists in all created things. (To) the question whether man is or is not free to realise that immortal *Brahman*... how he should perform the transient affairs of Actions in the *Maya*-world, in order to obtain the Realisation... the conclusions are drawn that bondage is not the characteristic feature of action, but of the mind. By performing the actions with a pure, that is, with a disinterested frame of mind, after having gradually reduced the attachment which one has for the fruits of action, the Realisation of the *Atman*, in the shape of an equable frame of mind, gradually saturates the corporeal organs, and complete Release is ultimately obtained."

Many modern thinkers saw the mind as a radio and thoughts as electromagnetic waves carrying information loaded signals. The mind can receive and transmit thoughts. This explains well how people are connected with strong mental bonds, though physically separated by large distances. It also explains the mental chasm between two people living under the same roof. Earlier considered esoteric, a phenomenon like telepathy makes sense with this understanding of the tuning of two minds like a radio. Expanding the analogy further, it is important that the radio is tuned well to the frequency of the transmitter and filters out all other frequencies. Through history and across traditions, it has been emphasised that free will is bestowed upon man by God so that he can deliberately, wilfully, and repeatedly use it to align with the will of God and become an instrument of God in the process, as brilliantly put by Saint Francis of Assisi (1182– 1226): "Lord, make me an instrument of your peace: where there is hatred, let me sow love; where there is injury, pardon; where there is doubt, faith; where there is despair, hope; where there is darkness, light; where there is sadness, joy."[3] Such a mind does not any longer remain a prisoner of this world, but becomes an agent of God's unfolding plan for humanity.

In this chapter, Lokmanya considers the next logical question, which is, whether by aligning our free will to the God's will and thereby accruing no further karma, one must stop participating in the affairs of the world or engage with it as an instrument of God? Does the will of God about a man end with his renunciation? Can the liberated soul be indifferent to the welfare of the world? Is it justifiable for a *samnyasi* to get lost in seclusion without caring anymore for the world? By becoming indifferent to what the world needs, will we not fall short of doing our duty to it?

The Realisation of the *Atman*, in its truest description, goes beyond an intellectual comprehension of the experience. It is not about seeking God, speculating, or theologically theorizing about God or his Ultimate Being-ness. The Realisation of the *Atman* means the first-hand, intimate, mystical experience of God's Presence or Oneness with the Universe. It is the being-ness with the Ultimate Being-ness, *Paramatman* itself.

If all that is being stated is accurate, it would seem that experiencing the Realisation of the *Atman* would be the end of a journey through countless lifetimes for the soul; it would be the individualised expression of Ultimate Being-ness, Consciousness, Spirit or God. What else is there? If, in the next moment, one would suddenly experience Enlightenment, would life come to an abrupt halt? Would an infinite field of light swallow up one's soul, with one's physical body vanishing as a result?

---

3 https://www.loyolapress.com/our-catholic-faith/prayer/traditional-catholic-prayers/saints-prayers/peace-prayer-of-saint-francis. Last accessed on 9 October 2017.

History is full of Self-realised people who appeared in different time-space coordinates to teach spiritually ignorant people, blinded with belief in religious dogma, the examples of how to live and deal with the world so as to evolve and not just live. Guru Nanak Dev (1469– 1539), Sant Kabir (1440-1518), Desmond Tutu (b. 1931); they are all Realised souls who made transformation of the people around them as their mission. As the legend goes, even Gautama Buddha, who initially decided to live in peace after attaining enlightenment, was asked by Lord Brahma to engage with the people, who live with 'dust in their eyes', and clear their vision. It is indeed a historic fact that Buddha travelled widely for forty-five years and dealt with kings, robbers, the arrogant and brute lay people, and even the courtesan Amrapali.

Buddha was unsure if he should teach his insights of enlightenment to anyone. The deity Brahma appeared before the Buddha and made him survey the world with Divine-vision and see human beings like lotuses at various stages of growth, some indeed likely to understand the truth. Buddha then decided to teach and carried out this mission for the next forty-five years, till his last day.

Sadhguru Jaggi Vasudev (b. 1957) puts it very succinctly, "If you want to work with anything, for example, let us say you want to drive your motorcycle or car. The better you grasp what the machine is, the more control and freedom it gives you as to what you can do with it... The more you know about this piece of life, which you refer to as 'myself', the better your grasp over this and the better your ability to handle it, which definitely gives you more access to life... Do not think of self-realisation as some weird thing that some yogi does in a Himalayan cave. It is not about that. It is just that you want to live your life with certain ease, you have to know this piece of life. The more you know about this piece of life, which you refer to as "myself," the better your grasp over this and the better your ability to handle it, which definitely gives you more access to life. In other words, self-realisation is a way of knowing this piece of life in a much better way than the way you currently know it."[4]

It is therefore clear that Self-realisation does not end the engagement of the Realised soul with the world. The question then arises that what sort of interaction the realised soul could have with the world of desires. One possible explanation is that Realised souls could express the energy of their 'Experience', enabling those around them to live better. But then, what makes a living better? It is seen across time and space that the expression of greater love and creativity has a radiating effect and it indeed engulfs the sentient beings around. So much so, that when one stumbles or appears to fail, the presence of a Self-realised person in one's life can raise one to a higher plateau of consciousness. In that way, the mere presence of Self-realised souls in the world is beneficial to the people. What could be this higher plateau of consciousness? The laws of physics don't change at 100 degrees Celsius, as they are exactly the same all the time. However, according to physicists, the consequences of the laws of physics change quite radically as we move from a liquid phase into a gaseous phase. The higher plateau of consciousness must be understood in the same sort of way.

Lokmanya writes, "It would not have been sufficient to say to Arjuna that after the Realisation of the *Brahman*, it is just the same whether one performs or does not perform 'Action'. A man, whose 'Reason' has become equable towards all created beings as a result of Knowledge, is not affected by the merit or demerit

---

[4] http://isha.sadhguru.org/blog/yoga-meditation/demystifying-yoga/what-does-self-realization-mean/. Last accessed on 5 December 2017.

of any action. 'Reason' is superior to 'Action' in all affairs of life. The definite injunction of the Blessed Lord to Arjuna was: Fight! (*yudhyasva!*)... The doctrine of the *Gita* has come into existence only in order to explain why a wise man must perform a particular act, notwithstanding the fact that he sees before his eyes terrible consequences of the same. This is, indeed, the most important feature of the *Gita*."

अन्तवन्त इमे देहा नित्यस्योक्ताः शरीरिणः ।
अनाशिनोऽप्रमेयस्य तस्माद्युध्यस्व भारत ॥१८॥

Only the material body is perishable (antavantah); the embodied soul within is indestructible, immeasurable, and eternal (anasinahaprameyasya, nityasya). For this reason, (Shri Krishna tells Arjuna) fight, O descendent of Bharat. (Bhagavad-Gita Chapter 2, Verse 18)

Lokmanya now returns to Chapter 3 of the *Bhagavad-Gita* and builds a rational argument preferring action to renunciation, after the realisation of the *Atman*. Lokmanya writes, "...in the commencement of the third chapter (of the *Gita*, Arjuna had told Shri Krishna), "If, in Your opinion, the desireless or equable frame of mind is superior to action, I shall make my 'Reason' pure like that of a *Sthitaprajna*; why do You compel me to perform a terrible act like war?""

ज्यायसी चेत्कर्मणस्ते मता बुद्धिर्जनार्दन ।
तत्किं कर्मणि घोरे मां नियोजयसि केशव ॥१॥

(A confused Arjuna asks Shri Krishna), O Keshava, if you consider knowledge (buddhih) as superior to action (karmanas), then why are you engaging me in this ghastly action (kimkarmani ghore mam niyojayasi)? (Bhagavad-Gita Chapter 3, Verse 1)

Lokmanya writes, "This question of Arjuna is not something new. In the Yoga-Vashistha, Shri Rama has asked the same question to Rishi Vashistha, and in the Ganesha-*Gita*, the king named Varenya has asked the same question to Shri Ganesha. It even appears from the works of Aristotle that this question had been raised in very ancient times in Greece, where philosophical ideas first originated (in the Western world)."

Throughout the history of human civilisation, thinkers have answered these questions in mainly two ways. One way traversed through abstract concepts such as being, knowing, identity, time and space. It can be called the metaphysical inquiry. The second way navigated through the moral principles that would govern a person's behaviour to take up an activity or not. Both ways are, indeed, valid. A true understanding of *Karma Yoga* lies not in choosing the right action over the wrong action, but taking action in an equable frame of mind when the two interests collide. And, an equable frame of mind is to act anchored in 'Reason', but not wavered by the favourable or unfavourable result of the action. In this way, the body and mind are actively employed in discharging the duties that fall to one's lot in life. Swami Vivekananda famously said, "The very reason for nature's existence is for the education of the soul... It is the worker who is attached to results who grumbles about the nature of the duty which has fallen to his lot; to the unattached worker, all duties are equally good, and form efficient instruments with which selfishness and sensuality may be killed, and the freedom of the soul secured."

Lokmanya writes, "The importance of the clear statement in the *Gita* that *karma karmajyayohyakarmanah*, action is superior to non-action, becomes clear to the reader."

नियतं कुरु कर्म त्वं कर्म ज्यायो ह्यकर्मणः ।
शरीरयात्रापि च ते न प्रसिध्येदकर्मणः ॥८॥

Perform your prescribed work (niyatam karma), since action is superior to inaction (karma jyayohyakarmanah). By ceasing activity, even your bodily maintenance (sharira yatraapi) will not be possible. (Bhagavad-Gita Chapter 3, Verse 8)

In this verse, we can see the high regard that Shri Krishna has for work. The work, in this context, is a person's *dharma*, his sacred duty. To perform what is expected of us is required. We cannot avoid it. To work is important because it will be our way of maintaining this body.

Before comparing the options of living the life of a renunciate and a life of action in the world, which has been a major theme of the *Gita*, Lokmanya briefly writes about Western philosophy, as if setting up a calibration mark.

He cites the French philosopher Auguste Comte (1798–1857), who was of the opinion that, "It is misleading to say that it is better to spend one's life in the contemplation of philosophy; and the philosopher, who adopts such a course of life, and abandons the doing of whatever public welfare it is possible for him to do, must be said to misuse the material which is at his disposal." Lokmanya also cites the English philosophers Herbert Spencer (1820–1903), John Stuart Mill (1806–1873) and others, who were of the same opinion as Comte. He writes, "But the modern materialistic philosopher Friedrich Nietzsche (1844–1900), has gone beyond all these philosophers. He has, in his works, so severely criticised those who are for giving up action, that according to him, it is not possible to refer to the supporters of Renunciation (*karma-samnyasa*) by any milder terms than 'fools of fools'."

According to Dr. S. Radhakrishnan, "Renunciation and detachment are closely related and are mentioned together. Through detachment, subjection of the self with its desires (is possible) and through renunciation, the state beyond all work can be reached. Because of this close relationship between renunciation and detachment, they are understood as one virtue that stands out above all others in the *Gita*. It is… an important virtue because it leads to peace, freedom and integration of the self (*jiva*) with the Self (*Atman*). Renunciation of the fruit is better than renunciation (of action) because, from the former (renunciation of fruit) flows peace…. Renunciation is not abstention from work, but absence of loathing and desiring. The true worker (*Karma Yogi*) is also the true renouncer (*nitya samnyasi*), for he does his work in a detached spirit… In the popular imagination, *samnyasa* is associated with men with shaven heads, robes of mendicants and a begging bowl, but this is a far cry from the idea of renunciation according to the *Gita*, which invites all men to the spiritual state of renunciation and not to external trappings of wandering mendicants. A life of renunciation implies a life of solitude and disciplined activity."[5]

यदा ते मोहकलिलं बुद्धिर्व्यतितरिष्यति ।
तदा गन्तासि निर्वेदं श्रोतव्यस्य श्रुतस्य च ॥५२॥

One who stays in seclusion (viviktashevee), eats very little (laghvah ashee), regulates speech, body and mind (yata-vak-kaya-manasah), considers meditation as supreme (dhyaanayogaparaha), is fully possessed (samupaashritaha) of dispassion (vairagyam). (Bhagavad-Gita Chapter 2, Verse 52)

Lokmanya writes, "The word '*samnyasa*' does not, in this place, mean 'not marrying', or 'giving up wife and children and wearing saffron-coloured robes'... though Bhishma was a celibate, he was taking part in politics till the moment of his death; and Shri Shankaracharya, after passing straight to the fourth state from the first state of celibacy; or, in Maharashtra, Shri Samartha Ramadasa, remaining a celibate mendicant for life, have brought about the salvation of the world by spreading Knowledge. The crucial point in the present place is whether, after having acquired Knowledge, a man should take part in all the activities of the world as duties and for public welfare, or should entirely give them up, looking upon them as illusory. He who takes part in these activities is the *Karma Yogin*, whether he has married or not, whether he wears white clothes or saffron-coloured clothes. In order to perform these activities, it is sometimes more convenient to remain unmarried or to wear saffron-coloured robes, or to go and live outside town. This is so because, by doing so, there is no obstruction in the way of applying one's whole time and energy to public welfare, as it does not entail the worry of maintaining a family. Though such persons may be ascetics according to the dress which they wear, yet, essentially they are *Karma Yogins*. On the other hand, such persons who look upon all worldly activities as useless, and abandon them and sit quiet, may be said to be ascetics, whether they have entered the fourth state of life."

---

5 Aloysius Michael, *Radhakrishnan on Hindu Moral Life and Action*, Concept Publishing Company, New Delhi, 1979, p. 62.

लोकेऽस्मिन्द्विविधा निष्ठा पुरा प्रोक्ता मयानघ ।
ज्ञानयोगेन साङ्ख्यानां कर्मयोगेन योगिनाम् ॥३॥

The Blessed Lord tells Arjuna about the two-fold ways to live a virtuous life (dvi-vidha)– the path of knowledge (jnana-yogena) for the empiric philosophers (samkhyanam) and the path of activity (karma-yogena) for the men of action (yoginam).
(Bhagavad-Gita Chapter 3, Verse 3)

Expounding on this *shloka*, Swami Vivekananda writes, "(Shri Krishna tells Arjuna), from ancient times, these two systems have come down to us. The *Samkhya* philosophers advance the theory of knowledge. The *Yogins* advance the theory of work... The vast majority of mankind choose... the way through the world, making use of all the bondages themselves to break those bondages. This is also a kind of giving up; only it is done slowly and gradually, by knowing things, enjoying things and thus obtaining experience, and knowing the nature of things until the mind lets them all go at last and becomes unattached. ...There is no cessation of work."[6]

Lokmanya writes that there have been commentators, in whose opinion it is impossible to attain Release unless a man renounces the world and abandons the ordinary activities of life. They have started commenting on the *Gita* with the preconceived notion that the sum and the substance of the doctrine propounded by the *Gita* pronounces that *Karma Yoga* is not an independent path of obtaining Release, but merely a preparatory part of the process. One must, in the beginning, perform actions in order to purify the 'Mind' to eventually go in for Renunciation. Renunciation is the paramount and the ultimate cult. Lokmanya then raises the question, "But if this meaning is adopted, then the importance of the word, *dvividha* (two-fold), in the statement of the Blessed Lord that the *Samkhya* (Samnyasa) and *Yoga* (Karma Yoga) are two kinds of cults in this world, is lost."

Lokmanya now goes on to explain that the word *Karma Yoga* can be interpreted in many different ways. The primary source

---

[6] Swami Vivekananda, *Complete Works*, *1.467 and 1.98*, Advaita Ashram, Seventh Reprint, Kolkata, 2016, p. 61.

of *Dharma* is the *Veda* and when we seek spiritual guidance from the *Veda* we are totally confused by the immensity, obscurity and complexity of the teachings! How do we deal with this vast resource of material? What is significant and what is not? What do I accept and what do I reject? It is in this context that one has recourse to the study of *Mimamsa*, or hermeneutics.[7] The *Gita* does not accept this. Scriptures are unnecessary for the man who has attained insight. The person who has Realised the Supreme passes beyond the range of the *Vedas* and the *Upanishads* (*shabdabramativartate*).

यदा ते मोहकलिलं बुद्धिर्व्यतितरिष्यति ।
तदा गन्तासि निर्वेदं श्रोतव्यस्य श्रुतस्य च ॥५२॥

When your intelligence has passed out of the dense forest of delusion (moha-kalilam), you shall become indifferent (gantasinirvedam) to all that has been heard and all that is to be heard (srotavyasyasrutasya cha)
(Bhagavad-Gita Chapter 2, Verse 52) (2.52)

त्रैगुण्यविषया वेदा निस्त्रैगुण्यो भवार्जुन ।
निर्द्वन्द्वो नित्यसत्त्वस्थो निर्योगक्षेम आत्मवान् ॥४५॥

The Vedas expounded on the threefold mode of material nature (traigunya), but do you become free? Be free from the pair of opposites (nirdvandvah) and firmly fix your mind in purity (nistraigunyah). Established in the Self (atmavan), do not care for the acquisition of the new and preservation of the old (niryoga-ksemah) of the worldly objects.
(Bhagavad-Gita Chapter 2, Verse 45)

Dr. S. Radhakrishna elaborates on *nityasattva* mentioned in this *shloka*, "Ritualistic practices necessary for the maintenance of worldly life are the results of the modes (of *Prakrti*). To gain the higher reward of perfection, we must direct our attention to the Supreme Reality. The conduct of the liberated, however, will be outwardly the same as

---

7 http://www.srimatham.com/uploads/5/5/4/9/5549439/mimamsa.pdf. Last accessed on 5 December 2017.

that of one who is in the *sattva* condition. His action will be calm and disinterested. He acts with no interests in the fruits of activity; not so the followers of the *karmakanda* of the *Veda*." [8]

The alternative interpretation of *Karma Yoga* could be the undertaking of actions for the purification of the 'Mind' and it is therefore seen as the preliminary preparation for Renunciation. The *Gita* does not accept this too. Action ought to be performed after one has acquired Knowledge, with a disinterested frame of mind, depending upon one's station and stage in life, to maintain order in the society and for the good of all people.

सक्ताः कर्मण्यविद्वांसो यथा कुर्वन्ति भारत ।
कुर्याद्विद्वांस्तथासक्तश्चिकीर्षुर्लोकसंग्रहम् ॥२५॥

(Shri Krishna tells Arjuna) As ignorant people (avidvamsah) perform their duties with attachment to the results (saktahkarmany), O scion of Bharat, so should the wise act without attachment (asaktah), for the sake of maintaining the world-order and good of the people (loka-sangraham)
(Bhagavad-Gita Chapter 3, Verse 25)

Mahatma Gandhi explains, "One must work. Just as ignorant people do, except that they work with attachment. We too must take up a pick-axe and work like them. A wise man should be industrious and work as hard as others; only he should work for the world disinterestedly, and without attachment. If we spin for the poor without attachment to our work, we will serve our own good and theirs. If we work in this spirit, we are persons of spiritual knowledge and, though working, we are doing nothing. Does a person who has kept the *ekadashi* fast commit a sin by cooking? He or she cooks in a disinterested spirit, for the children and guests."[9]

Contemporary *Bhakti Yoga* saint Swami Mukundananda clarifies, "In this verse, the expression *saktahavidvansah* has been used for people who are attached to worldly pleasures, but who still have full faith in the *Vedic* rituals, as sanctioned by the scriptures. They

---
8   S. Radhakrishnan, *The Bhagavad Gita*, HarperCollins Publishers, India, 2014, p. 134-135.
9   Mahatma Gandhi, *The Bhagavad Gita*, Jaico Publishing House, Mumbai, 2010, p. 107.

are called *avidvansah* (ignorant) because though they have bookish knowledge of the scriptures, they do not comprehend the final goal of God-realisation. Such ignorant people perform their duty scrupulously according to the ordinance of the scriptures, without indolence or doubt. They have firm faith that the performance of *Vedic* duties and rituals will bring the material rewards that they desire. If the faith of such people in rituals is broken, without their having developed faith in the higher principle of devotion, they will have nowhere to go."[10]

Lokmanya asserts, "It (*karma yoga*) can never be a preliminary preparation for Renunciation. The *Gita* clearly says that inasmuch as man has already acquired knowledge, desireless action does not become a source of bondage; and that the Release which can be obtained by Renunciation, can also be obtained by this *Karma Yoga*."

यत्साङ्ख्यैः प्राप्यते स्थानं तद्योगैरपि गम्यते ।
एकं साङ्ख्यं च योगं च यः पश्यति स पश्यति ॥५॥

Men of action reach the same status (tad yogairapi gamyate), which is obtained by men of renunciation (yatsankhyaih prapyate sthanam). Hence, those who see that the ways of renunciation and of action are one, truly see things as they are (yah pasyatisapasyati). (Bhagavad-Gita Chapter 5, Verse 5)

Dr. S. Radhakrishna explains, "The true renouncer is not he who remains completely inactive, but he whose work is done in a spirit of detachment. Renunciation is a mental attitude, the casting off of desire in work; true work is work with all desires renounced. There is no opposition between the two. When actions are performed by the wise man or the fool, the body (that is, the apparent doer) is the same, but the inward understanding is different (*prajnasya murkhasya ca karyayoge, samatvamabhyeti tanurna, buddhih*)."[11]

Bhasa, who was one of the earliest and most celebrated Indian playwrights in Sanskrit, has expounded this doctrine of the *Gita*, in the following words:

---

10 http://www.holy-bhagavad-gita.org/chapter/3/verse/25. Last accessed on 11 October 2017.
11 S. Radhakrishnan, *The Bhagavad Gita*, HarperCollins Publishers India, 2014, p. 205.

न ते न बुद्धिर्मम दूषणीया येन प्रकामं भवतास्मि हास्यः ।
प्राज्ञस्य मूर्खस्य च कार्ययोगे समत्वमभ्येति तनुर्न बुद्धिः ॥५॥

It is the mind, which has to be blamed. The same body performs ludicrous or virtuous actions, depending upon the mind (buddhi) of the person who is controlling the body.
(Avimaraka, Act 5, Verse 5)

Lokmanya focuses on the intention and declares, "My readers will see how the meaning in the original (*karma-yogo vishisyate*, the superiority of *Karma Yoga* is greater) is stretched and mutilated, where the original work and the commentators support different doctrines, and the commentators begin to comment on the original, in the firm belief that the doctrine supported by them is borne out by the original. Was not Shri Krishna or Shri Vyasa in a position to clearly say to Arjuna in plain Sanskrit, "O Arjuna, your question is improper"? But instead of doing so, it has been stated in numerous places, "*Karma Yoga* is superior".

Lokmanya maintained that the doctrine of *Karma Yoga* is not a new theory. The Law is so ancient that not even Shri Krishna was the great teacher who first propounded it. It is India's sacred heritage since time immemorial... *Karma Yoga* is the method, which leads to the attainment of both, material and spiritual glory.[12] Lokmanya unequivocally rejects the interpretation of Shri Shankaracharya and Shri Madhavacharya here, on the grounds that Shri Krishna made Arjuna a complete knower of the most secret doctrine (*itiguhyatamamshastram*) so that he could accomplish his mission of fighting the war against the wicked.

इति गुह्यतमं शास्त्रमिदमुक्तं मयानघ ।
एतद्बुद्ध्वा बुद्धिमान्स्यात्कृतकृत्यश्च भारत ॥२०॥

This most secret doctrine spoken by me (uktammaya) will make you enlightened to fulfill all that is to be accomplished (krita-krityah), O Bharat (Arjuna).
(Bhagavad-Gita Chapter 15, Verse 20)

---

12 B.G.TILAK, *Selected Documents*, vol. 3, 64, 65.

Lokmanya writes, "From this, it becomes abundantly clear that the best mode of life for a knower (*buddhi-man*), according to the Blessed Lord, is to continue to perform Action desirelessly, even after acquiring knowledge. Besides, even if Arjuna is, for the sake of argument, looked upon as ignorant, one cannot say that Janaka and other ancient *Karma Yogins*, as also the Blessed Lord Himself... were all ignorant... the *Gita* has expounded nothing but the doctrine of Action combined with Knowledge."

Contemporary Austrian-born American physicist Fritjof Capra (b. 1939) draws a parallel between Shiva's dance and the dance of subatomic particles. The rhythm of creation and destruction is not only the end of a season and the beginning of another; or the birth and death of all living creatures, but is also the very essence of inorganic matter where electrons ceaselessly move around the nucleus. Shiva's dance is indeed the dance of subatomic matter.

Capra famously declared, "Quantum theory thus reveals a basic oneness of the universe. It shows that we cannot decompose the world into independently existing smallest units. As we penetrate into matter, nature does not show us any isolated "building blocks", but rather, appears as a complicated web of relations between the various parts of the whole. These relations always include the observer in an essential way. The human observer constitutes the final link in the chain of observational processes, and the properties of any atomic object can be understood only in terms of the object's interaction with the observer."[13]

A hundred years ago, Lokmanya brilliantly wrote the same concept. He writes, "Not only men, but even the Sun and the Moon are continually performing action! Truly, as it is definite that *Karma* is nothing but creation, and that creation is nothing but *Karma*, we ourselves see that the activities of the world, that is to say, *Karma*, does not rest even for a moment... The Blessed Lord advises everybody in the name of Arjuna... *yah kriyavansapandithah*, i.e. that man is truly a learned man, who is a doer... since nobody in this world can escape *Karma*, one must perform all the duties which befall one according to one's own status in life, giving up the desire

---

13 http://www.azquotes.com/quote/364051. Last accessed on 11 October 2017.

of fruit... Matter (*prakrti*) will always go on performing its activities. When one gives up the egoistical idea that he is the performer of the Action, one is Released."

The Blessed Lord Himself takes incarnations from time to time for the universal benefit, for e.g. for "the protection of saints, the destruction of villains, and the re-establishment of religion (*dharma*)."

नियतं कुरु कर्म त्वं कर्म ज्यायो ह्यकर्मणः ।
शरीरयात्रापि च ते न प्रसिध्येदकर्मणः ॥८॥

For the protection of the good (paritranaya sadhunam) and the destruction of the wicked (vinasaya ca duskrtam), and for the establishment of order in the world (dharma-samsthapanarthaya), I do appear (sambhavami, in the human form) in every age (yuge yuge), and set things right for the good (samsthapana-arthaya). (Bhagavad-Gita Chapter 4, Verse 8)

Swami Vivekananda adds in his commentary of this *shloka*, "We read in the history of the world about prophets and their lives, and these come down to us through centuries of writings and workings by their disciples. Through thousands of years of chiselling and modelling, the lives of great prophets of yore come down to us; and yet, in my opinion, not one stands so high in brilliance as the life which I saw with my own eyes, under whose shadow I have lived, at whose feet I have learnt everything– the life of Ramakrishna Paramhamsa.... Whenever there is a decline of *dharma*, the rise of *adharma*, then I body myself forth... whenever you see a great soul struggling to uplift mankind, know that I have come..."[14]

As that man who has become a knower, has lost his 'mine-ness', he begins to perform all the activities in the world created by the *Ishvara*, with the mine-less feeling. This is the difference between the *Jnanin* and the *Ajnanin*. The Blessed Lord called these persons *tattva-vit*, or the knowers of the Truth.

---

14 Swami Vivekananda, *Complete Works*, *1.467 and 1.98*, Advaita Ashram, Seventh Reprint, Kolkata, 2016, p. 78.

तत्त्ववित्तु महाबाहो गुणकर्मविभागयोः ।
गुणा गुणेषु वर्तन्त इति मत्वा न सज्जते ॥२८॥

The knower of the Absolute truth (tattvavit) that the soul is distinct from gunas (vibhagayoh) never indulges (nasajjate) in sense gratification (guneshu).
(Bhagavad-Gita Chapter 3, Verse 28)

Mahatma Gandhi comments, "The point of this verse is, in the extremely difficult business of running this world, in the running of this intricate machine– the very thought of which is sufficient to make one's head spin– what is there that I can do? What strength do I have? I dare not touch a single part of it. Anyone who considers carefully how this world is kept going, will see that the different *gunas* are ceaselessly active and doing their work."[15]

Now comes the next question: What is this work? Swami Vivekananda explains, "What is this doing good to the world? Can we do good to the world? In an absolute sense, no; in a relative sense, yes. No permanent or everlasting good can be done to the world; if it could be done, the world would not be this world. We may satisfy the hunger of a man for five minutes, but he will be hungry again. Every pleasure with which we supply a man may be seen to be momentary. No one can permanently cure this ever-recurring fever of pleasure and pain. Can any permanent happiness be given to the world? In the ocean, we cannot raise a wave without causing a hollow somewhere else. The sum-total of the good things in the world has been the same throughout in its relation to man's need and greed. It cannot be increased or decreased. Take the history of the human race as we know to-day. Do we not find the same miseries and the same happiness, the same pleasures and pains, the same differences in position? Are not some rich, some poor, some high, some low, some healthy, some unhealthy?"[16]

Lokmanya writes, "The scients *(Jnanin)* are the eyes of the world. If they give up their duties, the world will become blind, and cannot but be destroyed. It is the scients *(tattva-vit* persons) who have to

---

[15] Mahatma Gandhi, *The Bhagavad Gita*, Jaico Publishing House, Mumbai, 2010, p. 110.
[16] http://www.sacred-texts.com/hin/kyog/kyog08.htm, p. 110. Last accessed on 11 October 2017.

make people wise and ameliorate their condition. However, such a thing cannot be done by mere verbal discourses and advice. We always see in the world that a person who merely preaches the Knowledge of the *Brahman* to those people who are not in the habit of behaving righteously, and whose minds are not purified, misapplies the knowledge by saying, "What is yours is mine, and what is mine is also mine."

Sant Tukaram (1608– 1650) says in simple words that our body is the temple of God. Inside is God in the form of the soul. Like there is sugar in sugarcane; just like that, God resides in our heart (soul).

Lokmanya cites Saint Tukaram:

जे कां रंजले गांजले । त्यांसि म्हणे जो आपुले ।
तोचि साधु ओळखावा । देव तेथेचि जाणावा ॥

Nobody owns up (responsibility of the) people who are unhappy and in distress. Only a saint empathises with them (as) he can see God in such people. (Tukaram Gatha, 960. 1-2)

पर उपकारी वेंचियेल्या शक्ती । तेणें आत्मस्थिती जाणीतली ॥

(Only) by investing one's life energy in doing good to others, the true state of the Atman can be realised. (Tukaram Gatha, 4563).

जगाच्या कल्याणा संतांच्या विभूती । देह कष्टविती उपकारे ॥

Saints are born for the welfare of the public. They use their bodies in helping others emerge out of their sufferings. (Tukaram Gatha, 929).

Lokmanya also cites fifth century Sanskrit writer Bhartrhari's words, '*svartho yasya parartha eva sa puman ekah satam agranah*', and describes a saint as a person who mirrors the needs and pains of others in his own self. The saints own no property. They wander from place to place, dispensing their divine knowledge. Saints possess nothing and even beg for their food. Accepting only what is needed for their bare maintenance, saints give the highest education, culture and enlightenment to the people, discriminating against none. They live by example and their presence in society inspires others to live a virtuous life and experience bliss in the process. Gurudev Rabindranath Tagore declares, "I slept and dreamt that life was joy. I awoke and saw that life was service. I acted and behold, service was joy."

Acquiring knowledge of the *Brahman* (*Brahmavidya*) emerges as the principal subject undertaken in the *Bhagavad-Gita*. In this process, the Blessed Lord first explains *Samkhya Yoga* and then *Karma Yoga,* with a description of *Dhyana Yoga* and *Bhakti Yoga* still later. In fact, the Blessed Lord tells Arjuna, "*bhakto'si me sakhacetirahasyamhy-etad-uttamam*"– you are devoted to me, and you are equally an intimate friend; that is why I disclose to you this highest secret of *Brahmavidya*. Lokmanya writes, "My readers will now appreciate the inner reason for the words, "*iti srimadbhagavadgitasu upanishatsu brahmavidyayam yogashastre*", used at the end of each chapter of the *Gita*... These words mean that it does not contain only the *Brahmavidya*, and that the principal object of the *Bhagavad-Gita* was to support only the Yoga or the *Karma Yoga*, out of the two paths of *Samkhya* and *Yoga* (the *Vedantic Samnyasa*, and the *Vedantic Karma Yoga*), which are included in the *Brahmavidya*... (this clearly establishes that) the *Bhagavad-Gita-Upanishad* is the most important treatise on the science of *Karma Yoga*... This also clearly explains why the *Bhagavad-Gita* was included in the *Prasthanatrayi*. If the *Gita* did not contain anything more than the *Upanishad* and the *Vedanta-Sutras*, there would be no point in including the *Gita* in the *Prasthanatrayi*."

Lokmanya elaborates, "The Vedic Religion is not to be looked upon as a one-handed man, that is, as being only in support of *Samnyasa*; and that although it has only one head, namely *Brahmavidya*, yet, *Samkhya* and *Karma Yoga*, which, from the point of view of Release, are of equal value, are its right hand and left hand respectively... there remains no opposition between the *Gita* and the *Upanishads*... as the *Upanishads* support the one path, and the *Gita* the other path, these two parts of the *Prasthanatrayi* are seen to be mutually cooperative like two hands, instead of being mutually antagonistic." Lokmanya now summarises a precise 13-point differentiation between the renunciation advocated by the *Samkhya Yoga* and the *Karma Yoga* of the *Bhagavad-Gita*, after a seeker has acquired *Brahma vidya* (knowledge of the *Atman*). *Karma-Samnyasa* (*Samkhya*) and *Karma Yoga* (*Gita*) resonate on three points. Lokmanya lists them as, "(1) Release is obtained only by Knowledge of the *Atman*, and not by *Karma*. The happiness of heaven, obtained by credulously performing sacrificial ritual, is inconstant. (2) In order to acquire the Knowledge of the *Atman*, the 'Mind' must be made steady, desireless, and equable by means of the control of the organs. (3) This path is eternal, and has the support of the *Shrutis*, as also of the *Smrtis*."

Lokmanya clearly points out the ten differences between the *Karma-samnyasa* of *Samkhya* and *Karma Yoga* of the *Gita* and declares, "In the same way, the *Gita* does not acquire the subordinate position of merely repeating what has already been said, which it would if it is only supporting what the *Upanishads* have maintained."

Samkhya: Break the bonds of the objects of pleasure, which please the organs, and be free.

Gita: Do not give up the objects which please the organs; but maintain your association with them apathetically, that is, desirelessly, and test the control you have over the organs. Desireless does not mean inactivity.

Samkhya: Action, which is a product of desire, is causative of sin and bondage. *Gita:* Lifeless (*achetana*) *Karma* does not bind or leave anybody; and the cause of bondage and unhappiness is the desire or the hope of reward existing in the 'Mind' of the doer.

Samkhya: Though action has to be performed until the 'Mind' is purified, it must ultimately be given up.

Gita: Even after the purification of the 'Mind', perform all actions courageously and enthusiastically, giving up the Hope for Fruit. One cannot give up *Karma* even if one wishes to. *Karma* is the Creation and it has no rest.

Samkhya: As *Karma* performed in connection with sacrificial ritual does not create bondage; there is no objection to its being performed during the status of a house–holder.

Gita: All actions, which are performed with a desireless frame of mind, or with the idea of dedicating them to the *Brahman*, are a great *Yajna* (sacrifice). Therefore, all duties, which are appropriate to one's own status in life, should be performed desirelessly, as pure duties; and these should be performed continually.

Samkhya: As the natural needs of the Body cannot be escaped from, it is not improper to beg, for earning one's livelihood, after having taken *Samnyasa*.

Gita: Begging for earning one's subsistence is also *Karma*, and that too, 'disgraceful'. If this *Karma* is to be performed, why not perform all other actions desirelessly? Besides, if the status of a householder is done away with, who is going to give you food?

Samkhya: After the Acquisition of Knowledge, no duty remains for your own benefit; and there is no necessity to act for universal welfare.

Gita: After the Acquisition of Knowledge, although no duty remains to you for your own benefit, yet, you cannot escape *Karma*. Therefore, whatever duties are enjoined by the *Shastras* should be performed with a selfless (*nirmama*) frame of mind, saying: 'I do not want it', and with an eye to universal welfare. No one can escape *Lokasmgraha* (universal welfare). For instance, see the life of the Blessed Lord Himself!

Samkhya: Nevertheless, persons of high authority may, till death, carry on their duties, after Acquisition of Knowledge, as was done by Janaka and others, but only as exceptions.

Gita: According to the arrangement of the four castes, which is based on the divisions of the qualities (*guna-vibhaga*), every one acquires by birth, great or small authority; and this authority, which is acquired according to one's own state in life (*dharma*), must be exercised till death, desirelessly and without exception, because this cycle of activities has been created by the *Parameshvara* for the maintenance of the world.

Samkhya: In any case, *Samnyasa* in the shape of abandonment of action is the best. The duties of the three other states are the means, or the preparatory stages, for the purification of the 'Mind'; and there is an inherent opposition between *Jnana* and *Karma*. Therefore, acquire purification of the 'Mind' as early as possible in the earlier stages of life, and after having acquired Knowledge, take ultimately to *Samnyasa* in the shape of Abandonment of action. If you have acquired purification of the 'Mind' with birth or in young age, there is no necessity of performing the duties pertaining to the state of a householder. The true state of *Samnyasa* consists in the literal abandonment of action.

Gita: It is true that by performing the actions pertaining to worldly life in the manner enjoined by the *Shastras*, one acquires the purification of the 'Mind'. But, purification of the 'Mind' is not the only use of *Karma*. *Karma* is necessary in order that the activities of the world should go on. In the same way, though there is an opposition between *Jnana* and desire-prompted action, there is none between *Jnana* and desireless action; and therefore, after the purification of the 'Mind', continue the actions prescribed for the various castes, abandoning the hope of the fruit of action, and desirelessly, till death, for the benefit of the world. This is the true *Samnyasa*; it is neither possible nor proper to literally abandon *Karma* (action) at any time.

Samkhya: Even after the abandonment of action, you must observe the rules of *sama, dama* etc.

Gita: After the Acquisition of Knowledge, take *Samnyasa* in the shape of abandonment of the fruit of action, and observe all the rules arising as a result of Self-identification (*atmaupamya*), except *sama, dama* etc.; and perform in a peaceful frame of mind, all the duties enjoined by the *Shastras*, till death, for the purpose of universal welfare. Do not give up desireless action.

Samkhya: Shuka, Yajnavalkya and others adopted this path.

Gita: Vyasa, Vashishtha, Jaigisavya (who had full knowledge of all his previous births, uninterrupted ten world sunsets (*Maha Pralaya*) in succession), and others, as also Janaka, Shri Krishna and others followed this path.

In the 304th *Adhyaya* of *Shanti Parva* of the *Mahabharata*, Yudhishthira asked Bhishma the difference between the *Samkhya* and the *Yoga* system of philosophy and whether one could be preferred over the other. Bhishma said, "The evidences of *Yoga* are addressed to the direct ken of the senses; those of *Samkhya* are based on the scriptures. I approve... both those systems of science... If practised duly according to the instructions laid down, both would, O king, cause a person to attain to the highest end. In both systems, purity is equally recommended, as also compassion towards all creatures, O sinless one. In both, again, the observance of vows has been equally laid down. Only the scriptures that point out their paths are different... By casting off, through the aid of *Yoga*, these five faults, viz., attachment, heedlessness, affection, lust, and wrath, one attains to Emancipation".[17]

Lokmanya concludes with Bhishma's assertion, "Both these paths or *Nisthas* are based on the Knowledge of the *Brahman*, and as the desireless-ness or peacefulness of the 'Mind' is a common factor in both, both the paths ultimately lead to Release. The important

---

17   http://www.sacred-texts.com/hin/m12/m12b128.htm. Last accessed on 12 October 2017.

difference between the two is that in the one case, *Karma* (action) is abandoned after *Jnana* (Knowledge), and in the other, desire-prompted (*kamya*) 'action' is abandoned, and 'desireless action' is continued."

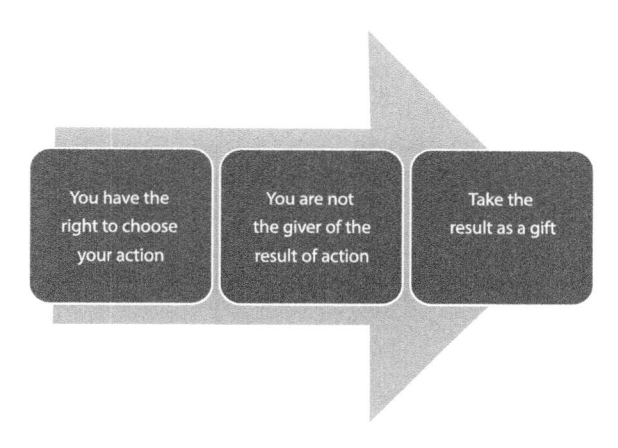

```
┌──────────────┐ ┌──────────────┐ ┌──────────────┐
│ You have the │ │ You are not  │ │   Take the   │
│right to choose│ │the giver of the│ │result as a gift│
│ your action  │ │result of action│ │              │
└──────────────┘ └──────────────┘ └──────────────┘
```

The moment you do an action, it leaves your hand– metaphorically speaking– and becomes part of the universe. And once Karma becomes part of the Universe, all the Universal laws will act upon the Karma. This is because everything in creation in acted upon by the laws of the Universe.

The *Samnyasa* could also be very hazardous. A.C. Bhaktivedanta Swami Prabhupada cautioned in Sri Chaitanya-Charitamrita, "You should not make yourself a show-bottle devotee and become a false renunciant– *markata-vairagya na kara loka dekhana.*"[18] It is, indeed, very common that people take up renunciation as an escape from the trials and tribulations of worldly life. This renunciation is not a mental act developing disinclination from the world, as it should be, but abandonment of duties. Some persons abandon action for fear of physical labour, though they have not acquired knowledge. This is called *rajasa tyaga*. The Blessed Lord tells Arjuna:

दुःखमित्येव यत्कर्म कायक्लेशभयात् त्यजेत् ।
स कृत्वा राजसं त्यागं नैव त्यागफलं लभेत् ॥८॥

---

[18] https://prabhupadabooks.com/cc/madhya/16/238?d=1&f=189313. Last accessed on 12 October 2017.

> *To give up one's prescribed duties because they are troublesome or cause bodily discomfort (kaya-klesa-bhayat), is renunciation in the mode of passion (krtvarajasamtyagam). Such renunciation is never beneficial or elevating (naivaphalamlabhet). (Bhagavad-Gita Chapter 18, Verse 8)*

Eknath Easwaran adds, "*Tamas* is great at renouncing responsibilities. Halfway through college, or when he has a family to support, he decides that the time has come to give up worldly life with all its problems and devote his time to contemplation, gardening, writing poetry, or enjoying a simple life. "I am not causing anybody any harm," he says, and on the surface it may seem true. But the mental state says point-blank, "I do not care. What matters is that I do what I like." *Rajas*, by contrast, gives up things when he is forced to, usually by pain. If he renounces martinis, it is not because he has got over his desire and turns it around; it is because he has developed an ulcer and drinking martini hurts. He gives up smoking because his cough has become too painful; because it is difficult even to breathe... We are all sent into life for one task; to enrich the lives of others. Anybody who takes from life without giving to others in return, is a thief."[19]

The *Bhagavad-Gita* gives a call for action when difficulties arise in life. It begins with the predicament of Arjuna, who is finding the task of fighting his teacher, elders and family members in a war, unpleasant and troublesome. He is inclined to leave the battlefield and accept defeat without fighting, which he rationalises as 'sin'. Shri Krishna rebuked Arjuna for this show of feebleness of the will. However, instead of giving a command to fight, the Blessed Lord undertakes the task of bringing about an internal transformation within him, and through that, gives the message of *Karma Yoga* to humanity. After hearing Shri Krishna, Arjuna realises that the purpose of the war is not to secure the kingdom of Hastinapur for his comfort and glory, but to annihilate the wicked who were in power and liberate people from the unjust rule of the tyrant.

Swami Muktananda writes, "Renunciation is definitely

---

[19] Eknath Easwaran, *The Bhagavad-Gita for Daily Living*, Jaico Publishing House, Mumbai, India, 2007, Vol. III, p. 387-389.

necessary for spiritual attainment. But the problem is that people's understanding of renunciation is very shallow and they consider it to be only the external abandonment of work. Such renunciation leads to hypocrisy in which, while externally donning the robes of a renunciant, one internally contemplates upon the objects of the senses. There are many *sadhus* in India who come in this category. They left the world with the noble intention of God-realisation, but because the mind was not yet detached from the objects of their senses, their renunciation did not bestow the desired fruits. Consequently, they found their actions did not lead them to a higher spiritual life at all. The defect was in their sequence– they strove first for external renunciation and later for internal detachment. The instruction of this verse is to reverse the sequence– first develop internal detachment and then renounce externally."[20]

Lokmanya cites Nrsimha-Purana to buttress knowledge (*jnana*) with Action (*karma*) as the right course of a human life. "Just as the movement of birds in the sky is made by two wings, so also is Release obtained by the combination of *Jnana* and *karma*, and perfection is not attained by only one of them."

यथाश्वा रथहीनाश्व रथाश्वाश्वैर्विना यथा।
एवं तपश्च विद्या च उभावपि तपस्विन: ॥९॥
यथान्नं मधुसंयुक्तं मधु चान्नेन संयुतम्।
एवं तपश्च विद्या च संयुक्ते भेषजं महत् ॥१०॥
द्वाभ्यामेव हि पक्षाभ्यां यथा वै पक्षिणां गति: ।
तथैव ज्ञानकर्मभ्यां प्राप्यते ब्रह्म शाश्वतम् ॥११॥

As horses without a chariot and a chariot without horses serve no purpose, so is the case with knowledge without action and action without knowledge. As honey mixed with the bitter herb makes a medicine, so also, penance combined with skill brings liberation. As birds fly using both of their wings, so also, the Brahman is realised by combining Jnana and Karma.
(Nrsimha Purana Adhyaya 61, 9-11)

---

[20] http://www.holy-bhagavad-gita.org/chapter/18/verse/9. Last accessed on 12 October 2017.

This chapter is concluded with the assertion, "I have so far proved that in order to carry on the activities of the mortal world or for universal welfare, the simultaneous combination of desireless action according to one's own qualification, and Release-giving Knowledge, is necessary according to the *Gita*... this path of *Karma Yoga* has been in vogue since ancient times, and was accepted by Janaka and others; and that it is also known as the Bhagavata religion, because it was extended further and revived by the Blessed Lord. It is now necessary, from the point of view of general welfare (*Lokasmgraha*), to deal with the question of how the seekers who follow this path, carry on their worldly activities simultaneously, along with the acquisition of the highest ideal of man. This subject is the theme of the next chapter."

ॐ

12

Guiding Souls

> In a process that is akin to a seed germinating suddenly, certain spiritual guideposts appear showing the way, or the right path. From a scientific perspective, the inner being of a person can be seen as an amorphous collection of thoughts, images, emotions, sensations, dreams, insights and inspiration. Add a little sensitivity to the relation between metaphor and reality and we can see them as products of the soul's continuous morphing.
>
> — A. P. J. Abdul Kalam

Lokmanya has so far supplied a powerful corrective to the overemphasis of *Jnana* and renunciation, which led to mere quietism of the Indian society and the way it crumbled before invaders. Lokmanya, in a long and sustained protest against the dangers of quietism, has brought out the unique feature of *Jnana*, as taught in the *Gita*, which is that it is never divorced from service to society. Unsympathetic critics of Hinduism have often ignored the *Lokasmgraha* message of the *Gita* and said that social service forms no integral part of the Hindu religion. They forget that service to society is fundamental to the very concept of Hindu *Dharma* as taught by the *Gita*.

As if coming down heavily on the egoistical way of renunciation and highlighting the merit of living a life of *nishkama karma*, Lokmanya opens this chapter with a verse from the *Shanti Parva* of the *Mahabharata*. Bhishma told the Pandavas and Shri Krishna and many sages, the story of a merchant named Tuladhara, who expounded *Dharma* to a Brahmin ascetic by the name of Jajali.

सर्वेषां यः सुहृन्नित्यं सर्वेषां च हिते रतः ।
कर्मणा मनसा वाचा स धर्मं वेद जाजले ॥९॥

The person who always treats all beings as friends and is engaged in doing what is good for all with deeds, thinks good of all and speaks kindly, has understood the Dharma and the scriptures (and not the intellectual rationaliser of doing what is good for him), O Jajali (Mahabharata, Shanti Parva, Adhyaya 254, Shloka 9).

Jajali was a Brahmin. He accrued great yogic powers by observing severe austerities. One such power was that he could stand immovably, like a wooden post, for months together, not even eating food or excreting. Once, a pair of birds made their nest in his thickly matted hair and laid eggs. In the course of time the eggs hatched, the small birds developed wings and left the nest. Jajali was bloated with pride and thought egoistically about who could be more privileged than him. But he was rebuked by a heavenly voice (*Akashvani*) telling him that he was not even equal in religious merit to the merchant Tuladhara living in the city of Kashi.

Insulted, angry but also curious, Jajali travelled to the city of Kashi, and looked for Tuladhara. He found him engaged in selling his wares. Jajali, secretly desiring to put down Tuladhara, asked him to explain to him about morality and the ways of knowledge. Standing with his head bowed in reverence to Jajali, Tuladhara said, "I am a petty businessman but my scales are perfectly even; I see every customer and even animals as equal. There is no difference for me between a clod of clay, a stone, and a lump of gold. I have no fear of anyone, nor does anyone fear me. I live like a wooden log floating upon the river waters." Jajali was humbled and his false pride collapsed.

Lokmanya writes, "That school of thought, according to which, nothing remains to be done by way of duty after a man has acquired the Knowledge of the *Brahman*… on that account, advocates giving up entirely the painful and insipid activities of a transient worldly life, with an apathetic frame of mind… can never think that *Karma*

Yoga, or the mode of life appropriate to the state of a householder, is a science which deserves consideration," and gave the title, 'The State and the Activities of the Siddha', to this chapter.

Emphasising the futility of Jajali's penance and profundity of Tuladhara's engagement with the world, Lokmanya questions those who believe that leading a worldly life till death is foolish, and consider it to be the highest duty of everyone in life to renounce the world as early as possible.

Swami Ranganathananda explains beautifully (while talking to government officials), "Do a clerk's work, not with a clerk's mind, but with the mind of a citizen of free India... The work becomes great when done by a great mind. The work becomes small, when done by a small mind. It is not the work that is great, it is the mind that is behind the work that makes it great. The mother cooks food for you, and the paid cook also cooks food for you. Cooking is the same, but the mind is so different between the one and the other. So, that is the most important thing as far as human beings are concerned. *Karma Yoga* deals with that subject. How to make this mind rich? How to make this mind pure? How to make this mind unlimited? That is the work we have to do."[1]

What is the purpose of the work? Why are we expending effort? Till such time that the work is done to earn money, to pass an examination, to accomplish some goal, to meet an objective; the work remains desire-driven and expands *karma*, and adds on the complexity, making the entrapment even denser. But when the effort is made with mindfulness of the larger picture in which the effort is made, the motive is not personal, not selfish, and the consequences are well-considered, the work becomes more engaged, more attuned to God's will, accruing no reactions and bindings to the doer. There is a beautiful saying of Confucius, which Dr. A.P.J. Abdul Kalam made very popular by quoting in his numerous speeches:

> *"If there is righteousness in the heart;*
> *There will be beauty in the character.*
> *If there is beauty in the character;*
> *There will be harmony in the home.*
> *If there is harmony in the home;*
> *There will be order in the nations.*
> *When there is order in the nations;*
> *There will peace in the world."*

So, righteousness of the heart and purity of the mind are fundamental. Those are the root causes for peace in the world that eventually manifest as political order and social harmony. Those who have got into the habit of arriving at a decision about morality merely by considering the external action, without attaching proper importance to mental purity, may consider this doctrine as strange.

---

[1] Swami Ranganathananda, *Universal Message of the Bhagavad Gita, Vol. 2,* Advaita Ashrama, Kolkata, 2015 (Seventh reprint), p.30.

But the *Gita* is very clear in establishing it in the form of the ideal of *Sthitaprajna* (Steady-in-Mind). But before Lokmanya takes it up, he takes a final view on the Path of *Samnyasa* and the Path of *Karma Yoga*, in terms of *Karma Yogin* being the example-setters before the ordinary people and the world, so that they are benefitted in the bigger business of *karma*, of which they are not even aware.

Lokmanya writes, "It has been shown in the last chapter that the most important doctrine laid down by the *Gita* is that the *Jnanin* must perform all the activities of life, with the help of the feeling of indifference to the world and the equability of the 'Mind' that results from the Realisation of the *Brahman*. When it is admitted that (1) the deletion of knowledge-full (*jnana-yukta*) action from the world will result in the world becoming blind and being destroyed; that (2) even *Jnanins* must desirelessly perform all the duties of worldly life, and so set before ordinary people a living example of a good and pure life, since it is the desire of the Blessed Lord that the world should not be so destroyed, and that its activities should go on without a hitch; and that (3) this path is the most excellent and acceptable of all, and so it becomes necessary to consider in what way such a *Jnanin* performs the activities of his worldly life because, as the life of such a *Jnanin* is nothing but an example set by him for other people... We have, therefore, in this way found a guiding soul, a preceptor who will give to us a visible reply, in the form of his own life, to the difficult question of the discrimination between what should be done and what should not be done (*karma-akarma-vichikitsa*), or, between what is a duty and what is not a duty (*karya-akarya-vyavasthiti*)... Such a preceptor was standing in life before Arjuna, in the form of Sri Krishna."

यद्यदाचरति श्रेष्ठस्तत्तदेवेतरो जनः ।
स यत्प्रमाणं कुरुते लोकस्तदनुवर्तते ॥२१॥

Whatever actions virtuous persons perform (acharati shreshthas), common people follow. Whatever standards (pramanam) they set, the entire world pursues them (lokas tad anuvartate). (Bhagavad-Gita Chapter 3, Verse 21)

It is stated in one place in the Narayaniya religion, that:

एकान्तिनो हि पुरुषा दुर्लभा बहवो नृप ॥५७॥
यद्येकान्तिभिराकीर्ण जगत् स्यात्कुरुनन्दन ।
अहिंसकैरात्मविद्भिः सर्वभूतहिते रतैः ॥५८॥
भवेत् कृतयुगप्राप्तिराशीःकर्मविवर्जितैः ॥५८॥

It is difficult to find many people who follow the Ekantika (Activistic) path. If this world is filled with Self-knowing, harmless Jnanins, who work for the general welfare, all desire-prompted actions will go away and the good old time (Krta Yuga) will indeed return! (Mahabharata, Shanti Parva, Adhyaya 336 Mokshdharma Parva).

Lokmanya writes, "It is the opinion of our philosophers that such a state of society existed in ancient times and that it will recur again… Western scholars say on the authority of modern history, that such a state of things never existed before, but it is possible that such a state of things may come into existence, sometime or the other in the future, as a result of the advancement of mankind. However, as I am not now concerned with history, I may, without being contradicted, say that, according to both opinions, every person in this state, which is supposed to be the highest or the most perfect state of society, will be fully a *Jnanin*, and every action of his is bound to be pure, beneficial and moral, or rather, the pinnacle of dutifulness."

Lokmanya cites the English biologist-philosopher, Herbert Spencer (1820– 1903), who emphasised the need for restrained conduct, in his book, *The Principles of Ethics.* Spencer famously said, "What a cage is to the wild beast, law is to the selfish man." Any conduct restrained within the required limits generates no aggressive passions, creates harmonious cooperation, and in this way, all people living together in a society get benefitted and live blessed in harmony. Lokmanya cites ancient Greek philosopher Plato (428– 348 BCE), who gave the idea of 'philosopher king', saying that ordinary people can't understand ethics and are better off by following the decisions of the philosophers. Lokmanya also cites another Greek philosopher, Epicurus (341–270 BCE), who called one as a real knower who is peaceful, equable, and probably always joyful. Neither does he do the slightest harm to other people, nor do other people harm him.

After citing various philosophers about where our ethical principles come from, and what they mean, and after examining issues of universal truths, the will of God, the role of reason in ethical judgments, and the meaning of ethical terms themselves, Lokmanya called the ability to perceive and constructively act on one's own emotions and the feelings of others as the kernel of all Ethics and termed the *sthitaprajna* concept given in the *Gita* as the most fundamental idea in this regard.

In the *Bhagavad-Gita*, the characteristics of the *Sthitaprajna* have been mentioned in the most articulate manner.

यस्मान्नोद्विजते लोको लोकान्नोद्विजते च यः ।
हर्षामर्षभयोद्वेगैर्मुक्तो यः स च मे प्रियः ॥१५॥

Those who are not a source of annoyance to anyone (udvijate) and who, in turn, are not agitated by anyone (advijate); who are equal in pleasure and pain (harsamarsa) and free from fear and anxiety (bhaya udvegair); such devotees of mine are very dear to me. (Bhagavad-Gita Chapter 12, Verse 15)

प्रजहाति यदा कामान्सर्वान्पार्थ मनोगतान् ।
आत्मन्येवात्मना तुष्टः स्थितप्रज्ञस्तदोच्यते ॥५५॥

Shri Krishna tells Arjuna, "When one discards all selfish desires and cravings of the senses that torment the mind (kamansarvan mano-gatan), and becomes satisfied in the realisation of the self (atmanyevatmanatushtah), such a person is transcendentally situated (sthita-prajnah). (Bhagavad-Gita Chapter 2, Verse 55)

समदुःखसुखः स्वस्थः समलोष्टाश्मकाञ्चनः ।
तुल्यप्रियाप्रियो धीरस्तुल्यनिन्दात्मसंस्तुतिः ॥२४॥

मानापमानयोस्तुल्यस्तुल्यो मित्रारिपक्षयोः ।
सर्वारम्भपरित्यागी गुणातीतः स उच्यते ॥२५॥

These are the people who are alike in happiness and distress (sama-duhkha-sukhah); who are established in the Self (svasthah); who look upon a clod, a stone, and a piece of gold (sama-lostasma-kancanah) as of equal value; who remain the same amidst pleasant and unpleasant events (priyaapriyodhiras) and who take their criticism and their praise with the same repose of mind (ninda atma-samstutih).
(Bhagavad-Gita Chapter 14, Verse 24)

These are the people who remain the same in honour and dishonour (manapamanayostulyas), who treat both friend and foe alike (tulyomitrari-paksayoh), and who have abandoned all desire-driven enterprises (sarvarambha-parityagi)– they are said to have risen above the three gunas (guna-atitah).
(Bhagavad-Gita Chapter 14, Verse 25)

ब्रह्मभूतः प्रसन्नात्मा न शोचति न काङ्क्षति ।
समः सर्वेषु भूतेषु मद्भक्तिं लभते पराम् ॥५४॥

One situated in the transcendental Brahman is full of joy (brahma-bhutahprasannatma). This person does not lament or desire (na socati na kanksati), and becomes equitably disposed towards all living beings (samah sarvesu bhutesu). This (way of living) is devotional service to Me (mad-bhaktim) and is the most beneficial (labhate param).
(Bhagavad-Gita Chapter 18, Verse 54).

Swami Ranganathananda explains, "Such a person (*brahma-bhutah prasannatma*) was being evolved from an ordinary person. Who was that ordinary person? *Vyaktibhutah*, (the one with) the feeling that I am a separate individual, with a separate ego... This is how we start our journey. We then proceed to the training of the mind and the elimination of the ego... How to handle this ego, this individuality in each of us?... All happiness, welfare and peace depend upon that one art– the art of handling this sense of individuality. Several occasions we have had before in our life where we collided with other individuals all the time... like a billiard ball colliding with other billiard balls... The whole subject of human development and fulfilment evolves from this particular theme: how to handle this focus of individuality within us, by which we can live happily and in peace with other people, and project that peace onto the outside world as well."[2] Dr. S. Radhakrishnan points out, "This verse is another indication that, for the *Gita*, disappearance of the individual in a featureless Absolute is not the highest, state but devotion to the Supreme Lord..."[3]

Lokmanya says, "However difficult the accomplishment of the state of *Sthitaprajna* may be, as it is evident from the description of such a man, but once this ultimate state is accomplished, this person does not need to be taught any laws about what should be done or should not be done (about Ethics). As the purest, the most equable and the most sinless frame of mind is the essence of morality, laying down laws of Ethics for such a *Sthitaprajna* would be as unreasonable as imagining that the Sun is surrounded by darkness, and holding up a torch to it. There may be a doubt as to whether or not a particular person has reached this highest of states."

It is important to understand the idea of a *Sthitaprajna* as a person endowed with Ethical Authority over the ordinary people of the world. In Christianity, there is this concept of prophetic ministry. Scriptures declare, "And he gave some apostles, and some prophets, and some evangelists, and some pastors, and teachers." (Ephesians 4:11). All five ascension gifts are equally important. We need the apostle. He is a spiritual father, architect, and builder. We need the soul-winning evangelist who reminds us of reaching the lost. We need the pastor who counsels, nurtures and comforts, and the teacher to instruct, tutor, and explain God's Word and ways. And we need the prophet, God's voice of edification, exhortation and comfort... We need the freshness of prophetic revelation, that life-giving rhema (divine messages) that comes through the prophet's

---

2 Swami Ranganathananda, *Universal Message of the Bhagavad Gita, Vol. 3*, Advaita Ashrama, Kolkata, 2015 (Seventh reprint), p.332.

3 S. Radhakrishnan, *The Bhagavad Gita*, HarperCollins Publishers, India, 2014, p. 440.

gift. Without that refreshing, we die a boring religious death and are not spiritually relatable to our generation. We all need the prophetic voice to come into the earth, that we might have a "living word" imparted into our lives."[4]

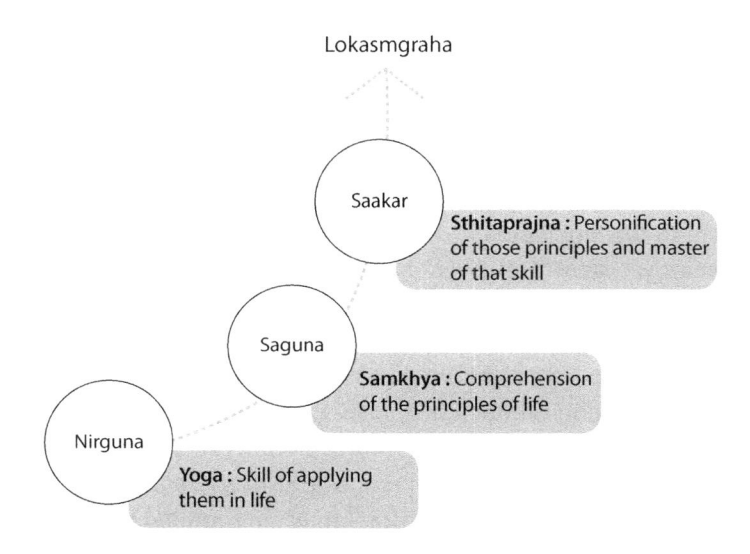

```
                        Lokasmgraha
                             ↑
                             ⋮
                          ┌──────┐
                          │Saakar│
                          └──────┘     ┌─────────────────────────────┐
                               ⋮       │ Sthitaprajna: Personification│
                               ⋮       │ of those principles and master│
                               ⋮       │ of that skill                │
                                       └─────────────────────────────┘
                       ┌──────┐
                       │Saguna│
                       └──────┘   ┌─────────────────────────────┐
                            ⋮     │ Samkhya: Comprehension       │
                            ⋮     │ of the principles of life    │
                            ⋮     └─────────────────────────────┘
              ┌───────┐
              │Nirguna│
              └───────┘
                       ┌─────────────────────────────┐
                       │ Yoga: Skill of applying      │
                       │ them in life                 │
                       └─────────────────────────────┘
```

In fact, it is the Gita that has coined the word Sthitaprajna... as the term itself tells (means) one having steadfast wisdom. But how could there be steadfast wisdom without subduing the senses? Hence, the sthitaprajna has been described as the embodiment of restraint. Restraint implies that the intellect is anchored in the Self and the mind and the organs are under the control of the intellect. The Sthitaprajna reins in all his organs and uses them in desireless and selfless action.[5]

In the Hindu religion, the *Sthitaprajna* seers perform these important functions. Lokmanya writes, "Once it (*Sthitaprajna* state) has been established, no proposition is indeed possible, except the Metaphysical examination, regarding the merit or de-merit of his (a *Sthitaprajna's*) actions, just as regal authority is vested in one independent person or a collection of persons. No desire exists in the mind of *Sthitaprajna*; and therefore, he is not induced to perform action by any motive, except the fact that it is a duty enjoined by

---

[4] http://www.jonasclark.com/index.php/12-functions-of-prophetic-ministry/. Last accessed on 14 October 2017.

[5] http://www.vinobabhave.org/index.php/talks-on-geeta/group1-2/chapter-2-col-120. Last accessed on 13 October 2017.

the *Shastras* and therefore, the words, sin or meritorious action, morality or immorality, can never be applied to the conduct of such persons, who are filled by a sinless and pure desire."

A *Sthitaprajna* could clearly see things that were going to happen soon. This made the *Sthitaprajna* assume a great responsibility, of undertaking the difficult task of delivering hard messages to people who were following the wrong course in their lives. A *Sthitaprajna* must declare very clearly to the heady people, the bad consequences of their arrogance, as in the *Sthitaprajna* state, one can see clearly, things that are going to happen soon.

People are always happy with things as they are– living in their bubble. They feel that their religion has made them safe. Their jobs, insurance cover, friend circle, connections and networks will come to their rescue, should something go wrong. This makes the *Sthitaprajna's* task much harder. Then, there are many false gurus. People like them because these false gurus validate the bad habits and behaviour of these people, telling them that there is nothing wrong with their lifestyle.

Finally, there are doubts. It is natural to have doubts when we have let other matters control our lives. The difficulties in life seem to be very great. A spiritual darkness descends upon our soul. We begin to doubt God's love for us. Some people may even doubt that God exists. It is for this, that the *Sthitaprajna* exists. The *Gita* provides through the *Sthitaprajna*, an important lesson for the world. Each person has some work to do in this world. There is no escape from that, as it is the reason for each one of us to exist. We must know this rationale and continue our work, irrespective of what happens. This is more important than achieving success. Danger is imminent when results become most important to us. Instead of considering our life as a responsibility to be an instrument of God, we start trying to prove our own worth.

Lokmanya writes, "Not only in the Vedic religion, but also in the Buddhist and Christian religions this principle (desireless action leading to peace) was accepted and even by the ancient Greek philosophers; and in the present age, Immanuel Kant, has, in his book on the science of Ethics, proved this by conclusive reasons.

When it has thus been proved what the unpollutable original spring or the stainless model of all rules of Morality is, such persons as want to scrutinise the fundamental principles of Ethics, or of the doctrine of Energism (*karma yoga*), must minutely examine the lives of such holy and stainless saints. That is why Arjuna has asked Shri Krishna, the following questions in the *Bhagavad-Gita*...."

कैर्लिङ्गैस्त्रीन्गुणानेतानतीतो भवति प्रभो ।
किमाचारः कथं चैताँस्त्रीन्गुणानतिवर्तते ॥२१॥

Arjuna asked Shri Krishna, "What are the characteristics of those who have gone beyond the gunas (gunanatito), O Lord? How do they act (kimacarah)? How do they go beyond the bondage of the three gunas (tringunanativartate)?"
(Bhagavad-Gita Chapter 14, Verse 21)

Dr. S. Radhakrishnan makes an important point here. He writes, "What are the marks of the *jivan-mukta*, of him who achieves perfection in the present life? The characteristics are more or less the same as those of the *sthitaprajna (Bhagavad-Gita Chapter 2, Verse 55)*, of the *bhaktiman*, devotee *(Bhagavad-Gita Chapter 12, Verse 13)* . From this, it is evident that the marks of perfection are the same, however it may be reached."[6]

Lokmanya explains, "As an assayer tests the golden ornament by comparing it with a sample piece of a hundred carat gold in his possession, so also is the behaviour of the *Sthitaprajna*, a test for deciding between the duty and the non-duty, the just and the unjust. The implied meaning of these questions is that the Blessed Lord should explain to Arjuna what that test was... The sum and substance of the advice given to Arjuna in the *Gita* is, 'It is not necessary to give up action, nor can you give it up; but, Realise the identity of the *Brahman* and the *Atman* and keep your Pure Reason (*vyavasayatmika buddhi*) equable like that of the *Karma Yogin*, so that your Practical reason (*vasanatmika buddhi*) will thereby also become pure, so that you will not be caught in the bondage of Karma.'"

---

[6] S. Radhakrishnan, *The Bhagavad Gita*, HarperCollins Publishers, India, 2014, p. 382.

Lokmanya now examines the life of the *Sthitaprajna* a little more minutely and explains the benefit for ordinary people. But before that he cautions, "One must also bear in mind that the *Sthitaprajna* is one who has to live in a society in this *Kalyuga*, in which almost all people are steeped in their own selfish interests. Because, however great and complete the Knowledge of a man may be, and whatever the state of equability of 'Mind' which he has reached, it will not do any good if he adopts the practice of harmlessness, kindness, peacefulness, forgiveness etc. in dealing with persons whose minds are impure, and who are caught within the toils of desire, anger etc."

Does this mean that moral standards go by the eye of the beholder? It can't be thus, as that would mean the humanity has no right way, no clear path, but drifts in the turbulent waters of time, without a compass. Each one of us, in our heart, knows when we are wrong. But what to do about it evades us. As religion has little left to offer beyond dogma and there are false gurus appearing and disappearing every season, there is no one sure way to know the difference between right and wrong. Our leaders talk grand visions and boastful ideologies, but hardly say anything practical and helpful. Where does the truth on matters concerning how to live a righteous life, lie? The *Gita* offers the state of *Sthitaprajna* as a definite answer. In the state of *Sthitaprajna*, a different attitude, marked by feeling of letting go of the past, a sense of contentment with the present, and a sturdier confidence in the future, automatically flourishes.

Lokmanya writes, "It need not be said that the rules of Right and Wrong, that are applicable to a society in which the majority of the people are of an avaricious nature, must be at least somewhat different from the rules of Right and Wrong and of Absolute Ethics, applicable to a society in which every person is a *Sthitaprajna*. Otherwise, saints will have to leave this world, and evil-doers will be the rulers everywhere. This does not mean that saints must give up their equable frame of mind. However, there could be various types of equability of 'Mind'. It is stated in the *Gita* that the hearts of saints are equal towards *brahmane gavi hastini*, i.e. Brahmins, cows and elephants."

विद्याविनयसम्पन्ने ब्राह्मणे गवि हस्तिनि ।
शुनि चैव श्वपाके च पण्डिताः समदर्शिनः ॥१८॥

The truly learned and humble (vidya-vinaya-sampanne) see with equal vision (sama-darsinah), a Brahmin, a cow, an elephant (brahmane gavi hastini), a dog (shuni), and a dog-eater (shvapake). (Bhagavad-Gita Chapter 5, Verse 18)

Dr. S. Radhakrishnan elaborates upon this *shloka*, "Great learning brings great humility (*vidyavinayasampanne*). As our knowledge increases, we become increasingly aware of the encircling darkness. It is when we light the candle that we see how dark it is. What we know is practically nothing compared to what we do not know. A little knowledge leads to dogmatism, a little more, to questioning, and a little more takes us to prayer. Besides, humility comes from the knowledge that we are sustained in existence by the love of God. The greatest thinkers of all ages were deeply religious men… the wise see one God in all beings and develop the quality of equal-mindedness, which is the characteristic of the Divine."[7]

But is this possible? This is the most difficult question in *Karma Yoga*. If the saints turns apathetic and tolerate selfish people without getting angry with them and turn a blind eye to the ills in society, just as an ostrich buries its head in the sand, could they qualify to be called as saints? Lokmanya cites Shri Samartha Ramadasa, "One should thoroughly understand and grasp the traditions (*guna*), stories (*katha*), stratagems (*chhal-bal*), strategies (*yukti*), circumstances (*prasanga*), intentness of pursuit (*sapeksha*), inferences (*tarka*), shrewdness (*dhurtapana*), diplomacy (*rajniti*), forbearance (*sahansheelta*), acuteness (*tikshanata*), generosity (*udarata*), metaphysical knowledge (*adhyatma jnana*), devotion (*bhakti*), aloofness (*aliptata*), indifference to the world (*vairagya*), daringness (*dharisht*), aspiration (*havyas*), determination (*kararipana*), firmness (*nigraha*), equability (*samata*), discrimination (*vivek*) and numerous other qualities of such *Jnanins*."

---

[7] S. Radhakrishnan, *The Bhagavad Gita*, HarperCollins Publishers, India, 2014, p. 210-211, 212.

खटनटासी खटनट । अगत्य करी ॥
(दासबोध १९.९.३० राजकारणनिरुपण-२)

One must deal with arrogant, superior and disdainful people with contempt; disrespectful people, with boldness; and traitors, with wickedness. (Dasabodha 19.9.30)

Lokmanya writes, "In short, when a man descends from the state of perfection to ordinary life, it is undoubtedly necessary to make some changes in the rules of 'Right and Wrong' which apply to the highest state... It is no use quarrelling with the permanent laws of Ethics. Although philosophers have mentioned some exceptions to the permanent laws of Ethics, they also mention penances for acting according to different exceptions... The true foundation of Ethics is the frame of mind and mode of life of the *Sthitaprajna Jnanin* (Steady-in-Mind scient)."

It is very fashionable nowadays to talk about individual needs of personal anatomy, personal entitlement, personal privileges, personal wealth and even personal gratification, more so among the young people, who are fortunate to earn large salaries due to globalisation and the information and communication technology sweeping the world markets. The value placed on the individual and all that goes with it– jewellery, cosmetics, consumption, entertainment bordering on addictions, and promiscuous relationships at the workplace– are highly misplaced and of no value whatsoever. These are intrinsically inadequate and ultimately self-defeating. Momentary assuagements bring along lifelong frustrations. Today, market, television and internet-driven shopping in particular, has created an unprecedented gap between human needs and individual desires. The market is generating unhappiness every time it stokes new desires in individual minds. The suffering of countless people, who mortgage their future earnings to the credit card companies, over useless pleasures and meaningless value objects, is humongous.

The commodification is, in some way, even more insidious than the characterisation suggests. Not just lifestyles, but even self-actualisation is packaged and distributed according to market criteria. Young children are made into 'commodities'; so many engineers, so many doctors, so many nurses, so many computer programmers, so many construction workers, even so many pharmacists and so many taxi drivers. Our schools, colleges and universities have become fishing trawlers of human resources for the consumption machine of modern economy. Our day-to-day lives are not shaped by values, but by the market forces operating on our minds through the television and free apps doled out on the Internet. This trend must be halted before it irreversibly breaks the boulder of society into individual sand particles, purposelessly and inconsequentially floating with the winds. Lokmanya categorically states, "Laws of Ethics have been made for the improvement of society. They have been made in order that the activities of society should go on, and that benefit should be acquired in this life and the next."

लोकयात्रा च द्रष्टव्या धर्मश्चात्महितानि च ।
एवं नरो वर्तमानः शाश्वतीरेधते समाः ॥१७॥

(External guiding factors such as) the advancement of society, doubt between what is right and what is wrong, and one's own benefit have always been considered while deciding on what is to be done by a person. (Mahabharata, Anushashan Parva, Adhyaya (Patra pariksha) 37, Shloka 17)

Lokmanya mentions Shibi, a king of the Lunar dynasty (*Chandra vansha*), for correctly discriminating between right and wrong. His story appears in the *Vana Parva* in *Mahabharata*, to emphasise the importance of keeping one's word and upholding *dharma.* The story is also told as a Jataka tale in Buddhist literature. As Shibi sat in the court one day, a pigeon sought refuge in his lap, while being chased by an eagle. Shibi wanted to protect the dove, but the eagle demanded the pigeon from the king, as it constituted his means of subsistence. Accepting the eagle's right, the king offered his own flesh in order to follow his *dharma* of protecting those who took refuge under him. Shibi cut and ripped flesh equal to the dove's weight from his thigh, but it did not weigh nearly as much as the dove, as per the 'test' planned by the gods. Shibi ended up putting his whole body on the weighing scale and passed the test. The hawk flapped its wings and rose in the air and swooped down, as if to peck at the king's flesh. People shut their eyes, unable to bear the spectacle. But to their surprise, they found Indra, the king of gods with the dazzling crown, standing in place of the hawk. He held Shibi's hand and helped him down the weighing scales.

The story beautifully presents the ideal of good kingship. A good king is one who is a protector to all his subjects. Protecting the dove is shown as not being enough, as this would mean starvation of the hawk. By offering his own flesh to the hawk, the king found a way to protect both, the dove and the hawk, even at the expense of his own life.

Contemporary Canadian philosopher Jeff Noonan neatly brings out the involvement of internal forces affecting the external factors. He writes, "My home is made of brick, but its being a home is not reducible to the material from which it is constructed. These bricks have been organised into a coherent structure to serve a definite purpose, and I have certain emotional dispositions towards this structure, that I do not have towards others. This structure, the purpose it serves, and my dispositions towards it, are all irreducible elements of the bricks forming a home." [8]

But then, society cannot survive on the attachments and aversions of individuals. Using an analogy, if one eats a piece of fruit in the expectation that it is nutritious, but it turns out to have been poisoned, then the external factor (poison) destroys the whole person along with his judgement. Values exist in this world till such time that they are life-supporting and give meaning to life. When the society is organised in such a way that it enables not merely the greatest benefit or advantage of the greatest number, but more coherently inclusive ranges of thought/experience/action, only then does life become better and freer for the people.

Lokmanya writes, "The question of whether a particular act is ethically proper or improper, can be considered in two ways: (1) by considering merely its external result, that is to say, its visible effect on the world; and (2) by considering the 'Reason' or the desire of the doer... in order that one's action should be pure, one's 'Practical Reason' has got to be pure, and in order that one's 'Practical Reason' should be pure, one's 'Pure Reason', that is, the reasoning faculty which discriminates between what ought to be done and what ought not to be done, has got to be pure."

In the absence of 'Pure Reason', the 'Practical Reason' can lead to beliefs and behaviours involving uncritical zeal or an obsessive enthusiasm culminating into the deadly force of fanaticism. Actions can be bogus. Hypocrisy of leaders; political, business and even religious leaders, is causing some of the biggest problems to the ordinary people. These attitudes have not only caused severe danger to the growth and well-being of the people, it has made them suspicious and non-believers of goodness. Homes are no longer peaceful, streets are no longer safe, and worse, children are no longer willing to be taught and led, and to serve. Hypocrisy of the rich, powerful and famous has made ordinary people unable to trust others, leave alone build effective relationships. The Reason of the

---

8 Jeff Noonan, *Materialist Ethics and Life-Value*, McGill-Queen's University Press, Montreal 2012, p. 21.

doer rather than the Action of the doer is indeed more important. The *Gita* places the root of Morality as the Reason and not the Action.

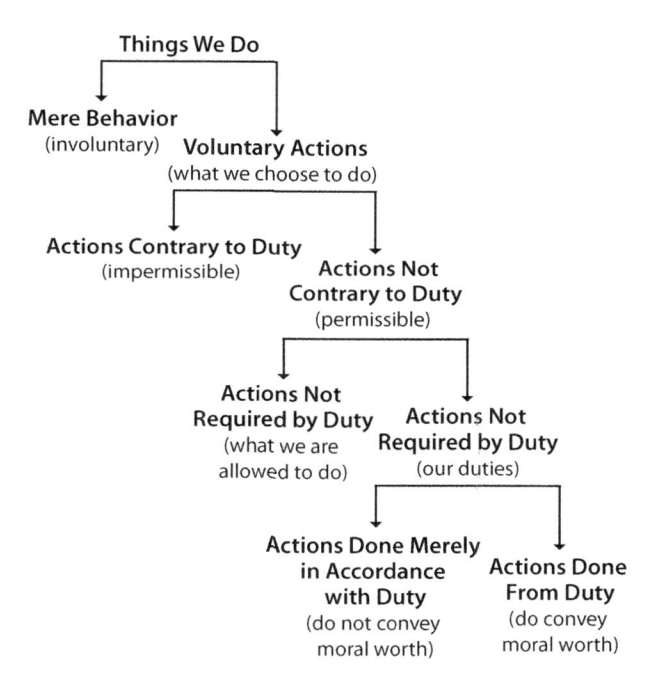

```
                    Things We Do
                         │
           ┌─────────────┴─────────────┐
           ▼                           ▼
    Mere Behavior              Voluntary Actions
     (involuntary)           (what we choose to do)
                                       │
                           ┌───────────┴───────────┐
                           ▼                       ▼
                Actions Contrary to Duty      Actions Not
                    (impermissible)         Contrary to Duty
                                              (permissible)
                                                   │
                                       ┌───────────┴───────────┐
                                       ▼                       ▼
                                Actions Not             Actions Not
                             Required by Duty        Required by Duty
                              (what we are             (our duties)
                              allowed to do)                 │
                                                   ┌─────────┴─────────┐
                                                   ▼                   ▼
                                           Actions Done Merely    Actions Done
                                             in Accordance         From Duty
                                               with Duty          (do convey
                                             (do not convey      moral worth)
                                              moral worth)
```

Classical Greek ethics of Plato and Aristotle give primacy to good character (virtue). Going by the principle of Utilitarian Ethics, the ends justify the means and the conduct which has the best results is declared right. The Bhagavad Gita teaches that our existence has a far nobler end than mere happiness. And Reason is declared as the basis of an action and not the good end. The will of a Sthitaprajna is not merely good as a means to something else, but good in itself.

अनुबन्धं क्षयं हिंसामनवेक्ष्यच च पौरुषम् ।
मोहादारभ्यते कर्म यत्तत्तामसमुच्यते ॥२५॥

Actions taken out of delusion (mohat), disregarding (anapekshya) the consequences (anubandham), loss and injury (kshayamhinsam) that they may cause, and without assessing one's capacity to implement them (anapekshya cha paurusham), spring out of the mental state of dullness (tamasamuchyate). (Bhagavad-Gita Chapter 18, Verse 25)

Such a person, who starts doing whatever he feels like, without reasoning, is said to be *tamasik* or devilish. Swami Mukundananda adds, "The intellects of those in *tamoguna* are covered by the fog of ignorance. They are oblivious to, or unconcerned with, what is right and what is wrong, and are only interested in themselves and their self-interest. They pay no heed to money or the resources at hand, or even to the hardships incurred by others. Such work brings harm to them and to others... (also) *Tamasik* action causes decay of one's health and vitality. It is a waste of effort, a waste of time, and a waste of resources. Typical examples of this are gambling, stealing, corruption, drinking, etc."[9] On the other hand, when a person is established in 'Pure Reason', proper and right actions are automatically performed and the person flourishes for his own good and the good of all others around him.

Lokmanya writes, "To express the matter in short, the doctrine of the *Gita* is that morality does not consist of material action only, but that it wholly depends on the 'Reason' of the doer. If a man, not realising the true principle underlying this doctrine, starts doing whatever he likes, he must be said to be a *tamasa* or a devil. Once the mind has become equable, it is not necessary to give the man any further advice about the propriety or the impropriety of actions. Bearing this principle in mind, Saint Tukaram had preached to Shivaji Maharaj, the sole doctrine of *Karma Yoga*, similar to the *Bhagavad-Gita*, in the *abhanga*:

कल्याणकारक अर्थ याचा एक । सर्वांभूतीं देख एक आत्मा ॥

This has only one merit-producing meaning;

There is only one Atman, that is, God in all created beings."
(Tukaram Gatha, 4428. 9)

There is a cart before the horse paradox here. How does one get to the equable 'Reason' so that his conduct becomes proper (*sadacharana*)? Is it proper action that emanates from 'Reason', or

---

9 www.holy-bhagavad-gita.org/chapter/18/verse/25. Last accessed on 14 October 2017.

'Reason' that is constructed out of consistent and incessant proper conduct? There is a famous saying in Myanmar Buddhism that human life is not a pagoda to be built for which the trellis of good conduct are erected. Human lives are indeed the trellis, which are used to build the pagoda that is the society. Human lives are indeed seen merely means to build a good society!

Lokmanya writes, "It is stated already in the commencement of the *Gita*, that because this (to make one's mind like that of a *Sthitaprajna*) is the highest ideal, one need not wait for performing action until that ideal has been reached. One should, in the meantime, perform all actions with as much unselfishness as possible, so that thereby the 'Reason' will become purer and purer, and the highest state of perfection will ultimately be reached, and one must not waste time by insisting on not performing any action until the perfect state of the 'Reason' has been reached."

नेहाभिक्रमनाशोऽस्ति प्रत्यवायो न विद्यते ।
स्वल्पमप्यस्य धर्मस्य त्रायते महतो भयात् ॥४०॥

In this path (of knowledge and renunciation of desire and taking up of action), there is no loss or adverse result (abhikrama-naso), and even a little effort in this way (sva alpam apy asya dharmasya) protects (trayate) one from great danger (trayate mahato bhayat). (Bhagavad-Gita Chapter 2, Verse 40)

The principle, enunciated in the *Isha Upanishad*, that a *yatra va asya sarvam atmavibhut* (the man for whom everything is in unison with the *Atman*) behaves towards others with a perfectly equable 'Mind', is now examined.

यस्तु सर्वाणि भूतानि आत्मन्येवानुपश्यति ।
सर्वभूतेषु चात्मानं ततो न विजुगुप्सते ॥६॥

To see all beings emanated out of one Supreme Self, and to see that Supreme Self in all beings; a person, by virtue of this perception, does not dislike anyone. (Isha Upanishad, Verse 6)

This same principle has been literally enunciated in the *Bhagavad-Gita*:

सर्वभूतस्थमात्मानं सर्वभूतानि चात्मनि ।
ईक्षते योगयुक्तात्मा सर्वत्र समदर्शनः ॥२९॥

The true yogis, skilfully uniting their consciousness with the God (yoga-yukta-atma), see everywhere with an equal eye (sarvatra sama-darsanah), all living beings in God and God in all living beings (sarva-bhuta-sthamatmanam). (Bhagavad-Gita Chapter 6, Verse 29)

Different people in the world have seen the Hindu concept of Self-realisation– knowledge of *Atman* as our real identity– differently. Some saw is it as a realisation of one's full potential, akin to a seed becoming a tree and not being wasted as a sapling, plant or by not even sprouting. Some others saw it as expressing one's creativity, using one's innate talents into art forms and skilful performances. On the other hand, many people, even in the Western societies, particularly the early Protestant Christian missionaries, saw it as a quest for spiritual enlightenment and to give back to society. The *Gita* very clearly laid down that man's fullness can only be reached when he expresses and interacts with the outside world and does not run away from the world in pursuit of the internal wholeness of the self.

Lokmanya writes, "The ultimate and the most comprehensive interpretation of the canon of Self-identification is that the highest idea of manhood and the most complete fructification of the arrangement of the four states of life consists in: (1) realising that family life is but the first lesson in the science of Self-identification, and (2) instead of being continually engrossed in the family, making one's 'Self-identifying Reason' more and more comprehensive, by substituting one's friends, one's relations, or those born in the same *gotra* (clan) as oneself, or the inhabitants of one's own village, or the members of one's own community, or one's co-religionists, and ultimately, all human beings, or all created beings, in place of one's family, thereby realising that, that *Atman*, which is within oneself, is also within all created beings; and that one should regulate one's conduct accordingly."

The philosophy of the *Karma Yoga* is an incredible integration of the internal and external worlds of a human life. Though the foundation of the *Karma Yoga* is the knowledge of the Supreme Self (*Atman*), it does not limit the purpose of life as the realisation of the inherent comprehensiveness of the *Atman* (*atma vaiputrananasi*). *Karma Yoga* calls for the regulation of one's activities, believing that the whole universe is one big family (*vasudhaiva kutumbakam*).

अयं बन्धुरयं नेति गणना लघुचेतसाम् ।
उदारचरितानां तु वसुधैव कुटुम्बकम् ॥७१॥

Those who discriminate people as others and mine are of a small mind. For the magnanimous people, the entire world constitutes one family. (Maha Upanishad, Chapter 6, Verse 71).

This concept, with no parallel in any other culture in the world, is not limited to peace and harmony among different races, societies, religious beliefs, political ideologies, or countries in the world, but conveys a truth that the whole world has to live as a family, with shared responsibility and resources. The false security of modern technology has thickened the delusion of the fragility of human existence on this planet. Modern children eating instant dinners cooked in microwave ovens do not even know that the food is not coming from the supermarket, not even from the field of a farmer, but from the Sun, which is 150 million kilometres away. Our ignorance that we are a part of a big system, of which even the Sun is a very small part, does not change the fact of our existential dependence on almost everything else around us– plants, animals, atmosphere, moon, planets, stars and so on.

Lokmanya writes, offering no excuse for the small-mindedness of a person, "Those ordinary persons, whose 'Mind' has not reached the state of equability, add their feeling of mine-ness (*mamatva*) to this law of Cause and Effect, and making the counterblow stronger than the blow, take their revenge for the blow; or, if the other person is weak, they are ready to take advantage of some trifling or imaginary affront, and rob him to their own advantage, under the pretext of retaliation. However, if a man, whose 'Mind' has become free from the feelings of revenge, enmity, or pride, or free from the desire of robbing the weak as a result of anger, avarice, or hatred, or free from the desire of obstinately making an exhibition of one's greatness, authority, or power, which inhabits the minds of ordinary people, merely throws back a stone that has been thrown at him, that does not disturb the peacefulness, non-inimicality and equability of his 'Mind'. It is, on the other hand, his duty, from the point of view of universal welfare, to take such retaliatory action, for the purpose of preventing the predominance of wrong-doers and the consequent persecution of the weak in the world."

सक्ताः कर्मण्यविद्वांसो यथा कुर्वन्ति भारत ।
कुर्याद्विद्वांस्तथासक्तश्चिकीर्षुर्लोकसंग्रहम् ॥२५॥

(Shri Krishna tells Arjuna), As ignorant people (avidvamsah) perform their duties with attachment to the results (saktahkarmany), O scion of Bharat, so should the wise act without attachment (asaktah), for the sake of maintaining the world order and for the good of the people (loka-sangraham)
(Bhagavad-Gita Chapter 3, Verse 25)

Every one is born in a world pre-existed and the world continues after one's exit out of it at the time of death. A life is therefore like a wave on the body of water and nothing more. It is therefore wise to see the world as a ground of individual life and not the other way round. Working for the well-being of all mankind and not self-feeding and aggrading is the real purpose of a life. This has been at the core of all religions. Lokmanya writes, "It is not that the *Karma Yogin Sthitaprajna* disregards the religious doctrines of behaving non-inimically towards everybody, not doing evil to evildoers, or not getting angry with those who are angry with one. But, instead of accepting the doctrine of the School of Renunciation that 'Non-inimicality' (*nirvana*) means inactivity or non-retaliation, the philosophy of *Karma Yoga* says that *nirvaira* means merely giving up *vaira* or the feeling of hostility and the desire to do evil. Inasmuch as nobody can escape *Karma*, one should perform as much *Karma* as is possible and necessary for the social welfare, without entertaining any evil desire, and as a matter of duty, and apathetically, and without Attachment. Therefore, instead of using the word *nirvaira* by itself, the Blessed Lord has placed the important adjective *mat-karma-krit* (perform duties for my sake) before it (in the *Gita*)."

मत्कर्मकृन्मत्परमो मद्भक्तः सङ्गवर्जितः ।
निर्वैरः सर्वभूतेषु यः स मामेति पाण्डव ॥५५॥

Shri Krishna tells Arjuna, "Those who perform all their duties for My sake (mat-karma-krt), who depend upon me (mat-paramah) and are devoted to me (mat-bhaktah), who are free from attachment, and are without malice towards all beings (nirvairahsarva-bhutesu); such devotees certainly come to Me (mam eti)." (Bhagavad-Gita Chapter 11, Verse 55)

This *shloka* brilliantly interlocks non-inimicality with 'desireless action' and provides a unique perspective to the spirit of devotion. The Blessed Lord is assuming the full and final responsibility for all the Action for Him, and with the idea of dedicating it to Him. Lokmanya cites examples from the *Dvapara Yuga*. Still upset and loathful, Vibhishana, the brother of Ravana, who was killed in war by Shri Rama, is hesitant to perform his funeral ceremony. Shri Rama tells Vibhishana:

मरणान्तानि वैराणि निवृत्तं नः प्रयोजनम् ।
क्रियतामस्य संस्कारो ममाप्येष यथा तव॥

Whatever desire to do evil (vaira) was there in the mind of your brother (Ravana), has come to an end, now that he is dead, just as My duty of punishing evil-doers has ended. Now I have no enmity with Ravana and neither should you. Therefore, cremate your brother's body (as a matter of duty, and apathetically, and without Attachment). (Valmiki Ramayana, Book 6 (Yuddha Kanda), Chapter (Sarga) 109. Shloka 25)

Here, Lokmanya brilliantly argues in favour of taking care of one's family, serving the society and the national pride, and not escaping from them in the name of living by 'Pure Reason' and justifying the apathy towards one's responsibilities, and escaping from the affairs of the world as a consequence of the realisation of the *Atman*. Lokmanya writes, "(as) it is not possible to do away with the lower floors of the building, when the higher floors are built... as the pick axe does not cease to be necessary because one has got a sword... as the fire does not cease to be necessary, because one has the sun... so also does patriotism, family, not become unnecessary, although one has reached the topmost stage of the welfare of all created things... patriotism and pride of one's family and other creeds are always necessary to the same extent as Equability of Reason."

Conflict of interests is the hallmark of human society. Starting from personal interests, to familial concerns, to castes, creeds, language, religion, and even the form of the God and the way God is to be worshipped, are the fault lines over which the affairs of the world operate. How to choose between the conflicting interests has been a constant theme of religious scriptures and philosophical writings. Lokmanya cites the *Mahabharata*, where Dhritarashtra wrongly chose the interests of his son, Duryodhana, over a war that eventually destroyed his entire clan. The famous lines of Dhritarashtra's brother, Vidura, are quoted:

त्यजेदेकं कुलस्यार्थे ग्रामस्यार्थे कुलं त्यजेत् ।
ग्रामं जनपदस्यार्थे आत्मार्थे पृथिवीं त्यजेत् ॥

One member of the family must be abandoned to protect a family; one family must be forsaken for the protection of a town. The town must be given up for the protection of the society and for protecting the Atman, this life (on earth) is better sacrificed.
(Mahabharata, Adi Parva, 115. 36)

Lokmanya writes, "When all things have been considered in this way, it becomes clear that the true duty of a *Jnanin* is (1) to keep their own 'Reason' free from objects of pleasure; peaceful, non-inimical, and equable, by Realising the identity of the *Brahman* and the *Atman;* and (2) without getting disgusted with ordinary ignorant people and accepting the state of abandonment of action (*karma-samnyasa*), to preach to people, whatever is proper for them; having regard for the prevailing conditions, and to place before their eyes the living example of a model moral life, in the shape of their own desireless adherence to duty, and (3) in that way, to place all on the path of betterment, as gradually and peacefully as possible, but at the same time, enthusiastically. This is what is done by the Blessed Lord by taking various incarnations from time to time. The sum and substance of the entire philosophy of the *Gita* is that scients should follow the same example, and should, at all times, continue to do their duty in this world desirelessly, and to the best of their abilities, and with a pure 'Mind', without an eye to the Fruit. They should also be willing to lay down their lives, if necessary, while they are doing so, and they must not, under any circumstances, fail in their duty. This is what is known as the universal welfare (*lokasmgraha*). This is the true *Karma Yoga*."

The philosophy of *Karma Yoga* places great emphasis on the presence of *Sthitaprajna* (Steady-in-Mind) people in the society, who function as an example in morally imperfect societies. They act like a calibration standard against which ordinary people test their own behaviour and modify their actions. There are no commandments, no manuals of do's and don'ts. It is startling to observe the emphasis that the Blessed Lord is laying on the freedom of the individual, which the later religions have systematically taken away from the people.

श्रेयान्स्वधर्मो विगुणः परधर्मात्स्वनुष्ठितात् ।
स्वधर्मे निधनं श्रेयः परधर्मो भयावहः ॥३५॥

It is far better to perform one's natural prescribed duty, though tinged with faults (sreyansva-dharmovigunah), than to perform another's prescribed duty (para-dharmat), though perfectly. In fact, it is preferable to die (nidhanamsreyah) in the discharge of one's duty, than to follow the path of another, which (action) is fraught with danger (para-dharmobhayavahah). (Bhagavad-Gita Chapter 3, Verse 35)

Dr. S. Radhakrishnan adds, "We have not all the same gifts, but what is vital, is not whether we are endowed with five talents or only one, but how faithfully we have employed the trust committed to us. We must play our part manfully, be it great or small. Goodness denotes perfection of quality. However distasteful one's duty may be, one must be faithful to it even unto death."[10]

Swami Ranganathananda explains, "Find out your own *dharma*, based on your mental disposition. *Shreyan svadharmo vigunah*– even though one's own *dharma* is not of a high quality, still it is the best for oneself... Like the individuality of one's thumb impression... There is a psychic individuality that is based on a certain bent of life, attitudes, reactions, likes and dislikes. All these constitute one's individuality; let one respect it and not imitate somebody else; don't be ashamed of yourself. This *shloka* refers to this need on our part to have faith in ourselves, confidence in ourselves, in one's own psychological disposition. One should change it for the better but should not exchange it, should not cast oneself in the mould of somebody else."[11]

Our philosophers have, never indeed, accepted the doctrine of balancing of self-interest and other's interest. *Svadharma* remained the hallmark of ethics in the ancient Indian society. It is a pity for the pea-hen to dance because the peacock does so. Upon seeing an eagle, swooping down, taking a prey in its claws and flying high up in the air, if a crow also attempts to do so, it is sure to come to grief. Therefore, acceptance of one's own *dharma* is fundamental. And it is only possible by nurturing equable reason. Lokmanya writes, "One must depend on the principle of an equable 'Reason', which is always alive in the hearts of saints; and that Equability of 'Reason' is the true root of the philosophy of *Karma Yoga*."

A very important point is now raised about the control of all organs of actions when the mind is constantly thinking of sensory objects. Lokmanya writes, "That man alone is the highest of men, whose Reason is pure. Rather, one may even say that the man, who,

---

10 S. Radhakrishnan, *The Bhagavad Gita*, HarperCollins Publishers, Noida, India, 2014, p. 168-169.
11 Swami Ranganathananda, *Universal Message of the Bhagavad Gita, Vol. 1*, Advaita Ashrama, Kolkata 2015 (Seventh reprint), p.313.

without having a pure mind, is only engrossed in the calculating discrimination between outward Actions, runs the risk of becoming a hypocrite." Though physically the person is absolutely quiet; his mind is desperately craving for objects. Many people outwardly renounce physical pleasures, take vows, but their mind is not settled in the ideal of equable 'Reason'. They keep on doing things in a subversive way by secret methods. The Blessed Lord declares them as *mithyachari* (hypocrites), in the *Gita*.

कर्मेन्द्रियाणि संयम्य य आस्ते मनसा स्मरन् ।
इन्द्रियार्थान्विमूढात्मा मिथ्याचारः स उच्यते ॥६॥

Those who restrain the external organs of action (karmendriyani samyamya), but continue to dwell on sense objects in the mind and brood (aste manasa smaran), certainly delude themselves and are to be called hypocrites, men of false conduct (mithya-acarah). (Bhagavad-Gita Chapter 3, Verse 6)

Dr. S. Radhakrishnan adds, "We may control outwardly our activities, but if do not restrain the desires which impel them, we have failed to grasp the true meaning of restraint."[12]

Swami Ranganathananda explains, "The honest way is: do you want this? Yes, I want it. The devious way is: I don't want it, but … seeking it by devious means. This kind of hypocrisy has come to us due to not understanding the high ideal of actionlessness, desirelessness, etc. In our present state, we can say honestly, yes, I want sense pleasure. There is no hypocrisy in it. I run after a thing, I seek it, I want it, but why be a hypocrite? When the mind develops, I will be able to say I don't want it, because I have achieved something higher within me. Then there will be no hypocrisy."[13]

Lokmanya takes a very pragmatic stand here. He writes, "Just as when a man is down with a very serious illness, its diagnosis or treatment is impossible without the help of a clever doctor, so also, will it be futile for an ordinary person to proudly imagine that he

---
12 S. Radhakrishnan, *The Bhagavad Gita*, HarperCollins Publishers, India, 2014, p. 153.
13 Swami Ranganathananda, *Universal Message of the Bhagavad Gita, Vol. 1*, Advaita Ashrama, Kolkata, 2015 (Seventh reprint), p.262.

will be able to arrive at a faultless decision between morality and immorality, without the help of saints... when there is a difficult and a doubtful situation."

But Lokmanya also advises to diligently seek Equability of Reason. He writes, "One must always increase the Equability of Reason' by constant practice, and when the minds of all the human beings in the world gradually reach the state of perfect Equability in this way, the *Krtayuga* will start, and the highest ideal or the most perfect state of the human race will be reached by everyone."

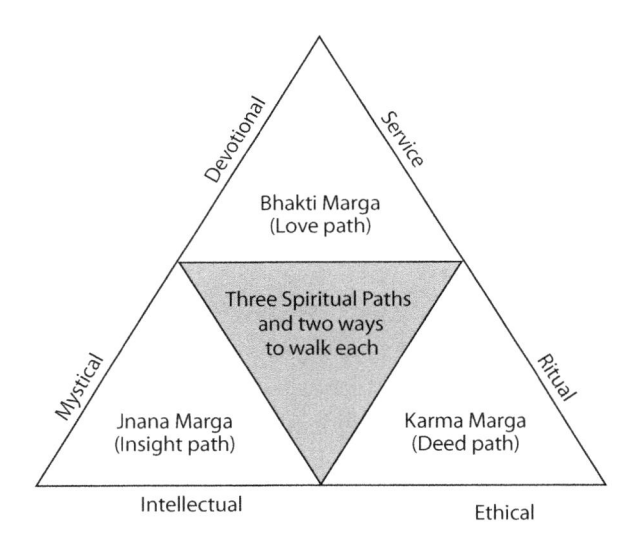

```
                        /\
                       /  \
                      /Dev.\ Service
                     /otional\
                    /          \
                   / Bhakti Marga\
                  /  (Love path)  \
                 /_____\
                /\                  /\
               /  \                /  \
              /    \  Three       /    \
             /      \ Spiritual  /      \
           Mystical  \  Paths   /        Ritual
           /          \ and two/          \
          /            \ ways /            \
         /              \ to /              \
        /  Jnana Marga   \  /  Karma Marga   \
       /   (Insight path) \/   (Deed path)    \
      /_____\
            Intellectual          Ethical
```

The Bhagavad-Gita extols three major margas or paths of skilled effort (Yoga), which help the aspirant frame his personal nature with the highest goal-realisation and union with Brahman, or the all-knowing and pervasive consciousness that governs the universe. Although each path is different, the destination is ultimately the same.

A *Sthitaprajna* looks upon the world as phenomena in which he has a definitive role of maintaining the order and progressing the evolution. As *Sthitaprajna* persons are few and rare, the ordinary people must develop certain qualities and nurture certain virtues keeping in mind the existence of an individual for the society and not the other way round. Living by this understanding only can one be truly happy in life. The *Gita* is unique in its astute comprehension of all possible spiritual paths and how to trek them. The *Gita* does not tell us in terms of do's and don'ts, it does not offer commandments, it asks you to anchor in to the Reason and light up your surroundings so that you can chose as well as walk your path.

Having completed a thorough examination of *Jnana Marga* and *Karma Marga,* Lokmanya now takes the reader to the *Bhakti Marga,* the "import of the *Gita,* which still remains to be dealt with".

ॐ

13

The Path of Devotion

तुम सुणो जी मुहांरो अरजी ।
भवसागर में बही जात हूं काढो तो थांरी मरजी ।
इण संसार सगो नहि कोई सांचा सगा रघुबरजी ॥
मात-पिता और कुटम कबीलो सब मतलब के गरजी ॥

Please listen to my plea. I am drowning in this world (*bhavsagar*); pull me out if you wish. Except the truthful and caring God (Raghubarji), no one is indeed trustworthy. Parents, family members and community; every one deals with me according to their interests.

Mira Bai

Work, apart from devotion or love of God, is helpless and cannot stand alone.

Ramakrishna Paramahamsa

Love is a little word, but contains so much to think about and can be felt in so many different ways. Normal human experience is woven around multiple forms of love– affection, appreciation, devotion, fondness, friendship, infatuation, lust, passion, respect, tenderness, yearning, worship, and so on. There is possessive love– the desire to possess objects, animals and even people. There is status love - love of name and fame, of wealth etc. There is aesthetic love - of the arts, music, and the love of nature. Above all, there is love for God– a sublime form of love. Saint-poet Kabir (1440– 1518), very beautifully says:

ढाई अक्षर प्रेम का, पढे सो पंडित होए ॥

The two and a half letters of the word 'love', contains the entire wisdom of the world.

Love for God is better called devotion. It is primarily giving oneself to the service of God through feelings, thoughts and deeds. Devotion involves a profound sense of loyalty and an intense feeling of regard. Humility is the hallmark of devotion. One consciously becomes small before God, and starts doing menial work without hesitation, for example, cleaning floors in a temple, or polishing the shoes of devotees in a Gurudwara. A majority of people develop devotion to the forms of God– idols, saints, animals, trees, and even rituals and talismans. A few persons can even feel the divine and become conscious of spiritual energy as the principle of life and can sense the spirit or presence of God, in every form.

A *Bhakta*, a person in devotional love of God, feels an emotional fulfilment in worshipping God or doing service to please God. This bonding leads to a progressive transformation that not only improves the outer deeds of the devotee, but even the body becomes transformed as the degree of love enhances. Spanish priest and theologian Saint Ignatius of Loyola (1491-1556), famously said, "Above all, remember that God looks for solid virtues in us, such as patience, humility, obedience, abnegation of your own will - that is, the good will to serve Him and our neighbour in Him. His providence allows us other devotions only insofar as He sees that they are useful to us." The periods of higher consciousness are felt more frequently and people even hear revelations and have *darshan* of the God forms.

Lokmanya opens this chapter with the words of Shri Krishna, in the *Gita*:

सर्वधर्मान्परित्यज्य मामेकं शरणं व्रज ।
अहं त्वां सर्वपापेभ्यो मोक्षयिष्यामि मा शुचः ॥६६॥

Abandoning all forms of rites and duties for my sake (sarva-dharmanparityajya mam), take refuge in Me alone (ekamsharanamvraja). I shall free you from all sins (aham tvam sarva-pāpebhyo mokshayishyami). (Therefore) do not fear (ma shuchah). (Bhagavad-Gita Chapter 18, Verse 66)

Lokmanya writes, "There is no doubt that realisation of the identity of the *Brahman* and the *Atman* is the only true reality and the ideal... (However), the path or manner of acquiring that Equability of Reason, is wholly dependent on the Reason itself. Ordinary persons feel a doubt as to how one can acquire that keenness of Intelligence by which that path or manner can be fully realised. If somebody's Reason is not so keen, that man must be considered as lost; and such a doubt is certainly not ill-founded. They say: if even the greatest of *Jnanins* have to say *neti, neti* (It is not this, It is not this) in describing that immortal highest *Brahman* (*Parabrahman*), which is clothed in the perishable *Name-d and Form-ed Maya*, how are ordinary persons like us to understand it?"

So devotion emerges as an easier path. Deep knowledge of the *Brahman* is brought closer to the person as an idol or a guru, and made palatable to the limited receptiveness of his senses and the capacity of comprehension of his mind. It is widely written and believed as true that the experience of the *Brahman* and the *Atman* can't be described and even those who felt it could never share the experience with others, neither through speech, nor writing. Lokmanya cites a story about this from the *Shruti* texts. He writes, "(a certain student) Baskali asked Bahva (his teacher) the question: "My lord, explain to me, please, what the *Brahman* is". Bahva would not give any answer. Though Baskali repeated the question, Bahva was still silent. When this happened three or four times, Bahva said to Baskali, "I have been all this while giving an answer to your question, and yet you do not understand it. What more can I do?"

दर्शयति चाथो अपि स्मर्यते ॥१७॥

The form of the Brahman cannot be described in any way, and therefore, remaining quiet and not giving any description of it, is the truest description of the Brahman. Have you now understood it? (Vedanta Sutra, 3. 2. 17).

It is indeed not possible for any man to realise the indescribable, unimaginable *Brahman*. The *Brahman* is incommunicable as it is absolutely different from the visible world. The words, "there is only one *Atman* in all created beings", therefore, remain an esoteric statement actually meaning nothing. There is no hope for the billions of people in the world of ever attaining the *Brahman*. Of course, there have been *rishis*, prophets and scients, who have described their realisation of the *Brahman*, and while there is no reason to doubt them, their descriptions are numerous and vary a lot. Swami Vivekananda very beautifully says, "There is only one thing real in the universe, which it calls *Brahman*; everything else is unreal, manifested and manufactured out of *Brahman* by the power of *Maya*. To reach back to that *Brahman* is our goal. We are, each one of us, that *Brahman*, that Reality, plus this *Maya*. If we can get rid of this *Maya* or ignorance, then we become what we really are."[1]

There are so many versions of experiencing the God and they come from so many widely varied sources, that the concept of faith in God has been separated from science. It is another matter that time and again scientists have been proven wrong, the 'facts' of one generation have turned into 'fallacies' of the next generation and the 'wild imagination' of one generation have turned into a 'normal fact' for the other generation. Though it is common to call faith a firm belief in something for which there is no proof, and equally common to hear that faith is belief without the need for any proof, it is indeed true that in a world of imperfect beings, inadequate senses, and partial experience, that mark every step of scientific inquiry, absolute certainty is as abstract a concept as faith.

Lokmanya writes, "Really speaking, it will be seen that Knowledge does not become complete or even fruitful without Religious Faith (*shraddha*). That all Knowledge is acquired merely by Intelligence, and that no other mental faculties are necessary for that purpose, is an idle belief of certain philosophers, whose minds have become crude as a result of a life-long contact with sciences, which are based on inferential reasoning."

---

1 http://www.swamivivekanandaquotes.org/2013/12/swami-vivekananda-brahma-quotes.html. Last accessed on 20 October 2017.

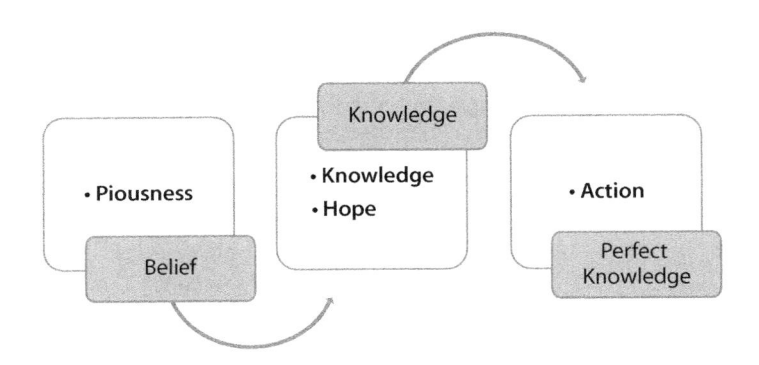

```
           ┌─────────┐
           │Knowledge│
           └─────────┘
  ┌──────┐  ┌─────────┐  ┌──────┐
  │•Piousness│ │•Knowledge│ │•Action│
  │          │ │•Hope     │ │       │
  │  Belief  │ │          │ │Perfect│
  └──────────┘ └─────────┘ │Knowledge│
                           └────────┘
```

Faith is the bridge between belief and knowledge. As a vehicle, faith moves one from belief to knowledge. Faith can never be blind, as it is born out of reason that captures the credibility of the evidence which produces it. We have faith in God because we give credibility to the narratives of the sages and seers. And the faithful actions of our ancestors have created knowledge that is most useful.

Our brains are conditioned from the moment we arrive in this world. Not only does the causal body accompany the soul in the new body, carrying along energy impulses loaded with consequences of the deeds in the earlier lives, but also, each sensory input– the touch of the mother, light, sound, smell– gets recorded in the nascent brain– in the very early life. As this information record keeps getting captured and stored in our brains, a very personalised system of thought is created, as beliefs of what is good and what is not good. Collectively, the same process creates the worldview of a family, a community, a society and even a nation and a race. It is through this worldview, and never directly, that we understand new information and evaluate our experiences in the world and our reactions and responses to it. It is important to understand that our beliefs and worldviews do not have any inherent validity beyond our brains. Each one of us carries within our heads, a model, based upon which, we construe the world around us.

Lokmanya writes, "Therefore, in order to perfect the knowledge which has been acquired by Intelligence, and in order that, that knowledge should be translated by means of the Intelligence, into behaviour and action, such knowledge has to always rely on Faith, Kindness, Affection, Love of Duty, and other inherent mental tendencies. That knowledge, which does not rely on the help of these mental tendencies, after they have been awakened and purified, must be looked upon as bare, incomplete, perversely inferential, and barren or immature. Just as a bullet in a gun cannot be fired without the help of gunpowder, so also, the knowledge which is acquired merely by Intelligence, cannot redeem anyone without the help of mental qualities like Love, Faith, etc."

Lokmanya cites the story of Shvetketu, stated in the *Chandogya Upanishad*. Shvetketu's father instructs him to bring the fruit of a banyan tree and asks him to see what is inside. When Shvetketu cuts open the fruit, he sees innumerable minute seeds or grains inside. His father again asks him to take one of the seeds and look inside it. Shvetketu sees nothing inside the seed and tells his father, "There is nothing inside the seed." Upon this, Shvetketu's father asks him how the tremendous banyan tree had sprung from that nothing which he saw inside, and asked him to put faith in this, rather than calling it nothing.

तँ होवाच यं वै सोम्यैतमणिमानं न निभालयस
एतस्य वै सोम्यैषोऽणिम्न एवं महान्यग्रोधस्तिष्ठति
श्रद्धत्स्व सोम्येति ॥६.१२.२॥

Then he (the father) said to him (Shvetketu), that subtle essence (which indeed creates a giant nyagrodha tree but), you don't see that, put faith (shraddhasva) there. (Chandogya Upanishad, Chapter 6, Section 12, Shloka 2).

Lokmanya explains with powerful similes, "If Faith is ultimately necessary in order to obtain the definite knowledge that the Sun is going to rise to-morrow morning, then it undoubtedly follows that after having gone by the cart-road of Intelligence as far as possible to completely realise the eternal, unending, all-causing, all-knowing, independent and vital Principle, which is the root of the entire universe, one has to go further, at least to some extent, by the foot-path of Faith and Affection. The woman, who a man looks upon as venerable and worshipful, because she is his mother, is looked upon by others as an ordinary woman, or, according to the scientific camouflage of words of Logicians, she is merely a matter of human female progestogens. From this simple example, one can easily understand the difference that is brought about by pouring the Knowledge acquired by mere inference, into the mould of Faith and Affection. For this very reason, the *Gita* declared, "the most excellent *Karma Yogin* from among all, is the one who has Faith".

योगिनामपि सर्वेषां मद्गतेनान्तरात्मना ।
श्रद्धावान्भजते यो मां स मे युक्ततमो मतः ॥४७॥

Even among all the yogis, he who abides by Me (mat-gatena) with his mind fixed on Me (antah-atmana) and with faith, (shraddhavan) renders to me his loving service (bhajate); he is considered by Me to be the best of the yogis (sa me yuktatamo matah). (Bhagavad-Gita Chapter 6, Verse 47)

An exact opposite of this is happening today. Knowledge is increasingly getting narrowly defined as information. An internet connection on mobile phones has created a cognitive deluge. We have information about almost everything for which we have either no direct experience or data to know its accuracy and thereby we are getting drowned in a false worldview. An unprecedented darkness is enveloping the collective consciousness of the people. The knowledge with which people deal today– be it business, medicine, agriculture - which is presented as scientific, accurate and seemingly trustworthy, has severe limits and is a product of vested, commercial and even extractive sources. This has taken a toll on the faith and confidence of people, who are swayed by false information and land up in difficult situations, for example, business losses, ill health and mental disorientation. Deception can never lead us to the truth. The more the emphasis is on expressing a 'fact', the more the chances are of it being the product of deceit. So, how one can deal with this? Lokmanya's words assume a greater importance than ever before. "If the only difficulty were that the quality-less *Parabrahman* is difficult to realise for ordinary persons, then that difficulty could be overcome by Faith or confidence, though there might be a difference of opinion among the intelligent persons. In such a case, we could judge for ourselves, which of these intelligent persons was more reliable, and then we could put our faith in his statements."

ध्यानेनात्मनि पश्यन्ति केचिदात्मानमात्मना ।
अन्ये साङ्ख्येन योगेन कर्मयोगेन चापरे ॥२५॥

Some try to perceive the one Supreme Soul (kecidatmanam) within their hearts (atmana), others, through meditation (dhyanena), some others try to do so through the cultivation of knowledge (sankhyena), while still others strive to attain that realisation by the path of action (karma-yogena). (Bhagavad-Gita Chapter 13, Verse 25)

What is that knowledge, by which, information offered for free can be tested– reinforced or refuted? Lokmanya provides the answer. It is our belief system, our anchor in to the cosmic intellect (*Prajna*) that can save one from such tribulations and eventual drowning in the deluge of information. Lokmanya writes, "Variety is indeed the universal characteristic of God's creation. No two leaves of a tree are alike; no two human beings have exactly the same fingerprints; no two human societies have the same features. Similarly, all souls are unique, and they have their distinctive traits that have been acquired in their unique journey through the cycle of life and death. Therefore, in the realm of spiritual practice as well, not all are attracted to the same kind of practice. The beauty of the *Bhagavad-Gita* and the Vedic scriptures is that they realise this inherent variety among human beings and accommodate it in their instructions."

And how do we get anchored in to *Prajna*? Swami Muktananda provides the answer as devotion to the God. He writes in his commentary on this *shloka*, "Here, Shri Krishna explains that some *sadhaks* (aspirants) find great joy in grappling with their mind and bringing it under control. They are attracted to meditating upon God, seated within their hearts. They relish the spiritual bliss that they experience when their mind comes to rest upon the Lord within them. Others find satisfaction in exercising their intellect. The idea of the distinction of the soul, the body, mind, intellect, and ego excites them greatly. They relish cultivating knowledge about the three entities– soul, God, and *Maya*– through the processes of *shravana, manan, nididhyasan* (hearing, contemplating, and internalising with firm faith). Yet others find their spirits soaring when they can engage in meaningful action. They strive to engage their God-given abilities in working for Him. Nothing satisfies them more than using the last drop of their energy in the service of God. In this way, all kinds of *sadhaks* utilise their individual propensities for realizing the Supreme. The fulfilment of any endeavour involving knowledge, action, love, etc., is when it is combined with devotion for the pleasure of God."

But what pleases the God? In the *Shrimad Bhagavatam*, there is a conversation between Narada Muni and King Prachinabarhi. The king is proudly engaged in performing animal sacrifices to please the God. Narada Muni chastises him and tells him that he is merely puffing himself up with false prestige by killing the animals that grew on the grass that covers the earth by the grace of the God. When God-consciousness is missing, one is simply engaged in false activities and false educational pursuits.

आस्तीर्य दर्भैः प्रागग्रैः कात्स्न्येन क्षितिमण्डलम् ।
स्तब्धो बृहद्वधानमानी कर्म नावैषि यत्परम् ।
तत्कर्म हरितोषं यत्सा विद्या तन्मतिर्ययाा ॥४९॥

The entire world is covered (ksiti-mandalam) with the grass (astiryadarbhaih) feeding animals. Foolish people feel proud by sacrificing these animals (stabdhobrhad-vadhan) as an offering to the God. They do not know that devotional service is the only way one can please the God (hari-tosham). We must educate ourselves to elevate our consciousness (sa vidya tan-matiryaya). (Shrimad Bhagavatam 4.29.49)

But how one can serve God, who is imperceptible? Devoting oneself to an imperceptible God is indeed a fundamental problem of mankind. Although different belief systems evolved, they did more harm than benefit. Interpreting belief systems other than the one we hold is, indeed, problematic. Philosophers then evolved the method of query to hold a rational view of things. To understand the world, full of mysteries, imagination was used and beliefs about countless seen and unseen external agencies and forces operating upon our lives got seeded in the collective consciousness. Over the centuries, religion and science kept diverging and eventually became incompatible with one another, particularly in the materialistically developed Western world. In India, however, many people could comfortably bridge this gap within their respective belief systems and also see no divide between real science and genuine spirituality. As science kept facing difficulties in the extrapolation of knowledge into unknown areas, both, within the human body and in deep outer space, spirituality offered great insights.

Anyone with a trained eye can easily observe various spurious forms of devotion amongst the people who throng temples, apply marks on their foreheads, wear talismans, count rosary beads and observe a great show of penance and austerity at certain times every year. These devotees are indeed infected with pride and worldliness and their minds can never lift past worldly concerns of winning and defeating, gain and loss. For them, devotion is a game of name and fame. Many of them even turn puritans. They self-assume authority of the guardians of the God and condemn real but often credulous devotees, especially among the poor and lowly.

Outwardly, there are scrupulous devotees who falsely believe in their imagined form of the God and belittle the other forms. Before Shri Shankaracharya's arrival, Hinduism had become a kaleidoscope of different God-forms. Kings were classified as followers of Vishnu, Shiva, or Shakti. The temples rose and fell in their status depending on the choice of the king. The collections of offerings by the devotees depended upon which god-form was favoured by the king. Even families and communities are divided based on the God-form they choose to revere. There are performer devotees. They perfect the art forms of devotion– dancers, singers, poets, and narrators (*katha-vachakas*). Deeply entangled in their art forms, but without a corresponding internal disposition, they live in hypocrisy and perform for a fee in the name of God and live comfortable, and even luxurious lives.

Inwardly, there are presumptuous devotees. They indeed show impressive outward devotion to God, but continue to sin without making any effort to amend their lives. They designate days to a particular God-form, observe a fast on that day but feast on all other days. Many of these devotees are indeed hypocrites who practice devotion only to appear holy in the eyes of others. And finally, most of them are interested devotees, who turn to God only when they want something. They even attempt to use God for their success and power and nothing more.

Lokmanya captures the entire spectrum when he writes, "Unless some perceptible thing has been seen, the human mind cannot conceive the idea of the Imperceptible. For instance, it is only after one has seen by one's own eyes the perceptible colours red, green etc., that the common and imperceptible idea of 'colour' comes into existence in the human mind, and not otherwise. You may call this the natural quality or the defect of the human mind. Whatever may be the case, as long as the embodied human being cannot get rid of this mental quality, there is no other way except to descend from the Quality-less into the Quality-full, and into the Perceptible Quality-full rather than the Imperceptible Quality-full, for purposes of Worship (*upasana*) or Devotion (*bhakti*). Therefore, the path of worshipping the Perceptible has been in vogue since time immemorial, and ultimately, in *Upanishads* like the *Rama-tapaniya* and others, the worship of the perceptible form of the *Brahman*, in the shape of human beings, is mentioned. In the *Bhagavad-Gita* also, this doctrine has been reiterated in the following logical form:

क्लेशोऽधिकतरस्तेषामव्यक्तासक्तचेतसाम् ।
अव्यक्ता हि गतिर्दुःखं देहवद्भिरवाप्यते ॥५॥

For those whose minds are attached to the unmanifest (avyaktasakta-chetasam), the path of realisation is full of tribulations (klesoadhikataras). Worship of the unmanifest is exceedingly difficult for embodied beings (dehavadbhih).
(Bhagavad-Gita Chapter 12, Verse 5)"

When we worship (*puja*), we are saying that God has worth,

that he is worthy (*pujya*) and we praise God as worth more than everything else put together. Worship done with the intention of seeking rewards is indeed the most shallow of all forms of worship. Praise, when done as an appendage to plea becomes flattery and loses all merit. True worship expresses the heart, true worship involves the mind, and above all, it involves the body. Mere giving praise upward with the hope of receiving instructions from above is indeed not worship but a wishful activity. Instead of raising our consciousness to the imperceptible, we remain mired in our whims and fancies.

Dr. S. Radhakrishnan adds in his commentary of this *shloka* a verse from the *Avadhuta Gita*:

येनेदं पूरितं सर्वमात्मनैवात्मनात्मनि ।
निराकारं कथं वन्दे ह्यभिन्नं शिवमव्ययम् ॥

The Immutable does not offer an easy hold to the mind and the path is more arduous. We reach the same goal more easily and naturally by the path of devotion to the Personal God, by turning Godwards all our energies, knowledge, will and feeling.[2]

Lokmanya explains, "That man, who wishes to concentrate his mind (*chitta*) on the Imperceptible (*avyakta*), suffers much, because, to the human being clothed in a body and organs, it is inherently difficult to reach this state of the imperceptible. This path of 'visible experience' is known as the 'Path of Devotion'.

Swami Mukundananda deliberates, "Why is the worship of the formless *Brahman* so difficult? The first and foremost reason for this is that we humans possess a form ourselves and we have been habituated to interacting with forms in endless lifetimes. Thus, while striving to love God as well, if our mind has a wonderful enchanting form to meditate upon, it can easily focus upon it and increase its attachment to the Lord. However, in the case of the formless, the intellect cannot conceive of it, and the mind and senses have no tangible object to relate to. Therefore, both, the endeavours of meditating on God and increasing the mind's attachment to

---

[2] S. Radhakrishnan, *The Bhagavad Gita*, HarperCollins Publishers India, 2014, p. 346-347.

him, become difficult... The *Jnanins*, who worship God as *nirguna*, *nirvishesh*, and *nirakar*, have to rely entirely upon self-effort for progress. On the other hand, the personal form of God is an ocean of compassion and mercy. Hence, devotees of the personal form receive the help of divine support in their *Sadhana*."[3]

There is a *Patanjali Yoga Sutra* cautioning that if we focus our mind on something very subtle, it is going to be a most unmanageable affair.

सूक्ष्मविषयत्वं चालिङ्गपर्यवसानाम् ॥४५॥

All the subtle metal formations eventually get settled in the Primary Matter, without any distinguishing mark. (As in pure consciousness there are no objects, thus, there can be no subtleties). (Patanjali Yoga Sutra 1.45)

Lokmanya writes, "When once the form of the *Parabrahman* has been defined by means of the Intelligence, concentrating the mind on its imperceptible form by means of thought, will be possible for an intelligent person. It is not that it is impossible, but inasmuch as this act of attaching the 'Mind' on the Imperceptible has to be accomplished with the help of Faith or Affection, one does not escape the necessity of Faith and Affection in this path. Therefore, from the philosophical point of view, even the worship of the *Satchitananda Brahman* (the *Brahman* which is eternal, conscious and joyful) must be included in the Path of Devotion, which is founded on love. Nevertheless, as the form of the *Brahman*, which is taken for the purpose of meditation in this path, is essentially imperceptible, and is accessible only to the 'Reason', i.e. only to *Jnanin*, and is the most important factor, it is common not to refer to this path as the 'Path of Devotion', but as The Contemplation of the Absolute Self (*Adhyatma-vichara*), the Worship of the Imperceptible (*avyakta upasana*) or simply Worship (*upasana*), or the 'path of knowledge'. Although the *Brahman*, which is worshipped, is required to be quality-full, yet, if one takes a perceptible, instead of an imperceptible form, and especially a human form, for worship, that makes it the 'Path of Devotion.'"

---

3   http://www.holy-bhagavad-gita.org/chapter/12/verse/5. Last accessed on 23 October 2017.

This way is a direct higher form of worship. Shri Hanuman worshipped Shri Rama and the Gopikas worshipped Shri Krishna in this direct way of pure worship of the God in His human form. If the human form of God is not available, the idol of the God is worshipped with a high intensity of love, but without any desire for gain for oneself. Mira Bai worshipped the statue of Shri Krishna; Ramakrishna Paramahamsa worshipped the statue of Kali, in this way. Their *bhakti* was as real as that of Shri Hanuman and the Gopikas. Shri Swaminarayan (1781–1830) declared that the God (*Purna Purushottam Narayan*) is always present on Earth in the form of the saint who has gone beyond the three qualities of *prakrti* (*gunantit satpurush*). The *gunantit satpurush* is the only pathway to God and to *moksha*. He is responsible for helping the *jiva* realise *Parabrahman*. I had the great fortune of meeting *gunantit satpurush* Pramukh Swamiji and *gunantit satpurush* Mahant Swamiji and have no doubt whatsoever about them as a direct access to God. One can worship God through pure service to the people in need. God is more pleased in this way.

Lokmanya clarifies, "It can be clearly seen, that (1) though the paths may be two, yet, since one attains the same *Parameshvara*, and ultimately acquires '*Equability of Reason*' through either path, these two paths are eternal staircases for rising to the same floor, which are used by different persons according to their respective qualifications; and that (2) the ideals do not become different because the paths are different. Out of these, the first step of one of the staircases is Intelligence, whereas the first step of the other staircase is Faith and Love. Now, whichever path is followed, the man acquires the same kind of Realisation of the same *Parameshvara*, and attains the same Release. Therefore, the doctrine that, "there is no salvation unless it is based on actually experienced Knowledge", is common to both the paths."

Swami Vivekananda famously said, "The perfected *Bhakta* no more goes to see God in temples and churches; he knows no place where he will not find Him. He finds Him in the temple as well as out of the temple; he finds Him in the saint's saintliness as well as in the wicked man's wickedness, because he has Him already seated in glory in his own heart, as the one Almighty, inextinguishable Light of Love, which is ever-shining and eternally present."

भक्त्या मामभिजानाति यावान्यश्चास्मि तत्त्वतः ।
ततो मां तत्त्वतो ज्ञात्वा विशते तदनन्तरम् ॥५५॥

Through devotion only one can know as much as I am in truth (yavan yas cha asmi tattvatah). Thereafter (tatah), having known Me in truth (mam tattvatah jnatva), he enters into Me (vishate tad-anantaram). (Bhagavad-Gita Chapter 18, Verse 55)

Contemporary spiritual practitioner of both Eastern and Western methods, Janaka (John) Stagnaro (b. 1960), very beautifully explains the intertwined *saguna bhakti* and realisation of the *nirguna* God, through a poem:

Hanuman bows to Ram,
Says I know we are One:
Always have been,
Always will be,
This my Heart knows without doubt.

But my Lord,
While I still see this body
And this world all around,
Let me play Thy servant.[4]

Lokmanya, after rejecting the bogus differentiation between *saguna* and *nirguna bhakti*, with the words, "Where is the sense of entering into the futile discussion as to whether the path of Knowledge is superior or the Path of Devotion is superior?" issues caution not to undermine the Path of Knowledge. He writes, "Devotion is only a path; that is to say, it is a means of acquiring Knowledge. It is not a *Nistha*. Therefore, in the beginning of the *Gita*, only the two *Nisthas* of *Jnana* (*Samkhya*) and *Yoga* (*Karma*) have been dealt with, and in

---
4 http://www.mindfulness-meditation-techniques.com/devotion-and-knowledge.html. Last accessed on 23 October 2017.

mentioning the various means, ways, ritual, or paths of acquiring the *Karma Yoga Nistha*, out of the two, the *Gita* has described the two sister paths of the Worship of the Imperceptible (*Jnana marga*) and the Worship of the Perceptible (*Bhakti marga*), which have been in vogue since times immemorial. It states that of the two, the Worship of the Imperceptible is fraught with difficulty, whereas the Worship of the Perceptible, or Devotion, is a path which is easier i.e., it is such that it can be followed by everybody."

The Path of Knowledge takes one to realise, sooner or later, that all people have the divine root. As they progress on this path, however, an egoistic thought captures their mind, not just at times, but most of the times, that they are now closer to the Divinity than others, and they start feeling entitled to the acknowledgement of the divine tremendousness and magnificence in their own selves. They even call themselves '*Bhagwan*'. Merit is in concealing the divine-connect and living by the will of God, what Dr. A.P.J. Abdul Kalam called as being established in a God-synchronous orbit. Making a show of the connect with the divine and calling oneself *Bhagwan* is no good.

India has recently (2016-2017) seen two mighty gurus convicted for the rape of their women devotees. Contemporary American author, Todd Tomasella, writes rather pungently, but most aptly about this phenomenon, "How terrible is this!– When the ambassadors of God... who are commissioned to teach the way to heaven, do, in fact, teach them the way to hell ---if it be asked... Ten thousand wise and honourable men; even all those, of whatever denomination, who encourage the proud, the trifler, the passionate, the lover of the world, the man of pleasure, the unjust or unkind, the easy, careless, harmless, useless creatures, the man who suffers no reproach for righteousness' sake, to imagine he is in the way to heaven. These are false prophets in the highest sense of the word. These are traitors both, to God and man."[5]

Lokmanya writes, "It is now necessary to point out a position of danger which exists in this easy, long-standing, and visible path of acquiring Knowledge. If not, there is a chance that an unaware wayfarer along the road may fall into that pit. This pit-fall has been

---

5 Todd Tomasella, *Deceivers & False Prophets Among Us: Riveting Insights Into the Dark World of Deception at Work in Today's Church*, AuthorHouse, Bloomington, USA, 2008, p. 4.

clearly defined in the *Bhagavad-Gita*, and that is the important point of difference between the Vedic Path of Devotion and other paths of Devotion. Although it is generally accepted that, in order that the human 'Mind' should become attached to the *Parabrahman*, and that a man should acquire an equable 'Reason' by means of the purification of the 'Mind', there must be some quality and perceptible object as a symbol (*prakrti*) of the *Parabrahman* in front of the Devotee, otherwise, the 'Mind' cannot become steady. As it is clear from history, there are grave disputes about what that symbol should be."

Swami Vivekananda described this aspect best. He declared, "Such a man becomes a world-mover for whom his little self is dead and God stands in its place. The whole universe will become transfigured to him… Instead of being a prison house, where we everyday struggle to fight and compete for a morsel of bread, this universe will then be to us a playground. Beautiful will be this universe then! How beautiful is this world! He alone has the right to say that it is all good. This will be the great good to the world resulting from such realisation, that instead of this world going on with all its friction and clashing, if all mankind today realise a bit of that great truth, the aspect of the whole world will be changed, and in the place of fighting and quarrelling, there would be a reign of peace."[6]

Lokmanya elaborates, "From the Metaphysical point of view, there is no place in the world where the *Parameshvara* does not exist. Even in the *Bhagavad-Gita*, after Arjuna had asked Shri Krishna which various objects he should meditate on, as being His Manifestations, the Blessed Lord has, in the tenth chapter, mentioned the 'Mind', out of all the organs, the Himalayas, out of all immoveable things, repetition of prayers, out of all *Yajnas*, Vasuki among the serpents, Prahlada among the demons, Aryan among the ancestors, Chitraratha among the *Gandharvas*, the Pipal tree out of all trees, the eagle among all the birds, Bhrigu out of the great Rishis, the letter 'A' out of all letters, and Vishnu out of all the various Suns, as being the numerous forms of Himself, which fill the moveable and the immoveable world on all sides." Shri Krishna has ultimately said:

---

[6] https://www.wisdomlib.org/hinduism/book/isha-Upanishad/d/doc122464.html. Last accessed on 25 October 2017.

The Path of Devotion

यद्यद्विभूतिमत्सत्त्वं श्रीमदूर्जितमेव वा ।
तत्तदेवावगच्छ त्वं मम तेजोंऽशसम्भवम् ॥४१॥

Whatever you see as beautiful, glorious, and powerful (vibhuti, srimat, urjitam), know it to spring from but a spark of my splendour (mama tejo-amsa).
(Bhagavad-Gita Chapter 10. Verse 41)

Dr. S. Radhakrishnan clarifies, "While all things are supported by God, things of beauty and splendour reveal Him more than others. Every deed of Heroism, every life of sacrifice, every work of genius, is a revelation of the Divine. The epic moments of a man's life are inexplicably beyond the finite mind of man."[7]

In the eleventh chapter of the *Bhagavad-Gita*, there is an instance when Arjuna tells the Blessed Lord that his illusion is now dispelled (*moho ayam vigato mama*) and pleads to see (*drastum icchami te rupam*) the Cosmic Form of the God (*darsayatmanam avyayam*). The Blessed Lord tells Arjuna that as it is not possible for the human eye to see the God (*na tu mam sakyase drastum anenaiva sva-chaksusa*), He would momentarily let him have the Divine eye (*divyam dadami te chaksuh*) to behold God's mystic opulence (*pasya me yogam aishvaram*).

Arjuna sees in God's universal body (*visveshvara vishva-rupa*) many, many forms-bellies, mouths, eyes-expanded without limit (*aneka-bahudara-vaktra-netramananta-rupam*). There is no end, there is no beginning, and there is no middle to all this (*nantam na madhyam na punas tava adim*). Arjuna can see that God is one (*tvaya ekena*), spread throughout the sky and the planets and all the space between them (*dyav a-prthivyor idam antaram*).

Arjuna also sees God as a blazing face with awful teeth of death (*damstra-karalani cha temukhani*). Two similes are offered here for the end of human lives - the rivers flowing into the sea (*yatha nadinam bahavo ambu-vegah samudram*) and insects flying towards the flame to get scorched (*yatha pradiptam jvalanam patanga*), perhaps to differentiate between the people who die living a good life (of a river) and silently merge into the ocean, and

---

7 S. Radhakrishnan, *The Bhagavad Gita*, HarperCollins Publishers, India, 2014, p. 317.

the people who live a desire-propelled fast life and die the death of insects, scorching themselves into the flame.

Arjuna could realise that all people are destined to die (*nihatah purvam eva*) and that he (as a warrior in the battlefield) was a mere instrument of the Lord (*nimitta-matram bhava*) for that to happen. He pleads with Shri Krishna to show His four-armed form, with a crowned head and with a club, wheel, conch and lotus flower in His hands (*kiritinam gadinam chakra-hastam icchami tvam drastum aham tathaiva tenaiva rupena chatur-bhujena*). The Blessed Lord now displays His real four-armed form, and at last returns to His two-armed human form, reassuring the fearful Arjuna.

Lokmanya writes, "(Shri Krishna) has given to Arjuna an actual experience of this proposition, by showing to him His Cosmic Form. If all the things or qualities to be seen in the world are only forms or symbols of the *Parameshvara*, how can one say that the Blessed Lord is in one of them and not in another, and who is going to say it? It becomes logically necessary to say that He is near and yet afar; existent and yet non-existent, also beyond both; the eagle, as also the serpent; the death, as also the one who dies; the one who creates obstacles, and the one who removes them; the one who creates fear, and one who removes it; the terrible and yet, the not-terrible; the pleasant and yet the unpleasant; the one who causes the rain, and the one who prevents rain from falling."

Taking every form as God's valid form, in the Hindu religion, there are significant differences in worship. There is codified, formal, ceremonial and ritualistic worship. But people also do worship in a casual and informal manner. Worship can be at times noisy and boisterous, almost like a theatrical performance with music and singing. There is also quiet and contemplative worship, where you can listen to the heart sounds and breathing of the worshipper. People worship in beautiful temples and also under trees and roadside shanties, with an idol doubled up as a *Mandir*. In the midst of such diversity, Hindu worship is perceived by an outsider as a matter of taste. Are all forms of worship valid? Or is there a differential, either by method or by the idol worshipped? The serious conflicts over worship are no surprise.

Shri Krishna helped Arjuna to gain the necessary insight to enable him to perceive The Lord, who was already in front of him, in the form he desired. Shri Krishna did not transform Himself into the Cosmic Form, but only bestowed His grace on Arjuna to enable him to perceive the Divine form of The Lord and hence Shri Krishna says, `Behold'. The stupendous self-revelation of Divine power is manifested to Arjuna, who understands the true meaning of the cosmic process and destiny. The vision is not a myth or a legend, but spiritual experience.[8]

Lokmanya writes, "If everything in this world is, in the same way, in part, a form of the *Parameshvara*, why should not such persons, at a stroke, grasp this all-pervasive form of the *Parameshvara*, and take for worship, in the beginning, any one of these numerous things, as a means or a symbol for Realising this imperceptible and pure form? Some may worship the 'Mind', others may perform the *Yajna* of wealth, others again, the *Yajna* of prayer, some may worship the eagle, others may worship only the sacred symbol *Om*, some may worship Vishnu and others Shiva, some may worship Ganapati, and others, Bhavani.

---

8   http://srimadbhagvatgita.blogspot.in/2013/07/bhagavad-gita-chapter-11-vishwaroopa. html. Last accessed on 24 October 2017.

Some, again, may look upon their parents as the *Parameshvara* and serve them, whereas others might choose for worship a form which is much more comprehensive, such as the Virata form, which is made up of all created beings. One may prescribe the worship of the Sun, whereas others may say that Shri Krishna or Shri Rama is better than the Sun. But, as the idea that all these Forms are fundamentally one and the same, has been lost sight of, as a result of Ignorance or Delusion, or as it is not to be found at all in some religions, a false arrogance sometimes arises as to the relative merits of these objects of worship, and that is when matters come to physical violence."

All people, therefore, need to cultivate a life with God that is growing and developing. What is not flowing and growing, is bound to stagnate and decay. Hinduism is a religion in which individuals are an integral part of the God. *Jiva* being the *amsha* of *Paramatman*, people are not just an association of individuals, but we are organically connected to one another. True faithful worship, however, does not come naturally to a majority of the human beings. The *Atman* yearns for the need for itself in human beings; that when they do not know the imperceptible God, they invent idols of gods, dogmatic religions, cults, and even false worship. The human mind, as a factory of idolisation, creates reasons to divide people and have a misplaced sense of superiority of one over the other.

Lokmanya writes, "If, for the moment, one keeps aside, out of consideration, the mutual conflicts between the Vedic, Buddhist, Jain, Christian, or Mohammedan religions, the history of Europe shows us that matters had come to the point of the worshippers of one and the same quality-full and perceptible Christ, murdering each other, as a result of the difference in ritualistic practices. Quarrels are even now going on among the worshippers of the Quality-full, on the ground that the deity worshipped by one is better than the deity worshipped by another, because the former is Formless, and the latter has a Form. Unless one explains whether there is a way of bringing these quarrels arising in the Path of Devotion, to a close, and if so, which that way is, the Path of devotion does not become free from danger and we shall, therefore, consider what the reply of the *Gita* is to that question."

The Blessed Lord has clearly given to Arjuna the advice that:

अव्यक्तं व्यक्तिमापन्नं मन्यन्ते मामबुद्धयः ।
परं भावमजानन्तो ममाव्ययमनुत्तमम् ॥२४॥

People lacking in intelligence (abuddhayah) believe that I have manifested out of My supreme state (mamaparam bhavam) which is immutable and unsurpassable (avyayam, anuttamam), into the human form (vyaktim apannam). (Bhagavad-Gita Chapter 7, Verse 24)

Swami Mukundananda elaborates, "Amongst the people who accept both aspects of God's personality, the debate sometimes ensues regarding which of these is the original form. Did the formless manifest from the personal form of God, or vice versa? Shri Krishna resolves this debate here by stating that the divine personality is primordial– it has not manifested from the formless *Brahman*. God exists eternally in his divine form in the spiritual realm. The formless *Brahman* is the light that emanates from his transcendental body."[9]

Dr. S. Radhakrishnan adds, "The forms we impose on the Formless are due to our limitations. We turn away from the contemplation of the Ultimate Reality to concentrate upon imaginative reconstructions. All gods, except the One Unmanifest Eternal, are forms imposed on Him. God is not among many… (He) stands beyond all forms, the immutable centre of endless mobility."[10]

Swami Ranganathananda cites a parable of Shri Ramakrishna Paramahamsa, in his commentary of this *shloka*. He writes, "A person took his diamond and asked a vegetable seller, 'How much will you give me for this diamond?' 'Only ten pounds of potatoes, nothing more.' Then he went to a cloth merchant. He offered him ten yards of cloth and nothing more. Finally, he went to a diamond merchant and asked him, 'How much will you give?' He replied, 'Ten thousand rupees shall I give you'. So also, in spiritual life, it is the same. When we try to judge others, always keep in mind the truth that the range

---

9   http://www.holy-bhagavad-gita.org/chapter/7/verse/24. Last accessed on 11 December 2017.
10 S. Radhakrishnan, *The Bhagavad Gita*, HarperCollins Publishers India, 2014, p. 263.

of one's experience conditions one's judgement. Within that range only does one estimate a person."[11]

Lokmanya declares, "The power of redemption, which is contained in the Path of Devotion, is not a power possessed by some living or lifeless image, or by a building of bricks and mortar. That belief, which every worshipper, for his own convenience, holds with reference to such an image, to the effect that it is the *Ishvara*, is the thing which really redeems. Let the symbol be of stone, or of metal, or of anything else; it can never be worth more than what it really is. Whatever may be your faith with reference to the symbol, it is the fruit of your Devotion that the *Parameshvara* gives you. Then, where is the sense of fighting that the symbol chosen by one is better than the one chosen by another? If your faith is not pure, then, however good the symbol may be, what is the use of it?"

Lokmanya cites Shri Samartha:

विषयी लोक श्रवणा येती । ते बायकांकडेच पहाती ।
चोरटे लोक चोरून जाती । पादरक्षा॥

People, for sensory appeasement, go to the temple on the pretext of listening to the sermons, but actually look at the women devotees. There are people who come to the temple with the intention of stealing; and they steal your shoes. That is their partake. (Dasabodha 18. 10. 26).

Lokmanya writes, "If idols of deities, or temples had any redeeming power in themselves, then even such sensual persons or thieves must attain Release. Some people believe that Devotion to the *Parameshvara* is only for the purpose of Release. However, those persons who wish to obtain some material or selfish object, must demote themselves to the worship of different deities. It is said in the *Gita* itself that such persons run after these deities with such selfish motives, and the idea that these deities, of their own accord, give you the reward of the worship, is philosophically incorrect."

---

11 Swami Ranganathananda, *Universal Message of the Bhagavad Gita, Vol. 2*, Kolkata: Advaita Ashrama, 2015 (Seventh reprint), p.257-258.

The Path of Devotion

कामैस्तैस्तैर्हृतज्ञानाः प्रपद्यन्तेऽन्यदेवताः ।
तं तं नियममास्थाय प्रकृत्या नियताः स्वया ॥२०॥

Propelled by material desires, different people worship different gods (yoyo yam yam tanum bhaktah). According to their own nature, they practice rites and rituals. (Bhagavad-Gita Chapter 7, Verse 20)

यो यो यां यां तनुं भक्तः श्रद्धयार्चितुमिच्छति ।
तस्य तस्याचलां श्रद्धां तामेव विदधाम्यहम् ॥२१॥

Whatever (God) forms a devotee worships with faith (shraddhay architum), I steady the faith of the devotee in that form (tam eva vidadhamy aham).
(Bhagavad-Gita Chapter 7, Verse 21)

Dr. S. Radhakrishnan elaborates, "The Supreme confirms the faith of each and grants the rewards each seeks. Exactly as far as the soul has risen in its struggle, does God stoop to meet it. Even seers, who were as profoundly contemplative as Gautama Buddha and Shri Shankaracharya, did not repudiate the popular belief in gods. They were conscious of the infinite number of possible manifestations. Every surface derives its soil from the depths, even as every shadow reflects the nature of the substance. Besides, all worship elevates. No matter what we revere, so long as our reverence is serious, it helps (one) progress."[12]

The *Vedanta* Philosophy of the Absolute Self considers the all-pervading *Parameshvara* as the ultimate provider of what is seen as coming from the deities worshipped with whatever desire.

फलमत उपपत्तेः ॥३८॥

The fruits of action (phalam) are from Him (ataha), this being the logical position (upapatte). (Brahma Sutra Bhashya of Shri Shankaracharya III.ii. 38)

---

12 S. Radhakrishnan, *The Bhagavad Gita*, : HarperCollins Publishers, India, 2014, p. 261.

The *Gita* endorses the same doctrine.

$$\text{स तया श्रद्धया युक्तस्तस्याराधनमीहते ।}$$
$$\text{लभते च ततः कामान्मयैव विहितान्हि तान् ॥२२॥}$$

With faith (sa taya shraddhaya), whichever god the devotee worships with whatever desire (labhate cha tatah kaman), My power alone provides (mayaeva vihitan hi tan). (Bhagavad-Gita Chapter 7, Verse 22)

Lokmanya clarifies, "Though the *Parameshvara* who gives the reward may, in this way, be One, yet, as He gives a different reward to each one, according to his good or evil intentions, the results of the worship of different symbols or deities are seen to be different from each other; and it is with this import in mind, that the Blessed Lord has said *shraddha mayah ayam purushah ya yat shraddhah sa eva sah.*"

$$\text{सत्त्वानुरूपा सर्वस्य श्रद्धा भवति भारत ।}$$
$$\text{श्रद्धामयोऽयं पुरुषो ये यच्छ्रद्धः स एव सः ॥३॥}$$

The existential truth of human beings (sattva-anurupa) shapes their faith (shraddha bhavati). Man is of the nature of his faith; what one's faith is, certainly that the person is (yo yacchraddhah sa eva sah). (Bhagavad-Gita Chapter 17, Verse 3)

Dr. S. Radhakrishnan elaborates, "(In this *Shloka*, the author of *Mahabharata*) takes up for consideration, a number of questions which probably aroused interests at that time, about faith, diet, sacrifice, asceticism, almsgiving, renunciation and relinquishment. *Sattva* is meant for *svabhava*, nature... Faith is the pressure of Spirit on humanity, the force that urges humanity towards what is better, not only in the order of knowledge, but in the whole order of spiritual life. Faith, as the inward sense of truth, points to the object over which fuller light is shed later. *Bhagavat* says that the fruit of worship follows the faith of the doer (*shraddha anurupam phalahetukatvat*). We are what we are on account of our past and we can create our future."[13]

$$\text{यान्ति देवव्रता देवान्पितृन्यान्ति पितृव्रताः ।}$$
$$\text{भूतानि यान्ति भूतेज्या यान्ति मद्याजिनोऽपि माम् ॥२५॥}$$

Worshippers of gods go to gods (yanti deva-vrata devan), worshippers of the ancestors go to the ancestors (pitrn yanti pitr-vratah), worshippers of ghosts take birth amongst such beings (bhutani yanti bhutejya), and My devotees come to Me alone (yanti mad-yajinoapi mam). (Bhagavad-Gita Chapter 9, Verse 25) (9. 25)

Dr. S. Radhakrishnan elaborates, "The shining gods, the spirits of the dead and the spirits in the psychic world all happen to be worshipped by men in different stages of development, but they are all limited forms of the Supreme and cannot give the aspiring soul the peace that is beyond all understanding. The result of worship is assimilation to the form worshipped and these limited forms give limited results."[14]

$$\text{ये यथा मां प्रपद्यन्ते तांस्तथैव भजाम्यहम् ।}$$
$$\text{मम वर्त्मानुवर्तन्ते मनुष्याः पार्थ सर्वशः ॥११॥}$$

In whatever way people surrender unto me (ye yatha mam prapadyante), I accept them. Everyone (knowingly or unknowingly) follows my path (mama vartma anuvartante). (Bhagavad-Gita Chapter 4, Verse 11)

Dr. S. Radhakrishnan elaborates, "The Hindu thinkers are conscious of the amazing variety of ways in which we may approach the Supreme, of the contingency of all forms. They know that it is impossible for any effort of logical reason to give us a true picture of the ultimate reality. From the point of view of metaphysics (*paramartha*), no manifestation is to be taken as absolutely true, while, from the standpoint of experience (*vyavahara*), every one

---

13 S. Radhakrishnan, *The Bhagavad Gita*, HarperCollins Publishers, India, 2014, p. 406-407.
14 *ibid*, p. 294.

of them has some validity.... The *Gita* does not speak of this or that form of religion, but speaks of the impulses, which are expressed in all forms, the desire to find God and understand our relation to Him.... The *Gita* affirms that though beliefs and practices may be many and varied, spiritual realisation, to which these are the means, is one."[15]

Faith (*shraddha*) is indeed a powerful mental force. Without faith, one cannot even make progress in any field of work beyond a point, leave alone faith in the God. Now, faith is not some one-time transaction; it takes time to grow. If one doesn't continue to grow faith in one's relationship with the God, one doesn't see God's hand guiding one's life and the lives of those around one and remains like a blindfolded person crossing a heavy-traffic road. Faith grows on itself. Whatever faith one has inside, indeed determines the outcome of the faith level one would have for the God at work around you. People, who don't have faith in God's moving this world, are mostly those who are resigned to live purposeless lives, merely for their livelihoods and family and are not looking for anything big, great or even miraculous to happen. Time and again, the Blessed Lord tells Arjuna that He loved it when people placed their full trust in Him. Just a little faith can grow on itself and can do amazing things in one's life and in the lives of those around one. But faith can also be misplaced, a force applied at a wrong point. Lokmanya writes, "The *Shaligram* is only a stone. If you entertain the faith with reference to it that it is Vishnu, you will reach the sphere of Vishnu. If you worship the same symbol, believing that it is some past being like a *Yaksha*, or a demon etc., you will reach the spheres of (these) past beings."

After correcting the focus on the God, how does one stay grounded in his faith in God? How does one apply it in the real life? Do reading scriptures, praying, observing rituals, festivals and fasting and visiting temples, make for enough expression of faith? The answer is a blunt no. Faith in the God involves the understanding that the God is the Real Doer (*karta*) of whatever happens in the world. Even bad things, ghastly things and apparently outrageous things carry a deep meaning. Faith is not like a seed kept in the pocket; the seed has to be sown, watered and protected, and then, over the years, it becomes a tree, giving fruits and shade to the believer.

---
15 *ibid*, p. 183-184, 185.

The best expression of faith in the God is the acceptance of one's reality and properly conducting one's life in this world. A faithful person watches what he thinks, what he says, what he does and ensures that the three are the same. Those who think one thing, say another and do some other thing, are indeed good for nothing. As mankind marches ahead, such people are thrown out and trampled underfoot by other people. It is not some injustice or punishment or cruelty on the part of the God, but the result of a disorientation of one's life and failure to act with integrity of soul, mind and the body. Symbols without faith hardly matter.

Lokmanya writes, "When, in this way, a difference has been made between the symbol, and the Faith with which that symbol is worshipped, no reason remains for quarrelling about the symbol, whatever that symbol may be. This is so because, the idea that the symbol is the god or *Parameshvara*, no more remains. That omnipresent *Parameshvara*, who gives rewards for all actions, looks only to the Faith of the devotees. Those persons, who have realised this principle of the Path of Devotion, do not obstinately insist, "That form of the *Ishvara* or the symbol which I worship, is the only true symbol, and other symbols are false". Rather, he has the charitable feeling that whatever may be the symbol that is taken, all those who worship the *Parameshvara* through that symbol, reach the one and the same *Parameshvara*."

किं पुनर्ब्राह्मणाः पुण्या भक्ता राजर्षयस्तथा ।
अनित्यमसुखं लोकमिमं प्राप्य भजस्व माम् ॥३३॥

How much meritorious work the Kings and sages would have done to be in their position (kim punar brahmanah punya bhakta rajarsayas tatha)! But they too seek this goal (of emancipation out of their troubles) with devotion. Therefore, having come to this transient and joyless world, engage in devotion unto me (bhajasva mam). (Bhagavad-Gita Chapter 9, Verse 33)

A.C. Bhaktivedanta Swami Prabhupada says, "This world is not a happy place for anyone -*anityam asukham lokam*, this world is temporary and full of miseries... This world is temporary, but there is another world, which is eternal. This world is miserable, but the other world is eternal and blissful... The devotional service of the Supreme Lord is the only process by which all problems of all classes of men can be solved."[16] Eknath Easwaran adds, "Just because someone is cultured, or wealthy, or has led a good life, he or she is not barred from going far on the spiritual path. In my experience, those who have undergone all the discipline it takes to become scholars, doctors, engineers, lawyers, artists, and scientists can take to meditation very easily. All they have to do is take the energy, concentration, and effort they used to achieve excellence in their field and turn it towards the supreme goal of life... Once they understand how to harness their capabilities through the practice of meditation, such people can grow to great spiritual heights."[17]

Lokmanya writes, "In short, the doctrine of the *Gita* is that, in the same way that the moment a man acquires the desire of practicing *Karma Yoga*, he is drawn towards complete perfection, so also, in the Path of Devotion, when once the Devotee has consigned himself to the *Parameshvara*, the Blessed Lord Himself gradually increases his *Nishtha*, and makes him ultimately realise His own form. By this knowledge (and not by blind faith), the devotee of the Blessed Lord ultimately attains Release."

"This skill of Vedic religion, of harmonising the natural inclination of the human mind towards the Visible or the perceptible, with the recondite doctrines of philosophy, is not to be seen in the Philosophy of Devotion of any other people. When these people once attach themselves to some quality-full form of the *Parameshvara* and thus come into the sphere of the Perceptible, they remain entangled in that sphere. Not being able to see anything besides that form, vain glory about their own quality-full symbol, takes hold of their minds. When this happens, they wrongly begin to differentiate between Philosophy on the one hand, and the Path of Devotion on the other. But, as the dawn of philosophy had taken place in India from extremely ancient times, there is seen no conflict between Devotion and Spiritual Knowledge in the religion of the *Gita*. Whereas the Vedic Path of Knowledge is chastened by Devotion, the Vedic Path

---

16 https://asitis.com/9/33.html. Last accessed on 30 September 2017.
17 Eknath Easwaran, *The Bhagavad Gita for Daily Living*, Jaico Publishing House, Mumbai, India, 2007, Vol. II, p. 198.

of Devotion is, likewise, chastened by Knowledge. Whichever Path is taken by man, he ultimately attains the same excellent state."

"The sense of Equality appearing in the Philosophy of Devotion is taught by the *Gita*. It enables one to easily grasp the Knowledge of the identity of the *Brahman* and the *Atman* mentioned in the *Upanishads*. This is done without sacrificing the ordinary activities of worldly life, and without establishing any difference between the four castes or the four stages of life, or the communities, or even between men and women. One then understands the true import of the summing up of the Religion of the *Gita*, made by the Blessed Lord, in the last chapter of the *Gita*. He says, "Give up all other religions (*dharma*) and surrender yourself solely to Me; I shall redeem you from all sins, do not be afraid."

सर्वधर्मान्परित्यज्य मामेकं शरणं व्रज ।
अहं त्वां सर्वपापेभ्यो मोक्षयिष्यामि मा शुचः ॥६६॥

Surrender all your duties (sarva-dharman parityajya) before Me, come to Me alone and I will give you shelter (mam ekam sharanam vraja). Do not grieve (ma shuchah), for I shall liberate you from all sinful consequences (sarva-papebhyo Mokshayisyami). (Bhagavad-Gita Chapter 18, Verse 66)

Dr. S. Radhakrishnan elaborates, "We should willingly yield to His pressure, completely surrender to His will and take shelter in His love. If we destroy confidence in our own little self and replace it by perfect confidence in God, He will save us. God asks us for total self-giving and gives us in return, the power of the spirit, which changes every situation... If we have to realise our destinies, we must stand naked and guileless before the Supreme. Now and then, we vainly try to cover ourselves up and hide the truth from the Lord... The followers of Shri Ramanujacharya look upon this verse as the *charma shloka* or the final verse of the *Gita*."[18]

Swami Ranganathananda declared this *shloka* as the conclusion of the spiritual message of the *Gita*. He writes, "Philosophy is what imparts wisdom to human life. Textbook philosophy does not do

---
18 S. Radhakrishnan, *The Bhagavad Gita*,: HarperCollins Publishers, India, 2014, p. 406-448-449.

that, but a deeper vision of truth is what gives to philosophy its high value. With that philosophy, one can find one's way in life. It is like a lamp which throws light on our path and shows us the way."[19]

Lokmanya clarifies, "The word *dharma* has been used here in the comprehensive meaning. It means that, all the practical paths or means, which have been shown for acquiring the highest excellence of the Self, while following the ordinary activities of life, are *dharma* (duty)... (as) there is a likelihood of the mind becoming confused as a result of its being caught in the various paths of the worship of different symbols, the final and definite assurance of the Blessed Lord, not only to Arjuna, but to everybody, in the name of Arjuna, is that, one should give up all the various paths of Purification of the 'Mind', and should "surrender oneself solely to Me; I shall redeem you from all sins, do not be afraid."

Even the Saint Tukaram makes his ultimate prayer to God, which entails the annihilation of diverse kinds of *dharma*, in the following words:

जळो ते जाणीव जळो ते शाहाणीव । राहो माझा भाव विठ्ठलापायीं ।
जळो तो आचार जळो तो विचार । राहो मन स्थिर विठ्ठलापायीं ॥

Let the knowledge be burnt, and burn with that, the wisdom. My Faith at the feet of Vitthala (Shri Krishna) can never be destroyed. Let religious practices be burnt, and burn every contemplation, Let my mind be anchored on the feet of Vitthala.
(Tukaram Gatha, 3464)

Lokmanya closes this chapter in these lyrical words, "This is the pinnacle of definite advice, or of prayer. 'Devotion' is the last sweet mouthful out of the golden dish of the *Shrimad Bhagavad-Gita*. We have taken this mouthful of Love; now let us take the final sip of water (*aposni*) and prepare to rise from the feast."

ॐ

---

[19] Swami Ranganathananda, *Universal Message of the Bhagavad Gita, Vol. 3*, Advaita Ashrama, Kolkata, 2015 (Seventh reprint), p.355.

14

The Train of Thought

> As a single footstep will not make a path on the earth, so a single thought will not make a pathway in the mind. To make a deep physical path, we walk again and again. To make a deep mental path, we must think over and over the kind of thoughts we wish to dominate our lives.[1]
>
> *Henry David Thoreau*

In the thirteen chapters of this book so far, Lokmanya has expounded the doctrine of the *Bhagavad-Gita* as two-fold. One is to acquire the state of Equability of Reason. This is possible when one realises the reality of the *Atman*. It can be done following the Path of Knowledge or the Path of Devotion. The other is to perform whatever duty befalls one in this world with the mental state of Equability of Reason. Indeed, Lokmanya presented the *Gita* differently to the reader to convey these two points, as best said by the American poet Henry David Thoreau (1817–1862)– "Just as to make a deep physical path, we walk again and again on that, similarly, to make a deep mental path, we must think the thoughts over and over again." In this chapter, Lokmanya connects his argument of the two-fold doctrine of the *Bhagavad-Gita*, built up in the preceding chapters, to the eighteen chapters of the *Gita*.

There are three ways of understanding a doctrine– logical, empirical, and anecdotal. Lokmanya used all the three methods to emphatically establish the Secret of the *Gita* as the Action befallen on one in this world, with Equability of Reason. Weaving in the stories told and retold by hundreds of generations of Indian

---

[1] https://www.goodreads.com/quotes/29754-as-a-single-footstep-will-not-make-a-path-on. Last accessed on 25 October 2017.

people, quoting from scriptures, the *Shastras*, and even the works of the Western philosophers, and building up a sound logic through them, Lokmanya created a powerful guide-post for the people who value their lives and aspire to excel in their chosen fields and harness their innate talents. In the Indian philosophical system, the three methods are seen as two approaches leading to the truth - going by the experiences and insights of the ancestors contained in the *Puranas* (the *Pauranika* method), and logically arranging and putting forward all the pros and cons of the doctrine under discussion i.e., the scientific (*Shastriya*) method. Lokmanya has followed both paths and converged them to the two-layered secret of the *Bhagavad-Gita*.

Lokmanya writes, "My readers must first remember that the *Gita* was preached by one omniscient, all-powerful, prosperous, and highly revered *Kshatriya* to another powerful archer-warrior, in order to induce the latter to perform his duties according to the law of warriors, at a date when our India was well-known on all sides as enjoying the happiness of Spiritual Knowledge, material wealth, worldly success, and complete self-government... But whatever advice is given, it is necessary that there should be some occasion for giving it; and in order that the advice given should be fruitful, a desire to receive the Knowledge of that advice must, in the first place, have arisen in the mind of the disciple."

The first chapter of the *Gita* presents the occasion for Shri Krishna to offer advice to Arjuna. The two streams of one dynasty– the Pandavas and the Kauravas– are confronting each other in a battlefield. It is not a heat-of-the-moment situation; the conflict has been brewing over for many years. The decision to go to war was preceded by intense negotiations and even a last-ditched diplomatic effort by Shri Krishna himself. All the kings ruling different parts of *Bharatvarsha* were approached by the warring parties and armies were recruited in a well-organised manner. Even Shri Krishna offered his help to the Pandavas and Kauravas in the war. The Kauravas opted for Shri Krishna's army and the Pandavas opted for Shri Krishna's guidance. Shri Krishna, thus, took up the role of a charioteer to the most distinguished Pandava warrior, Arjuna.

The Train of Thought

When the fight was about to start, Arjuna requested Shri Krishna to take his chariot in the middle of both the armies, in the standoff situation. Upon seeing his relatives and friends on both sides and realizing their imminent death, Arjuna, a well-trained professional warrior, developed cold feet.

Lokmanya writes, "When Arjuna saw the realistic vision of the destruction of the entire clan by this internecine war, even a great fighter like him felt unhappy, and he said, "Alas! Are we going to bring about this terrible destruction of our own clan in order that we should get the kingdom? Is it not better to beg?" A dejected Arjuna said to Shri Krishna, "It does not matter if I am killed by my enemies, but I do not wish to commit terrible sins like patricide, or the murder of one's preceptors, or be the destructor of the entire clan, even if I were to get the kingdom of the three worlds." His body began to tremble, he lost control over his limbs, his mouth became dry, and with a very unhappy face, he threw down his bow and arrows and sat down in his chariot."

It is very clearly brought out that this was not a question of 'to fight or not to fight', as the conflict had been brewing over many years and all efforts of reconciliation had failed. It was not a question of Arjuna suddenly turning compassionate and averse to killing people, for which he had been trained since childhood. The point was the attachment that had sprung up in his heart upon seeing his family members and relatives on both sides, and their imminent death in the ensuing war. A warrior, most skilled and famous for his skill in killing the enemy, is wavering from his professional duty; a soldier running away from the army upon hearing of his deployment in the war. The situation is like a singer getting stage fright, a surgeon losing his confidence in the operation theatre, a cricket player throwing away his wicket without even facing the first ball.

Lokmanya writes, "This part of the story is mentioned in the first chapter, which is called the '*Yoga* of the Dejection of Arjuna', because, although the whole of the *Gita* deals with only one subject matter, namely, 'the philosophy of *Karma Yoga* included in the cult (*vidya*) of the *Brahman*', the subject matter principally described in each chapter is looked upon as a portion of this philosophy of *Karma Yoga*, and each chapter is, with reference to the subject matter in it, called *this Yoga*, *that Yoga*, etc. And all these *Yogas* taken together make up the entire 'Philosophy of *Karma Yoga* included in the cult (*vidya*) of the *Brahman*'."

Therefore, the message of The *Gita* has been established right in the first chapter, that this life is meant for action. Life is neither meant for renunciation nor for devotion. Lokmanya writes, "If one does not clearly understand at the outset, what the question before one's own self is, one also cannot clearly understand the answer to the question. If the sum and substance of the *Gita* is to be understood as being that one should abandon worldly life, and take either to Devotion to the Blessed Lord, or to the Path of Renunciation, then there was no necessity to give that advice to Arjuna, as he was ready to give up the terrible warfare of his own accord and go begging round the world."

Lokmanya writes, "Shri Krishna said to Arjuna in the beginning of the second chapter, "O Arjuna, whence have you got this disastrous idea (*kashmala*)? This impotency (*klaibya*) is unworthy of you! Your reputation will go to dogs! Therefore, give up this weakness (*daurbalya*) and stand up to fight!" But when, in spite of that advice, Arjuna reiterated his previous unmanly tale of woe, and said to Shri Krishna, with a pitiful expression on his face, "How shall I kill such great and noble-souled persons like Bhishma, Drona, etc.?",... Shri Krishna saw that Arjuna was completely under the sway of this despondence; and smiling a little, He started imparting Knowledge to him…"

अशोच्यानन्वशोचस्त्वं प्रज्ञावादांश्च भाषसे ।
गतासूनगतासूंश्च नानुशोचन्ति पण्डिताः ॥२॥११॥

While you speak words of wisdom (prajna-vadan), you are mourning for that which is not worthy of grief (ashochyan). The wise lament (anushochanti) neither for the living nor for the dead (gatasun-agatasunsh-cha). (Bhagavad-Gita Chapter 2, Verse 11)

The genesis of the Bhagavad-Gita is Arjuna's predicament to fight the war. When do we end up with a "real difficulty" in decision-making? How will we react under such conditions? The greatest motivation to read the Gita lies here. If Arjuna, who faced a miserable situation, could redeem himself from this and get back in the thick of action, we will also be able to get motivated enough to face some of the toughest challenges in life.[2]

Lokmanya writes, "Arjuna wanted to act like a *Jnanin* (scient), and was boasting about Renunciation of Action; and therefore the Blessed Lord commences His advice with the description of the two paths (*Nisthas*) of 'Abandonment of Action' and 'Performance of Action', which were being followed in the world by *Jnanins*; and first tells Arjuna that whichever of the two paths was adopted by him, he would yet be wrong... The Blessed Lord first says to Arjuna, "Inasmuch as the *Atman* is imperishable and immortal according to the Philosophy of the Absolute Self expounded in the *Samkhya*

---

2 http://www.iimb.ac.in/sites/default/files/22%20Reality%20of%20difficult%20decision%20making%20situations.pdf. Last accessed on 25 October 2017.

School of philosophy, this idea that you are going to kill Bhishma, etc. is erroneous in its very inception. The *Atman* is neither killed, nor does it kill. Just as a man changes one set of clothes and puts on another, so does the *Atman* give up one body and take up another; that is all... (and then tells) give up the *Karma*-vision that 'I am killing and he is dying'; and perform that Action which befalls you in the course of life, with the idea that you are merely doing your duty, so that you will incur no sin whatsoever."

Lokmanya writes, "...The root of the whole of the exposition of the *Gita* is in the second chapter." In this chapter, the central principle of the *Karma Yoga* is established in the decision whether a particular action is good or bad. In a stark departure from earlier works, the *Gita* calls the purity or impurity of the Practical Reason (*vyavasatmika buddhi*) of the doer, rather than the external effects of the Action, as the criteria of taking up an Action or abandoning it. Desire-prone actions are impure; desireless and duty-bound actions are pure.

दूरेण ह्यवरं कर्म बुद्धियोगाद्धनञ्जय ।
बुद्धौ शरणमन्विच्छ कृपणाः फलहेतवः ॥४९॥

Stay away (durena) from reward-seeking actions that are certainly inferior to works performed with the intellect (buddhi-yogat). Seek refuge in divine knowledge and insight (buddhau sharanamanvichchha). Miserable are those who seek the fruits of their works (kripanah phala-hetavah).
(Bhagavad-Gita Chapter 2, Verse 49)

Now, in order to purify the Practical Reason, the Discerning Reason (what is duty bound) has to be strengthened by means of concentration.

व्यवसायात्मिका बुद्धिरेकेह कुरुनन्दन ।
बहुशाखा ह्यनन्ताश्च बुद्धयोऽव्यवसायिनाम् ॥४१॥

Practicing discrimination with the intellect (vyavasaya-atmika) is one-pointed. But the intellect of those who are irresolute (avyavasayinamis) is infinitely many-branched

(bahu-shakhahyanantah) (and therefore inffective).
(Bhagavad-Gita Chapter 2, Verse 41)

The above two facts, namely, the Practical Reason and the Discerning Reason, get converged in giving up the desire-pronged activity of Vedic *Karma* (sacrificial *Yajnas*) and performing Action desirelessly, as the authority of a man is limited to undertaking a particular action, but not upon the result of that Action, which emerges out of a very complex process (intertwined with Law of Karma and divine grace), which is beyond human comprehension.

कर्मण्येवाधिकारस्ते मा फलेषु कदाचन ।
मा कर्मफलहेतुर्भूर्मा ते सङ्गोऽस्त्वकर्मणि ॥४७॥

You have a right only to perform your prescribed duties (karmany-evadhikaraste), but never to the fruits of your actions (ma phaleshu kadachana). Never consider yourself to be the cause of the results of your activities (ma karma-phala-heturbhuh), nor be inactive (akarmani).
(Bhagavad-Gita Chapter 2, Verse 47)

The person whose Reason has become equable in this way, is called *Sthitaprajna* (Steady-in-Intellect) and his intellect is situated in the Divine Consciousness (*samadhi-sthasya*).

श्रुतिविप्रतिपन्ना ते यदा स्थास्यति निश्चला ।
समाधावचला बुद्धिस्तदा योगमवाप्स्यसि ॥५३॥

When your intellect ceases to be allured by the fruitive sections of the Vedas (shruti-vipratipanna) and remains steadfast in divine consciousness (sthasyatinishchala), at that time, you will then attain the state of Yoga (tadayogamavapsyasi).
(Bhagavad-Gita Chapter 2, Verse 53)

The rest of this chapter describes the life of a *Sthitaprajna* and it is established that the intellectual state of a *Sthitaprajna* is, indeed, the state of being merged in the *Brahman* (*Brahmi* state).

The third chapter opens with another dilemma of Arjuna. He asks Shri Krishna that if Reason is superior to Action, then why is he being asked to engage in war. He may reason out why war should not be carried out. Or, he may make his Reason equable and then abandon action without violating the *Samkhya Yoga*. Lokmanya writes, "This question (of Arjuna's, at the beginning of the third chapter of the *Gita*) is answered by the Blessed Lord by saying, "It is true that I have mentioned the two paths of *Samkhya* and *Yoga*; but no man whosoever (he may be) can entirely give up Action. So long as he is clothed in a body, Matter (*Prakrti*) will by its inherent nature, compel him to perform Action.... Therefore, go on performing Action, for if you do not do so, you will not be able to even to obtain food. Action has been created by *Parameshvara*, not by Man.""

नियतं कुरु कर्म त्वं कर्म ज्यायो ह्यकर्मणः ।
शरीरयात्रापि च ते न प्रसिध्येदकर्मणः॥८॥

Constantly perform your duties (niyatamkuru karma tvam), since action is certainly superior to inaction (karma jyayo hi yakarmanah). By ceasing activity, even your bodily maintenance will not be possible (sharira-yatrapi cha tenaprasiddhyet). (Bhagavad-Gita Chapter 3, Verse 8)

Lokmanya writes, "As nobody can escape Action, one comes to the necessary conclusion that such Action must now be performed desirelessly for the benefit of others... Bearing this in mind, Janaka and other *Jnanins* have engaged in Action since ancient times. I (the Blessed Lord) am doing the same... bringing about *lokasmgraha* (universal welfare), that is, putting people on the path of self-amelioration, by placing before their eyes a good example in the shape of one's conduct."

Contemporary *Gita* teacher and Founder of Vedanta Trust Smt. Jaya Row writes, "Arjuna asks– What is it that takes me away from my chosen path and makes me do the things I ought not to do? Shri Krishna answers– It is desire, it is anger, born of the quality of *rajas,* passion. The enemy is within, not out there. Yet, you waste precious time and energy in trying to deal with external forces.

Desire comes in three shades– *sattva* (purity), *rajas* (passion) and *tamas* (darkness)... Blending poetry with philosophy, Krishna describes how these three kinds of desires shroud the *Atman*, the divine spark in you. *Sattva* is like smoke around fire. The brilliance and splendour of the *Atman* shines forth in a *sattvik* person. *Rajas* covers the *Atman* like dust on a mirror. Selfishness and ego blur the image of the Self. You are unable to see Divinity in a *rajasika* person. *Tamas* is like an embryo in the uterus. Not only does it completely cover Divinity, but it also takes time for you to emerge out of lethargy and indolence... Rise to a higher desire, the lower will lose its hold over you. He concludes with a highly inspiring message– Kill the formidable enemy in the form of desire by rising to the highest desire, that of Self-Realisation. The warrior in Arjuna is provoked, and responds."[3]

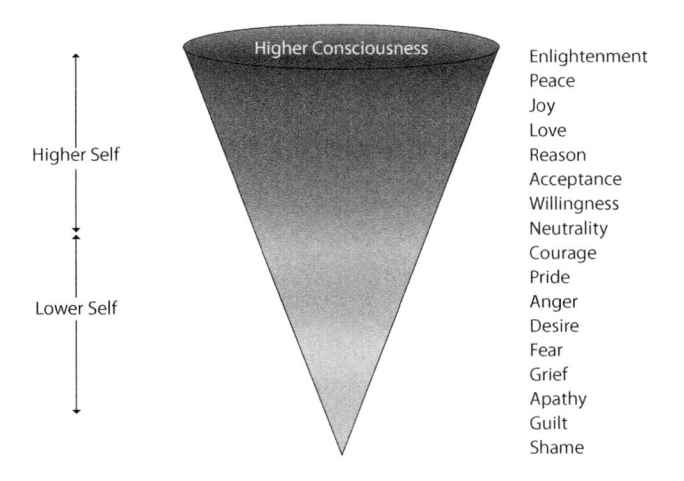

Higher Self / Lower Self

Higher Consciousness

Enlightenment
Peace
Joy
Love
Reason
Acceptance
Willingness
Neutrality
Courage
Pride
Anger
Desire
Fear
Grief
Apathy
Guilt
Shame

British theosophist and spiritualist, Paul Brunton (1898–1981), famously said, "Saints and sages, thinkers and philosophers, priests and scientific inquirers have tried for centuries to understand the enigmatic nature of the human soul. They find man a paradoxical being; one capable of descent into the darkest abysses of evil, and yet, equally capable of ascent to the sublime heights of nobility. They discover two creatures within his breast– one related to the demons and the other related to the angels."[4]

---

3   http://vedantavision.org/bhagavad-gita/summary-of-chapters/bhagavad-gita-chapter-iii.html. Last accessed on 25 October 2017.

4   Paul Brunton, *The Secret Path: A Technique of Spiritual Self-discovery for the Modern World*, Pilgrims Publishing, Varanasi, 2002.

The rise of consciousness from the lower self to the higher self is a brilliant idea given in this chapter of the *Gita*. The culmination of the process comes in becoming an instrument of God. All actions are done in the God-consciousness and accrue no karmic consequences. Lokmanya writes, "The Blessed Lord, by saying, 'Dedicate all Actions to Me', gives the first glimpse (*sutauvacha*) of the central principle of the Path of Devotion, namely, to perform all Actions with the idea of dedicating them to the *Parameshvara*.

मयि सर्वाणि कर्माणि संन्यस्याध्यात्मचेतसा ।
निराशीर्निर्ममो भूत्वा युध्यस्व विगतज्वरः ॥३०॥

Perform all works as an offering unto Me, with the thoughts resting on God (adhyatma-chetasa). Therefore, free from the hankering for the results of the actions, and taking no ownership (nirashirnirmama) and without any mental fever (vigata-jvarah), fight (yudhyasva). (Bhagavad-Gita Chapter 3, Verse 30)

ये मे मतमिदं नित्यमनुतिष्ठन्ति मानवाः ।
श्रद्धावन्तोऽनसूयन्तो मुच्यन्ते तेऽपि कर्मभिः ॥३१॥

Those who constantly abide by my teachings (ye me matamidam nityamanutishthanti) faithfully (shraddha-vantah) and give up a flawed/fault-finding approach/attitude/perspective, they are also released from the bondage of karma (muchyante teapi karmabhih). (Bhagavad-Gita Chapter 3, Verse 31)

Moving further into the next chapter, Lokmanya writes, "Nevertheless, this subject matter has not yet been exhausted in the third chapter, and the fourth chapter has been started for further dealing with the same subject. In order that Arjuna should not think that the disquisition made so far was something new, which the Blessed Lord invented merely for the purpose of inducing him to fight, Shri Krishna, in the beginning of the fourth chapter, mentions the tradition of *Karma Yoga*, i.e., of the Bhagavata or Narayaniya religion, in the Krta Yuga. The Blessed Lord said to Arjuna that in the beginning of the *Yuga* (*aadau*), he had taught this Path of *Karma*

Yoga to the Sun-god Vivasvan, who passed it on to Manu, and Manu, in turn, instructed it to Ikshvaku, and that it had been lost in the interim, and therefore, He was now preaching the same *Yoga* (the Path of *Karma Yoga*) to Arjuna... (When Arjuna) rejoins by asking how the Blessed Lord could have been in existence with Vivasvan, the Blessed Lord has accounted for His several incarnations by saying that He had to take those incarnations for protecting saints and destroying evil-doers and establishing true religion."

यदा यदा हि धर्मस्य ग्लानिर्भवति भारत ।
अभ्युत्थानमधर्मस्य तदात्मानं सृजाम्यहम् ॥७॥
परित्राणाय साधूनां विनाशाय च दुष्कृताम् ।
धर्मसंस्थापनार्थाय सम्भवामि युगे युगे ॥८॥

Shri Krishna tells Arjuna: Whenever and wherever there is a decline in righteousness (yadayada hi dharmasya glanirbhavati) and an increase in unrighteousness (abhyutthanamadharmasya), at that time, I manifest myself on earth (tadaatmanam srjamy aham). (Bhagavad-Gita Chapter 4, Verse 7)

Dr. S. Radhakrishnan explains, "*Dharma* literally means mode of being. It is the essential nature of being that determines its mode of behaviour. So long as our conduct is in conformity with our essential nature, we are acting in the right way. *Adharma* is nonconformity to our nature... God does not stand aside when we abuse our freedom and cause disequilibrium. He does not simply wind up the world, set it on the right track and then let it jog along by itself. His loving hand is steering it all the time... The conception of *dharma* is a development of the idea of *Rta*, which connotes cosmic as well as moral order, in the *Rig-Veda*."[5]

For the protection of the good (*paritranaya sadhunam*) and the destruction of the wicked (*vinasaya ca duskrtam*), and for the establishment of order in the world (*dharma-samsthapanarthaya*), I do appear (*sambhavami*, in the human form) in every age (*yuge yuge*) and set things right for the good (*samsthapana-arthaya*). (Bhagavad *Gita* Chapter 4, Verse 8)

---

5 S. Radhakrishnan, *The Bhagavad Gita*, HarperCollins Publishers, India, 2014, p. 179.

In Verse 16, Shri Krishna tells Arjuna the secret of action - what is action and what is inaction *(kim karma kim akarmeti)*, by knowing which one becomes free yourself from material bondage *(pravakshyami yaj jnatva mokhyase ashubhat).*

Smt. Jaya Row writes, "Verses 24 to 30 give a unique method of worshipping God 24/7. The entire gamut of human activities is divided into twelve parts and each is converted to *Yajna*, worship. Shri Krishna applied the *Yajna* process of offering and kindling to all of life's activities, thus reminding us of God in our everyday routine. This is a far more practical method of worship than pulling ourselves out of our daily schedule to engage in prayer, which, at best, can only be done periodically. The endeavour is to instil the thought of the Divine, while worldly activities are being accomplished. Worship has to be 24/7. A casual, occasional thought of God is of no use as it gets nullified by the bulk of material pursuits. Yet, it is not possible for the average person to give up mundane actions to engage in worship."[6]

Shloka 34 in this chapter gives the qualities of a good student as well as an ideal guru.

तद्विद्धि प्रणिपातेन परिप्रश्नेन सेवया ।
उपदेक्ष्यन्ति ते ज्ञानं ज्ञानिनस्तत्त्वदर्शिनः ॥३४॥

Learn the Truth by approaching a spiritual master (tad viddhi pranipatena). Inquire from him with reverence and render service unto him (pariprashnena sevaya). Only such an enlightened Saint, who has seen the Truth (jnaninahtattva-darshinah), can impart knowledge unto you (upadekshyantite)
(Bhagavad-Gita Chapter 4, Verse 34)

Smt. Jaya Row adds, "A well-prepared student is like a dry matchstick. A mere suggestion is enough to light up and gain Enlightenment. The mediocre student is like a damp matchstick. Intense effort and hard work by the student fail to ignite wisdom and inspire his life."[7]

---

6 https://www.speakingtree.in/blog/bhagavad-gita-chapter-iv, Last accessed on 25 October 2017.

7 *ibid*

The chapter ends with Shri Krishna's inspiring words:

तस्मादज्ञानसम्भूतं हृत्स्थं ज्ञानासिनात्मनः ।
छित्त्वैनं संशयं योगमातिष्ठोत्तिष्ठ भारत ॥४२॥

Therefore, with the sword of knowledge (jnana asina), cut asunder the doubts that have arisen in your heart (chhittvaenam sanshayam) due to ignorance, O scion of Bharata, establish yourself in the Yoga and stand up for war (yogamatishthauttishtha).
(Bhagavad-Gita Chapter 4, Verse 42)

Swami Ranganathananda adds, "This doubt, *hrtstham*, 'that is creeping in your heart', crippling your life and action; destroy that doubt. *Ajnanasambhtam*, 'born out of *Ajnana* i.e., ignorance or spiritual blindness'. That is creating doubts and uncertainties in your mind. Therefore, destroy it. How to destroy it? *Jnana asina*, 'by making *jnana* into a sword', cut across the jungle of doubts and confusion in you."[8]

Lokmanya writes, 'It is true that the reasons as to why action should be performed, that is the necessity of the *Karma Yoga*, have been explained in the third and fourth chapters. However, in the second chapter, after explaining the knowledge contained in the *Samkhya* philosophy, the Blessed Lord has said over and over again that 'Reason' was superior to action, so it now becomes necessary to explain which of these two paths is superior, because if one says that both the paths are of equal importance, it follows that people are free to choose whichever of the two paths they prefer and that it is not necessary to follow only the path of *Karma Yoga*. This very doubt came into the mind of Arjuna and he has, in the beginning of the fifth chapter, said to the Blessed Lord, do not mix up the two paths of *Samkhya* and *Yoga*, but tell me definitely which of the two is superior, so that it will be convenient for me to act accordingly. The Blessed Lord has removed the doubt of Arjuna by saying that though both the paths are equally productive of Release, yet the path of *Karma Yoga* is the better one of the two."

---
[8] Swami Ranganathananda, *Universal Message of the Bhagavad Gita, Vol. 12*, Advaita Ashrama, Kolkata, 2015 (Seventh reprint), p.489.

संन्यासः कर्मयोगश्च निःश्रेयसकरावुभौ ।
तयोस्तु कर्मसंन्यासात्कर्मयोगो विशिष्यते ॥२॥

Both, the paths of renunciation of actions and working in devotion, lead to the supreme goal (nihshreyasa-karau). But undertaking of Actions (with devotion) is superior to renunciation of actions (karma-sannyasat karma-yogovishishyate).
(Bhagavad-Gita Chapter 5, Verse 2)

Emancipation out of the perpetual birth-death-rebirth cycle is the real goal of spiritual aspirants. However it is never a one life endeavour and span several life times. Even a *yogi*, who has controlled his senses and mind, can have many desires for which he must act. Only by separating one from the desires he stops hating or running away from things and people. He is now unmoved by the pairs of opposites in the world and guiltless of his action. Action therefore precedes meditation. Upon successful mediation only can one act desirelessly and dedicate all actions to *Brahman*. His life becomes the life of a flower, it blossoms at the right time, spreads fragrance silently and falls away uneventfully.

Shloka 13 in Chapter 5 of the *Bhagavad-Gita* gives a powerful metaphor of the human body as a city of nine gates (*nava-dvare pure*).

सर्वकर्माणि मनसा संन्यस्यास्ते सुखं वशी ।
नवद्वारे पुरे देही नैव कुर्वन्न कारयन् ॥१३॥

Having renounced all activities by the mind (sarva-karmani manasa sannyasyaste), such people reside happily in the city of nine gates (nava-dvare pure), free from thinking they are the doers or the cause of anything (naiva kurvanna karayan).
(Bhagavad-Gita Chapter 5, Verse 13)

Shloka 18 tells very powerfully, how divine knowledge bestows a vision so different from physical sight that it can see diametrically contrasting species and life forms with an equal eye.

विद्याविनयसम्पन्ने ब्राह्मणे गवि हस्तिनि ।
शुनि चैव श्वपाके च पण्डिताः समदर्शिनः ॥१८॥

The truly learned and humble persons (vidya-vinaya-sampanne), see with equal vision (sama-darshinah), a Brahmin, a cow, an elephant, a dog, and a dog-eater (brahmane gavi hastini shuni cha evashva-pake).
(Bhagavad-Gita Chapter 5, Verse 18)

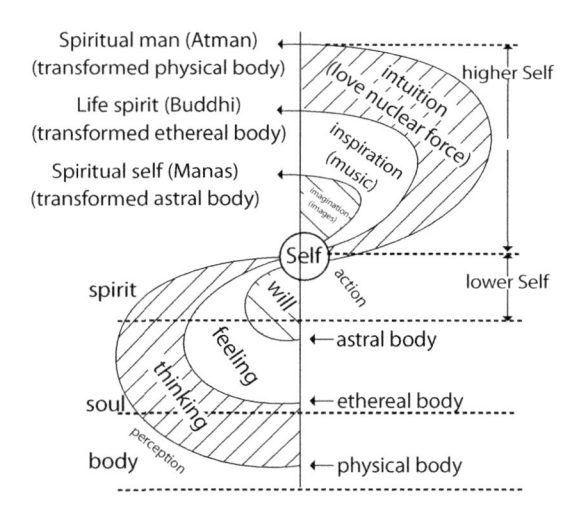

The Mind spans over a wide spectrum - Over mind (Mahat), Intuition (Buddhi), Illumined Mind (Prajna), Higher Mind (Pure Reason), and Thinking Mind (Reason). Except the Thinking Mind, the four higher planes are eternally pre-existent, and constitute the modes or qualities of the Absolute (Satchitananda), of the nature of pure Being, Consciousness, and Bliss.

Swami Muktananda writes, "When we perceive things through the perspective of knowledge, it is called '*prajna chakshu*', which means 'with the eyes of knowledge'. Shri Krishna uses the words '*vidya sampanne*' to the same effect, but he also adds '*vinaya*', meaning 'humbleness.' The sign of divine knowledge is that it is accompanied by a sense of humility, while shallow bookish knowledge is accompanied with the pride of scholarship."[9]

---
9 http://www.holy-bhagavad-gita.org/chapter/5/verse/18. Last accessed on 25 October 2017.

This concept of the *Bhagavad-Gita* was explained in a different terminology by Austrian philosopher Rudolph Steiner (1861-1925) and other theosophical mystics, who defined the lower emotional body as sentient soul; mental/intellectual body/layer as intellectual soul; and the three higher transpersonal or spiritual levels, namely, spiritual self (faculty of imagination), life spirit (faculty of inspiration), and *Atman* (faculty of intuition), as the higher self.

In the sixth chapter, Shri Krishna continues the comparative evaluation of *Karma Yoga* (practicing spirituality while continuing the worldly duties) and *Karma Samnyasa* (practicing spirituality in the renounced order) from chapter five and recommends the former. Lokmanya writes, "The Blessed Lord has here explained in what way that Equable Reason can be acquired by which one can obtain success in the practice of *Karma Yoga*. In the very first *shloka*, the Blessed Lord has expressed His firm opinion that the man who performs all Action, which fall to his share, as duties, and without entertaining the hope of fruit, is the true *Yogi*, or the true *Samnyasi*. ... He then goes on to explain the principle of the Independence of the *Atman*. He says that whatever Action has to be performed in the shape of control of the organs, for steadying the mind, according to the philosophy of *Karma Yoga*, must be performed by oneself. If one does not do so properly, one cannot blame anybody else."

अनाश्रितः कर्मफलं कार्यं कर्म करोति यः ।
स संन्यासी च योगी च न निरग्निर्न चाक्रियः ॥१॥

Those who perform prescribed duties without desiring the results of their actions (anashritah karma-phalam) are actual renunciates and yogis, not those who have merely ceased performing sacrifices or abandoned bodily activities (na niragnir na chakriyah). (Bhagavad-Gita Chapter 6, Verse 1)

This *shloka* is very important. It had become a practice that when someone entered the renounced order of life, all the ritualistic activities were given up to the extent that one would not touch fire even for the purpose of cooking food, and live on alms instead. People started glorifying themselves as living only on fruits, or on milk, or only on breath, or even wear no clothes (*phalahari babas, dudhahari babas, pavanahari babas, naga babas*) as a testimony of their renunciation. In this *shloka*, the Blessed Lord dismisses all these concepts. He says that such external acts of asceticism do not make anyone either a *samnyasi* or a *yogi*.

The Blessed Lord called for a conscious and steadfast effort to make one's mind Equable towards all created beings.

सर्वभूतस्थमात्मानं सर्वभूतानि चात्मनि ।
ईक्षते योगयुक्तात्मा सर्वत्र समदर्शनः ॥२९॥

One united in consciousness with God (yoga-yukta-atma), sees with equal eye, all living beings in God and God in all living beings (sarva-bhuta-sthamatmanam sarva-bhutani chatmani).
(Bhagavad-Gita Chapter 6, Verse 29)

यो मां पश्यति सर्वत्र सर्वं च मयि पश्यति ।
तस्याहं न प्रणश्यामि स च मे न प्रणश्यति ॥३०॥

For those who see me everywhere (yo mam pashyati sarvatra sarvam) and see all things in me (mayi pashyati); for them I am never lost, nor are they ever lost to me (aham na pranashyami sa cha me na pranashyati). (Bhagavad-Gita Chapter 6, Verse 30)

Swami Muktananda writes, "When the mind is purified, one is able to perceive the self as distinct from the body, mind, and intellect. For example, if there is muddy water in a glass, we cannot see through it. However, if we put alum in the water, the mud settles down and the water becomes clear. Similarly, when the mind is unclean, it obscures perception of the soul and any acquired scriptural knowledge of the *Atman* is only at the theoretical level. But when the mind becomes pure, the soul is directly perceived through realisation."[10]

At this juncture, Lokmanya makes a very crucial comment. He writes, "Some persons are of the opinion that the exposition of *Karma Yoga* has come to an end here, that is, at the end of the

---

10 http://www.holy-bhagavad-gita.org/chapter/6/verse/20. Last accessed on 13 December 2017.

sixth chapter. Thereafter, the Blessed Lord has described the Path of Knowledge and the Path of Devotion as two 'independent' paths. They say that the paths are mutually independent, or are the same in importance as the *Karma Yoga,* but different from it, and as such, proper to be followed as alternatives for the Path of *Karma Yoga.* The Path of Devotion has been described from the seventh to the twelfth chapters and the Path of Knowledge, in the remaining six chapters (thirteenth to the eighteenth), equally dividing the *Gita* in this way, six chapters each allocated to Action (*karma*), Devotion (*bhakti*) and Knowledge (*jnana*), and the *Gita* becomes equally divided among the three paths. But this opinion is wrong."

The seventh chapter begins with these words of the Blessed Lord:

मय्यासक्तमनाः पार्थ योगं युञ्जन्मदाश्रयः ।
असंशयं समग्रं मां यथा ज्ञास्यसि तच्छृणु ॥१॥

Hear how, with the mind attached (asakta-manah) to Me (mayy) and surrendering to Me (mat-ashrayah) through the practice of yoga, you can know Me completely, free from doubt.
(Bhagavad-Gita Chapter 7, Verse 1)

Lokmanya writes, "The Yoga (mentioned in the first *shloka* of the seventh chapter) is necessarily the *Karma Yoga,* which has been described in the first six chapters; and this means that now, that is, from the seventh chapter, the Blessed Lord is starting a description of that path or the '*vidhi*', by which, the complete knowledge of the God can be acquired while a man is practicing this *Karma Yoga.*"

ज्ञानं तेऽहं सविज्ञानमिदं वक्ष्याम्यशेषतः ।
यज्ज्ञात्वा नेह भूयोऽन्यज्ज्ञातव्यमवशिष्यते ॥२॥

I shall now reveal unto you fully, the spiritual illumination (jnana) and the phenomenal knowledge (vijnana). (By knowing these two) nothing else remains to be known (anyatjnatavyam) or anything unknowable (avasisyate) (does not remain) in this world. (Bhagavad-Gita Chapter 7, Verse 2)

Dr. S. Radhakrishnan adds, "We must have not merely knowledge of the relation-less Absolute, but also of its varied manifestations. The Supreme is (very much present) in the man and the nature, though these do not limit Him."[11]

Lokmanya writes, "In the seventh chapter, the consideration of the perishable and the imperishable world, that is, the entire Cosmos, has been started." Earth, water, fire, air, space, mind, intellect, and ego– are the eight components of God's material energy and the *Gita* calls them the inferior energy of the God and the *jiva* (soul energy) as the superior energy.

अपरेयमितस्त्वन्यां प्रकृतिं विद्धि मे पराम् ।
जीवभूतां महाबाहो ययेदं धार्यते जगत् ॥५॥

Such is my inferior energy (apara). But beyond it, I have a superior energy. This is the jīvaśakti (the soul energy), which comprises the embodied souls, and is the basis of life in this world (yayedam dharyate jagat). (Bhagavad-Gita Chapter 7, Verse 5)

The Blessed Lord further says that He is the source of the entire creation (*aham kritsnasya jagatahprabhavah*), and into Him, the world again dissolves (*pralayastatha*). There is nothing higher than God and everything rests in God, like beads strung on a thread (*sutremani-ganaiva*). However, the people in this world are unable to know the God as supreme and eternal (*param avyayam*), as they are deluded (*mohitam*) by the three modes of the material energy (*tribhirguna-mayairbhavair*).

At the end of this chapter, the Blessed Lord declares that He is the governing principle of the *adhibhuta* (field of matter) and the *adhidaiva* (the celestial gods), and the *adhiyajna* (the Lord all sacrificial performances). The three terms would be fully explained in the eighth chapter.

अधिभूतं क्षरो भावः पुरुषश्चाधिदैवतम् ।
अधियज्ञोऽहमेवात्र देहे देहभृतां वर ॥४॥

---

[11] S. Radhakrishnan, *The Bhagavad Gita*, HarperCollins Publishers, Noida India, 2014, p. 249-250.

The ever-changing physical world is called adhibhuta and it is perishable (kshara). My universal form (bhavahpurushash) presides over the celestial gods (adhidaivatam). I am the Lord of all sacrifices (adhiyajnah) and am certainly here in the heart of all bodies (aham evatra dehe deha-bhritam). (Bhagavad-Gita Chapter 8, Verse 4)

Smt. Jaya Row writes, "Shri Krishna then goes on to highlight the power of thought. You are a product of your thoughts. You sculpt your own future by guiding your thoughts towards your goal. If the goal is worldly, you remain caught up in the vagaries of the world. The spiritual journey begins by redirecting your thoughts from material pursuits to spiritual aspirations. Once this is done, make an effort to master the senses. Follow the practices of *Karma Yoga* (path of action), *Bhakti Yoga* (path of devotion) and *Jnana Yoga* (path of knowledge). It is through these practices that the mind becomes calm and free from desire. If you have invested your thoughts in the spiritual ideal, you break free from the cycle of birth and death to merge with *Brahman*."[12]

The eighth chapter includes a brilliant allegory of the two, bright and dark paths that always exist in this world. The way of light leads to liberation and the way of darkness leads to rebirth - the six months of the sun's northern course, the bright fortnight of the moon, and the bright part of the day; and the six months of the sun's southern course, the dark fortnight of the moon, the time of smoke, and the night. The way of light leads to liberation and the way of darkness leads to rebirth. The *Gita* resonates here with the *Pavamana Mantra* in the *Brihadaranyaka Upanishad* (1. 3. 28.)

असतो मा सद्गमय ।
तमसो मा ज्योतिर्गमय ।
मृत्योर्मामृतं गमय ॥
ॐ शान्तिः शान्तिः शान्तिः ॥

Lead me from falsehood to truth,

---

12 http://www.speakingtree.in/blog/bhagavad-gita-chapter-viii. Last accessed on 26 October 2017.

Lead me from darkness to light,
Lead me from death to immortality
Let there be Peace! Peace! Peace!
(Brihadaranyaka Upanishad (1. 3. 28.))

Lokmanya writes, "In the ninth chapter, the same subject matter is continued and it is said that Realisation by means of Devotion to the tangible form of the intangible *Parameshvara*, which has, in this way, filled the entire universe, and surrendering oneself to Him wholly and solely, is the easy or royal and practically experienceable path of Realising the *Brahmanand*; that this very path is also known as the 'king of all cults' and the 'king of all mysticisms.' Nevertheless, the Blessed Lord does not forget to mention every now and then in these three chapters (7, 8 and 9), that the person who is following the Path of Spiritual Knowledge or the path of devotion, must continue performing action, which is the most important principle in the path of *Karma Yoga*."

Verse 22 in this chapter provides the famous motto of the 'Life Insurance Corporation of India' - '*yoga-ksemam vahamy aham*'.

अनन्याश्चिन्तयन्तो मां ये जनाः पर्युपासते ।
तेषां नित्याभियुक्तानां योगक्षेमं वहाम्यहम् ॥२२॥

Those persons who start seeing them never separate from Me and worship Me regularly (nitya abhiyuktanam) and centred their thinking around Me (chintayanto mam), I provide them what they lack and preserve all that they already have. (yoga-ksemamvahamy aham). (Bhagavad-Gita Chapter 9, Verse 22)

Dr. S. Radhakrishnan adds, "God takes up all the burdens and the cares of His devotees. To become conscious of divine love, all other love must be abandoned. If we cast ourselves entirely on the mercy of the God, He bears all our cares and sorrows. We can depend on His saving care and emerging grace."[13]

Swami Muktananda writes in his commentary of this *shloka*, "God offers motherly assurance to souls who surrender exclusively

---
[13] S. Radhakrishnan, *The Bhagavad Gita*, HarperCollins Publishers, India, 2014, p. 292-293.

to him. The words used are *vahami aham* (I personally carry the burden of maintaining my devotees)... This can again be understood through the same analogy of the mother and child. A new born baby is fully dependent upon its mother, who takes care of the baby's welfare entirely. The baby simply cries whenever it needs anything; the mother cleans it, feeds it, bathes it etc. But when the baby becomes a five-year old child, it begins doing some actions for itself. In this way, as the boy keeps assuming more responsibilities, his mother keeps relinquishing her responsibilities. God's law is exactly the same. When we act from our independent will, thinking that we are the doers of our actions, and depend upon our own prowess and abilities, God does not bestow His grace. He merely notes our *karmas* and gives the result. When we surrender partially to him and partially depend upon material crutches, God also partially bestows His grace upon us. And when we offer ourselves exclusively to Him, *mamekam sharanam vraja*, God bestows His complete grace and takes full responsibility, by preserving what we have and providing what we lack."

यत्करोषि यदश्नासि यज्जुहोषि ददासि यत् ।
यत्तपस्यसि कौन्तेय तत्कुरुष्व मदर्पणम् ॥२७॥

Whatever (yat) you do, whatever you eat (karoshi), whatever you offer to the sacred fire (juhoshi), whatever you bestow as a gift (dadasi), and whatever austerities (tapasyasi) you perform, do them as an offering to me (tat kurushva mad-arpanam).
(Bhagavad-Gita Chapter 9, Verse 27)

शुभाशुभफलैरेवं मोक्ष्यसे कर्मबन्धनैः ।
संन्यासयोगयुक्तात्मा विमुक्तो मामुपैष्यसि ॥२८॥

By dedicating all your works to me, you will be freed from the bondage (mokshyase karma-bandhanaih) of good and bad results (shubhaashubhaphalaih). With your mind attached to me through renunciation, you will be liberated and will reach me (mam upaishyasi). (Bhagavad-Gita Chapter 9, Verse 28)

This straightforward deal offered by the Blessed Lord in the *Gita*, "If you do my work, I will take care of you," is unparalleled in any other religion in the world.

The tenth chapter contains the narration of the Blessed Lord to help Arjuna to know God's magnificent and resplendent glories. Arjuna, by this time, has been initiated into the science of *bhakti* (Chapter 9) and knows a little about God's opulence. The Blessed Lord expounds further on it to enhance his devotion.

यद्यद्विभूतिमत्सत्त्वं श्रीमदूर्जितमेव वा ।
तत्तदेवावगच्छ त्वं मम तेजोंऽशसम्भवम् ॥४१॥

Whatever (*yadyad*) you see as opulent, beautiful, glorious (*vibhutimatsattvam shrimadurjitam*), know it to spring from (*sambhavam*) a spark of my splendour (*mama tejo amsha*)
(Bhagavad *Gita* Chapter 10, Verse 41)

अथवा बहुनैतेन किं ज्ञातेन तवार्जुन ।
विष्टभ्याहमिदं कृत्स्नमेकांशेन स्थितो जगत् ॥४२॥

What need is there for all this detailed knowledge (jnatenatava), O Arjuna? Simply know that by one fraction of my being situated here (ekanshenasthito), I pervade and support (vishtabhyaaham) this entire creation (kritshsnamjagat).
(Bhagavad-Gita Chapter 10, Verse 42)

Lokmanya writes, "After explaining to Arjuna in the tenth chapter, the statement made by Shri Krishna earlier, that "the entire Cosmos has sprung from Me, and is My Form", by saying that every one of the excellent things in the world is an incarnation of the Blessed Lord, and giving many examples, the Blessed Lord, at the desire of Arjuna, actually shows him, in the eleventh chapter, His Cosmic Form, and proves to him the truth of the position that the *Parameshvara* is all-pervading, by placing before Arjuna's eyes such Cosmic Form."

The hallmark of the eleventh chapter is the Cosmic Form (*Vishvarupa*). Arjuna could now see the totality of creation in the body of the God of gods. Arjuna also sees the three worlds trembling in fear of God's laws and realises that God is also the destroyer of the three worlds.

तस्मात्त्वमुत्तिष्ठ यशो लभस्व
जित्वा शत्रून्भुङ्क्ष्व राज्यं समृद्धम् ।
मयैवैते निहताः पूर्वमेव
निमित्तमात्रं भव सव्यसाचिन् ।।३३।।

(Shri Krishna tells Arjuna) Therefore, get up (uttistha) and attain honour! Conquer your foes (jitva shatrun) and enjoy prosperous rulership (bhunksva rajyam samrddham). These warriors stand already slain by me (mayaivaite nihatah purvameva), and you will only be an instrument of my work (nimitta-matram). (Bhagavad-Gita Chapter 11, Verse 33)

Dr. S. Radhakrishnan elaborates, "We need not look upon the whole cosmic process as anything more than the unfolding of a predetermined plan, the unveiling of a ready-made scenario... The radical novelty of each moment of evolution in time is not inconsistent with Divine Eternity. The ideas of God are worked out through human instrumentality. If we are wise, we so act that we are instruments in His hands. We allow Him to absorb our soul and leave no trace of the ego. We must receive His command and do His will, with the cry, 'In your will, is our peace'. Behind this world of spare-time, interpenetrating it is the creative purpose of God. We must understand that supreme design and be content to serve it. Every act is a symbol of something far beyond itself."[14]

This chapter establishes beyond doubt that only a devotee can see the human form of the God. Studying *Shastras* or performing *yajnas* cannot access it.

भक्त्या त्वनन्यया शक्य अहमेवंविधोऽर्जुन ।
ज्ञातुं द्रष्टुं च तत्त्वेन प्रवेष्टुं च परन्तप ।।५४।।

O Arjuna, by unalloyed devotion alone (bhaktyatuananyaya) can I be known as I am, standing before you (evam-vidhah).

---

14 S. Radhakrishnan, *The Bhagavad Gita*, HarperCollins Publishers, India, 2014, p. 332-333.

Thereby, on receiving my divine vision (jnatumdrashtum cha tattvena), O scorcher of foes (parantapa), one can enter into union with me (praveshtum).
(Bhagavad-Gita Chapter 11, Verse 54)

The small twelfth chapter, containing only 20 *shlokas*, further emphasises the path of loving devotion over all other types of spiritual practices. Lokmanya writes, "Arjuna, in the beginning of the twelfth chapter, asks the Blessed Lord the question whether the worship of the *Parameshvara* should be the worship of the perceptible form or of the imperceptible form. To this, the Blessed Lord replies that the perceptible form described in the ninth chapter is easier, and after describing the state of the highest devotee of the Blessed Lord as being similar to that of a *Sthitaprajna*, described in the second chapter, He closes his statements."

The Blessed Lord tells Arjuna the path of *Bhakti*. Fix your mind on Me and surrender your intellect to Me (*mayi buddhi mniveshaya*). If you are unable to fix your mind steadily on Me, then practice remembering me with devotion (*abhyasa-yogenatato mam*) while carrying on with your worldly affairs. If you cannot practice remembering Me with devotion, then just try to do service to the needy (*mat-karma paramah*) for My sake (*mat-artham*). If you are unable to even work for Me in devotion, then try to renounce the fruits of your actions (*phala-tyagam*) and be grounded in the *Atman* (*yata-atma-vaan*).

The Blessed Lord now declares in most direct way the grading of devotion:

श्रेयो हि ज्ञानमभ्यासाज्ज्ञानाद्ध्यानं विशिष्यते ।
ध्यानात्कर्मफलत्यागस्त्यागाच्छान्तिरनन्तरम् ॥१२॥

Better than mechanical practice (abhyasa) is knowledge (jnanam); better than knowledge is meditation (dhyanat). Better than meditation is renunciation of the fruits of actions (karma-phala-tyagah), for peace immediately follows such renunciation (tyagatshantihanantaram).
(Bhagavad-Gita Chapter 12, Verse 12)

Swami Mukundananda adds, "Many people are at the level of mechanical practice. They perform the rituals enjoined by their religious creed, but do not engage their mind in God. When they purchase a new house or a new car, they call the *Pundit* to perform the *puja* (worship) ceremony. And while the *Pundit* performs the *puja*, they sit and talk in the other room or sip a cup of tea. For them, devotion is nothing more than performing the empty ritual. It is often performed by way of ceremonial habits that have been passed on from parents and elders. Performing rituals mechanically is not a bad thing, for after all, something is better than nothing. At least such people are externally engaging in devotion."[15]

Lokmanya takes a pause here as the twelfth chapter concludes and reiterates his position that, "It is not possible to divide the *Gita* into three independent portions dealing with Energism, Devotion, and Spiritual Knowledge; yet, some people think that it is easy to divide the Spiritual and worldly knowledge described from the seventh chapter, into the two divisions of 'Devotion' and 'Knowledge'; and they say that the second division of six chapters deals with the 'Devotion'... this opinion is wrong; because the seventh chapter starts with Spiritual and worldly knowledge of the perishable and imperishable world, and not with the Devotion... (also) we find statements in different places in the subsequent chapters, preaching Devotion."

Lokmanya writes, "After the physical eyes of Arjuna had got the actual experience that the *Parameshvara* occupies and pervades the whole of the *Brahmanda* (Cosmos), that is to say, the perishable and the imperishable universe having seen the Cosmic Form of the *Parameshvara*, the Blessed Lord explains in the thirteenth chapter, the doctrine of the Body and the *Atman,* namely, that the same *Parameshvara* occupies the body (*pinda*), that is to say, the body of man, or *kshetra*, in the shape of the *Atman*, and that the knowledge, that is to say, knowledge of this *kshetrajna*, is also the knowledge of the *Parameshvara*".

It is obvious that the tread of Devotion continues beyond the twelfth chapter *dhyanena atmani pashyanti* (seeing the *Atman* by meditation).

---
15 http://www.holy-bhagavad-gita.org/chapter/12/verse/12. Last accessed on 26 October 2017.

ध्यानेनात्मनि पश्यन्ति केचिदात्मानमात्मना ।
अन्ये साङ्ख्येन योगेन कर्मयोगेन चापरे ॥२४॥

Some try to perceive the one Supreme Soul (kecidatmanam) within their hearts (atmana), others through meditation (dhyanena), some others try to do so through the cultivation of knowledge (sankhyena), while still others strive to attain that realisation by the path of action (karma-yogena).
(Bhagavad-Gita Chapter 13, Verse 24)

य एवं वेत्ति पुरुषं प्रकृतिं च गुणैः सह ।
सर्वथा वर्तमानोऽपि न स भूयोऽभिजायते ॥२३॥

Those who understand the truth about the Supreme Soul, creating the individual soul, material nature, and the interaction of the three modes of nature (vetti purusam prakrtim cha gunaih saha), will not take birth here again (bhuyohabhijayate) in spite of their activities, in every way, whatever state of life they may be in (sarvatha vartamanopi).
(Bhagavad-Gita Chapter 13, Verse 23)

Having first described the *Parameshvara* on the authority of the *Upanishads*, by the words, '*anandi mat param brahma*' etc., it is shown later that Body and the *Atman* has been included in the *Samkhya* exposition of *Prakrti* (matter) and *Purusha* (spirit); and it is ultimately said that he who realises the difference between *Prakrti* and *Purusha*, and realises the all-pervading *Paramatman* with *jnana-chakshu* (spiritual eyes) is truly Realised. But even in this, the thread of action has been kept in the texture by saying, "Everything is done by the Matter (*Prakrti*) and the *Atman* is not the doer, and by realising this, action (*karma*) does not create bondage.

After establishing the distinction between the soul and the material body in the thirteenth chapter, the subject matter of this *jnana* is continued in the fourteenth chapter, and the position that there is only one *Atman* or *Parameshvara* is further reinforced by explaining the presence of diversity of life-forms on earth and other entities in the Cosmos as the play of material energy. In the fourteenth chapter, the nature of the material energy is explained as the source of the body and its elements, the mind and the matter.

The total material substance, *Prakrti*, is my womb (*mama yonih*). I impregnate it (*dadhamy aham*) with the individual souls, and thus, all living beings are born (*sambhavah sarva-bhutanam tato bhavati*). The material energy consists of three modes (*gunas*)– goodness (*sattva*), passion (*rajas*), and ignorance (*tamas*). These modes bind the eternal soul to the perishable body (*nibadhnanti dehe dehinam avyayam*). Those who serve me (*sevate*) with unalloyed devotion (a*vyabhicharena bhakti-yogena*) rise above the three modes of material nature (*sa guna nsamatityaitan*) and come to the level of *Brahman (brahma-buyaya kalpate*).

Lokmanya writes, "In the fifteenth chapter, there is, in the beginning, a reference to the description of the *Parmeshvara* as a tree."

Smt. Jaya Row writes, "In this short yet immensely deep chapter, Shri Krishna expounds the nature of *Brahman.* The universe, with its millions of galaxies, is *kshara*, the perishable aspect of *Brahman*. The imperishable substratum of the perishable world is *Akshara*. Shri Krishna brings in a third concept here, that of *Uttama Purusa* or highest Self, and completes the picture."[16]

द्वाविमौ पुरुषौ लोके क्षरश्चाक्षर एव च ।
क्षरः सर्वाणि भूतानि कूटस्थोऽक्षर उच्यते ॥१६॥

There are two kinds of beings (dvaupurusau) in creation, the kshar (perishable) and the akshar (imperishable). In the material world, everything perishes. The spiritual world is infallible. (Bhagavad-Gita Chapter 15, Verse 16)

उत्तमः पुरुषस्त्वन्यः परमात्मेत्युदाहृतः ।
यो लोकत्रयमाविश्य बिभर्त्यव्यय ईश्वरः ॥१७॥

Besides these (the kshara and the akshara), is the Supreme Divine Personality (uttamahpurushah), who is the

---

16 http://vedantavision.org/library/articles/the-supreme-self.html. Last accessed on 13 December 2017.

indestructible Supreme Soul (parama-atma). He enters the three worlds as the unchanging controller and supports all living beings. (Bhagavad-Gita Chapter 15, Verse 17)

Lokmanya writes, "In the sixteenth chapter, it is said that men are divided into those possessing divine wealth and those possessing ungodly wealth, in the same way as there arises diversity in the world by different constituents of Matter (*Prakrti*). There is a description of how they act respectively (what their *karma* is), and what goal they ultimately reach."

The divine (*daivi*) nature comprises of fearlessness (*abhaya*), purity of mind (*sattva-sanshuddhi*), knowledge (*jnana*), skill (*yoga*), steadfastness (*vyavasthiti*), charity (*dana*), control of the senses (*dama*) and sacrifice (*yajna*), self-study (*svadhyaya*), austerity (*tapas*), straightforwardness (*arjavam*), non-violence (*ahimsa*), truthfulness (*satyam*), absence of anger (*akrodha*), renunciation (*tyaga*), peacefulness (*shanti*), restraint from fault-finding (*apaishuna*), compassion toward all living beings (*dayabhuteshu*), absence of covetousness (*aloluptvam*), gentleness (*mardava*), modesty (*hrih*), lack of fickleness (*achapala*), vigour (*teja*), forgiveness (*kshama*), fortitude (*dhriti*), cleanliness (*shaucham*), bearing enmity toward none (*adrohah)* and absence of vanity (*atimanita*).

The qualities of those who possess a demoniac (*asuri*) nature are hypocrisy (*dambhah*), conceit (*abhimana*), anger (*krodha*), harshness (*parushya*) and ignorance (*Ajnana*). These people do not comprehend what actions are proper and what are improper; consequently, they possess neither purity, nor good conduct, nor even truthfulness. They consider that there is no absolute truth, no basis and no God to control their behaviour. To them, the world is created from the combination of the two sexes, and sexual gratification (*kama-haitukam*) is its only purpose. Possessed by their fantasies, trapped in a web of delusion, and addicted to sensual pleasures, they sink into the murkiest hell (*narakeahuchau*). In another striking allegory, three gates of the hell are named.

त्रिविधं नरकस्येदं द्वारं नाशनमात्मनः ।
कामः क्रोधस्तथा लोभस्तस्मादेतत्त्रयं त्यजेत् ॥२१॥

Self-destruction for the soul (nashanamatmanah) is hell with the three gates (tri-vidham narakasyedam dvaram)– lust, anger and greed. Therefore, all should abandon these three (tasmādetattrayam tyajet). (Bhagavad-Gita Chapter 16, Verse 21)

The divine qualities lead one towards liberation (*vimokshaya*), while the demoniac qualities are the cause for a continuing destiny of bondage (*nibandhaya*).

Lokmanya writes, "The seventeenth chapter contains an Exposition, in reply to a question of Arjuna, of how the diversity resulting from the different constituents of three-constituted *Prakrti* is also to be seen in devotion, charitable gifts, sacrificial ritual, austerity etc., and in the end, the word 'tat' in '*Om-Tat-Sat*', the symbol of *Brahman*, has been explained as meaning 'action performed desirelessly'; and '*sat*' as meaning action, which, though good, has been performed desire-fully; and it is explained that this common symbol of the *Brahman* also supports the path of *Karma Yoga*."

The eighteenth and the final chapter of the *Bhagavad-Gita* is the longest. It begins with a question about two commonly used Sanskrit words, *samnyasa* (renunciation of actions) and *tyaga* (renunciation of desires). Lokmanya writes, "As the stage of asceticism, described in the *Smriti* texts, finds no place in the *Karma Yoga*, and as Arjuna felt a doubt that there was likely to be a conflict between this *Karma Yoga* and the *Manu Smrti* and other *Smrti* texts, he has, in the commencement of the eighteenth chapter, asked the Blessed Lord for an explanation of the difference between *Tyaga* (Abandonment and *Samnyasa* (Renunciation). To this, the Blessed Lord has replied that as the etymological meaning of the word '*Samnyasa*' is 'to leave,' and as the Hope of Fruit is left in the *Karma Yoga*, though the *karma* is not left, *Karma Yoga* is essentially a *Samnyasa*."

The Train of Thought

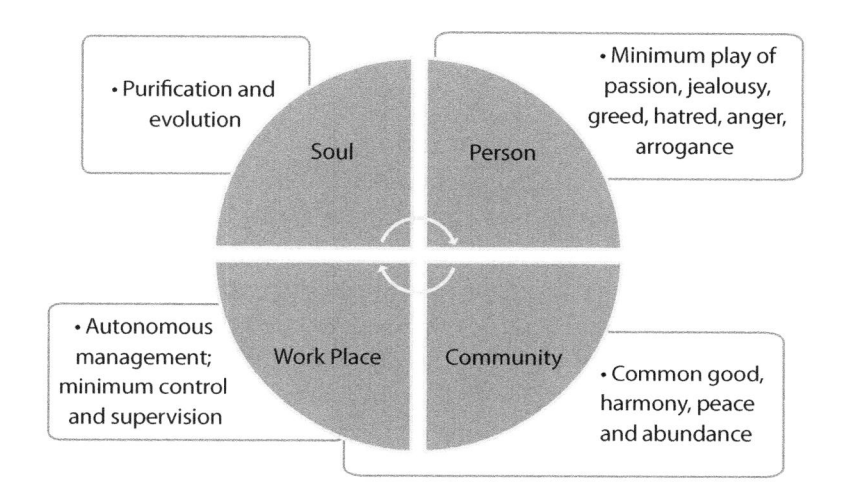

- Purification and evolution — **Soul**
- Minimum play of passion, jealousy, greed, hatred, anger, arrogance — **Person**
- Autonomous management; minimum control and supervision — **Work Place**
- Common good, harmony, peace and abundance — **Community**

Karma Yoga and Jnana Yoga both support each other in expanding the human heart from its narrow confines of Me and Mine. When one succeeds in orienting one's life to doing good to others, selfish motives disperse like clouds in the wind.

The Blessed Lord then leaves us to do as we wish. There are no commandments, orders that must be obeyed, or decrees that ought to be accepted without question. The message of *Gita* is advisory based on a logic, and most careful study of scriptures and observations upon the tradition.

इति ते ज्ञानमाख्यातं गुह्याद्गुह्यतरं मया ।
विमृश्यैतदशेषेण यथेच्छसि तथा कुरु ॥१८ ६३॥

Thus, I have explained to you this knowledge that is more secret than all secrets (guhyadguhyataram Maya). Ponder over it deeply, and then do as you wish (yathechchhasi tatha kuru).
(Bhagavad-Gita Chapter 18, Verse 63)

Dr. S. Radhakrishnan elaborates, "*Yatha icchasitathakuru*: do as you choose. God is seemingly indifferent, for He leaves the decision to Arjuna's choice. His apparent indifference is due to His anxiety that each one of us should get to Him of his own free choice. He constrains no one since free spontaneity is valuable. Man is to be wooed and not coerced into cooperation. He is to be drawn, not driven, persuaded, not compelled.... He is ever ready to help us when we stumble, comfort us when we fall. God is prepared to wait in patience till we turn to Him... even error is a condition of growth."[17]

The principles of *Gita* invoke contemplation. The narrative invites the reader to examine life from different angles. Lokmanya presented an exhaustive repository of scriptures– *Vedas, Upanishad, Samhitas, Itihaas,* poetry and invites present generation to experiment with them and draw its own conclusions. Only such an inquiry will make people live by these principles. The most esoteric truths presented in the *Gita* provide even to the layperson a sense of liberation and he can see the world beyond suffering. *Gita* is a great inspiration to live a life of authority and responsibility as that of a king, but think with a dispassionate mind and remain unnerved in adversity like a *samnyasi*. The *Gita* asks us to respond to the reality presented before us anchored in the cosmic intelligence and be a part of the evolution of human race, not react out of fear and run away from it to end up in an opportunity wasted only to return in a lower life form later.

Lokmanya emphasises, "From the continuity of the eighteen chapters of the *Gita* which has been mentioned above, it will be seen that the *Gita* is not a *potpourri* of three independent *Nisthas* of Action, Devotion, and Spiritual Knowledge, nor a blanket made up by sewing together pieces of linen, silk and embroidery; but that this very fine and costly texture in the shape of the *Gita*, which bears the name of '*Karma Yoga*', has been woven from the beginning to the end, with 'a mind which has fully engrossed in *Yoga*', after the threads of cotton, silk and embroidery had been properly placed in their respective places."

---

17 S. Radhakrishnan, *The Bhagavad Gita*, HarperCollins Publishers, India, 2014, p. 445-446.

Lokmanya concludes this chapter on the most systematic and accurate thought process behind the *Bhagavad-Gita* with the following words, "The *Parameshvara* intends the world to go on, and from time to time He takes incarnations for that purpose. The Path of carrying on the activities of the worldly life, with a desireless frame of mind, even after the acquisition of knowledge, which has been preached by the Blessed Lord in the *Gita*, is the most proper path to be followed in the *Kalyuga*".

ॐ

15

The Code of Creation

> The religion of the *Gita* does not maintain any distinction between classes, castes, countries, or any other distinction, but gives Release to everyone in the same measure, and at the same time, shows proper forbearance towards other religions, is thus seen to be the sweetest and immortal fruit of the tree of the Vedic Religion.
>
> *Bal Gangadhar Tilak*

Lokmanya opens the fifteenth and the final chapter with the first line of the seventh *shloka* in the eighth chapter of the *Gita*:

तस्मात्सर्वेषु कालेषु मामनुस्मर युध्य च ।
मय्यर्पितमनोबुद्धिर्मामेवैष्यस्यसंशयम् ॥७॥

Therefore, in all times, remember Me (tasmat sarveshu kaleshu mam anusmara) and do your worldly duty with your body (yudhya cha). With mind and intellect surrendered to me (mayi arpita-mano-buddhir), you will definitely attain Me without a doubt (mam eva eshyasi asanshayam).
(Bhagavad-Gita Chapter 8, Verse 7)

Lokmanya writes, "Whether one considers the continuity of the various chapters (train of thought, as presented in the earlier chapter), or dealt with it according to the logical method of the *Mimamsa* School, it follows clearly that (i) the various interpretations, which have been put on the *Gita* by doctrine-supporting commentators... are not correct; and that (ii) harmonising the Monistic (*Advaita*) *Vedanta* of the *Upanishads* with the Philosophy of Devotion, and in this way accounting for the mode of life of great and noble people, or, to mention the matter briefly, *Karma Yoga* fused with Spiritual Knowledge and Devotion, is the true purpose of the *Gita*."

Swami Ranganathananda writes, "*mam anusmara yudha cha*, 'meditate upon Me and carry on the battle of life'... that is the special message of the *Gita*... We are all working people. In the midst of work can we realise the Divine? Yes, we can. The Divine is our own nature. Realising Him is our birthright. Everybody can realise Him. That is how the Supreme Divinity has been presented in the *Gita*."[1]

Swami Mukundananda adds, "Keep your mind attached to me, and do your worldly duty with your body." This applies to people in all walks of life– doctors, engineers, advocates, housewives, students, etc. In Arjun's specific case, he is a warrior and his duty is to fight. So he is being instructed to fulfil his duty, while keeping his mind in God. Some people neglect their worldly duties on the plea that they have taken to spiritual life. Others excuse themselves from spiritual practice on the pretext of worldly engagements. People believe that spiritual and material pursuits are irreconcilable. But God's message is to sanctify one's entire life."[2]

Mystic poet and saint Kabir (1440-1518) provides a powerful allegory on how God must be remembered while engaging with the world.[3] It is common in villages, even now in some remote areas, for the women to go in a group to fetch water from a pond, fill it in an earthen pitcher, and carry it on their heads while walking and taking together. They even have another pitcher under their arm. They are not walking on a road but on the uneven ground. While they are walking, busy in their small talk, their mind is fixed on the pitcher full of water they are carrying. They are walking in such a way that the water in the pitcher does not even slosh. A *Karma Yogi* lives like this. All actions are performed, all interactions are done, but the mind, the thoughts all the time remain on God.

---

1 Swami Ranganathananda, *Universal Message of the Bhagavad Gita, Vol. 2*, Advaita Ashrama, Kolkata, 2015 (Seventh reprint), p.288.
2 http://www.holy-bhagavad-gita.org/chapter/8/verse/7. Last accessed on 28 October 2017
3 https://hindividya.com/kabir-ke-dohe-hindi/

> सुमिरन की सुधियों करो, ज्यों गागर पनिहारी ।
> हाले डोले सुरति में, कहैं कबीर विचारी ॥

Remain ever mindful of God as is the water-carrying lady, who is mindful of (not allowing water to splash out of) her pitcher while carrying it on her head (and apparently busy), talking to others, says Kabir after contemplation.[3]

The linking of day-to-day work with worship is the great departure that the *Gita* took from the Vedic ways that over centuries digressed in to dogmatic rituals. The priest class had turned greedy and started offering *Yajna* services as remedies for misfortunes as well as promises to aspirants. Lokmanya writes, "...mechanical ritual, which is devoid of Spiritual Knowledge, can never satisfy an intelligent person, and if one considers the philosophy of the *Upanishads*, not only is it difficult to grasp for people of ordinary intelligence, as it is based purely on Reason, but the *Samnyasa* (renunciation) advocated by it, conflicts with universal benefits (*lokasmgraha*)."

There is a popular *shloka* expressing the predicament of worldly life.[4] People desire good outcome of their actions and all good things in life but shy away from performing good acts and deeds as they find them bothersome and even unpleasant. No one wants misfortune and problems and yet, people merrily indulge in unwholesome acts and deeds, unmindful that these will eventually bring them sorrow and regret.

> पुण्यस्य फलमिच्छन्ति पुण्यं नेच्छन्ति मानवाः ।
> न पापफलमिच्छन्ति पापं कुर्वन्ति यत्नतः ॥

Man desires good results (punyasya phala michchanthi), but does not perform good deeds (punyam ne chchanthi). Man does not like bad results (na paapa phala michchanthi), yet plunges into sinful acts (paapam kurvanthu).[4]

The true spiritual knowledge therefore, is to know what is right for you and work accordingly. Desiring one thing and doing the

---

[4] https://sanskritstudy.blogspot.in/2014/06/lesson-69.html

opposite of it is indeed foolishness. As actions can't be avoided, it essential they are done with the right frame of mind. To enable that right frame of mind, the *Gita* provides a brilliant solution of desireless action. But the desires would not go just by wishing for this. Devotion is therefore prescribed to shield the mind from unwholesome desires, as does a firewall in the computer keep the viruses and malwares away. Lokmanya writes, "Therefore the Blessed Lord preached in the *Gita* that the philosophy of life-long desireless action is based on spiritual knowledge, in which the highest importance is given to Devotion, so as to effect a fusion between Intelligence (*jnana*), Devotion (*bhakti*), and physical capacity (*kartavya*), and so as to enable the ordinary affairs of the world to be carried on satisfactorily...."

The incessant conflict between philosophical doubt and moral standards has troubled man since time immemorial. Each one of us knows the constant dialogue that goes on and on in our minds - to do or not to do, to take or leave, to fight or let go, and so on. English poet William Blake (1757–1827) famously wrote, "If the doors of perception were cleansed, everything would appear to man as it is, Infinite. For man has closed himself up, till he sees all things thro' narrow chinks of his cavern."[5] Our powers of perception are indeed quite dim relative to the vast and complex truths of the world around us.

Lokmanya explains, "Which action is righteous, meritorious, just, or beneficial, and which, on the other hand, is unrighteous, improper, unjust or harmful, can be explained in two ways. One way, and the easier one, is to say that if a particular thing is done in a particular way, it is right, and if it is done in another way, it is wrong. Injunctions like 'Do not cause death', 'Do not steal', 'Speak the truth', 'Act righteously', etc. and are of this kind. These injunctions or courses of conduct are definitely laid down in the *Manu-Smriti,* and other *Smritis* and in the *Upanishads*. But man is a rational animal; he is not satisfied with such didactic injunctions, and he naturally feels a desire to understand the true reason as to why they were

---

5   William Blake, *The Marriage of Heaven and Hell*, 1790, p. 215. It is a series of texts written in imitation of biblical prophecy but expressing Blake's own intensely personal Romantic and revolutionary beliefs.

laid down. He naturally thinks over and finds out the eternal and fundamental principle at the bottom of these rules of conduct."

In his earnest quest to know the existential truth, French philosopher Rene Descartes (1596–1650) tried to arrive at a sound, certain, indubitable foundation upon which a new, more scientifically correct worldview could be built. To this end, he sought to reject all existing opinions, which he felt, were nothing more than the opinions of other people's minds. Instead of finding the ground of his existence, Descartes sunk himself in the bottomless pit of "cogito ergo sum," or "I think, therefore I am". As he went on he realised that every one of his opinions and observations could also be doubted and rejected, as he did for the others.

People can doubt every thing and yet they have to face life and deal with it. We may have hundreds and thousands of doubts about the nature of truth, including taking a position that everything is subjective as well as speculative and there is nothing like a true position, but we still have to live and make daily decisions about how to move on with other people, earn a livelihood in the world and sleep in peace. So what could be the basis on which we make our decisions to manage our lives? Lokmanya adds, "Going to the bottom of worldly morality in this way, and finding out the underlying fundamental principles is the purpose of philosophy (*shastra*). Merely putting together the rules is known as *achara samgraha* (the code of conduct). Such a code relating to the path of action is found in the *Smrti* texts and the *Bhagavad-Gita* contains a conversational (*pauranika*), but philosophical (*shastriya*) disquisition on the fundamental principles of that code. Therefore, it is more proper to say that the subject matter of exposition in the *Gita* is the science of Karma Yoga (*Karma Yoga Shastra*)...."

Lokmanya further elaborates, "In the times of the *Upanishads*, and also afterwards, there were *Jnanins* like Janaka and Shri Krishna... and the key note (in the writings about their lives) was *Karma Yoga* or the philosophy of worldly life; and in order to explain this principle, subtle points of righteous or unrighteous conduct have been dealt with in several places in the *Mahabharata*, and ultimately, the *Gita* has dealt with those principles of Ethics, which have been responsible for the maintenance of the world consistently with the viewpoint of Release. There are also many such instances in the other *Puranas*. However, as all other expositions on the subject turn pale by the side of the brilliance of the *Gita*, the *Bhagavad-Gita* has become the most important work on the philosophy of *Karma Yoga*."

Well-versed with the Western literature, Lokmanya was aware and appreciative of the philosophical pluralism and uncertainty about existential truths and morality of worldly affairs. While Lokmanya rejected the assertion of thinkers like Greek philosopher Protagoras (490–420 BCE) that there is nothing like absolute knowledge and "man is the measure of all things", he found in the Western philosophy an opportunity to refine his own understanding of the principles of the *Gita*.

Lokmanya writes, "Yet, it cannot be said that this exposition of the doctrine of the *Gita* is complete, unless one compares the ethical principles propounded by the Western philosophers with the fundamental spiritual principles of the 'doable' and the 'not doable' enunciated in the *Gita*. In making this comparison, it is also necessary to compare the Philosophy of the Absolute Self in the East with such philosophy in the West. But the knowledge of Absolute Self in the West has not gone much beyond our knowledge. As this fact is commonly accepted, there is not much of a necessity to compare the Eastern metaphysical philosophy with the Western Metaphysical philosophy. The only thing, which remains, is the comparison of the Eastern with the Western science of Ethics or *Karma Yoga*, which science according to many has not been expounded by our philosophers. But the consideration of even this one subject is so comprehensive that it will be necessary to write an independent treaty in order to deal with it exhaustively. Yet as I did not consider it proper to omit this matter altogether… I have touched upon some of the most salient and important points in that subject in this concluding chapter."

Is it only our thinking that there is an objective higher code, to which we are all subject, but there is no such code? We just think that ethics are objectively based, whereas they are societal checks and balances created, modified, even scrapped in different spaces and times. Do moral rules exist just because we are agreeable to them? What about others who disagree, care a boot, and go on with life the way it suits them? Greek philosopher Pyrrho (360– 270 BCE) who travelled with Alexander's army to India even declared that as things are indifferent, immeasurable and inarbitrable, neither our sensations nor our opinions tell us truths or falsehoods.

Lokmanya answers, "As the words 'Righteousness' and 'Unrighteousness', or 'Morality' and 'Immorality', can, strictly speaking, be applied only to the actions of intelligent beings, it can be realised, after a little consideration, that Morality does not rest only on action, but rests on Reason. This is what is meant by saying: *dharmo hi tesham adhiko vishesah* (knowledge of right and wrong is the specific quality of man, that is, of intelligent beings)... in as much as the wrongs committed by men in a moment of insanity or unknowingly, are considered forgivable by people, or even according to law, one has to necessarily consider, in the first instance, the Reason of the doer, that is to say, the motive with which he did the act, and whether or not he had realised the consequences of the act, when one is determining the righteousness or the unrighteousness of the doer."

Another Greek philosopher Aristotle (384-322 BCE) stated in his Law of Non-Contradiction that one cannot say of something that it is and that it is not in the same respect and at the same time. What does it mean for morality? In any given moral dilemma, there can be any number of components, which ultimately lead to a more moral, immoral, or amoral judgment. Therefore, there are degrees of right and wrong determined by intent and circumstance. Lokmanya writes, "It is not difficult for a rich man to give large sums of money in charity as he wishes. But although this act of his may be good, yet one has to decide the true moral value of it, and such value cannot be determined merely by considering the fact of this gift made in an off-hand way. One has to consider whether or not the Reason of that rich person was governed by the religious faith (*Shraddha*)."

To be rich and to be virtuous are two different things. There are very wicked people who succeed in amassing great wealth by wrong means and stage acts of charity purely for the sake of creating a good image in the society. The essence of charity lies in the intent to sacrifice. A small charitable act of a poor stretching beyond his already meagre means surely merits more than a grand feast hosted by a king for the poor, because in the case of the king, there is no sacrifice made. When the poor Sudama brought the insignificant gift of three fistful measure of beaten rice to his friend Shri Krishna, not only did the Blessed Lord accept it with love and start eating it right in front of him, but the Lord also gave Sudama everything he needed in return of his small gift given with a pure intent. The story of a mongoose is cited to further emphasise this point. Lokmanya writes, "At the end of *Mahabharata*, after the entire question of righteousness and unrighteousness has been dealt with, there is a story which very well brings put this position."

Pandavas are naturally pleased after winning the horrendous *Mahabharata* war and getting their kingdom back. They perform the customary *Aswamedhika Yajna* and on the concluding day, Yudhishthira, basking in glory and radiating pride stands to distribute gifts to the people assembled there. To every one's surprise, a mongoose, with half of its body golden, appears from nowhere and starts rolling in the ash of the *Yajna Kunda*. After a while, it shakes its head in disappointment. When Yudhishthira asks the mongoose why it is shaking its head like that, the half golden mongoose replies, "I came here to turn the remaining half of my body golden, but alas it is not possible!" Yudhishthira asks how half of its body had turned golden in the first place.

The mongoose narrates an equally strange story. "Once, I was wandering in the home of a very poor Brahmin family. After performing the *Yajna* with their limited means when they were about eat their food, some unexpected guest arrived and as there was no other food to give him, the family gave their food to the guest and remained hungry without even uttering a word. Very pleased at the sight of their generosity and their magnanimity even with whatever little they possessed, I smeared myself in the ash of their *Yajna Kunda* and half of my body became golden as it is now. With a wish to turn the other half of my body golden too, I visit places wherever *Yajnas* are performed and roll over in the ash. But never could I find again the sacredness of that poor family's *Yajna*. I came here with lot of expectation, but alas here also it did not happen!"

Yudhishthira is humbled. In a flash, his face turns pale and pride evaporates. He realises that all the riches and wealth he is going to distribute to the guests, though apparently generous, are insufficient in purity as there is no sacrifice involved on his part in giving them away. This story mentioned in the *Mahabharata* is the testimony of the steadfastness of the Indian mind in adversity and generosity of the heart of the Indian people to share even if they have little.

Lokmanya writes, "...Though the merit of the act of the Brahmin might not, in the opinion of the writer of Mahabharata, have been greater than the Yajna of Yudhishthira, yet, he certainly looked upon the ethical or religious merit of both as at least the same. Even in ordinary life, we follow the same principle, and consider the moral merit, of a millionaire giving a thousand rupees for a pious object, as the same as that of a poor man who gives one rupee by way of subscription.... In the exposition of Morality made in the Mahabharata, while the story of the mongoose was being told, it is said:

सहस्रशक्तिश्च शतं शतशक्तिर्दशापि च ।
दद्यादापश्च यः शक्त्या सर्वे तुल्यफलाः स्मृताः ॥

A man who owns a thousand giving a hundred, a man who owns a hundred giving ten, or someone according to his ability, giving only a drink of water, all these acts are of the same merit and equally beneficial.
(Mahabharata, Ashvamedhika Parva, Adhyaya 90, Shloka 96)

The same is the purport conveyed by the sentence "*patram pushpam phalam toyam...*" in the *Gita*:

पत्रं पुष्पं फलं तोयं यो मे भक्त्या प्रयच्छति ।
तदहं भक्त्युपहृतमश्नामि प्रयतात्मनः ॥२६॥

If one offers to me with devotion a leaf, a flower, a fruit, or even water (patram puspam phalam toyam), I delightfully partake (tad aham asnami) of that article offered with love by my devotee in pure consciousness (prayata-atmanah).
(Bhagavad-Gita Chapter 9, Verse 26)

This principle has been adopted not only in our religion, but also in Christianity. Lokmanya shares a story from the Bible:

"As Jesus was sitting opposite the treasury, He watched the crowd placing money into it. And many rich people put in large amounts. Then one poor widow came and put in two small copper coins, which amounted to a small fraction of a denarius. Jesus called His disciples to Him and said, "Truly I tell you, this poor widow has put more than all the others into the treasury. For they all contributed out of their surplus, but she out of her poverty has put in all she had to live on." (Mark 12. 41-44)[6]

Lokmanya writes, "If one considers the effect of impurity of the

---

6 http://biblehub.com/bsb/mark/12.htm. Last accessed on 28 October 2017.

Reason on the moral merit of an action, that is when the Reason is not pure, it will be seen that killing a man who has attacked you for murdering you, and killing a rich traveller for the sake of his money, are ethically entirely different." Lokmanya cites German poet Friedrich Schiller's drama *'William Tell'*.

"William (Wilhelm) Tell is a renowned hunter of the Canton of Uri. Tell, a pacifist, avenges the oppression of the Swiss people by slaying the ruthless governor, the representative of the emperor of Austria. Tell's skill as a marksman is tested when he is ordered by the governor to shoot an apple off the head of his son at seventy paces. Arrested despite his obedience, Tell, in another feat of daring, escapes from the boat that carries him to imprisonment, gets his crossbow, and slays the evil governor.[7]

There are several ways to evaluate Actions. We evaluate Actions from the moral point of view. It can be done in two very different ways. Actions can be examined if these are morally right or wrong, but these can also be judged as morally good or bad. Both evaluations could be logically independent of each other. How to distinguish between the morally right and the morally good? Here enters the concept of the motive of the doer. Take for example, a doctor is faced with a situation whether to tell his patient that he is going to die with his cancer in less than a year's time. Should he tell him right away as truth-telling is morally right, and it is none of the doctor's business to worry about the effect of this revelation upon the psychology of the patient? But it is not the motive of the doctor to plunge the patient into despair. He must give his patient the opportunity to prepare himself and his family for the end and engage him in the treatment; even it is not going to make any difference. Lokmanya writes, "The Equable Reason of the *Sthitaprajna* is a combination of the steadiness of Pure Reason and the purity of Practical Reason."

Contemporary philosopher Paul Boghossian in his brilliant article in *the New York Times - The Maze of Moral Relativism*[8], explains, "Relativism about morality has come to play an increasingly important role in contemporary culture. To many

---

[7] https://www.enotes.com/topics/william-tell/characters. Last accessed on 28 October 2017.

[8] https://opinionator.blogs.nytimes.com/2011/07/24/the-maze-of-moral-relativism/. Last accessed on 29 October 2017.

thoughtful people, and especially to those who are unwilling to derive their morality from a religion, it appears unavoidable. Where would absolute facts about right and wrong come from, they reason, if there is no supreme being to decree them?" Paul Boghossian termed it as nihilistic response. He writes, "When we decided that there were no such things as witches, we didn't become relativists about witches. Rather, we just gave up witch talk altogether... There is no half-way house called 'moral relativism,' in which we continue to use normative vocabulary with the stipulation that it is to be understood as relativised to particular moral codes. If there are no absolute facts about morality, 'right' and 'wrong' would have to join "witch" in the dustbin of failed concepts." He concludes, "A would-be relativist about morality needs to decide whether his view grants the existence of some absolute moral facts, or whether it is to be a pure relativism, free of any commitment to absolutes. The latter position... is mere nihilism; whereas the former leads us straight out of relativism and back into the quest for the moral absolutes."

Lokmanya writes, "The Blessed Lord did not ask Arjuna to consider how many persons would be benefitted or how many persons ruined by the war being carried on. On the other hand, the Blessed Lord has said, "Whether Bhishma will die or Drona will die as a result of the war, is a minor consideration. The principle question is with what frame of Reason one is going to enter the fight. If your Reason is like that of a *Sthitaprajna*, you will incur no sin if Bhishma and Drona are killed while you are performing your duty. You are not fighting with a Hope of Fruit. You have only asked for a share of that kingdom to which you have acquired a right by birth. To avoid the war, you have not failed to take it lying down as much as possible. But you saw that there was no other alternative. For this you are not to blame at all. It is your duty to acquire these rights ultimately by fight, in the interests of the public welfare, according to the religion of the Kshatriyas, instead of wasting time in begging like a Brahmin."

The correct answer to a moral question is never easy. When there appears to be no good answer to a hard moral question, and even scriptures fail to settle the debate, where do we rest our search? Einstein famously established that there is no such thing as absolute motion or absolute rest. Whether something is moving or at rest is relative to a space-time frame of reference. Something may be at rest in one such frame of reference and moving in another. Lokmanya writes, "But though the Reason is thus considered to be the superior factor in deciding what is right and what is wrong, it becomes necessary to explain what is meant by Pure Reason. As both, the Mind and the Reason are evolutes (*vikara*) of Matter (*prakrti*), they can inherently be of three kinds– *sattvik, rajasik*, and *tamasik*. Therefore, the *Gita* has declared '*Sattvik* Reason' as 'Reason' in the philosophy of *Karma Yoga*. The '*Sattvik* Reason' is also known as the *'Equable Reason'*, which recognises and realises the unity or identity of the *Atman,* which inhabits all created things."

The story of Markandeya is now shared. Markandeya was born to Mrikandu after he performed *tapas* to Lord Shiva, who gave two options to his father - He may have many children who would live long, but as ordinary people of average intelligence, like sand particles on a river bank, or, he could have only one son, immensely brilliant, but living a short life of a blazing meteor. The child would have a brilliant mind, but live for only sixteen years. Mrikandu opted for a son with brilliant mind. His wife gave birth to a son. Even at the time of its birth, the infant was radiating intelligence. The blessed couple named the child Markandeya.

As Markandeya grew up, his parents apprised him of the situation. Instead of wasting his appointed life of sixteen years in merry-making, Markandeya went to a quiet place on the bank of the Tungabhadra River and entered in to a severe penance to please Lord Shiva. He controlled his mind with great devotion. On the appointed day of his death, Markandeya embraced the *Shivalinga* and said. "I am taking refuge in you. What can Yama do to me when you are beside me?" In a moment of indiscretion, Yama cast his *pasha* and the rope on Markandeya and the *Shivalinga* together. When Yama pulled the rope it broke the *Shivalinga* into two, and Lord Shiva himself emerged out of it.

The Lord said, "Yama, you must use reason. You should know how to treat different people in different situations in different ways. Further, you behaved in a very arrogant way in discharging your duty. You have to use your discretion and deal with a situation according to its merit. This boy *tapasvi* is my devotee.

He has conquered death by the power of his *tapas*. His fame has been established in this world forever, and he is going to become immortal. But in order to not break the 'order of the universe', Markandeya will forever remain sixteen-years-old. Yama had no choice except to leave the place.

Lokmanya writes, "In the book on the Bhagavata religion called *Narada Pancharatra*, which is later in date than the *Gita*, Markandeya Rishi says to Narada Muni:

मानसं प्राणिनामेव सर्व्वकर्मैककारणं ।
मनोऽनुरूपं वाक्यंच वाक्येन प्रस्फुटं मनः ॥८॥

The 'Mind' is the only cause (the root cause) of all the actions of mankind. As the 'Mind' is, so does the man speak; a man's 'Mind' expresses itself in what he says.
(Narada Pancharatra, Adhyaya 7, Shloka 8)."

Lokmanya writes, "The Mind is the only cause (the root cause) of all Actions of mankind. As the Mind is, so does the man speak; a man's Mind expresses itself in what he says. In short, the mind comes first, and then all Actions take place. Therefore, Buddhist writers have also accepted the doctrine of the *Gita* relating to Pure Reason for distinguishing between the 'Doable' and the 'Not-doable'. For example, in the well-known Buddhist work on Morality known as *Dhammapada*, it is stated right in the beginning..."

मनःपूर्वङ्गमा धर्मा मनःश्रेष्ठा मनोमयाः ।
मनसा चेत्प्रदुष्टेन भाषते वा करोति वा ।
तत एनं दुःखमन्वेति चक्रमिव वहतः पदम् ॥१॥

(The mental) natures are the result of what we have thought, are chieftained by our thoughts, (and) are made up of our thoughts. If a man speaks or acts with an evil thought, sorrow follows him (as a consequence) even as the wheel follows the foot of the drawer (i.e. the ox which draws the cart).[9]

---

9   S. Radhakrishnan, *The Dhammapada*, Oxford University Press, Oxford India Paperbacks, New Delhi 1996, p.58.

"Time, in the story of Markandeya is represented by Yama since time brings death and dissolution to all things, but Shiva brings death to time itself. So, He is called Mahakala or Mahakalabhairava. As He alone is beyond death and time, Shiva is called Maha Mrityunjaya, the great Conqueror of Death."[10]

I have used here the Sanskrit translation of the original *Suktas* written in Pali done by Mahapandit Rahul Sankrityayan (1893–1963). Similarly, Buddhist writers have also accepted the corollary drawn from the *Upanishads* and in the *Gita*, that the *Sthitaprajna*, whose mind has become completely pure and desireless, cannot afterward be guilty of any sin, and that whatever he does, he is free both from sin and merit. It is stated in many places in Buddhist works that the '*arhat*' that is, the 'man who has reached the state of perfection', is always pure and sinless.

मातरं पितरं हत्वा राजानौ द्वौ च क्षत्रियौ ।
राष्ट्रं सानुचरं हत्वानघो याति ब्राह्मणः ॥५॥

---

10 http://shivadarshana.blogspot.in/2008/02/story-of-markandeya.html. Last accessed on 29 October 2017.

Having slain mother (craving), father (self-conceit), two warrior-kings (eternalism and nihilism), and destroyed a country (sense organs and sense objects) together with their treasures (attachment and lust), without grieving goes the holy man. Verse 294 (Chapter 21, Verse 5)[11]

Lokmanya writes, "Therefore, when one says that equability of Reason must always inhabit the Conscience, it is not necessary to also say that one should take into proper account the welfare of the greatest number. ...Morality is the inherent nature of the Conscience, which is pure, loving, equable, or in short, which is endowed with the *sattva* constituent (of *prakrti*)... those persons who have not overcome their selfish natures, become crafty, scheming, or hypocritical. The whole of society is likely to suffer to that extent... In the *Karma Yoga* one has to ultimately rely on the equability of Reason, which is expressed in external Actions, and which remains unchanged even in time of adversity. The true test of Righteous Action is Knowledge-full and ultimate Pure Reason, or rectitude, more comprehensive, more correct, and more faultless than Western intuitionists or materialistic doctrines."

Lokmanya finally sets asides the Intuitionists or Materialists on the philosophy of Ethics by Western writers and takes a final look at the metaphysical viewpoint of the Western philosophers and establishes that Purity of Reason is considered of greater value than Action itself as in the *Gita* by many Western philosophers. Lokmanya starts with the German philosopher Immanuel Kant (1724 -1804) and then discusses the ideas of the English philosopher Thomas Hill Green (1836–1882) and then the German philosophers Arthur Schopenhauer (1788–1860) and Paul Jacob Deussen (1845–1919).

Lokmanya writes, "For instance, take the *Metaphysics of Morals* and other books written by (Immanuel) Kant. Although Kant has not adopted the doctrine of the unity of *Atman* in all created beings, yet after minutely considering the question of Pure Reason and Practical Reason, he has come to the conclusions that: (1) rather than determining the ethical value of any particular act by considering its external results, how many persons will benefit and to what extent,

---

[11] Acharya Buddharakkhita, *The Dhammapada: The Buddha's Path of Wisdom*, Buddhist Publication Society, Kandy, Sri Lanka, 1985, p.68.

one should determine that value by considering to what extent the 'Practical Reason' (*vasana*) or desire of that person is pure; (2) this desire (emanating out of the 'Practical Reason') of a man can be considered to be pure, stainless, and independent, only when instead of being engrossed in the happiness of the organs, it remains continually within the control of the 'Pure Reason', regarding the Duty and the Non-Duty; (3) there is no necessity of laying down rules of Morality for that man whose desire has become purified in this way, as a result of the control of the organs, after it has been so purified; these rules are necessary only for ordinary persons; (4) when the desire has been purified in this way, whatever acts it inspires the man to do, are dictated after considering "what will happen to me, if some one else does to me what I do to him", and (5) this purity or independence of desire cannot be accounted for, unless one leaves the world of action and enters the world of *Brahman*."

Thomas Hill Green disagreed with the concepts of empiricism and biological evolution a craze of his times, and declared that man cannot be simply the result of natural and social forces. Lokmanya writes, "In his book *Prolegomena to Ethics*, Green first laid down that the inaccessible Principle, which saturates the external world, that is the Cosmos is partly incarnated in the shape of the *Atman* in the human body. He has later on laid down the propositions that it is the intense Desire of that permanent and the independent Principle in the human body, namely the *Atman*, of Realizing it's most comprehensive, social, and all-pervading form, which indeed compels human beings to perform good actions. The permanent and unchanging happiness of man lies in this Realisation, whereas the happiness afforded by objects of pleasure is non-permanent."

Schopenhauer in his book, *The World as Will and Representation* saw the world having a double-aspect, namely, as 'Will' and as 'Representations'. And like two sides of a coin, both 'Will' and 'Representations' are one and the same reality. Schopenhauer used the metaphor of electricity and a spark to explain the relationship between force and its manifestation. Friedrich Nietzsche writing on the ideas of Schopenhauer brings out, "Mankind must toil unceasingly to bring forth individual great men: this and nothing else is its task." One would like to apply to society and its ends a fact that holds universally in the animal and vegetable world; where progress depends only on the higher individual types, which are rarer, yet more persistent, complex and productive. But traditional notions of what the end of society is, absolutely bar the way."[12]

Strongly influenced by Arthur Schopenhauer, Paul Deussen was a friend of Friedrich Nietzsche and Swami Vivekananda. He even Sanskritised his name to 'Deva-Sena' as a mark of his admiration for Hinduism. Lokmanya writes, "Deussen was a follower of Schopenhauer. He has adopted *in toto* the doctrine of Schopenhauer that, "It is impossible to destroy unhappiness, unless desire is destroyed, in as much as desire is the cause of worldly life. It is the duty of every one to destroy desire,"... He has clearly shown in his book... *Elements of Metaphysics*... how all principles of Ethics can be substantiated on the basis of this Metaphysical proposition. Desireless action is the sign and the result of the destruction of desire. He wrote, "Abandonment of action is totally unnecessary for destroying desire. In fact, whether desire has been destroyed or not can be proved by nothing so well as by actions performed desirelessly for the benefit of the other. Deussen has laid down the proposition that, desirelessness of the 'Mind', is the root of proper behaviour and morality; and he has at the end of his argument quoted the verse *'tasmad asaktah satatam karyam karma samachara* (in the *Bhagavad-Gita*), which shows that he must have thought of this argument by reading the *Gita*."

तस्मादसक्तः सततं कार्यं कर्म समाचर ।
असक्तो ह्याचरन्कर्म परमाप्नोति पूरुषः ॥१९॥

For this reason constantly perform your duty (satatam karyam karma samachara) and act without attachments (asaktah) to them. Actions done in this way only lead one to the realisation of true purpose of human existence (param apnoti purusha).
(Bhagavad-Gita Chapter 3, Verse 19)

Lokmanya writes, "Whatever may be the truth, the fact that these ideas were universally current in our country long before Deussen,

---
12   https://en.wikisource.org/wiki/Schopenhauer as Educator. Last accessed on 29 October 2017.

Green, Schopenhauer, and Kant, and even possibly hundreds of years before Aristotle, is not a small matter."

In the *Pauranika* texts of Hinduism, there are four child sages (*Kumaras*) mentioned. Mind-born creations of the Brahma, they are named as Sanaka, Sanatana, Sanandana and Sanatkumara. They wander in all realms - material as well as spiritual - with the purpose to teach whoever is interested. There is a famous story discussed in *Vedanta* parlance. After worldly knowledge is accomplished– written, heard, all arts, sciences, one must seek a preceptor, who is Self-realised with humility and know Self-knowledge from him as it is revelatory and experiential in nature.

When Narada Muni approached the *Kumaras*, he said knew the four *Vedas*, the *Itihasa Purana*, the grammar, ancestral worship, all sciences and all arts. Sanatkumara told Narada Muni that whatever he had learned, were all names. Narada Muni was then given the knowledge of the *Brahman*, and it was called the *Upanishad*.

Shri Shankaracharya writes, "In matters coming within the range of experience, a knowledge of means of attaining the good and avoiding the evil is easily available through perception and inference... A man who believes that there is a Self (*Atman*), which gets into relation with a future body, seeks to know the means of attaining the good and avoiding the evil in connection with that body. Hence, the ceremonial portion of the *Vedas* is introduced to acquaint them with these details. But the cause of that desire to attain the good and avoid the evil, i.e., ignorance regarding the Self, which expresses itself as the idea of one being the agent and experiencer, has not been removed by the opposite, the knowledge of the nature of the Self as being identical with *Brahman*. Until that is removed, a man prompted by such natural defects of his as attachment or aversion to the fruits of his actions, proceeds to act even against the injunctions and prohibitions of the scriptures, and under the powerful urge of his natural defects, accumulates in thought, word and deed a good deal of work as iniquity, producing harm, visible and invisible. This leads to degradation down to the state of stationary objects. Sometimes, the impressions made by the scriptures are very strong, in which case he accumulates in thought, work and deed a great deal of what is known as good work which contributes to his well-being... For knowing the Supreme *Brahman* that is the indwelling Self, he should go... to a teacher, versed in the *Vedas* and absorbed in *Brahman*."[13]

Lokmanya writes, "Many persons are under the impression that *Vedanta* means giving up family life and entering the dry process of acquiring Release. But this idea is not correct. The *Vedanta* philosophy has come into existence for considering as scientifically as possible such deep and difficult questions such as: (1) going beyond whatever can be actually seen in the world and determining who man is; (2) determining what the Principle at the bottom of the universe is; (3) defining the relation between man and the Principle, and what the highest ideal of man in this world is, having regard to that relation; (4) finding out the mode of life which must be adopted by man in order to reach that ideal; or (5) in what way, which ideal can be reached, etc., and strictly speaking, the whole of Ethics, or the consideration of how men should behave towards each other in worldly life, can be seen as a part of this profound philosophy."

Contemporary physician-philosopher P. J. Mazumdar writes, "*Karma Yoga* is not without its moral guidelines. But this is different from that of other religions. Hinduism does not have the ten commandments of Christianity or the moral guidelines of the Koran. It recognises that such strict rules would not be applicable for all persons at all times. *Karma Yoga* instead shows us how to achieve moral guidelines by changing our personality. It tells us, not what to do, but how to do it. It teaches us to have always a *Sattvik* attitude, free from cruelty, lust, anger, etc. If we can maintain *Sattva*, then we will automatically know what action to do in a particular situation. Moral evil in Hinduism is not that which goes against the guidelines of particular texts but that which goes against a *Sattvik* character and follows *tamas* or *rajas*. *Sattvik* people can never do anything evil, they will always do that which is morally right, since they will not be blinded by hunger, anger, selfishness, etc. They will refrain from evil even when all the forces of society are forcing them to do it. Nor again will they shirk from doing anything, which needs to be done, even when the entire world is against it. This is the message of

---

[13] Sudhakshina Rangawami (Translator), *The Roots of Vedanta: Selections from Sankara's Writings*, Penguin India, New Delhi, 2012.

the *Karma Yoga*. When we know how do things in a larger context, we will know how to do the individual things also, and be guided into making the correct decision at each step."[14]

Lokmanya writes, "Although the Buddha had in the beginning preached the inactive path of renunciation, yet, soon thereafter there was a reform in the Buddhist religion consistent with the *Karma Yoga* of the *Gita*. It was preached that Buddhist ascetics should not remain in the woods, in solitude, but should continually exert themselves for the propagation of religion and for public good. History proves that as result of this reform, societies of energetic Buddhist ascetics reached Tibet in the North, Burma, China and Japan in the East, Celon in the South and Turkmenistan and the adjoining European countries like Greece, etc., in the West. If keeping in view the question of Release aside for the time being (and working in the world), Equability of Reason is accepted as important, as being the moral principle involved in the discernment of the Doable and Not-doable, it also becomes necessary to briefly consider why and how other paths arose in the Philosophy Ethics, in addition to that of the Metaphysics of the *Gita*."

Lokmanya cited the German-American author Paul Carus (1852–1919), who famously referred to himself as "an atheist who loved God" and his own philosophy as "Religion of Science."[15] In 1894, Carus published *The Gospel of Buddha* modelling it on the New Testament and telling the story of Buddha through parables in the Bible way. Deeply familiar with the Easterners' Mind, Carus saw laws of nature as a part of a creator God's design and therefore reasoned that as there is divinity in the cosmic order, so it is in this human world on planet earth.

Lokmanya quotes Carus from his book *The Ethical Problem*, "A man's ideas about the fundamental principles of Ethics vary according to his idea of the mutual relationship between the Body and the Cosmos. Unless there is some definite belief regarding the inter-relationship between the Body and the Cosmos, no question

---

14 P. J. Mazumdar, *The Circle of Fire: The Metaphysics of Yoga*, North Atlantic Books, Barkley, California, 2009.

15 https://theendlessfurther.com/buddha-the-atheist-who-loved-god-and-the-other-james-baldwin. Last accessed on 29 October 2017.

of Morality can truthfully speaking arise. It is possible that we may behave morally, although we may have no definite belief as regards this inter-relation. However, as this behaviour will be like something done in sleep, it would be more proper to refer to it as some bodily activity resulting from bodily laws, instead of referring to it as moral behaviour." For example, a tigress is ready to sacrifice her own life for protecting her cubs, but we do not say that it is a moral act, instead we call it as her inherent nature."

Lokmanya writes, "(Carus)... very nicely explains how several schools of thought have arisen in the matter of principles of Ethics. Because, that principle which solves the questions, "Who am I?" "How was the world created?" "What is my use in the world? etc., is the principle by which every thinking person ultimately decides the question on how he is to behave towards other people in his life. But these questions cannot be answered in the same way in different countries and at different times."

Lokmanya now takes a long-view on the evolution of Ethics in the West. He writes, "According to the Christian religion, which is in vogue in Europe, the Creator of man and the Universe is quality-full *Parameshvara* mentioned in the Bible and it is stated there that He first created the world, and laid down the Commandments of moral conduct for man. Christian philosophers were originally of the opinion that these Commandments, which were laid down consistently with the idea relating to the Body and the Cosmos mentioned in the Bible, were the root of all Morality. However, when it was found later that these Commandments were insufficient to meet all the ordinary activities of life, it came to be maintained that the Almighty (*Parameshvara*) had given Conscience to man in order to supplement or clarify these Commandments. However, as they later on realised the difficulty wherein a thief and an honest man do not have the same kind of Conscience, there came into vogue the opinion that although the Will of the Almighty was the foundation of Ethics, yet His Will had to be ascertained by considering in what the greatest good of the greatest number lay."

Lokmanya writes, "Ever since the day on which the human being came into existence in this world, man has been keeping his conduct pure with the help of his own intelligence, according to the circumstances of his country and of his times. Those high-principles and noble-minded people who have come to birth from time to time, have laid down rules for the purification of behaviour in the shape of inspirational commands according to their own ideas. The philosophy of Ethics has not come into existence for breaking up these rules and making new rules. Rules of Ethics such as, "Do not commit murder", "Speak the Truth", "Do good unto others", etc., have been in vogue since the ancient times. Whatever school of ethical thought is taken, the rules of Ethics, which are now in vogue, are everywhere more or less the same. The only differences, which arise in these rules, are regarding the form of the exposition of those rules. The statement of Paul Carus that the chief reason for these differences is the difference of opinion regarding the construction and inter-relation of the Body and the Cosmos is seen to be true.

The Indian civilisation respected the individual human being as the whole cosmos in miniature. This verse of the *Chandogya Upanishad* provides a brilliant imagery:

यावान्वा अयमाकाशस्तावानेषोऽन्तर्हृदय आकाशः ।
उभे अस्मिन्द्यावापृथिवी अन्तरेव समाहिते ।
उभावग्निश्च वायुश्च सूर्याचन्द्रमसावुभौ
विद्युन्नक्षत्राणि । यच्चास्येहास्ति यच्च नास्ति सर्वं
तदस्मिन्समाहितमिति ॥८.१.३॥

As this outer space extends so far extends the inner space (antar hrday akasha). Within it indeed are contained both heaven and earth (dyava-prthvi), both fire and air, both sun and moon, lightning and the stars. Whatever there is of him in this world and whatever is not, all that is contained within it (yac chayhasti yac cha nasti sarvam tad asmin samahitam iti).[16]
(Chandogya Upanishad, VIII.1.3).

Where is the need for a man therefore to feel small, insufficient and above all helpless? All inequalities of the world, harsh

---

16 S. Radhakrishnan, *The Principal Upanishads*, HarperCollins Publishers, India, 21st Impression (2010), p. 492.

conditions, difficulties, get defeated once the inner powerhouse of divinity is contacted. Austrian neurologist and a Holocaust survivor Viktor Emil Frankl (1905-1997) puts it so brilliantly, "Ultimately, man should not ask what the meaning of his life is, but rather must recognise that it is he who is asked. In a word, each man is questioned by life; and he can only answer to life by answering for his own life; to life he can only respond by being responsible... In some ways, suffering ceases to be suffering the moment it finds a meaning, such as the meaning of a sacrifice. It did not really matter what we expected from life, but rather what life expected from us. We needed to stop asking about the meaning of life, and instead to think of ourselves as those who were being questioned by life– daily and hourly. Our answer must consist, not in talk and meditation, but in right action and in right conduct. Life ultimately means taking the responsibility to find the right answer to its problems and to fulfil the tasks which it constantly sets for each individual."[17]

Steadiness of mind amidst adversity comes from the presence of eternal inside. The Blessed Lord called this mental stage as free from attachment, fear and anger.

दुःखेष्वनुद्विग्नमनाः सुखेषु विगतस्पृहः ।
वीतरागभयक्रोधः स्थितधीर्मुनिरुच्यते ॥५६॥

One whose mind remains undisturbed amidst misery (duhkhesv anudvigna-manah), who does not crave for pleasure (sukhesu vigata-sprhah), and who is free from attachment, fear, and anger (vita-raga-bhaya-krodhaha), is called a sage of steady wisdom (sthita-dhir munir). (Bhagavad-Gita Chapter 2, Verse 56)

Dr. S. Radhakrishnan cites *De rerum natura* (On the Nature of Things) a poem of Roman philosopher Lucretius (99– 55 BCE): "Religion does not consist in turning unceasingly towards the veiled stone, nor in approaching all the altars, nor in throwing oneself prostrate on the ground, nor in raising the hands before the habitations of gods, nor in deluging the temples with the blood of the beasts, nor in heaping vows upon vows; but in beholding all with

---
17 Viktor Frankl, *Man's Search for Meaning*, Washington Square Press, New York, 1985.

a peaceful soul... It is self-mastery, conquest of desire and passion that is insisted on."[18]

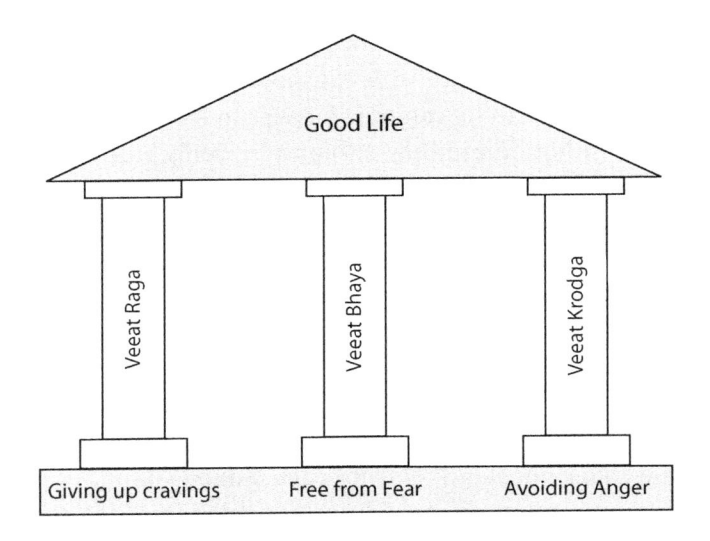

```
                  Good Life
         ┌──────────┬──────────┐
         │          │          │
      Veeat      Veeat      Veeat
       Raga      Bhaya      Krodga
         │          │          │
   Giving up    Free from   Avoiding
   cravings       Fear        Anger
```

Sthitaprajna mental state emerges out of not getting swayed by the sorrows life brings forth (dukheshu anudvigna manaha), not hankering for objects of pleasure (sukheshu vigata spruhaha) and freedom from attachment, fear and anger (vita-raga-bhaya-krodhaha). The intellect has to remind the mind about it every moment.

Lokmanya writes, "The *Gita* therefore says that whether worldly life is productive of happiness or of unhappiness, if one cannot give up worldly affairs even if one wants to do so, there is no sense in considering whether they produce happiness or unhappiness. Whether there is happiness or unhappiness, one must consider it a great fortune, that one has got a human birth. It is the duty of every human being to suffer whatever fate befalls him without allowing his heart to be discouraged... to perform whatever portion of Action has fallen on one's shoulder."

With an intent to sow seeds of discord in the society, certain vested interests have been criticising the *Gita* for what they saw as perpetuating the caste system in the Indian society. Nothing can be

---
18 S. Radhakrishnan, *The Bhagavad Gita*, HarperCollins Publishers, India, 2014, p. 141.

further than the truth. The *Bhagavad-Gita* does not talk of a caste system, but a four strata system of social organisation:

चातुर्वर्ण्यं मया सृष्टं गुणकर्मविभागशः ।
तस्य कर्तारमपि मां विद्ध्यकर्तारमव्ययम् ॥१३॥

I created the four categories of occupations (chatur-varnyam) according to difference in people's qualities and activities (guna-karma-vibhagasah). Although I am the creator of this system (kartaram mam), know Me to be the non-doer and eternal (akartaram avyayam). (Bhagavad-Gita Chapter 4, Verse 13)

Dr. S. Radhakrishnan clarifies on *Chaturvaryam*, the four-fold order: "The emphasis is on *guna* (aptitude) and *karma* (function) and not *jati* (birth). The *Varna* or the order to which we belong is independent of sex (gender), birth, or breeding. A class determined by temperament and vocation is not a caste determined by birth and heredity... An ancient verse - *antyajo viprajatish cha eka eva sahodarah, ekayoniprasutas cha ekashakhena jayate*– points out that the Brahmin and the outcaste are blood brothers."[19]

Swami Mukundananda adds, "The *Vedas* classify people into four categories of occupations, not according to their birth, but according to their natures. Such varieties of occupations exist in every society. Even in communist nations where equality is the overriding principle, the diversity in human beings cannot be smothered. There are the philosophers who are the communist party think tanks, there are the military men who protect the country, there are the farmers who engage in agriculture, and there are the factory workers."[20]

The Vedic philosophy dealt with the imperative stratification of the society in a much more scientific manner. The concept of material operating its three modes (*gunas*) was extended to the modes of livelihood of the people. Those who have a multitude of the mode of goodness (*sattva*) should take up knowledge work and engage in teaching and worship. People with passion (*rajas*) as

---

19 S. Radhakrishnan, *The Bhagavad Gita*, HarperCollins Publishers, 2014, India, p. 186.
20 http://www.holy-bhagavad-gita.org/chapter/4/verse/13

their dominating mode mixed with a smaller amount of the mode of goodness should rule and take up governance and military duties. Those who possess the mode of passion mixed with some mode of ignorance (*tamas*) should go for business and they form the trading, industry and the agricultural class. Lastly, people with a dominant mode of ignorance should become the working class– peasants, factory workers, weavers, tailors, barbers, etc. This classification was neither meant to be according to birth, nor was it unchangeable. India had a great warrior in Parshurama born to *Brahmin* parents, a great sage in Vishwamitra who was born in a *Kshatriya* family. Aitreya Mahidasa, Lopamudra, Matanga, Valmiki, Shabri, Kabir, Raidas, Narsi Mehta, Tukaram, Swami Vivekananda... they are most revered by all people for their great spiritual and social work, irrespective of the caste they were born in to.

The *Gita* makes a very clear mention of *swa-dharma* in this aspect.

श्रेयान्स्वधर्मो विगुणः परधर्मात्स्वनुष्ठितात् ।
स्वधर्मे निधनं श्रेयः परधर्मो भयावहः ॥३५॥

Glory is to them who perform their personal duty (swa-dharmah), though tinged with faults, than to perform other works however perfectly. In fact, it is preferable to die in the discharge of one's duty, than to follow another path, under fear.
(Bhagavad-Gita Chapter 3, Verse 35)

स्वे स्वे कर्मण्यभिरतः संसिद्धिं लभते नरः ।
स्वकर्मनिरतः सिद्धिं यथा विन्दति तच्छृणु ॥४५॥

By fulfilling their duties, born of their innate qualities (sve sve karmany abhiratah samsiddhim), human beings can attain perfection (sva-karma-niratah siddhim). Now hear from me how one can become perfect by discharging one's prescribed duties. (Bhagavad-Gita Chapter 18, Verse 45)

Dr. S. Radhakrishnan elaborates, *"Sve sve karmany abhiratah:* devoted each to his own duty. Each of us should be loyal to our feelings and impulses; it is dangerous to attempt work beyond the level of our nature (an untrained surgeon performing an operation, an untrained pilot flying aircraft, a person disconnected from the people ruling over them, for example), our *svabhava*. Within the power of our nature, we must live fully to our duty."

Lokmanya writes, "All persons– farmers, carpenters, ironmongers, agriculturists, grain-dealers, merchants, Brahmins, clerks, etc.– must keep their various activities pertaining to their respective position in life. And thereby carry out the maintenance and uplift of the world in the same way as Arjuna. ...When every one in this way sticks to whatever profession or position in life is by birth, with a desireless frame of mind, he the doer does not thereby commit any sin. All actions are essentially the same. The fault if any lies in the Reason of the doer, and not in the Action. When a man performs all actions after equalising his Reason, he thereby only performs the worship of the *Parameshvara*, and not having committed any sin, he ultimately attains Release."

The message of the *Gita* is to live in the world in a way that your work becomes your worship. Constant awareness of the presence of the *Parameshvara* in everything can make it happen. Our minds become a*Git*ated and restless only when we work with a selfish motive and demand out of our effort what we want. Work performed in the attitude of worship not only purifies but also calms the mind. It is a simple way to obtain peace of mind and enduring happiness not only for ourselves but all those around us.

यतः प्रवृत्तिर्भूतानां येन सर्वमिदं ततम् ।
स्वकर्मणा तमभ्यर्च्य सिद्धिं विन्दति मानवः ॥४६॥

The God from whom all beings have their origin (yatah pravrittir bhutanam), by whom this entire universe is pervaded (yena sarvam idam tatam), worshipping Him (tam abhyarchya) with his own proper duty (sva-karmana), man finds perfection (siddhim vindati manavah) (Bhagavad-Gita Chapter 18, Verse 46)

Lokmanya writes candidly, "I proclaim to everybody... perform lifelong your several duties. Thereby perpetually worship the deity in the shape of *Paramatman* (the highest *Atman*). Because, therein lies your happiness in this world and in the next. And on that account, the mutual conflict between, Spiritual Knowledge (*Jnana*), and Love (*Devotion*) are done away with, and the single *Gita* religion, which preaches that one's life (based on desireless action) should be turned into a Sacrifice (*Yajna*) (lived in the spirit of doing good to others around), contains the essence of the entire Vedic religion. When hundreds of energetic noble souls and active persons were busy with the benefit of all created things, India was blessed with the favour of the *Parameshvara*, and reached the height not only of Knowledge but also of prosperity. When this ancient religion lost following in our country, India reached its present fallen state."

Lokmanya concludes the book in a soulful manner with these words: "We therefore now pray to the *Parameshvara*, at the end of this book, that there should come to birth again in this country such noble and pure men as will worship the *Parameshvara* according to this equable and brilliant religion of the *Gita*, which harmonises Devotion, Spiritual Knowledge, and Energism. I end this Exposition of the Mystic Import (*Rahasya*) of the *Gita* by addressing to my readers the following hymn, with a prayer that in case of any omission or excess in this book, they should rectify such mistakes with Equable vision:

समानी व आकूतिः समाना हृदयानि वः ।
समानमस्तु वो मनो यथा वः सुसहासति ॥
यथा वः सुसहासति ॥

Common you (worshippers), be in your intention, common be (the wishes of) your hearts; common be your thoughts, so that you will acquire the strength of unity... (Rig-Veda Samhita, Mandala 10, Sukta 191) [21]

The words '*yatha vah sushasati*' are expressed twice, to indicate that the book is hereby concluded.

More than 100 years have passed since Lokmanya wrote these

---

21 H.H. Wilson, *Rigveda Samhita (English Translation according to Bhashya of Sayanacharya)*, Parimal Publications, Delhi, 2014, p. 579.

words. India has gained independence during this period and made tremendous progress as a nation in the world. There are signs of awareness amongst people against *tamasik* forces that immobilised the once vibrant and flourishing Indian civilisation. However, with the advent of the information and communication technology, the Indian people are suffering from the cognitive surplus reaching them through ubiquitous electronic media. Young minds are inundated with materialistic art, music, and literature and the neo-rich and the youth are embracing hedonistic lifestyles. The mission of Lokmanya was to remind the Indian people about the secret of the harmonised Devotion, Spiritual Knowledge, and Energism, shared with them by the Blessed Lord, which remains unchanged and assumes even greater significance in the present time.

Lokmanya represents an exhaustive embodiment of the sublime Divine Message that Shri Krishna communicated to Arjuna in order to deliver the human race from the swamp of ignorance to the purity of light. An image, authentic as well as comprehensive, this Message is therefore only attainable through careful study and profound analysis of both backgrounds and issues of such a scholarship and brilliance of expression. Lokmanya indeed sealed the Nectar of timeless wisdom treasured in the *Bhagavad-Gita* for the coming generations of Indian people and those who want to find solace in the ideals of Indian civilisation.

I see Lokmanya like the Sun; he radiated the brilliance of the Indian civilisation. I see my mentor-teacher, Dr. A.P.J. Abdul Kalam, as the Moon who shone in the reflected light of the heritage embodied by Lokmanya. I am not even a meteor, but have dared nevertheless to share my destined fraction of a second of 'light' with the young people of my country and to share with them the greatness that is their inheritance. The driving force of the Indian people is 'knowledge'. Reflection and self-correction is woven into our DNA. Our freedoms reside within us. The luckiest people on the Earth are the people who are born in India.

॥ ॐ तत्सत् ब्रह्यार्पणमस्तु ॥

This is dedicated to the *Brahman*, the Ultimate Reality in the universe that transcends and comprehends all other beings. *Shrimad Bhagavad-Gita* is the most lucid exposition of the Ultimate Reality before humanity and Shri Bal Gangadhar Tilak appeared on this planet to decode the exposition of the Ultimate Reality for *lokasmgraha* (benefit of humanity).

ॐ

Epilogue

God created man to work.
Work is man's greatest duty.

Man is nothing,
He can do nothing,
Achieve nothing, fulfil nothing, without working.
Work is man's most dependable function.

If you are poor– work.
If you are rich– work.
If failure discourages you– work.
If success encourages you– work.

You have been burdened with unfair responsibilities– work.
You have been entrusted with deserving responsibilities– work.
You have not been paid fairly– work.
You have been paid handsomely– work.

When dreams are shattered– work.
When faith falters– work.
When future appears bleak– work.
When hope seems dead– work.

Work is the greatest stress-buster.
Work is the mightiest morale-booster.
Work is an equally effective disease fighter.

If you neglect your work,
you invite worry, fear, doubt and debt.
Work is the greatest solution for all problems.

So, work, work, work,
And work desirelessly, with a purpose!

Anonymous

Image Bibliography

Ch. 1
p. 52- *https://en.wikipedia.org/wiki/Matsya#/media/File:The_fish_avatara_of_Vishnu_saves_Manu_during_the_great_deluge.jpg* (Mahabharata Vol. 2 by Pt. Ramanarayanadatta Shastri, Gorakhpur Gita Press)
p. 55- Conceptualized by Arun Tiwari, redrawn by Madhumita Shinde
p. 60- Conceptualized by Arun Tiwari, redrawn by Madhumita Shinde
p. 62- *http://devaayathana.blogspot.in/2015/03/saints-of-maharashtra-devotees-of.html* (Sant Dnyaneshwar- Painting by Raghuvir Mulgaonkar)
p. 68- Conceptualized by Arun Tiwari, redrawn by Madhumita Shinde

Ch. 2
p. 81- *http://pooranagarwal.blogspot.in/2015/07/blog-post_87.html*
p. 84- *https://en.wikipedia.org/wiki/Ganges_in_Hinduism#/media/File:Ravi_Varma-Descent_of_Ganga.jpg* (Descent Of Ganga– painting by Raja Ravi Varma)
p. 87- *http://collections.lacma.org/node/243743* (India, Himachal Pradesh, Nurpur, circa 1760-1770. From the Nasli and Alice Heeramaneck Collection (M.82.42.8))

Ch. 3
p. 99- Conceptualized by Arun Tiwari, redrawn by Madhumita Shinde
p. 105- *http://ritsin.com/draupadi-swayamvara.html/*
p. 107- *http://www.britishmuseum.org/research/collection_online* (1880,0.2073)
p. 117- Conceptualized by Arun Tiwari, redrawn by Madhumita Shinde

Ch. 4
P. 121- The Mauryan Empire, c. 250 BCE (*https://erenow.com/books/Warinworldhistory/12.html*)
p. 136- Yama teaching Nachiketha, Sankara Mutt at Rameshwaram (*https://en.wikipedia.org/wiki/Katha_Upanishad#/media/File:Yama_teaches_Nasiketha.jpg*)

Ch. 5
p. 151- The cursed Yayati begs forgiveness of Shukracharya, *https://en.wikipedia.org/wiki/Yayati#/media/File:Yayathi_ka_Shap.jpg*, Mahabharata. Published by Geeta Press, Gorakhpur.
p. 161- Conceptualized by Arun Tiwari, redrawn by Madhumita Shinde

Ch. 6
p. 171- *http://www.watchwordtest.com/Images/balances.png*
p. 181- *https://commons.wikimedia.org/wiki/File:Aurora_Riding_in_Her_Chariot_MET_DP807708.jpg*
p. 177- *http://tripurashakti.com/nidra/*

Ch. 7

p. 193- *http://www.yoganandaji.org/board/picture.php?albumid=4&pictureid=51*
p. 196- *http://www.swamij.com/images/prakriti.gif*
p. 203- Conceptualized by Arun Tiwari, redrawn by Madhumita Shinde
p. 207- Samarth Ramdas Swami - *https://commons.wikimedia.org/wiki/File:Samarth_Ramdas_swami.JPEG*

Ch. 8

p. 223- *https://xgeronimo.wordpress.com/2008/07/21/evolution-of-human-consciousness-map/*
p. 231- *http://steve.myers.co/gifs/caduceus.gif*
p. 235- *http://www.deinayurveda.net/wordpress/2009/07/kundalini-the-mystical-tree/*

Ch. 9

p. 252- *http://www.kheper.net/integral/Absolute_and_Manifestation.html*

Ch. 10

p. 273- *http://clipart-library.com/clipart/318360.htm*
p. 277- *https://hinduism.stackexchange.com/questions/3073/what-are-five-layers-pancha-kosha-of-human*
p. 285- Krishna and Pandavas along with Narada converse with Bhishma who is on bed of Arrows, Mahabharata, [Gorakhpur Geeta Press], *https://commons.wikimedia.org/wiki/File:Krishna_and_Pandavas_along_with_Narada_converse_with_Bhishma_who_is_on_bed_of_Arrows.jpg*
p. 292- *http://www.inner-light-in.com/2015/03/karma-theory-in-hinduism/*

Ch. 11

p. 303- *http://thedailyenlightenment.com/wp-content/uploads/2011/07/121.jpg*
p. 317- *http://devaayathana.blogspot.in/2015/03/saints-of-maharashtra-devotees-of.html* (Sant Tukaram- Painting by Raghuvir Mulgaonkar)
p. 323- Conceptualized by Arun Tiwari, redrawn by Madhumita Shinde

Ch.12

p. 329- Sage Jajali is honoured by the Vaishya Tuladhara, *https://commons.wikimedia.org/wiki/File:Sage_Jajali_is_honoured_by_the_Vaishya_Tuladhara.jpg*, Author: Ramanarayanadatta astri, Volume: 5, Publisher: [Gorakhpur Geeta Press]
p. 336- Conceptualized by Arun Tiwari, redrawn by Madhumita Shinde
p. 343- *https://commons.wikimedia.org/wiki/File:Kindness_of_Shibi.jpg*, Author: Ramanarayanadatta astri, Volume: 2 Publisher: [Gorakhpur Geeta Press]
p. 345- *http://www.wutsamada.com/alma/modern/*, Survey of Western Philosophy II, Modern Philosophy, INSTRUCTOR: Larry Hauser, *http://www.wutsamada.com/alma/modern/kant2_files/image001.jpg*
p. 356- Conceptualized by Arun Tiwari, redrawn by Madhumita Shinde

Ch. 13
p. 362- Conceptualized by Arun Tiwari, redrawn by Madhumita Shinde
p. 377- *http://www.Bhagavad-Gita.us/wp-content/uploads/2012/09/Gita-1-1.jpg*

Ch. 14
p. 393- Fifty centuries ago, on India's Battlefield of Kuruksetra, Krishna showed His bewildered friend Arjuna t he science of the self. *http://back2godhead.com/wp-content/uploads/2013/11/1978-09-021.jpg*
p. 397- Conceptualized by Arun Tiwari, redrawn by Madhumita Shinde
p. 403- *http://www.kheper.net/topics/Anthroposophy/selflevels.gif*
p. 419- Conceptualized by Arun Tiwari, redrawn by Madhumita Shinde

Ch. 15
p. 430- *https://commons.wikimedia.org/wiki/File: Mongoose_comes_to_Aswamedha_of_Yudhisthira.jpg*, Author: Ramanarayanadatta astri Volume: 6, Published by Geeta Press, Gorakhpur.
p. 436- The powerful ascetic Shiva defends his devotee Markandeya from Yama, the god of death, First printed by Ravi Varma Press in 1910. *https://en.wikipedia.org/wiki/File:Raja_Ravi_Varma,_Markandeya.jpg*
p. 446- Conceptualized by Arun Tiwari, redrawn by Madhumita Shinde

Printed in Great Britain
by Amazon